D0214794

OTHER VOICES: HIDDEN HISTORIES OF LIVERPOOL'S POPULAR MUSIC SCENES, 1930s-1970s

Dedicated to Roger Eagle and Albie Power

Other Voices: Hidden Histories of Liverpool's Popular Music Scenes, 1930s-1970s

MICHAEL BROCKEN
Liverpool Hope University, UK

ASHGATE

© Michael Brocken 2010

All rights reserved. No part of this publication may be reproduced, stored in a retrieval system or transmitted in any form or by any means, electronic, mechanical, photocopying, recording or otherwise without the prior permission of the publisher.

Michael Brocken has asserted his right under the Copyright, Designs and Patents Act, 1988, to be identified as the author of this work.

Published by
Ashgate Publishing Limited
Wey Court East
Union Road
Farnham
Surrey, GU9 7PT
England

Ashgate Publishing Company
Suite 420
101 Cherry Street
Burlington
VT 05401-4405
USA

www.ashgate.com

British Library Cataloguing in Publication Data
Brocken, Michael.
  Other voices : hidden histories of Liverpool's popular music scenes, 1930s-1970s.
  – (Ashgate popular and folk music series)
  1. Popular music – England – Liverpool – History – 20th century. 2. Music – Social aspects – England – Liverpool – History – 20th century.
  I. Title II. Series
  781.6'4'0942753–dc22

Library of Congress Cataloging-in-Publication Data
Brocken, Michael.
  Other voices : hidden histories of Liverpool's popular music scenes, 1930s-1970s / Michael Brocken.
        p. cm.—(Ashgate popular and folk music series)
  Includes bibliographical references.
  ISBN 978-0-7546-6793-3 (hardcover : alk. paper)
  1. Popular music—England—Liverpool—History and criticism. I. Title.

  ML3492.B76 2010
  781.6409427'53—dc22

                                                                    2009030046

ISBN 9780754667933 (hbk)
ISBN 9780754699170 (ebk)

Mixed Sources
Product group from well-managed forests and other controlled sources
www.fsc.org Cert no. SA-COC-1565
© 1996 Forest Stewardship Council
FSC

Printed and bound in Great Britain by
MPG Books Group, UK

Contents

General Editor's Preface

The upheaval that occurred in musicology during the last two decades of the twentieth century has created a new urgency for the study of popular music alongside the development of new critical and theoretical models. A relativistic outlook has replaced the universal perspective of modernism (the international ambitions of the 12-note style); the grand narrative of the evolution and dissolution of tonality has been challenged, and emphasis has shifted to cultural context, reception and subject position. Together, these have conspired to eat away at the status of canonical composers and categories of high and low in music. A need has arisen, also, to recognize and address the emergence of crossovers, mixed and new genres, to engage in debates concerning the vexed problem of what constitutes authenticity in music and to offer a critique of musical practice as the product of free, individual expression.

Popular musicology is now a vital and exciting area of scholarship, and the *Ashgate Popular and Folk Music Series* presents some of the best research in the field. Authors are concerned with locating musical practices, values and meanings in cultural context, and may draw upon methodologies and theories developed in cultural studies, semiotics, poststructuralism, psychology and sociology. The series focuses on popular musics of the twentieth and twenty-first centuries. It is designed to embrace the world's popular musics from Acid Jazz to Zydeco, whether high tech or low tech, commercial or non-commercial, contemporary or traditional.

Derek B. Scott,
Professor of Critical Musicology
University of Leeds, UK

Introduction

Capital of Culture – is anybody listening?

In 2003, Liverpool, the city of my birth successfully won the privilege to become the European Capital of Culture for 2008. In order to promote and gain support for this year-long event a new brand was born, 'Liverpool08'. The aim of the Liverpool Culture Company and Liverpool City Council was for '…the Liverpool08 brand [to] capture the dynamism and creativity of Liverpool and support Liverpool's quest to become a world-class city by taking full advantage of the Capital of Culture opportunity' (Liverpool08, 2005). The announcement was in effect a proposition: that Liverpool as a city could re-energize itself around different combinations of cultural symbols: music, drama, various creative and performing arts, community-related events, historical narratives, and so on. According to this matrix, if presented refreshed, 'art' tourism could not only re-vitalize the city, culturally, but could also reinvigorate its commerce – while at the same time perhaps give Liverpudlians a renewed sense of shared identities and experiences.

Hitherto Liverpool's re-use of previously well-known cultural formulae had not been altogether successful. The city had attempted to re-present previous cultural successes (principally those made by popular music) but had not thrown them into an inspired relief or combined such images with other exciting, even incompatible, concepts. It was argued by some that Liverpool had more recently become accustomed to presenting stale, repetitive and weary representations of cultural artefacts and (to paraphrase the Liverpool Cultural Ambassador Joe Flannery's comments re the Mathew Street Festival cancellation debacle in 2007) had the tendency to 'flatter' the taste of a visiting public rather than excite it. Flannery continued:

> At times in the past it has seemed to me that the city council has been playing a game of 'catch-up' with popular tastes. It took Liverpool over ten years to accommodate the idea that the Beatles could be a tourist attraction and that popular music should be taken seriously. After they rather grudgingly decided this was the case, they have laboured at it and appeared to some to be out of touch. (Flannery to Brocken, 2007)

Perhaps instead of expressing the spirit of the times, Liverpool as a city had attempted to reflect a static Beatles-related tourist market – and had largely failed.

So, in some respects the European Capital of Culture victory invited Liverpool's city fathers to consider undoing its previous (often homogenous) re-presentations and stereotypes and also question the representations that visitors had absorbed with respect to its past – a past that at times the city had not appeared to have negotiated particularly well.

Liverpool dealt with some incredibly difficult cultural and economic challenges throughout the last half of the twentieth century, but it could be argued that some of these problems were of its own making. From my own experiences as a Liverpudlian living in the city between 1954 and 1971, again between 1976 and 1980, and then working there regularly between 1994 and the present day, few appeared to be listening to those of us who had embraced popular culture as a meaningful expression of identity. To be sure, the keepers of the keys to the city had finally acknowledged in the 1990s that popular music in the shape of the Beatles, Eric's Club, the 1980s pop and dance music artistes, etc had all in their way drawn attention to Liverpool, but they only appeared to recognize these indicators as waves of consumption. Indeed, such activities were viewed by some city councillors as commodities that re-appeared every so many years in some kind of cyclical or 'serialized' form. Throughout the decades between the 1960s and the 1990s Liverpool's city fathers tended to turn an essentially deaf ear to those who suggested that the diversity and authenticity of Liverpool's popular music streams were identity-giving, had also promoted Liverpool to the world in a positive manner, and had actually helped to avert the decline of the city's infrastructure.

The council's actions did, at times, seem baffling: the building housing the Cavern club was knocked down for a ventilation shaft that never materialized; other venues such as the Flying Picket were forced to close through a deplorable lack of funding. Still more such as the Royal Court Theatre were mutilated, with its stalls seating removed, and allowed to fall into disrepair – the Watch Committee even banned the showing of the movie *Woodstock* in the city centre in 1971. One might propose that Liverpool's very composition had been increasingly sapped by the cultural stereotypes cast by the city's own dubious and outmoded political power squabbles. Of course, this malaise had not escaped the public's gaze. By 2003 the general call from those attempting to both preserve and innovate was that 'enough was enough'. Liverpool's administrators needed to *listen* in order to develop a degree of cultural self-reflexivity for the twenty-first century.

As I write this (January 2009), the European Capital of Culture year has drawn to a close and while the main objective of the 'Capital of Culture' programme could be viewed as an attempt to highlight the diversity of culture within Liverpool, a rather 'singular' cultural countenance has remained disconcertingly steadfast. Despite several recent attempts to re-configure popular music space in the city (for example via organizations such as Creative Bias, Novas, River Niger Arts, and the Merseyside Music Development Agency) together with a little contemporary national and international success for artists such as the Zutons, the Coral, and the Dead 60s, most of the *visible* music-making in Liverpool has tended to prolong old (perhaps outmoded) popular music genre stereotypes: white males with guitars. The more diverse musical motifs that represent Liverpool's vibrant migrant communities continue to be partially hidden and indeterminate, while others have been all but effaced. Indeed, whether (e.g.) a Black Liverpudlian with an Irish/West African background, a white working class youth, or a middle class orthodox Jew actually recognize themselves culturally via any of the Capital of Culture 2008 representations is anybody's guess – maybe, maybe not. It is little wonder, in fact, that the neo-Situationist exhibit *La Machine* 'spider' so enthralled the Liverpool public and was hailed as the year's greatest success. This at least allowed Liverpudlians to reclaim their streets for a few days during the summer of 2008 and question art's artificial separation from life and its institutionalization at one and the same time. By so doing, exhilaration was evident in the faces of those who took to the streets. One excited Liverpudlian, Dawn Mensah informed the BBC that prior to *La Machine*'s arrival she found it difficult to relate to the goings on in her own city. From the moment the spider arrived in Liverpool she hardly left the streets and now feels that the city in part belongs to her again.

Liverpool is described by some as a migrant or 'edgy city' (Higginson and Wailey, 2006). This attractive but to a certain extent homogenizing concept suggests that there exists an uncontested authentic tradition, a culture related to struggle. But this of course is a simplistic evaluation of a cultural environment within which a series of complex hate-love attitudes towards modern life has saturated the existences of its people. Liverpool continues to be a city of enormous social and economic contrasts that Capital of Culture year cannot (indeed should not) smooth away. For example, while it is true to say that throughout the twentieth century the city of Liverpool rode several dramatic economic and cultural roller coasters, its methods and approaches for both survival and surrender were as a consequence of its existence as an exchange and a treasury, not simply a bastion of working-class culture. In many respects Liverpool was one of this country's first post-industrial cities, for the decline of Empire deeply affected Liverpool's exchange-based prosperity at a time (the mid-twentieth century) when other cities were on the rise; so much so, in fact, that the population almost halved in the last 50 years of the twentieth century. This scenario was additionally fractured by increased specialization of jobs over the remaining 25 years of the century, the speed with which technology advanced, and the overall lack of economic and cultural investment by central government in the north-west of England – reinvention was, therefore, an absolute necessity. But this combined image of tragedy – of seemingly inextricable contradictions – was in fact counter-balanced to some extent by Liverpool's post-industrial entrepreneurial histories and contexts where especially in the post-WWII era myriad one-man businesses emerged from those who wished (in local parlance) 'to work for themselves'. Once set in motion these cultural processes acquired their own momentum and developed their own logics. In the process multiple new realities and possibilities for many Liverpudlians were spawned.

For example during the mid-1960s my own father went from being a somewhat down-at-heel bread roundsman working for Blackledge's Bakery in Bootle to a self-employed wholesaler with a high level of business acumen. By the 1970s, many such self-employed agents kept Liverpool trading during outwardly severe economic circumstances. In the wholesale marketplace traders such as Lockwoods, Market Meats, and Tranfoods fed the area, while in the local music businesses individuals such as Alan Richards, Roger Eagle, Ken Testi, Alan Cottom, Norman Killon, Diane Caine, Joe Flannery, Alan Peters *et al* sole-traded with some degree of success. Thus, the subjectivization of Liverpool's cultures into one of 'edgy' resistance brought on by commercial 'failure' has, itself, failed to acknowledge the potential for reproduction through re-subjectivity. Sadly, the cultures of the self-employed continue to be somewhat hidden as far as representations of Liverpool are concerned and it was only in more recent times (e.g. *Cunard Yanks* film first shown at the Liverpool Philharmonic Hall 21 June 2007) that Left-thinkers had to reconsider that they did not have an exclusive right to administer a history that excluded the upwardly-mobile such as 'Cunard Yank' Richie Barton.

So, despite the aforementioned 'post-industrial' tag and perhaps reflecting its self-employed alumni, Liverpool was never really an 'industrial' city, as such, but one built on trade and exchange. But its breathtaking pace of development, the multiplication of its material wealth mixing dangerously with seriously underdeveloped customs of contingency (e.g. the Mersey Dock Board frequently spent money where it should not have been spent, thus starving other areas of funds) meant that Liverpool found itself at first lagging behind and then seriously out of step with the wealth production of the more advanced commercialized cities across the world. So, for those of Liverpool's workforce who witnessed, first-hand, serious cultural divisions via labour and race a neo-Marxist position existed – perhaps at times for them everything solid truly did appear to 'melt into air'. Indeed the cultural separations in Liverpool's geography – from relatively wealthy Woolton Village in the south of the city, to relatively impoverished Netherfield Road in the north – merely served to illustrate that base, superstructure and dialectic materialism were less theory and more reality. For some in Liverpool, everyday life splintered into isolated pockets of time and space, and such issues were co-dictated by the cultural geography of a given area and how that area related to the city's former prosperity, the jobs market and the ageing demographic. For the self-employed, however, a release from the tyranny of dependency on such work patterns illustrated that micro-businesses (many built around the aforementioned wholesaling of comestibles and popular music) could help bring about a relative freedom.

Liverpool, therefore, is not only a city of great cultural contrasts, but also ideological and figurative contradictions of vast proportions. More recently, and perhaps as a consequence of these complex cultural authenticities and differences, there has developed an everyday life-culture made up on the one hand of bourgeois thrills, transitory fashions, and ineluctable sporting authenticities (the spectacular society) and on the other, dislocation and fragmentation where people's existences have few life-world associations, are restricted by demographics and a lack of education, and contain a developed victim culture. Regrettably in Liverpool it seems that only a few post-industrial signs are capable of giving meaning and value and negative associations abound concerning artistic signifiers. There has not been a self-reflexive revolution or a general freedom brought about by artistic self-expression, by any means. One might even suggest that all forms of politics as recognized in Liverpool (whether of the personal or party variety) have to some extent, failed. Together with all of the associated problems of long-term urban neglect, this has contributed to a facade with which some cultural observers still concern themselves. Yet, to repeat, paradoxically Liverpool's unique demographics and cultural geography also guaranteed great prosperity for some, exemplified across the city and on the Wirral peninsula by an almost impervious bourgeoisie and its accompanying fortresses of fringe suburbia.

Popular music

From 1963 onward this ambiguous, ambivalent (in fact, downright confusing) cultural scenario was supplemented by intense national (and then international) media scrutiny following the advent of 'Merseybeat'. Many have tried to find 'meanings' and sources from which this popular music font emerged but in doing so have merely stereotyped not only the city, but also its hoards of disparate musicians via overarching narratives of one form or another. Nik Cohn's image of 'Lennon rampage[ing] though Liverpool like some wounded buffalo, smashing everything that got in his way' (Cohn, 1970:123) is typical of the stereotypes brought about in part by rock's and Lennon's auteur status. Such stereotyping stems from a lack of historical understanding and the privileging of descriptive statements over analytic ones. This leads inexorably to a lack of historical explanation. Some popular music writers appear unable to explain the synchronic historical significance of diverse popular music soundtracks because by narrowing their focus they rely upon that old adage of 'causes and consequences'. For these writers historical lineage and legacies appear most important. But, as historian Arthur Marwick (1998) suggests, we simply cannot make mechanistic distinctions between causes and effects. Effects immediately become causes of further effects and 'periods' must be challenged in terms of both continuity and discontinuity, not simply 'legacies'. Yet such a linear music legacy continues to surround the city of Liverpool. Liverpool has, apparently, nurtured a popular music arsenal supposedly directly linked to a singular identity of the city 'created' in the early years of the 1960s. We are thus sold an illustration of Liverpool – and its habitus – 'providing' the world with popular music as if it were a gift. This is an exclusive rather than inclusive image, selective rather dispassionate, elitist, rather than democratic. Such apparently clearly defined musical legacies are problematic, for musical common identity is difficult to locate and can never be secure.

As a consequence of such formalistic narratives, other popular music histories concerning the city of Liverpool and its people have suffered from partial obscurity. If, for example, in Capital of Culture Year 2008 one were to make the claim that Liverpool's country music scene was as equally vital as the one surrounding rock 'n' roll music, or if one were to suggest that the folk scenes in and around Merseyside were matched only by those of London, the (perhaps rock-ist) commentator might possibly laugh, lose interest, and retreat back into his/ her manuscripts – principally because these particular 'roads' do not, on first examination, appear to lead to the Beatles (but of course in a roundabout way, they do). The Beatles might have appeared to some to have swept away the apparent mediocrity of previous popular music soundtracks, but by the time of their demise as a group they still stood closer to these preceding and co-existing soundtracks than they did to the music that followed. John Lennon was to say in an interview with *Rolling Stone*'s Jann Wenner shortly after the dissolution of the Beatles that he 'always likes simple rock. There's a great one in England now, "I Hear You Knocking". I liked "Spirit in the Sky" a few months back. I always liked simple rock and nothing else' (Lennon to Wenner, 1971:30). While we must not allow a disaffected Lennon to speak for the rest of the former Beatles, this comment suggests to us that his status as an iconoclastic musician is at the very least questionable.

So, while Beatles' history has become something of a dominant discourse, the writers of interminable expositions of these musical 'everymen' appear at times less interested in explicit probes for methodological clarity, and more concerned with tid-bits of information that can be bolted on to *a priori* theses (e.g. 'what *did* Lennon and Epstein get up to on that holiday in the sun? and how can it fit our pre-determined ideas?'). Such historiography inducts people into a specific kind of passing of 'secure' information (runes, even) where it is questionable whether anybody writing is at all interested in what *you* the reader actually thinks. Thus, an almost undeniable legitimacy and control of discursive space emerges that foregrounds a rather bland, myopic, linear-chronological narrative. Even ancillaries are marshalled for significance, so that listening to (say) Arthur Alexander is somehow of greater significance than listening to (say) Jim Reeves. Now that the immediately pre and post-WWII eras are slipping inescapably beyond living memory, it is the duty of popular music historians to challenge such deterministic narratives and assumptions before they also inexorably solidify as myths and legends.

The varying and variable popular music scenes that existed in twentieth-century Liverpool (of interest to all popular music historians quite simply because they were important to those involved) reveal a great deal. They were among the most important symbols of change and stasis in the shifting cultural temperatures of mid-twentieth-century Liverpool, being representations of race, class, gender, sexuality, economics, authenticity, and affect. It is usually acknowledged that this was indeed the case for rock 'n' roll, but it is seldom revealed that, for example, country music, the cabaret or folk 'scenes' performed similar duties – so, why not? After all should it not be acknowledged that any identity is ambiguous with a multiplicity of sources? Cannot identity be ascribed to any symbolic representation? Indeed, might one not posit an argument that these 'other' musical activities were of equal importance quite simply because they also involved countless listeners?

The very complexity of such diachronic and synchronic behaviours and meanings should not be ignored. We must listen to both the attentive and inattentive listener – who knows, in the process we might even get to know a little more about the Beatles, themselves.

Mike Brocken

Chapter 1

Looking back, not through – an overview: 'Beatlesology' and historicism

More often than not we reinvent the world that has been lost and then invest in this reinvention a much greater significance than was actually the case at the time. History and historiography, privileged by this matrix, can develop an awesome personality of its own. 'Beatlesology' has indeed done so, for there are literally hundreds of texts – including many 'vanity'-style publications – that place each writer at the centre of the narrative. According to this paradigm, there now appears to be so many crucial figures in Beatles history that it is difficult to find anyone at the periphery. For some in Liverpool the meaning of life apparently once centred around knowing this group of individuals. One might suggest that the historicism of the popular music-past via such a minuscule historical sample as the Beatles and their immediate milieu can only ever be a limited way of thinking about that past, especially when local conditions and peculiarities influence all outcomes in many disparate, decisive ways. To produce so many works about the Beatles that specifically concern themselves only with the group, seemingly at the expense of practically everything else, is (at least to this writer) a rather eccentric way of domesticating and veneering the streams of diachrony that not only co-existed but pre-existed them. It appears, at times to be rather like attempting to place the entire history of popular music on the head of a pin. This kind of historicism can be compared with those reductionist histories that propose that all developments can be explained by fundamental principles (such as economic determinism or acts of genius). No history is safe from the ravages of time and people and places disappear, so it is surely self-deceiving to think that artistic achievement can be studied in either a financial or creative bell jar.

Beatles history, as it has come to appear, is in danger of becoming a meta-narrative form in which we read more of the person making the inquiry than we do of the Beatles, or indeed their environment. All popular music historians should attempt to maintain a conversation within the broader cultural field that has given such creativity shape and the phrase 'discourse analysis' can be used in the sense that it relates and recounts ideas about history to contexts, interactions, cognition, and power. Also the use of the phrase 'discourse of history' suggests that, rather than seeing Beatles history as a given subject from which one can simply learn, like watching a series of brightly coloured lantern slides passing before our eyes, it can be conceived as a series of ways of organizing the past in directions that are openly and frequently contested. This discourse therefore includes and excludes, it centres and marginalizes, and reveals both the explicit and the implicit in ways that contest the powers behind the meta-narratives. Using the term 'discourse' comes to indicate that Beatles history is never anything other than diachronic and synchronic fragments. This information should not be news to many Beatles writers, were they not so enamoured of their subjects, so unreceptive to theory, and so wrapped-up in the notion of 'truth'. One might even suggest that such 'Fab Four' meta-narratives are fundamentally misconceived and doomed to disappoint.

A singular history of artistic achievement can never truly be written. The relatively different speeds at which society absorbs, rearticulates and gives any artistic shape space and meaning allow for different readings: different epiphanies, acceptances and refusals; art, and its relationship with the cultural environments within which it is given multifarious meaning, is a moving target. We might describe this relationship in cultural terms as 'significant creative space' – creative space to which we can assign a mark of identity, be it a name, a history, or a culture: in short we ascribe political significance to the creativity and our canons are then formulated. However there are problems with such marks of identity when we attempt to historicize the same, for firstly we often see the creativity as relatively stable and assign to it a status of stasis rather than kinesis – we do not allow any other forms of significance (or space) to come into view. We erroneously ascribe distinct 'othernesses' to events that actually emerge from and receive uneven sustenance within, the overarching culture (e.g. the very history of the Beatles). Furthermore we tend to focus on narrow concepts of identity (such as subcultures) only to universalize their value and meaning – as if all people received encoded information at one and the same time and decoded it similarly. Finally we tend to acknowledge historically our creative universe by reversing ourselves out of the present, fashioning 'flawed' heroes, and perhaps even admonishing certain characters for moving away from our canon (even when we know that creative time is kinetic and subject to fluctuation).

This work intends to highlight several identity-giving 'significant creative spaces' around which important spheres of meaning and sound revolved in Liverpool between the pre-WWII era and the late-1970s. The work calls to attention several contexts that the usual rock, pop, or indeed Beatles-related narratives have fallen short of recording and contesting, such as domestic and collective listening practices, record shops as arbiters of co-creative taste cultures, concepts surrounding pejorative genre descriptors and cultural geographies as socio-political delineators of musical authenticity, etc. The illumination of disparate popular music discourses has been overshadowed by an over-concentration on selected genres, idealized images, and the creation of a popular music 'universal standpoint' concerning meaning and value (in Liverpool and elsewhere) where no such universality actually exists. There are always several generic fields of play at one and the same time, and these invite the historical researcher to draw different conclusions on popular music value. The case studies introduced below illustrate that in Liverpool during this important period of the twentieth century, real people in real places interacted with several discrete and interlocking popular musical scenes – sometimes at one and the same time.

Trad jazz – you don't see me

> People go on about Liverpool being symbolized by the Beatles and things like
> that. Well you can keep that sort of thing. For me Liverpool is symbolized by the
> Merseysippi Jazz Band. (Steve Voce in Thompson, 1994:10)

Musical 'taste' cannot be shepherded, is almost entirely contingent and reliant on
the vagaries of mood, time, place and space. Similarly, popular music reception
strategies cannot be pre-planned or constructed like a historical 'military operation'
– and cannot be historicized, as such. Therefore the partially hidden practices of
musicians and receivers somewhat out of canonical focus ought to be investigated
in order to delve into chance, convergence and kinetic taste cultures. For the
popular music historian a great challenge of recording historical significance via
such conjunctures remains. Arthur Marwick states:

> Neat equations, still less general laws, do not figure in the historian's work. The
> interactions, convergences, 'feedback loops', uncovered by historians testify
> rather to the significance in their subject, as in the natural sciences, of 'chaos'.
> (Marwick, 1998:16)

As an example of such idiosyncrasy (indeed 'chaos') let us briefly consider the
records of (from Merseyside) the Merseysippi Jazz Band – perhaps the longest
running British traditional jazz band of all time. This band was by no means prolific
in the recording stakes, preferring instead to earn a part-time living from what they
loved most – playing jazz, but between 1954 and 1958 they were signed with
Carlo Krahmer's tiny London-based Esquire label; it appears that these records
were not always easy to obtain. Liverpool jazz fan Arthur Critchley recalls:

> I ordered a copy of a Merseysippis EP in the mid-1950s from Rushworth &
> Dreapers – about 1955, I think, but could I get it? I went to the shop every
> Saturday for a month to see if it had arrived but nothing doing. Eventually I got
> an address for the label, wrote direct and sent them a postal order and it arrived
> within a week. (Critchley to Brocken, 2006)

A good piece of oral testimony, to be sure, but what can be learnt? Well, in the first
instance that hearing certain sounds on record was not always easy in post-WWII
Merseyside. This judgment is confirmed by renowned Dylanologist Michael Grey
who hails from Birkenhead. At the *Robert Shelton Conference* held at The Bluecoat
Arts Centre in Liverpool in 2001 Grey discussed a time when one might request a
record from a Birkenhead record shop only to be told that it was either (a) in the
charts and had therefore sold-out or (b) wasn't in the charts, and so not in stock.
This might of course be something of an exaggeration – but perhaps not by much.
Actually getting to hear a piece of recorded music in the immediate post-war era in
Liverpool could be a rather fraught (yet ultimately exciting) experience. This was

unquestionably not always the fault of the record shop because all sounds took a lot longer to permeate society. However, the monopoly of the record industry by only a few record companies such as Decca, EMI, Pye, and Philips, together with the domination of the public broadcasting system by the BBC (and to a lesser extent Radio Luxembourg) meant that the unusual or archaic often went unheard by swathes of people. This was even the case on ('magical') Merseyside where, if one believes the myths, records turned up in Liverpool via Cunard vessels months before they were even made, never mind released. Such information informs us that popular music's relationships with and battles against cultural practices are contingent.

For example, we can see that according to the above Critchley-Grey template in Liverpool and Birkenhead, record collecting was frustrated by the *un*availability of certain sounds and created important social and even postal networks surrounding the consumption and production of music (what might have been advertised as being available on record, and what actually was available could be two completely different things). So, for some, records were conditional representations of immanence, difference, and diversity and as such viewed as holding great symbolic value: they were certainly not simply 'functional artefacts'. For the MJB listening to records was central to new ways of learning to play musical instruments and in understanding different cultures; actually having a recording deal was not especially important to them. However, diachronically participation in such record consumption was not open to all: class and income greatly discriminated between those music consumers who were able to afford records and those who were not. For my father, the apparently simple act of purchasing new records was beyond his income range, hence for him the equally symbolic convergence of radio (and later television).

BBC broadcasts were demarcated by judgements based around various class-based perspectives of popular music; genres such as traditional jazz were aired as representations of authenticity, and the musical interests of certain 'young people'. The MJB duly benefited, regionally and (at times) nationally from this exposure. But in some households (such as my own), inverted class judgements were at play. My father felt patronized by a great deal of the output of the BBC and only listened to the Light Programme when there was no alternative. When ITV arrived in 1955, it was this TV channel, rather than any offering from the BBC, that became the dominant arbiter of taste in the Brocken household. The point here is that even allowing for the BBC's exposure of trad jazz, the genre was not ubiquitous among UK listeners. In our living room it was not even instantly 'recognizable' amid the sound quotients offered by the Light Programme where one was more likely to hear Al Martino than Mick Mulligan, Perry Como rather than Ken Colyer, and the Merseysippi Jazz Band was a completely unknown quantity.

Arthur Critchley's comments also ask us to consider Esquire as a 'commercial' enterprise, for if distribution was such a problem, was Esquire actually commercial in the real sense of the word, or more like a club or society (as were, to begin with, Tempo and Topic)? It appears that funding for the Esquire sessions were minimal and royalties non-existent, yet the 'Merseysippis' continued to record for Krahmer until the latter decided not to record any more British artists in 1959. This, one feels, had more to do with the jazz status, rather than the business acumen, of the label. Sales were in all probability not a great motivator for at least three of those four years, however having reduced to such a minute level that according to Krahmer they 'just do not warrant further expenditure' (Krahmer in Leigh, 2002:108), it seems clear that financial expediency won out. But it was probably all of little consequence to the band: the 'Merseysippis' made far more money out of gigs and BBC recording sessions. In those pre-M6 days London was about as far away from Merseyside as one could get (even on the train) and although exciting, recording sessions were costly both in time and money, especially when sales were so weak. Ultimately neither the band nor Krahmer appear to have lost a great deal of sleep over the dissolution of this recording agreement.

Prior to the Esquire deal, the Merseysippi Jazz Band organized their own recording session. But this was not necessarily to do with the idea of making a 'trad jazz record' for a specialized, independent market, in line with other independent labels such as Tempo and Esquire. In fact the MJB did not appear to have been making any kind of specific statement at all. MJB member John Lawrence informed Spencer Leigh 'We just wanted the kick out of making a record and we weren't expecting to sell them' (*ibid:*103). This first Merseysippi Jazz Band record was a limited edition 78 rpm of 'Moose March' and 'Friendless Blues' – recorded by Johnny Roadhouse at his Decibel Studios in Manchester in 1952. In those days, purchase tax had to be added to any record run of over 100 so only 99 were pressed. The band received 8 copies and the rest were sold, here and there. Retrospectively, this can perhaps be seen to have been a significant event for it was probably the first such recording by a Liverpool jazz band, but it was by no means a 'commercial' enterprise and was hardly earth shattering news at the time; the fact that the band could actually afford to record this one-off single is, conceivably the most revealing historical signifier. The MJB recordings were not only rooted in somewhat purist (perhaps even 'alternative') musical traditions, but also in visible social and material conditions. This recording activity informs us that one mode of enquiry open to us is a consideration of trad jazz's somewhat middle-class, suburban roots and this could be further corroborated by the fact that although the 'Merseysippis' were an adept band working in a niche market, and could have turned professional at any time, they decided against this avenue.

So, the Merseysippi Jazz Band was part of a decidedly *ad hoc* state of affairs and, together with the memories of Arthur Critchley and Michael Grey, this information almost inadvertently captures taste cultures, retail and wholesale apathy, the tribulations of independent recording labels and studios, together with issues surrounding class and the somewhat unknown direction of trad jazz in the early-mid 1950s. This historical information simply cannot be ignored and its presence counsels the researcher to avoid prescriptive judgements before embarking upon research. There are few social subjects capable of forcing through a redistribution of sensibilities; even though one might suggest that the Beatles were such a group of individuals, the nature, content, goals, organization and affect of not only their creative work, but also of others needs to be scrutinized in order for this assertion to be made with any degree of confidence. It should be conceded that the many musical 'scenes' to which the Beatles did not effectively subscribe, have equal significance in any discourse analysis *of* the Beatles.

Folk music on Merseyside: several northern songs

Liverpool's dalliances with popular music forms neither began nor ended with beat, or traditional jazz, music. Consider, also, another other important 'scene' in late-1950s Liverpool: the one surrounding folk music. For writers of history attempting to record meaning in and of the production and reception of popular music, folk music historicism continues to be a major challenge (see Brocken, 2003). For some, it is hard to make sense of a lot of history without using some kind of idea of 'fractured' (thus realistic) causation, and folk music historiography abounds in such fractures (e.g. writers such as Karl Dallas (with Laing, Denselow and Shelton), 1975, Fred Woods, 1979, Niall MacKinnon, 1993). One might even suggest that a kind of reverse *avant garde* exists in the folk scene where a pre-selected distant image of a past appears more authentic than the vividly inauthentic immediately preceding past. In this kind of mythologized history there seems to be a custodianship of discourse: one is almost inducted into a specific type of dialogue where nobody is particularly interested in what is said as long as it is compatible with, and can be articulated by an approved discourse. Derived from this mode of thought, the historical nature of a great deal of popular music historicism established in the 1960s has also reinforced a certain type of historical conventional wisdom surrounding conflict culture. Some popular music historiography, greatly influenced by folk binary oppositions, has been structured as containing hierarchies and meritocracies based around authenticities contra to the so-called formalized (actually disorganized) structures of the music industry. Here the 'creative' pop musician is an 'artist' in the 'folk sense' – containing the 'one man against the world' stereotype that continues to contaminate a great deal of popular music writing.

More recently, some popular music writers (e.g. Moy, 2000, Beadle, 1993, Reynolds, 1990, 1998) have adapted to concepts that suggest a life under conditions of permanent and incurable uncertainty without an over-arching meta-narrative to which we should all reference. According to this matrix a musical life exists in the presence of an unlimited quantity of competing authenticities, unable to prove their claims to be grounded in anything more solid and binding than their own historically-shaped conventions. However, folk causations still channel interpretive disparities to represent 'the real' often according to a pre-determined template. The result is that, in folk histories the abandonment of causation seldom occurs, for pre-scribed folk historiography has tended to be linked with ideas constructed by Marxist (and it must be said cod-Marxist) historians about the dialectic process of history being determined by struggle and alienation; this is linked with concepts about production rather than consumption as the primary determinant of the condition of history. However, the historical realms within which Liverpool's folk scenes emerged are far more complex than this.

It had already occurred to well-known independent broadcaster and documentary maker Daniel Farson in his work *Beat City* (broadcast by Rediffusion, 24 December 1963), that variable and disparate histories both preceded and existed side-by-side with the 'explosion' of music-making in and around the Liverpool of the 1960s. Notwithstanding some truly phony pronouncements in *Beat City*, to his credit Farson identified a thriving folk music community. He focused in particular on the events at Gregson's Well pub in Low Hill where the Spinners held court and by doing so, claimed that 'folk music was a natural feature of the Liverpool scene – springing from [...] sea shanties' (Farson, 1963, ATV). Farson also used Jacqueline MacDonald's version of Frank Kelly's 'Liverpool Lullaby' as part of his soundtrack. The Spinners and Jacquie MacDonald subsequently enjoyed international distinction as folk music popularizers (the latter as part of the duo Jacquie and Bridie) but they represented only the tip of a multiplicity of folk music discourses that had evolved in Liverpool throughout the 1950s and 1960s.

Even a cursory glance at the Spinners' 'audience' (if that is the correct word) in Farson's 'Gregson's Well' TV section suggests (like the above information re the MJB) that a distinct middle-class market existed for this style of music. Farson recognized this and juxtaposed his illustration with another – this time of two pub singers perhaps from the Scotland Road or Vauxhall Road areas of the city singing Jim Reeves' 'Welcome to My World' – these were clearly worlds that seldom, if ever, collided. Farson's suggestion was that while folk music in Liverpool was embraced by the political Left, this was not a product of the working-class culture it so dearly wished to represent. The Spinners' folk club was indeed distinctly bourgeois, as were the various folk clubs that existed from the late-1950s to the 1970s at the University of Liverpool, but although a dominant force, was but one of numerous socio-cultural and musical shades within the spectrum of Liverpool folk scenes.

For example, there were politically aligned clubs, vaguely suburban Left folk clubs, an anarchist element (as evidenced by the presence of Stan Ambrose), folk elements to both the Anglican (e.g. the Crofters) and Roman Catholic churches, plus an evangelical element via the visiting Fisher Folk collectives. A pro-I.R.A element existed, plus a populist end of the folk continuum that was drawn to folk music as representing a kind of nautical-cum-patrimonial sod, particularly evident on the Wirral. So, one unitary folk scene did not exist and one should perhaps advocate that there existed a constellation of different folk sounds and meanings that (equally) represented different uses for folk music under divergent cultural circumstances. The expression 'folk scene' appears self-explanatory but remains genuinely enigmatic.

Indeed, the very folk music one might hear in (say) the Magazine pub in New Brighton was very different from that in (say) the Coffee House pub in Wavertree. In the former, singing was often unadorned and unaccompanied, carrying the weight of anti-commercialist Marxist discourse. In the Coffee House the atmosphere was far more affective and a variety of sounds permeated the room (from shanties on the one hand to singer/songwriter material on the other) so that the music's consumption was less directed. On the Wirral, clubs were equally diverse with, for example, the Boathouse at Parkgate having an English country dance band theme via the resident B's Band, Bob Buckle's club at the Central Hotel in Birkenhead featuring guests and guitarists (everyone from Nigel Denver to Ralph McTell), and so on. Some folk-oriented singers, such as Billy Maher, worked on the perimeters of these folk music 'scenes' on Merseyside and did not see the folk club as central to their activities. Maher believed in taking such music to different venues rather than forcing people to pass along an administered pathway. For others, however, the very presence of a folk club was regarded as pivotal – for them, it was the place and space where authenticity was enacted. If the task of the popular music historian is to reconstruct 'reasons' for past actions, then these have to be unpredictable, erratic, impulsive. Prescription histories of a unitary folk revival do not even get close to an understanding of the multifaceted feeders required to support a variety of scenes in and around such a city as Liverpool at the height of the folk revival in the 1960s and 1970s.

So, Daniel Farson's 'discovery' of a folk scene surrounding the Spinners and Jacqui and Bridie represented only a small facet of factionalist folk *scenes* on Merseyside. There were many rifts and these were to some extent geographic (in some cases actually divided by the River Mersey), class-based (not really working-class, but decidedly middle-class), at times quasi-religious and political, but all contingent of changing, converging and diverging demographic needs and demands. Folk histories are by nature empiricist, they are committed to the idea that somehow via the establishment of social oppositions, the musical past can be objectively re-created by believers. Perhaps rather than constantly looking for empiricist oppositions, folk music historians should spend more time uncovering how musical/cultural spaces converge and develop, and how changing forms of creativity fill such spaces at different times.

Rhythm Clubs: your mother did know, but can't remember

The inter-war dance band 'scene' in Liverpool is a further example of how differences of place and space are of great significance to the popular music historian. The outward image of inter-war dance music on Merseyside is that it was parochial and dependent upon bands playing strictly for dancing patrons (see Jenkins, 1994). Certainly, several local bands and musicians – including Jim McCartney (father of Paul) and Walter Richards (father of Alan – see later) – were very popular in certain specific social spaces within Liverpool. Wally Richards, for example, played not only local halls, but also tea dances with Harry Rosen's Band at Lewis' Department Store in Liverpool city centre. But Wally was at heart, a 'jazzer', and backed several important visiting Black jazz musicians at the Liverpool Philharmonic Hall, such as Coleman Hawkins. Wally had an extensive record collection and enjoyed listening to music with friends and relatives, and playing at local Rhythm Clubs. Certain spaces and places, then, were linked via the act of attentive, communal listening to ideas concerning jazz experimentation. Drummer Jack Terry testified to the significance of one Liverpool-based Rhythm Club of the 1930s:

> I ran this Rhythm Club in town in Renshaw Street. Quite a gathering of people used to come and we put record recitals on, jazz record recitals, and different musicians used to come along and bring their instruments. At the end, round 10 o'clock we'd have a bit of a jam session. Everyone would join in and we'd improvise on all the standard tunes of the day. This went on every Sunday.
>
> I also used to run a drum club in the afternoon, and there was a guitar player who used the same room for teaching guitar. We had a lot of good times there on a Sunday night. If a band was coming to (say) the Empire or the Shakespeare, to play for the week, we'd send a letter to the agent and mention that the musicians were invited along, just to have a listen. We'd get some beer in for them and it was amazing. They'd bring an instrument along with them and join in (Terry in Jenkins, 1994:56)

This quote from an interview conducted several years ago by the Institute of Popular Music in Liverpool asks, perhaps unwittingly, important questions about uncertainty and direction. For example, how do such gatherings of musicians re-define tastes? What criteria are used to relegate certain musical practices (such as tea dances)? How do we then historicize the importance of such collective musical value judgements (are they truly collective?)? It is possible for new relations to develop around differing sounds, for new symbolic representations to emerge concerning moves towards new musical relationships. But on a practical level how are such 'new' sounds heard? How are ideas of authority formed? If 'new' sounds become canonized: under which criteria? (perhaps the comfort of an uncontested 'jazz superiority') There should appear within this rather disorderly jazz realm an analysis into the popular music already incorporated into the fabric of British society, especially via the BBC and the record industry. This would invite enquiries concerning what it meant to be a British 'jazzer' during these periods – whether amateur or professional – and whether jazz was seen as oppositional.

The history of jazz is coterminous with and inextricably linked to the history of radio and records. Jazz musicians have always depended on these media forms, the repertoires of all dance bands were deeply affected by 'wireless' broadcasts, and the very act of listening (and dancing) to music on the radio was an important aspect of life for millions. The act of listening to and collecting records during the 1930s was increasingly considered by some to be an important taste culture in its own right. The growth of the sound picture as a habitual system of communication was actively encouraged by the *Melody Maker* and although radio reception was at first a domestic affair, jazz enthusiasts came to form Rhythm Clubs with the sole intention of listening to and learning from authentic recordings in order to develop their hobby – which might also include playing. To paraphrase Parsonage (2005), the first reference to Rhythm Clubs appeared in a *Melody Maker* of 3 June 1933 in a letter from Mr James P. Holloway concerning what the *Melody Maker* labelled 'Hot Circles'. Indeed the first Rhythm Club in the UK was entitled 'The Melody Maker Club No. 1' and met in the west-end of London.

By May 1935 there existed a body entitled the British Federation of Rhythm Clubs and Nott (2002:199) notes 90 clubs in existence. Perhaps those indulging in Rhythm Club and other such collecting activities began to feel that they constituted a music subculture. They certainly made demands upon the record industry to release jazz recordings in greater numbers, and even approached the BBC with new ideas about broadcasting such music. As a consequence a noticeable shift in the styles of jazz being played began to take place in late-1930s' Liverpool. Some dance band members, possibly rather bored and stultified by the outpourings of the radio media and the strict tempo tastes of dancers, turned to Rhythm Clubs. Bert Jayston recalled to this writer:

> I started by listening to anything I could get my hands on but then after picking up a bit of piano and then a few records, I started to refine my tastes. I enjoyed Benny Goodman's music and tried to hear that whenever I could, although I don't recall much of it on the radio. I used to go to the Rhythm Club at Chauffeurs in Hope Street on a Sunday afternoon. We'd listen to this stuff on the gramophone and try to vamp it ourselves. It could be hard work and sometimes we'd make a bit of a mess of it but seemed more alive than the stuff we were playing at dances. By the time I'd decided to take it seriously and consider going pro, I got called up for the Navy and that was that. (Jayston to Brocken, 2002)

In retrospect we might suggest that Bert's comments marked a small beginning for the later trad jazz movement – but this would not have been at all clear at the time and we should not dragoon such events to serve later purposes. Instead we can state that the development of amateur and professional jazz performing was a result of advances in both recording and radio technology. In both cases but especially regarding recording, the technology allowed closer scrutiny of the music as a text, and for the likes of Bert Jayston this made the step from being a collector to being a performer relatively painless. These jazzers probably saw their work primarily as fun and perhaps part of a continuing debate about the nature, function, and quality of jazz and jazz-related music. One might claim that jazz represented an alternative storage of knowledge which generated different meanings from those hermetically sealed popular tastes in and around the Liverpool dancehalls of the 1930s. But even this would be a rather empiricist statement to make. Jazz was constructed meaningfully for those involved and there were checking mechanisms for validating their readings – and that's about as far as we should be prepared to go.

But investigations into Rhythm Clubs are revealing. If nothing else they suggest that Liverpool's maritime claims on musical tastes are somewhat mythological and indeed passive. Via actively listening to records, radio, movies and indeed each other, budding jazz musicians were able to develop creative spaces across the city in a most pro-active of ways. These spaces were constantly supplemented by even more records, jam sessions and journals such as *Melody Maker*, and encouraged many young people of the 1930s to develop 'on the hoof' interests into the hitherto uncharted musical waters of jazz.

Skiffle and Liverpool: the continuing story of Lonnie Donegan

Lonnie Donegan was an unquestionable influence on young Liverpudlians in the 1950s, but I have written elsewhere (2006) that his work is grossly under-rated, especially by rock writers. I have also suggested that Donegan was a champion of a way of making music – skiffle – that appealed to a great many young people at specific moments in time and that his style of music appealed to an even wider variety of listeners and practitioners because he represented popular music social mores. Donegan held aspirations as a mainstream artist, and we should not hold this against him for it was this apparently 'inauthentic' mainstream that brought Donegan to the fore, not the albeit creative 'underground' spaces of trad jazz and skiffle. Lonnie Donegan openly conspired in his own success and was neither a provider of a musical '*ur*-history' for a rock music narrative, nor a prototype 'beatnick' for later generations to corral into position. He existed in the late-1950s as a figure of unquestionable synchronic and diachronic significance, not only for the benefit of later historians, but for many people at those moments in time – he was a pop star.

Donegan's ideas were typically oxymoronic. One the one hand he claimed to be something of a purist, on the other he tended to guess his way through his sources. For example he once described in an interview with BBC Radio Merseyside's Geoff Speed that a skiffle party reminded him of the idea of 'Phil the Fluter's Ball' – an Irish stereotype in song. The kind of music at the US skiffle parties was in Donegan's words only 'roughly parallel to what we were doing, so we called it skiffle, but we just did it for variety' (Donegan to Speed, BBC, 1971). One might argue, therefore, that skiffle was in a sound sense a sketchy conjecture far closer to the models that had preceded it than it was to rock 'n' roll and rhythm and blues. The noise levels and the singing styles of skifflers such as Donegan were far more European tonal than African-American, so one might propose that the perceptions of 'difference' surrounding skiffle were formulated within the institutionalized European tone model framework of musical ambience (if not 'knowledge', as such). Articulations of 'difference' were actually based on 'similarities' and skiffle was for some a kind of acceptable, organic 'Light' music (the singing style, the beat, and decibel level of Elvis Presley probably signified a real difference). However rather than considering skiffle via sound alone, we should also concern ourselves with how the genre questioned the rather ethnocentric cultural models of popular music that were presented in Britain in the 1950s.

It is unclear whether his actions were witting or unwitting, but Lonnie Donegan certainly fore-grounded previously subordinated and marginalized cultural discourses and traditions. Indeed, the social perspective offered by skiffle – which musically inhabited a space somewhere between white and black histories – is of considerable political and theoretical interest. Donegan's material was fascinating in that a proportion of it dealt with slavery in some form ('Take This Hammer', 'John Henry', 'Rock Island Line', etc). Listeners were therefore to a degree in collusion with both the musical and social conjunctural opportunities presented by and within the songs, and were able to assess them in comparison to the economic, cultural and ideological constraints comprising the modern world at that time. Despite being musically formed out of existing tonal codes and volumes, skiffle was seen as defiantly different by some, a revolt largely by middle-class youth against the hegemonic middle-classes themselves. Skiffle had much to do with fragmentation, heterogeneity and with the articulation of difference and marginality that we often associate with life today. While it was undoubtedly a fetish for the middle-classes, it was also instrumental in expanding access to a musical form previously the domain of the musical elitist – some of whom were no doubt migrants from Bert Jayston's Rhythm Club era.

In Liverpool, the owner of the Cavern club Alan Sytner recognized distinct class differences between those who came to listen to jazz, to skiffle, and those who were drawn to rock 'n' roll. It is well recorded that, as a modern jazz fan he couldn't have cared less about skiffle and in point of fact disliked and discouraged rock. He regarded himself as a sophisticated 21-year-old and noted that 'there were very marked demographics according to the night of the week and what was being put on' (Leigh, 2002:92). So what was skiffle doing at the Cavern? Some might suggest that it was merely a tolerated offshoot of trad jazz, but Donegan's national popularity does not confirm this constricted idea. We should instead attempt to contextually understand the presence of Liverpool-based skifflers listening, jamming and riffing at a Cavern gig without any recourse concerning what came before or, for some, what was to follow. For example, one ex-skiffler told this writer some years ago that he:

> went to the Cavern because of Donegan. The way I saw it at that time in Liverpool was that there was nothing happening for me as a young teenager; when I heard skiffle I really liked it and decided to see if there was anything local. Well I didn't find anything – maybe I wasn't looking hard enough. But then I found out about a national competition at the Cavern – so I went. For me the Cavern was responding to the *national* popularity of skiffle. Skiffle was pop to me – I knew nothing about it being part of the jazz scene or anything like that. (Bethell to Brocken, 1999)

There was even a branch of the 'Lonnie Donegan Skiffle Club' based *at* the Cavern. Skiffle was clearly both contemporaneous and retrospective; of today and yesterday, but served a multitude of purposes for those involved: stretching from signifyin' Black America to signifying success on the Hit Parade.

Country music in Liverpool: there are places *not* remembered

I recall my father saying to me that after he had returned to Liverpool in 1947 from the army he barely recognized the place. Nevertheless wanting (in his words) 'a quiet life' he knuckled down and got on with things. My father identified with the mobility of over seven years of army service, and for him this contrasted sharply with the rather stultifying sameness that pervaded the city he previously knew during the 1930s. So much so, in fact, that he frequently spoke nostalgically about his formative years in Liverpool before 1939.

This thinking marked several post-WWII discourses surrounding music appreciation in Liverpool. Specifically, there was a tendency to knit the inter-textuality of 'Americana' with the austerity of post-war Liverpool. This perspective is worthy of further consideration when observing the significance of country music affiliation and activity in the Liverpool of the post-WWII era. Most popular music researchers interested in the Beatles and/or Liverpool are aware of the importance of country music in the city – in particular, references to Hank Walters crop up in such texts (e.g. Leigh, 1991, McManus, 1994, Cohen 2005, 2007, etc); but how did country music form an alliance with day-to-day life in Liverpool?

Perhaps it had something to do with the fact that particular Liverpudlians chose to invest a small part of their aspirations into a small part of American history – the settlement of the western wilderness (at least as it was presented by the media systems of the day). The last frontier of the 1800s became not merely a source of excitement and romance, but also one of inspiration. The West, and 'its' music, was seen as providing a set of unique and imperishable core values such as individualism, self-reliance and a positive sense of right and wrong. These values had a tendency to merge with concepts about release through the controlling of one's own working day – a crucial feature of local life in the post-WWII era, at least up until the late-1980s. So, as a construct of the imagination brought about partially by aspects of the media of the time (such as film, records, and radio), the creation of ideas associated with the West in Liverpool is of some significance. Of course there was also an irony, for this assemblage of fragments of images had little to do with US history, *per se* (it was, of course, impossible to actually get into these other times in this or any other way).

We manufacture history and rely on what Steiner describes as 'axiomatic fictions' (Steiner in Jenkins, 2003:49). By this he means constructions brought about by powerful contemporary assumptions concerning what constitutes historical 'knowledge'. Beliefs about the West and 'Going West' became, effectively, a function myth. The West became a timescape of romance and when in the post-WWII era, Liverpool as a city was seen relatively unable or unwilling to resolve its inherent social problems, the glue with which Liverpudlians held things together came to include such sets of illusions. Of course, if enough people believe illusions, they become 'truth': hence a partial explanation for the practical uses of country music in Liverpool. Maybe this is one of the reasons why a young Ralph ('Hank') Walters, described by some as the instigator of country music on Merseyside, was so inspired by the music of Hank Williams – for some, Williams was a kind of singing John Wayne. Certainly the kinds of popular music, media worlds and creative cultural spaces that both pre-dated and surrounded Liverpool country singer Hank Walters require further investigation from this point of view, for when any 'birth' of a scene is attributed to one man – even implicitly (Cohen, 2007:72) one is left with a hagiographical image from which it is difficult to reverse. One should ask, instead, more questions about how such function myths worked for Liverpudlians, how they were mediated and how they then related to place. By doing so, the oppressive certainties offered by Merseybeat historiography are modified. For numerous people on Merseyside, it wasn't all about rock 'n' roll: at least to the exclusion of everything else.

For Mick O'Toole, country music lyrics represented a break with the youth music of the day, in some respects reflecting the 'adult' pathway chosen by Nashville 'countrypolitan' instigators Steve Sholes and Chet Atkins. Mick informed this writer that he came to prefer the lyrics of country songs because 'they appeared to be at least saying something'. Conversely, however, there were also musical signs that enabled him to move comfortably between the country and rock genres – usually by way of Elvis Presley (and Hank Snow): Presley's 'first L.P. was such a great mix of rock 'n' roll and country; I'd read everything about him; knew about his country roots and could tell the difference in the songs even then. Having suffered through Dennis Lotis and Dickie Valentine on the BBC Light Programme the excitement of Elvis was just unbelievable'(O'Toole to Brocken, 2008).

Many country music fans in the Liverpool of the 1950s and 1960s also appeared to prefer their music in pubs rather than clubs, as Daniel Farson also noted in his 1963 ITV documentary, but Hank Walters' club The Black Cat was an exception for it did not appear to have the posturing of a 'night club' *per se*. Mick O'Toole also recalled 'A proper 'night out' in those days meant going into town rather than local; Hank's club *was* in town but was also 'local' in that it was always a good night, often with a guest band as well as the Dusty Road Ramblers (Walter's group), and they would do half the night each; but it wasn't like going to a night club – not that there were many in Liverpool at that time' (*ibid*). Mick O'Toole discusses this country world in both a genre and geographic sense. The very location of the Black Cat (being 'in town') legitimized the venue and by existing in a night club on London Road, Hank Walters' country nights were not considered 'parochial' in the geographical sense. But they enjoyed the status of parochial events in the cultural sense – important signifiers for some fans of country music.

These comments perhaps help us to understand how all UK country music activities have been largely excluded from popular music studies histories, for they are difficult to pin-down. The more empiricist popular music writers have a tendency to demarcate practically everything via genres, with the accompanying suggestion that rooted authenticity effectively 'speaks for itself'. But genres are floating, shifting signifiers that relocate and reassemble in the most diverse of places. Country music was re-routed and reassembled in Liverpool as a localized activity, a kind of 'counter' to counter-cultural higher consciousness. Ironically, one of the most cherished qualities of country music activity in Liverpool surrounds its 'autonomy'. This discourse of self-sufficiency includes the *lack* of authenticity awarded to it by rock-ist critics, revels in the mediation of the function myth of the West, and is unflinchingly associated with local and international commercialism. These motifs also contribute positively to the Liverpudlian self-reliance theme: as an attribute of great local value.

Cabaret and Liverpool: filed away as 'bad', yes it is

The word 'cabaret' has probably never represented a British genre of music, as such, for it stands in the place of other words such as 'variety' or 'assortment' and is associated with terms such as 'atmosphere' and 'ambience'. Musically, it stands for diversity suggesting comedy, song, dance, and theatre. Culturally, cabaret defines a performance venue: a restaurant or nightclub with a stage, an audience sitting at tables (often dining or drinking) and performances being introduced by a master of ceremonies. But in the UK the word has also been anchored as a mode of expression. For some it refers to music residing firmly in the 'mainstream' or even 'Bad Music' zones. Alongside UK country, cabaret music can be reviled by critics and ignored by scholars – despite, (or perhaps because of) widespread popularity.

So what of the seemingly negative associations with the 'mainstream'? Much popular music dialogue is suspicious of mainstream music activity, as if it were contaminated. This issue is not only one of representation, in that what we regard as mainstream is usually that which is presented to us from the core of the music industries, but also one of reportage in that commentators of popular music activity often see the auteur as the *bona fide* centre of popular music's efficacy; this view also carries with it the perception of the popular as art. But, paradoxically once it becomes possible to repeat 'auteur-ship', the process begins whereby that auteur-ship is in danger of becoming itself 'traditional' – a place where it is *accepted* as art – a complex, ambiguous proposition. Therefore, not only is it increasingly difficult for contemporary artists to continue to regard non-mainstream activity as autonomous, but there can be no evasion of studies of the definitions and parameters of so-called mainstream popular music. In fact, given the mainstream's ability to process itself inexorably towards the obsolete, our marking of such a paradigm is probably of greater value to the historian than the mantras espousing the universal emancipatory nature of authentic music. As Simon Frith writes:

'What is at issue is not its immediate qualities of effect, but the opportunities it offers for further interpretation, for a reading, for a reading against the grain. And from this perspective even the judgement that something is "bad" is really a political rather than an aesthetic assessment' (Frith, 1996:14). The mainstream as 'bad' should not be avoided, but reconsidered and re-contextualized. The everyday act of judging things as 'good' and 'bad' can reveal ideological implications of vast proportions; but distaste for the middle-of-the-road does not justify exclusion from historical narratives. Studies of, for example, the cabaret scene across the UK reveal much about contemporary British society.

Liverpudlian Alan Richards has been and always will be unapologetically 'mainstream'. As a teenage pop song writer in the early 1970s he gradually moved into cabaret work and thence to studio and A&R management. From this position he set in motion a record label in Liverpool that could be described as one of the first acts of 1970s UK record label decentralization. However, this is seldom recorded, as such, because the label (Stag Music) involved itself only in a peripheral way with rock music and when it first began to establish itself in 1973 it was in direct response to Liverpool's healthy cabaret scene. Stag Music has never received the attention it deserves from popular music historians because approaches to popular music histories are based around dominant oppositions, distributed as if they were agreed by everyone. It was thus 'agreed' that the cabaret circuit was seen to belong to someone called 'them', whereas the rock and folk scenes belonged to 'us' – but who were/are 'them and us', exactly? To its credit *Melody Maker* did publicize this localized activity in 1974 thanks to the work of former Clayton Square Mike Evans, who noted in an article entitled 'Stag Keep It Local':

> They said it should have happened years ago. When Brian Epstein first struck gold on the Merseyside music scene, they said it should have been done then. A Liverpool-based recording set up for local artists, decentralising the business from the traditional London axis in the same way as the American industry has always had its network of independents scattered throughout every city in the country. (Evans, *Melody Maker*, 13 July, 1974:17)

This reads rather like an article from two years hence, when punk rock began to gestate and labels such as Stiff, A Step Forward and Chiswick emerged in London, but Stag was concerned with Liverpool's vivid cabaret scene; presumably an irrelevance for those rock writers in the 1970s who preferred to speculate on Liverpool's popular music Parausia.

If the Stag Music record label was Liverpool's first recording label certain questions need to be asked: why did it exist? What of its releases? And why have we seldom heard of it? The Stag Music label created a platform for musical comedy artists such as Tom O'Connor to be known at first regionally and then nationally. But by doing so, it existed relatively outside the pronounced internality of the music industry at that point in time (1973). Point-of-sale techniques were usually frowned-upon by the major industry players precisely because they entrepreneurially unpacked the formal chains of command – those self-sustaining distribution systems erected to legitimize the industry's own antiquated procedures. Any such legitimization process inevitably comes under pressure if it cannot absolutely provide a transcendent standard of validity and the existence of Stag Music suggested that this validity was at best questionable and probably not even applicable. For example, O'Connor's album *Alright Mouth!* sold over 40,000 copies, but at no time registered on the album charts. It gained exposure via a distribution deal with Woolworth's but while not carrying a full price tag (yet not being licensed to a recognized 'budget' label) existed out-with the data compiled for assembling the album charts. So we have further open-ended questions that abandon the myth of authenticity surrounding Liverpool and its music. The presence of the Stag Music label leads us to not only discursive enquiries concerning Liverpool's cabaret scene, the popular music significance of the 'chicken in a basket' circuit, but to the very relevance of the record industry model and its still antiquated distribution network – a point of great relevance today with the demise of Entertainment UK and Pinnacle.

While Beatles-related narratives might have us believe that, by the 1970s, Liverpool was a 'special place': unique, liberal, ethnically mixed, and culturally diverse producing many popular music hybrids, it was probably like any other city that enjoyed a taste for the mainstream. This taste culture was successfully catered for by the likes of Stag Music and its links with local cabaret lounges such as the Wooky Hollow, the Rumford Coach House and Russell's. In the 1970s these cabaret clubs served people almost nightly and so local acts became prime topics of conversation and reputation. Cabaret artists therefore were not only powerful metaphors for sophistication, but also locality, and local identity: paradoxically authentic in the 'rock sense'. This mainstream cabaret scene was like all good popular music activities, a function of context and perspective, not inherently about being consciously anything other than entertainment. This 'mainstream' motif only succeeds in universalizing very important local and time-related activities, and lashing together wide-ranging interests into a totalizing concept inherent of liberalist popular music discourse. This ahistorical act propels people from the past into a controlling discourse of the present from which they cannot, obviously, escape. Indeed one of these controlling discourses concerns cabaret's supposed position as a stepping stone to national fame: this was never really the case – in fact occasionally quite the reverse was to take place. For example, hero of Liverpool's Wooky Hollow club, Lovelace Watkins, was already a 'star' of sorts around the UK cabaret circuit long before he emerged as 'new talent' on TV – and ITV did not serve him well, for the atmosphere surrounding his live performances could not be reproduced in a commercial TV studio and his career slipped as a consequence of such exposure. Another example might be that of the ever popular 'Star Turn' from the northeast of England. Star Turn was immensely popular in Liverpool, selling out such clubs as the Montrose on a regular basis in the 1980s with his ironic takes on club MCs and Jive Bunny 'megamixes', but he was a specialized act in a clearly identified market and could not transfer well to other forms of media. Although Liverpool's cabaret scene probably did inhabit what some might describe as a 'safer' middle ground, it triumphed by eluding the very pigeon-holing that has so dogged rock homilies; to be sure, cabaret music was never disguised as anything else.

R&B on Merseyside: Yer blues (or soul?)

As the 1963 success of the Beatles and other local rock groups such as Gerry and the Pacemakers, the Swinging Blue Jeans and the Searchers intensified, so too did the glare of the media gaze, bringing national attention to a previously largely forgotten city – a positive development, one might suggest. There was, however, a downside to this renaissance. For example, by 1964, the Beatles, having already been lured away from the city, were followed by a posse of younger hopefuls. For most of these would-be pop stars, an encouraging light flickered only briefly and dimly in the afterglow of that first wave; soon, day jobs or unemployment called most of them back to reality. It was a period of great creativity and indigenous pride, but one, also, of tremendous disappointments. The late Albie Power, bass player with the Kirkbys (who frequently played away from Liverpool) informed this writer that his days with the band were full of mixed emotions:

> Once back in Liverpool we struggled even to get a gig at times. This might be after we had been playing in the Midlands with the Spencer Davies Group, the Hellions or the Uglys. We could command good money in Birmingham and would be well received, but even though we would return to Liverpool whenever we could, we found that work there was hard to find by '65, '66; I felt I was effectively unemployed when I came home. We had quite a bit of chart success in Finland of all places but we were pretty anonymous back home. It was good to get back to see a football match however! (Power to Brocken, 2003)

Looking back, perhaps the one indisputable outcome of these adventures was a confirmation of shared separation and alienation. Certainly, complex social strategies to deal ironically with what appeared to be an increasingly ironic world were erected by many of Merseyside's young people at that time. Ultimately the city that 'produced' the Beatles was unable to offer Albie a musical lifeline; later, it could not 'resurrect' his music career. Albie was one of the many young men who, having married in the late-1960s, decided to pack-in playing music as a living, and move out of Liverpool to an overspill estate in Cheshire. One might argue that residues of such feelings still permeate Liverpool's victim culture to this very day.

Some young post-Beatles Liverpool groups played a brand of R&B far closer to the sounds of the Rolling Stones and the Pretty Things than 'Merseybeat', as such. These groups initially reflected a 'fresh' trend that had its musical origins away from Merseyside altogether. By late-1964 the Clayton Squares were probably one of the best groups around with lead singer Terry Hines having a great growling baritone in some ways reminiscent of Howling Wolf himself. Long-time R&B advocates the Roadrunners were formed when the Beatles were still playing locally (George Harrison once cited them as the best group in Liverpool) – and were for a while the only Liverpool-based R&B group. The Roadrunners were also fans of Howlin' Wolf and became popular with the art school and university student audience in Liverpool. They secured a Sunday night residency in the basement of Hope Hall (now the Everyman Theatre restaurant). Hope Hall, by 1964, was an 'art house' cinema with a licensed bar downstairs and was close enough to the School of Art and the University of Liverpool to attract students. The Roadrunners were joined by the Hideaways, the Cordes, and the Almost Blues by the beginning of 1964. The Hideaways took their name from the Hideaway, an art school-oriented coffee bar near the Pier Head. It was here that they received their first bookings. The Cordes and the Almost Blues were part of a grammar school breed of groups that flourished in the mid-1960s and signified an incursion into the previously working-class domain of beat groups. Les Johnson, principally of another grammar school-based group, the Detonators, now recalls that interest in blues and R&B was a class-based issue. For Les, 'blues never really made it in Liverpool as it did elsewhere because there was something very class-based about it. Some people would say we were musical snobs' (Johnson to Brocken, 2009).

However, whereas Les's interests in Sonny Terry and Brownie Magee eventually took him into the alternative poetry-cum-music scene of late-'60s Liverpool (and beyond), the Cordes seemed to resolve such high art/low art dichotomies by involving themselves in the musical 'grey areas' where R&B and soul music flowed together. Despite both 'R&B' and 'soul' monikers being constructions of the music industry at different times, for fans in Liverpool these genres were not the same, and did not represent the same value systems. One Liverpool musician interviewed by this writer stated that for him R&B represented 'something more earthy'; for another, soul was 'divided up between the [US] north and the south and the south was more like R&B'; another simply claimed that 'Jimmy Reid was Blues, Bobby Parker was R&B and Otis Redding was soul – it was a generational thing'. By 1966, in the established nightclub venues of Liverpool, the more groups played popular soul music rather than obscure R&B, the better. Such bands appealed far more to dancers and as a consequence received more bookings. The Cordes 'went soul' and were joined by the Almost Blues and the Fix. As a 'standalone' sound then, R&B in Liverpool became a thing of the past almost as quickly as it had become the bedrock of repertoire.

Some R&B groups never left Liverpool; others having left never returned as working artists. The Clayton Squares were a prime example of this latter development, joining the Don Arden stable only to get lost in a sea of similar bands in the Metropolis. The Mojos, the Riot Squad and the Cryin' Shames also suffered a similar fate. As these London-locked groups disbanded many individuals such as Mike Evans, Tom Evans, Judd Lander, Terry Hines, and Lewis Collins moved on, artistically. Perhaps this was a good thing, for by 1966 it was quite evident to any of these young men returning home that Liverpool was saturated with aspiring groups – many of whom were below standard, semi-pro and, given a different set of musical/social circumstances, would never have survived. At times, these latter groups were even accused of lowering the musical benchmark so much that band fees deflated to an unsustainable level. By the end of the decade there were far fewer bands in Liverpool and this dearth was brought about by the aforementioned glut in the market, poor playing standards, and the ubiquitous deejay.

Tastemakers in Liverpool: tell me what you hear

> The day you bought the record, where you were, what you were wearing and who was in your heart, will be etched into your soul, as well defined as the grooves that are pressed into your record. (David Lashmar to Pettit, 2008:61)

The R&B scene in Liverpool would not have been possible without the opportunity to hear relatively 'obscure' sounds emanating from the US, and while the BBC to this day holds itself up as a bastion and arbiter of all good taste, it should be recorded that the Corporation paid scant attention to R&B until groups emerged singing repertoires of such sounds. Instead, as with Rhythm Clubs in the 1930s, the importance of listening and record collecting should never be underestimated when considering how these new sounds came to the attention of young people in the post-WWII era. Like their 1930s jazz forebears, young R&B fans and musicians used recordings to learn about African American music. Les Johnson:

> If I were to try to recount to you how many times I listened to the likes of 'Boom Boom' or 'Hideaway' just to get the sound right I'd be here all day. I found it quite easy to pick up the bass notes but it also depended on the quality of record player I was using. The songs were often 12-bar blues, so that was OK, but could be far more complicated that you'd think. I remember listening to Bobby Parker's 'Watch Your Step' over and over again trying to get it right. In the end I just gave up and played it as I called it – and that was fine. But records, well they made *all* the difference – if you could get your hands on them! (Johnson to Brocken, 2009)

One might posit the theory that this is why much of this scene was effectively rather bourgeois, for few without the required record player, records and instruments could have culturally invested on such a concentrated level. On the other hand it might also draw our attention to the growing importance of hire purchase among working-class families in the 1960s. Hessy's Music Store, for example, was well-known for its somewhat reckless dabbling with the hire purchase market, with store manager Jim Gretty arranging loans for budding musicians who had little or no chance of paying them off.

The retailing of popular music in Liverpool is by and large a partially-hidden history. Instead, the romantic notion of Cunard Yanks bringing home armfuls of (e.g.) Little Richard records from the USA is favoured for the emblematic and romantic status it brings to Liverpool. The Cunard Yanks story is just that – a story, and tales such as these are the very substance of urban myths and legends. Although Cunard Yanks undoubtedly existed and did bring home recordings from their trips, these tended to be (in the case of Richard Barton) jazz and (for others) mostly country and western LPs and OST albums. It has been reported that other merchant seamen working for other shipping lines brought home R&B records. Rita Martelli, cousin of Eddie and Chris Amoo of the Real Thing, makes such a claim. Furthermore, records were sold at the US Air Base at Burtonwood, near Liverpool and a number of these filtered into the Liverpool 8 area of the city. But most of the songs that ended up being covered by the Beatles and their Merseybeat cohorts were actually available for purchase in the UK – usually on 45s bearing the labels of London-American, Pye R&B International, Oriole, and Top Rank. London-American, having taken over from Vogue as Decca's subsidiary to access the US independent market, was recognizable via its black and silver label. During the late-1950s and early-1960s licence deals were negotiated by Decca with labels such as Aladdin, Duke, Peacock, King, Jamie, Atlantic, Cadence, Specialty, Philles and Motown. Many such records failed to reach the British Top Twenty, and so could be found in the deletion bins of city-centre shops such as NEMS, Rushworth and Dreapers, and Woolworth's, or in second-hand shops such as Edwards' and Willdridge's. From here they travelled into the hands of many aspiring musicians. Of the 24 cover versions actually released on record by the Beatles up until 1966, 15 had previously been available in Liverpool on the London-American label, alone.

In Liverpool, then (and despite the myth of origin surrounding US records), certain record shops, record departments (and the ubiquitous radio) were constitutive of transforming listening practices. Different genres of music became more culturally audible by the existence of retail record shops caring about selling music that people had (or had not) heard on the radio. This is not 'romantic', in the 'Cunard Yank' sense, but is perhaps somewhat more realistic in that ordinary people can be seen participating in an *ad hoc* distribution system of shops, coffee bars, and venues – even radio and television. By highlighting retailers and broadcasting we partially abandon hagiography in popular music histories and identify that popular music is not singular but eclectic, perhaps even directionless and amorphous. For example, how many times have we disappeared into a record shop with the intention of purchasing one record, and materialized with another? How many times, in fact, have we ventured into a record shop without *any* idea of what we were going to purchase? Via the retailing of records we have evidence of reception strategies based on not only attentive listening to records but also the ability to pick and choose from the surface of broadcasting in a contingent fashion. In this latter case it is obvious that the reception of music cannot be explained by the use of information that may not have been parlance at that time (later paradigms, for example, concerning rock's authenticity). Mick O'Toole informed this writer:

> I had a go at buying anything – especially if it was cheap. How do you get to find out unless you experiment? Sometimes I didn't know what I was buying until I got it home. At other times I might have heard a piece of music on the radio. On other occasions I'd buy something because it was recommended in my 'bible' – the NME. And then again I would buy Elvis's singles as soon as they came out without hearing them. That's the way it was. I didn't work things out like a military operation. (O'Toole to Brocken, 2009)

By over-determining the outcome of historical events via the imposition of apparent 'known' results, we actually encourage fixity in our historical enquiries. Fixity and fluidity are always at odds in enquiries into popular music praxis and empathy is often used to suggest purpose and balance, constructing us as active agents in our own interests. But this does not fully explain the history of popular music reception. In an odd kind of way the unknown (or is it unknowable?) always remains of equal historical value. Record shops and radio provided both a site and a spatial horizon across which yet to be realized affiliations and disaffiliations occurred; they represented fragmentariness, arbitrariness, mutability and inconstancy – chance as much as choice. Such casual moments are charged with great significance and show how record retailing is indeed a mosaic: the closer one gets to it, the more complex it becomes. Retailers were highly significant in the historical processes of popular music-making in Liverpool; transmitting important musical and social ideas through time and space. They interacted at different speeds with technology, and harnessed relations with political beliefs and socialization practices.

One might describe records shops as facilitators or 'tastemakers'. In 1950s and early-1960s Liverpool the impulses of the record collector were also sustained by individuals who were able to tap into popular music's somewhat cyclical developments, taking into account perhaps older values and practices and applying them to the 'new'. Nationally Larry Parnes, Joe Meek, and Jack Good were indeed key individuals. But one such character who has remained on the periphery of Beatles historiography is Joe Flannery. I have written elsewhere (Brocken in Inglis, 2000) how Flannery was able to digest and rearticulate important personal meanings from local activities surrounding rock 'n' roll; in this volume Joe represents not a hagiographical figure without whom the world would be a different place, but a noteworthy individual who, by occupying certain spaces (creative, entrepreneurial, domestic) at given moments in time, was briefly at the heart of the Beatles narrative. It was Flannery who handled the Pete Best affair and his comments perhaps shed a different light on explanations concerning Best's enforced departure from the Beatles.

Socialization, reception: what goes on?

> Going into the Stadium was like entering another world. It was a place 'beyond'
> Liverpool and all of its musical hang ups; it was like moving to London for a
> couple of hours and feeling like you were getting in touch with what was really
> going on. (Les Parry to Brocken, 2008)

For many in 1950s Liverpool popular music epitomized the cult of the coffee bar.
Most youngsters were still living at home and many were desperate to get out for
at least an evening or two each week. Prior to the mid-1950s the word 'teenager'
barely existed, but by the time social scientist Margaret Mead was attempting to
describe the differences between younger and older generations, terms such as
'teenager' and 'the generation gap' had gained wider currency. Throughout the
1950s the media used expressions such as 'teenager' to define (or homogenize
– take your pick) a new generation unaffected by WWII and unconcerned about
British propriety. Average unemployment figures were below 2 per cent during the
1950s and many young people, although often stuck in dead-end jobs, were finding
that they had disposable income. They came to define themselves via their creative
consumption of music, clothing, hairstyles, etc. To help add a little excitement,
coffee bars sprouted up right across Britain, giving teenagers further opportunities
to redefine themselves, socially.

In Liverpool in the late-1950s and early-1960s, coffee bar and youth club culture
was central to several musical activities. The now famous Casbah in West Derby
hosted live sessions that included appearances by the Quarry Men, the similarly
world-famous Jacaranda in Slater Street opened of an evening for 'arty' types, and
the Kardomah cafe on the corner of Whitechapel and Button Street held court for
'musos' well beyond the initial rock 'n' roll 'era'. Capaldi's Cafe in Kensington
(close to Edwards' second-hand record shop) was also of great significance, as was
the aforementioned Hideaway Coffee Bar near the Pier Head. Youth clubs also
served in uniting young people around collective purposes. There were several
important Liverpool youth clubs that encouraged music and arts such as the Old
Swan Boys Club, the Co-Op Pathfinders clubs, and various Methodist youth
sections, not to mention the ubiquitous Scouts, Cubs and Brownies. The Boys
Brigade was also very important in Liverpool for giving several budding musicians
a musical leg-up in marching bands and there were several local instrumental
groups such as accordion and mandolin bands. Socialization rituals surrounded
this music activity as it emerged from different creative spaces, for it was no use
playing if there was nobody listening. To begin with, both the Cavern and the
Mardi Gras venues were not licensed for the sale of alcohol and were little short
of extended coffee bars. Both venues attracted young people who were curious
to hear forms of popular music in an environment that gave space to collective
practices. Issues concerning musical high watermarks and incompetence were far
less important than the experiences such creative spaces enveloped. However, by
the late-1960s such socialization patterns and spaces in Liverpool were contracting,

and a perhaps less adventurous musical canon – one based around the playing of records – came to govern transmission and reception.

By at least 1967 Liverpool was no longer dominated by live music, but by rules and standards based around obedience to a sound. Soul music, on record became the standard by which all live music was judged. Perhaps once it becomes possible to replay the genre via the development of half decent sound systems in the mid-1960s, a pre-recorded standard of excellence emerged as a dominant force and many groups were unable to realize this sound. Black Liverpool bands such as the Harlems, the Buzz Brothers, the Chants, and the In-Crowd found that, in a sound sense, they were competing, not simply with other groups, but with the listeners' preferences for the recorded originals. As clubs became licensed and gigs reduced exponentially, discotheques filled the gaps. The dominant carrier of this quotient was the Tamla Motown label and by 1968 any deviation from the Motown sound ratio at certain venues in the city was tantamount to subversion. Deejays thus became important tastemakers in their own right and Billy Butler, for example, known for his affiliations to certain styles, came to be associated with an 'elite' taste culture. Butler was to later inform this writer:

> I think dancing to live music became more of a problem as bands went 'heavy'. So the deejay in-between sets tried to lighten things up. There would then be requests like 'play that one again, Bill', and I would know what people liked. When people were paying more to get into because clubs were licensed, you wanted to keep them happy. Groups couldn't keep their interest in the same way and soul music – particularly Motown – came to be the club sound of late-'60s Liverpool. (Butler to Brocken, 1996)

Despite the great strides that had been made by recorded sound to expand taste cultures, it could be argued that in Liverpool clubs of the very late-1960s, records were re-consumed into activities that were deprived of such diversity. Affiliations, compounded by decisions, affinities, schemes, and conventions, came to be highly demarcated, even somewhat conventional, with distinct controlling principles of sound, dress, behaviour, length of hair, and musical tastes.

This conventionality, however, was nightmarish for a minority of young people on Merseyside, and came at a time when rock culture was progressively reclaiming its inter-textual nature. Ged McKenna told me that 'it could be tough at times – certainly walking home after a rock gig at the Liverpool Stadium could be problematic when confronted by a load of Motown-loving skins' (McKenna to Brocken, 2009). Radio deejay Roger Lyon of BBC Radio Merseyside also stated that 'running the gauntlet of taste cultures in Liverpool proved difficult; if you did not like Motown and didn't wear a Barathea blazer and Como shoes, you were thought-of as odd' (Lyon to Brocken, 2009). These comments illustrate that there have been periods of time in Liverpool's musical history when popular music conformity came to dominate taste cultures. At such times one can identify the importance of the word-of-mouth approach to hearing new sounds. Because of the personal nature of the communications between individuals, product information communicated in this way enjoyed an added a layer of credibility; this was further supplemented by a growing specialized retail (e.g. Probe Records) and venue (e.g. Liverpool Stadium) network, and, in the process, another turn in the cycle of popular music taste cultures took place.

For example, by 1970 there were three linked rock venues in Liverpool that thrived on what might be described as word-of-mouth and around each venue a scene existed, something that could not have been 'invented' from within the music industry, as such. By the late-1960s most of the city clubs had gone over to an adult-oriented approach, geared to an over-eighteen drinking clientele, and the last thing they wanted in the way of live music was increasingly amp-laden and volume-oriented groups playing long guitar solos. But three venues in particular openly supported this 'underground' musical activity: The Moonstone pub in St John's Precinct, O'Connor's Tavern on Hardman Street and downstairs at the Cavern on Mathew Street, and significant value came to be placed on word-of-mouth transmission, as a 'buzz' was naturally generated around such places. Perhaps, once popular music procedures become persistent and somewhat formalized, some then look away to sources more meaningful, more inspirational (but also ultimately replayable). The recurring nature of popular music practice is never far from the historian's gaze.

Summary

The foreword of this volume suggested that Liverpool's variegated musical cultures have previously been portrayed as homogenous, and that via 'Capital of Culture' some kind of cultural re-identification had been called-for. However even such cultural reconsiderations contain enemies within – those of temporal linearity and unity. We are sadly mistaken if we trust the efficacy of only one popular music discourse. Instead, a tangled web of relationships exists between what has been written and what actually happened. If we are to understand the cultural cauldron within which the Beatles and their music fomented, we must ensure that we do not narrow our own vision. The significance of the emergence of the Beatles in Liverpool is that it was surrounded by several sincere synchronic and diachronic creative spaces, which, in turn, reflected and refracted social mores and folkways. It is not that the Beatles were special people, or that Liverpudlians are special people – quite the reverse: we are all, to some extent, the Beatles, and culture is permeable to unpredictable times (past, present, and future). There has never existed a cultural artefact that was unprecedented and like all of us, the Beatles were a little of 'this' and a little of 'that' at one and the same time. Through its diminishing focus, Beatles historiography has become shorn of meaning in the historical sense. Because of the propensity for Beatles' historians to replay reductive linear narratives, the Beatles represent for some meaningless pop iconography, a group indicative of a transparently over-elevated past era ('the sixties, man') that, increasingly, few really care about. At the very least, the popular music historian must attempt to reinstall meaning.

The historical investigation of any unprecedentedness should cast 'new' light on the socio-cultural environments within which artistic cultures have emerged and developed. If all artistic innovation is actually a complex relation between, not only that art and its past, but also the way that art is re-presented, then we should beware of writing histories that represent a kind of absolute break with any pre-history or present tense. The more we uncover routes into the past, the more we see that such apparent 'breaks' with history are seldom anything more than '*a priori*' ideologies in the minds of those making the enquiries. Thus discourse analysis (a wide-ranging historical approach to analysing written or spoken language) can reveal that popular music activity is an evocation of difference *and* similarity, of revolt *and* unity. All of these concurrent social, cultural and musical strands require investigation if we are to at least begin to understand the roles of people, cities, scenes, places and spaces, and how these all interact with popular music.

Chapter 2

Antediluvian images? Popular music and parochial space in inter-war Liverpool

After the war I felt like this wonderful music had all but been forgotten. Times had certainly changed and people and music had moved on. Sadly, many band leaders had retired and I don't think many people wanted to be reminded of the dance music from before the war.

(Clive Garner to Brocken, 1997)

Historical determinism

A great deal of popular music historicism still appears to lie on two rather simplistic ahistorical myths. The first, expressed in the analogy of authenticity, is linked to great and unprecedented new works, which creates an idea that there was a kind of break with all history together with a harmony of reception for 'something new', an interpretation of music as a text with a central meaning. The second mythical pillar actually contradicts the first but is used in tandem, that being the analogy of the precursor or *ur*-history where 'other' forms of music only appear to exist to feed into one central and apparently more significant sound (in the case of skiffle: the work of the Beatles, Merseybeat, etc). The two propositions then 'support' the proposal that the later sound exists as the universally acknowledged superior form of music to that which acts *as* the precursor. For this writer, both myths form the ideological basis of 'rock obedience' to what might be described as the *Rolling Stone* 'school' of rock journalism that was once considered so revolutionary but is now somewhat institutionalized as a discourse. Such historical determinism shows us how abundant and diverse pathways, initially offered as an avenue of reform, become teleological deterministic and insensitive to different approaches. Binary oppositions are produced concerning good and bad music, authentic and inauthentic artists, and alternative and mainstream tastes. Such fables run throughout most rock-ist texts while continuing to be reliant only upon concepts of judgement.

The theory of 'cultural capital' expanded in the work of Pierre Bourdieu (1984) might help to explain why this is the case. For Bourdieu all goods, material and symbolic, eventually present themselves as rare and worthy of being sought after in particular social formations. To paraphrase Bourdieu, this invests symbolic significance in specific taste cultures. While Bourdieu principally discusses institutionalized education practices, we have to acknowledge that education in the broader sense is not restricted to such institutions, and varying types of social networks achieve power from the passing of specialized information. The aforementioned mythical pillars surrounding popular music historiography have not only formed a basis for rock taste-making over the past 30 years, but also under-pinned rock's legendary 'fractured' social status. For example, while the British 'return' to New Orleans trad jazz signals, for many rock historians, a moment of disjuncture, feeding the notion of alternativity, one also might suggest, that this 'alternative' history was merely another of many artistic 'returns' of the late nineteenth and twentieth centuries made by British artists looking to work with pre-existing traditions. The list of those attempting musical 'returns' is vast, but includes such diverse artistes as Ralph Vaughan Williams, George Butterworth, Ken Colyer, Bert Lloyd, the Beatles, Vince Hill, Status Quo, Shakin' Stevens, and Amy Winehouse.

Reinterpretation

Of course, all of these artistic 'returns' were to some degree inventive (not mere replication). Indeed, Lonnie Donegan's national successes can in part be attributed to the balance between what was musically surprising and already known, between the new and the acknowledged. Such a 'return' is seen by some as revolutionary because, being older than the immediate past, it is considered as an endorsement of an overturning of the values of that immediate past (ironically, the past that put these ideas into place). This is actually how a great deal of artistic 'innovation' operates. Donegan, for example, reused a sonic formula confirmed by previous ambient characteristics, but at the same time threw this formula off-balance by combining it with other innovations (such as improvements in recorded sound). By doing so, he reflected both the spirit of the market and the spirit of the times, the *zeitgeist*. These two features are by no means incompatible.

Reinterpretations via 'returns' are constitutive of the schema of renewing past conventions in popular music. In the case of skiffle in the years between (say) 1956 and 1959, young musicians found a freedom to explore popular music as a meaningful way of both extending sound possibilities and creating relationships between different aspects and echelons of British and American society. This became noticeable on a national scale as a contemporary awareness of musical form became inextricably linked to social expression, media growth, and cultural re-evaluation. Popular music became a much more pronounced vehicle for aesthetics, and developed alongside a critical regionalism, which retained a sense of the possibilities of heterogeneous traditions to move forward. Admittedly, it is difficult to catch this sense historically, for the sonic image that is left behind imposes itself between the real and the imaginary, upsetting what might have been a contemporary, contextual balance between the two. We have, instead, not only an exponential, linear unfolding of images, but also an exponential (indeed self-referential) unfolding of the media surrounding the images. The unending problem for the historian, then, lies in an unwrapping (not discarding) of over-determinations wrought by a procession of writings caught up in their own presence (if you will, in their own game).

Liverpool: myths, consumption

A mythological place is one where a particular culture is described as existent but all but lost; here, yet not here. Unlike fictional places, mythological places are often considered tangible – places of lost authenticities and dispersed communities with scientific, historical or archaeological evidence, as well as myths and legends, to suggest that they existed and are awaiting rediscovery or clarification about their location. The end of WWII brought about an unquestionable consciousness of place thus mythology to Liverpool, a sense of 'location' evoked by the various dislocations and destructions of war itself. Due to the Blitz many places no longer physically existed, or else did exist but in vastly different ways. In the popular imagination of some occupying such cities as Liverpool partially lost places where location was in jeopardy and terminal decline close at hand came to dominate discourse.

Contemporary legends consisting of stories thought to be factual by those circulating them came to concern the very politics of place. Like all folklore, urban legends are not necessarily false, but they are often indistinct, embellished, or sensationalized through time. Historian Tony Lane, for example, discussed how mythologies of Liverpool's waterfront and docklands, created images of 'the idealized seafarer [...] regarded as the ultimate expression of what it means to be a man' (1987:10). Documentary maker Daniel Farson described Liverpool as a 'hard drinking, hard fighting [...] hardly pleasant' city (Farson, 1963). Comedian Ken Dodd discussed an imaginary group of 'People in Liverpool liv[ing] their lives in a higher gear than most people' (Dodd to Leigh, 1991:30), whereas broadcaster Roger Hill described certain Liverpool music as 'riverine music [...] being away yet wanting to return [...] Liverpool talking to itself [in a state of] grief' (Hill to Cohen, 2007:57). Novelist P. Willis-Pitts (2000) even advocated that the city was 'a fifth Beatle'. Such images have encouraged a hagiography of place with uncritical and even reverential streams of thoughts flowing along a river of social estrangement, further re-mythologizing the myth, as it were. When popular music was pushed to the centre, the hagiography grew even stronger:

> I knew there was a city called Liverpool but I didn't know that there was anything special about it until I got to Hamburg. This was the first time I heard the word 'Scouse' and I didn't know what it meant. The Liverpool musicians used to bring over [copies of] *Mersey Beat* and I was fascinated. Here was a whole musical world that had nothing to do with the rest of the country. *Mersey Beat* was a revelation and it even published a hierarchy of local stars. (Frank Allen in Leigh, 1991:9)

And

> Brian Epstein had a policy that he would get you any record you asked for, if
> it was in his power to do so. The groups would tell us about the new American
> singers and Brian would find the records. My collection got very interesting
> because of the records I bought from NEMS. I had a flat in Lincoln when I was a
> rep and I could weep 'cause I left them there – Chan Romero, Betty Everett and
> many others – in a huge pile and I hope that someone who appreciated them got
> hold of them. (Sue Johnston, *ibid*)

Whatever one feels about the veracity of these statements, both quotes above
suggest a degree of exceptional culture: that Liverpool was (as Paul Du Noyer
[2003] advocates) a kind of 'Wondrous Place'. Here, Du Noyer suggests that there
existed a 'special' cultural lineage between all musical forms to have come out of
the city. P. Willis-Pitts (2000) even compares working-class Liverpool experiences
with those of Black Americans and proposes that the social and musical conditions
in Black-American communities structurally resonated with working-class
Liverpool youth – which in turn made them (and not others) 'special'. Both works
are not without their significance, Du Noyer's text is particularly useful in that
it attempts to value connections between music trends and localities, but the
submission that in this 'wondrous place' distinct taste cultures emerged, in contradistinction to popular music major narratives, and were brought about by alienated
sensibilities, is imaginary and only serves to further amplify rather than contest the
indigenous chauvinisms and contemporary legends expressed above.

These 'exclusive' images are far too limited a base to comprehend the complex
webs and discourses surrounding popular music in Liverpool. In practical terms
alone the population of Liverpool has always been kinetic, and seismic transient
shifts of people both in and out of the city have taken place over long periods
of time. In practical terms, then, there has never existed *one* population of
Liverpool, but several more or less 'in transit'. Thus any singular 'artistic' (indeed
political) lineage or sensibility is very tricky to locate. It is within this inward-
outward migratory patterning of urban life that music tends to form kinetic
routes, rather than static roots. Images of musical sensibilities rooted in struggle
and opposition, providing a dialectic vehicle for change (or 'grief') do not fit
the realities of Liverpool's performance-past and parochial music-making. Such
theories overestimate negative musical responses to capitalism and underestimate
the 'reality' of common social bonds being created between social classes via the
consumption of entertainment artefacts. Liverpool as a city will always be unique
(in the sense that it is geographically not located elsewhere), but as with elsewhere,
patterns of consumption, rather than production, arbitrated reality. Needs were
constructed on the hoof, and, because they always signified something socially,
every single purchase articulated the realities of its users.

Discourse histories surrounding popular music consumption, therefore, remain
perhaps the best ways of understanding those concerned, rather than obsessions

concerning the politics of production. What is actually at stake here is the historicity, the genuineness, of claims concerning Liverpool's musical authenticity. Liverpool offers us the opportunity of investigating some kinds of transient historical continua. This has to include variables, it has to trace networks, and it does not limit itself generically to certain forms of music-making (e.g. rock 'n' roll) at the expense of others. Music is very much an expression of time as much as it is of cultural space; its significance is both historical and plural. So, before moving on to discuss trad jazz and skiffle in Liverpool in the next chapter, there follows an exploration into a particular Liverpudlian popular music 'moving target'. If skiffle and rock 'n' roll were 'precedented' to a degree by soundscapes that almost invited their presence, we need to look briefly at these sounds, both generally and more specifically with regards to the city of Liverpool.

Dance Bands and the BBC

In the summer of 1921, British pianist Jack Hylton began recording with the Queen's Dance Orchestra. This was significant work, for Hylton displayed to those British music lovers fortunate enough to afford such recordings that dance band arrangements of popular fox trots and one-steps did not have to be the domain of American bandleaders. As with most histories of twentieth-century British entertainment there was the usual battle between British artistic sovereignty and the incursions made by Americans. A great deal of sheet music for sale in the UK in the immediate post-WWI era was American in origin, and even some of the generic dance band music offered by majors such as Columbia (and their budget imprint Regal) and HMV (likewise, Zonophone) was American. Following Hylton, however (and for at least the next two decades), British musicians proceeded to produce dance music of a very high quality and the dance halls throughout the country were full of young people fox trotting, quick stepping and lindy hopping. For the most part the musical material remained American (the popularity of such songwriters as Berlin, the Gershwin brothers, Porter, etc was undeniable), but British dance band music was also used as part of the trend towards minimizing American influences. For example Barnard (1989:9) suggests that some of the larger dancehalls actually banned dances such as the Charleston, and the UK Musician's Union frowned upon Americans working in the UK. Both pro and anti-American processes, therefore, were well under way by the time the BBC became a public corporation via Royal Charter in 1927.

In the very early years of the BBC (before the charter), the booking policy of the company (rather than 'Corporation') was based upon the proximity and availability of the 'quality' bands playing in local West End nightclubs and hotels. In London's sophisticated settings such as the Kit Kat Club, the Savoy Hotel, the Café Anglais and the Monseigneur Restaurant, bands such as those led by Lew Stone, Bert Ambrose, Roy Fox, and (the American) Carroll Gibbons, regularly pleased their fans with distinctive arrangements of both 'sweet' and 'hot' sounds.

The Savoy Hotel's bands of Gibbons (notably the Savoy Orpheans) played a somewhat unobtrusive and easy-paced music, with a high quotient of melody and a distinct lack of bass. Carroll Gibbons, it seems, was an extremely influential tastemaker. He went to HMV as head of Light Music in 1928 and led the in-house 'New Mayfair Dance Orchestra' on records. After a short spell back in the USA, Gibbons re-formed the Orpheans in 1931 and led them for the rest of his life (d. May 1954). Despite his US origins, many considered Gibbons' BBC broadcasts, like those of Ambrose and Henry Hall, quintessentially part of the fabric of British society. Regionally, however, despite several tours by the big names from London, purveying dance music was largely the responsibility of local professional, semi-professional, and amateur bands. Liverpool was no exception and throughout the 1930s enjoyed a variety of thriving large and small venues, music shops and innumerable different musicians.

Nevertheless, during WWII (and despite the indisputable popularity of the London-based dance bandleaders on BBC radio) the status of these BBC-supported bands began to wane somewhat in favour of popular vocalists, a new wave of US bands such as those led by Glen Miller and Artie Shaw, and (for some) Dixieland Jazz (a genre many dance band musicians tended to play in jam sessions). By the end of hostilities in 1945 it became evident that the days of the dance bands were drawing to a close. It appears that to the vast majority of people, the dance band era was not only gone but also forgotten. The emergence of new sounds in the UK during the war (ostensibly those broadcast by American Forces Network radio), and the need for people in the post-WWII era to start afresh, coupled-with technological developments in vinyl, tape and broadcasting made these pre-war sounds somewhat archaic, and representative of a bygone era in British popular music. Subsequently, particularly in the wake of rock 'n' roll and skiffle, it was as if popular music history regarded this important era as a musical and social palimpsest, layering contemporary experiences over a seemingly faded and 'irrelevant' past.

Liverpool: dancehalls and dancing

It has been claimed that the city of Liverpool has the unique distinction of having opened not only the largest variety theatre in Britain – The Olympia on West Derby Road – on 24 April 1905, but also the very first *palais de danse* in the country when in May 1913, the Tournament Hall on Edge Lane was converted into the Carnival Hall and Palais to serve the Liverpool Exhibition. The Olympia still stands to this day and has enjoyed what might be described as an 'eventful' history. The venue opened with a spectacular equestrian revue 'Tally Ho', direct from the London Hippodrome. Pictures on the Bioscope were an added attraction to the programme. Seating was provided for 3,750 in stalls, dress circle, upper circle and gallery levels, plus 12 private boxes. It originally sported a vast stage, an ornate interior decorated with elephants and Indian panelling, and was designed to house circus events – the elephant, horse and lions' accommodation still survives below the stage, as does the 42 feet diameter water tank used for aquatic shows. The Olympia was commandeered as a naval depot during WWII and later became both a cinema and a Locarno. In recent years it has even presented caged-fighting. The *palais de dance* hall on Edge Lane, however, was only open for one summer. Nevertheless it appears to have been an eventful few months that included an International Ragtime Contest, and many novelty nights such as the Grass Widow's Ball. There were also New Boston Nights, Farmyard Carnivals, and exhibitions of the 'Liverpool Glide'. An attempt to turn this venue into a Winter Garden failed when the Justices refused a licence, and the hall closed for business in November 1913. According to Malcolm Munro, the first manager of the Grafton Rooms, during its brief existence the Carnival Palais was possibly the largest ballroom in England. Munro knew what he was talking about; he was a significant figure in the development of dance halls throughout the Merseyside region. Before managing the Grafton in 1924, Munro was associated with the first of the new post-WWI *palais* on Knowsley Road (Bootle) in 1922. He then moved to oversee the reopening of the Wellington Rooms (later renamed the Embassy Rooms) in Mount Pleasant in January 1923.

The Grafton

The Grafton Rooms with Malcolm Munro at the helm were opened on Saturday 9 February 1924 on the site of an old fairground next to the Olympia on West Derby Road, and proved to be an immediate success. This was despite the fact that in the years following the end of WWI, Liverpool witnessed a slow decline in the popularity of theatres and dancehalls – the Olympia, for example, closed for a period in 1925. Nott (2003:118) records that in 1931 11 theatres and musical halls existed but that by 1934 Caradog Jones' *Social Survey of Merseyside* (1934) found that almost half of these had closed. So even the opening of the Grafton Rooms was something of a gamble and its existence as a thriving business was actually in the face of a severe downward spiral in the local inter-war (entertainment) economy. The ballroom was built to accommodate 1,200 dancers and there were few expenses spared with a sunken, fully sprung oak dance floor, a luxurious balcony and a handpicked band (some, stated the *Liverpool Echo*, coming from the Savoy in London). The 'Echo' went on to state that the Grafton 'supplies a long-felt want, and it supplies it magnificently' (the editors, *Liverpool Echo*, 9 February, 1924).

Throughout the 1930s Malcolm Munro was able to build upon initial enthusiasm for the Grafton, despite the downturn in the entertainment business. He appears to have kept customers happy by instigating all sorts of novelties and entertainments, including talent and open-microphone competitions. Munro was to later write that he saw the Grafton Rooms as 'the most consistent provider of all the amenities of entertainment' and for a period of at least six years, the Grafton claimed to be a dance hall without compare across the UK. This was a mighty pronouncement, especially given the overall popularity of dancing during the mid-1930s and the prominence of London as the centre of popular music activity, but the Grafton's profile was certainly high at this time, as one cursory glance through the musical press of the day would testify. Here, one could find regular mentions of the Grafton's 'Old Tyme' dance presentations.

The Grafton's resident bandleader, Wilf Hamer greatly contributed to this national popularity and 'Wilf Hamer's Band' built a substantial following. In a classic example of the aforementioned artistic 'return' the Grafton became renowned for these 'Old Tyme' nights. Wilf Hamer developed this burgeoning scene by re-orchestrating many Victorian and Edwardian measures to suit modern instrumentation and syncopation. By doing so, he and Malcolm Munro created the 'Hamer's Melodious Memories'. Munro arranged a programme consisting of nineteenth and twentieth-century sequence dances and Hamer worked on re-arranging a large stock of pianoforte music, pirated and otherwise, which Munro had accrued throughout the previous ten years. These included original Veletas, Lancers, Barn Dances, Military Two-Steps, Polkas, and Waltzes. The following excerpt from a *Liverpool Echo* article in 1932 displays what a success the 'Old Tyme' nights had become. Dancers were prepared to travel long distances for the Grafton experience:

OLD-TIME ENTHUSIASM

Liverpool is becoming a centre for old-time dance enthusiasts, and I learn from Mr Malcolm Munro, of the Grafton Rooms, that patrons come from as far afield as Fleetwood and Hanley to the Tuesday and Thursday gatherings at this hall. Perhaps we shall soon have 'Old Tyme' excursion trains. Much of the success of these dances is due to the delightful orchestrations by Hamer and his Band. Tonight they have a novelty styles the 'Parisian Underworld Waltz'. (the editors, *Liverpool Echo*, 1932)

These 'Old Tyme' nights were highly profitable (all of the band parts, for example, were out of copyright) and their impact brought about a real level of financial security to the venue in difficult times. They even paved the way for an old-time dance revival. Commencing on 19 February 1929, 'Old Tyme Night' at the Grafton became very popular. Up to a thousand people attended each Tuesday night, and the revenue generated meant that £4,000 was paid off the Grafton overdraft in only a few years. The old-time revival spread not only through Liverpool and district, but all over the country and teachers, dance promoters, and dancehall directors came to discuss with Munro how they too could capitalize on this new craze. It was taken up at Nottingham Palais De Danse; at the Oxford Galleries, Newcastle; the Marine Gardens in Edinburgh and by bandleaders Jack Fallon and Billy Merrin, amongst many others.

This 'new/old 'scene' scarcely touched London, demonstrating that the musical 'cabal' of the Metropolis was probably far less in touch with popular musical activity across the regions than it thought it was. In fact London had to wait another decade-or-so for an old-time revival when Harry Davidson and his radio feature 'Those Were the Days' was networked all over the British Isles, and bandleader Geraldo also broadcast a series of 'old time dance music' entitled 'Dancing Thro'; but it was Munro and Hamer that helped to instigate the entire 'Old Tyme Dancing' genre. The BBC North Region was somewhat reluctant to give the inventive Wilf Hamer's Band a broadcast but this finally came in November 1935. Two other memorable radio programmes followed on St Patrick's Night and New Year's Eve 1936; but this was several years after he had initiated the craze at the Grafton Ballroom. However, Wilf Hamer's untimely death in July 1936 from pneumonia came as a great shock to all involved at not only the Grafton but in the broader 'old time' dancing community. Nevertheless his wife Mary valiantly continued to lead the band. Malcolm Munro was to later recall that:

> A major disaster occurred in July [1936] in the passing away of Wilf Hamer after a short illness. His wife, formerly Mary Daly, who was associated with the Embassy Rooms as leader of the 'Embassy Bohemians' and a noted solo pianist, took over her husband's baton in Rhyl in best 'show must go on' tradition, returning to the Grafton in October as Mrs Wilf Hamer. (Munro in Jenkins, 1994:41)

Tragically, Mary Hamer had given birth to her third child shortly after the death of her husband:

> Wilf was with his band playing in Rhyl, but caught pneumonia and came home. He was very ill – I think he was only home about a fortnight when he died. I was in the nursing home and the baby was born on June 29th; Wilf died on the day I was due to be released from the nursing home, and soon after that I took the band. I had to go straight to Rhyl from the nursing home. I went to Rhyl and finished the season until September when the band finished the contract they had, and then I came back to the Grafton Rooms and from then on I stayed for 20 years. (Mary Hamer to Garner, *BBC Radio Merseyside*, 1988)

There is little doubt that any micro-retrospective reveals many different popular music activities that, in turn, constitute grounds for further research. In the case of the Grafton it is obvious that a vibrant popular musical scene surrounded such a purpose-built venue. However with its links being less to do with blues, jazz or anything especially American, and with its existence as an 'inter-war' activity, it has slipped beneath the radar of much popular music enquiry. Furthermore, while ballroom dancer and bandleader Josephine Bradley is acknowledged as an important female bandleader during the 1930s, there is seldom any attention given over to the significance of women in regional inter-war popular music activities such as band leading. For Mary Hamer to have taken over the Grafton resident band when she did was heroic enough, but Mrs Hamer then proceeded to lead the Grafton band well into the 1950s – up to and beyond the arrival of rock 'n' roll. And, if one looks hard enough, there is even a Beatles connection. Ian Hamer and his brothers Stuart and George all began their musical careers at the Grafton Ballroom in Liverpool in the band run by their mother, Mary. After National Service in the RAF, Ian joined Carl Barriteau's band and then, in 1954, Oscar Rabin. Following this he was a jazz soloist in the Vic Lewis Big Band and in the group led by the Kirchin Brothers. He was with Tubby Hayes from 1955 to 1956, beginning a close association that was to last until Hayes's death in 1973. Apart from his jazz vocation, Hamer was, like his father, a master craftsman, and was constantly in demand to play with the most eminent popular music performers of the 1960s and 1970s. He played on the Beatles' 'Got to Get You into My Life' session and backed Bing Crosby, Tom Jones, Dusty Springfield, Shirley Bassey, Barbra Streisand, James Last and Matt Munro amongst many others. Hamer played lead trumpet with the BBC *Top of the Pops* band for more than 20 years.

The New Brighton Tower and the Gaumont-British Rialto

The Grafton Rooms contained one of the largest ballrooms on Merseyside, and justifiably garnered a national reputation. However it faced stern competition from New Brighton's Tower Ballroom completed in 1900. The Tower Ballroom was one of the largest in the world, with a sprung floor and dance band stage. The orchestra had at various times as many as 60 registered players, and well over 1,000 couples could dance without over-crowding. The room was decorated in white and gold, and adorned with emblems of the many Lancashire towns from whence most of the holiday-makers came. There was also a balcony with seats to watch the dancers below, and behind this was an open space where couples could learn to dance. The Rialto, on the other hand (on the corners of Parliament Street and Princes Avenue in Liverpool 8) was re-developed in 1927 when its owners Szarvasy-Gibbons were taken over by General Theatres and again by Gaumont-British. This was another beautiful complex with film theatre, ballroom and restaurant spaces. Accompanist Sid Hurst later identified to the Institute of Popular Music Leverhulme research team (hereafter IPM) in 1994 the differences between the Rialto and the Grafton:

> The Rialto was slightly more refined, I would say, as it was a complex, you see. There was a restaurant and everything; they did lots of dinner dances. The one thing that the Grafton didn't do was dinners, nothing like that. The Rialto was the one. You could have dinner dances and in my recollection the tables were all down one side. The clientele was slightly 'uppish' at the Rialto, though far more people went to the Grafton. Of course there was also the Tower in New Brighton – it was one of the biggest ballrooms in the area – a beautiful ballroom. Liverpool people went over the water to the Tower. It was alive, New Brighton.

> Not like today. You used to go on the ferries: it was only 1/- return. (Hurst to
> Jenkins, 1994:20)

These ballrooms were very professional and by the mid-1930s Liverpool had at
least ten such halls. J.B. Priestley observed in 1933:

> [...] Neon lighting and flashing signs. Cinemas, theatres [...] dance halls, grill
> rooms, boxing matches, cocktail bars, all in full glittering swing. The Adelphi
> Hotel had dressed up for the evening, was playing waltzes, and for the time
> being did not care a fig about the lost atlantic trade. (Priestley, 1934:249-50)

Not only were there luxurious establishments such as the Grafton Rooms, the Rialto
(and the State) Ballrooms, but also a few smaller halls in each district catering for
local dances once or twice each week. In fact every community enjoyed use of
some kind of meeting hall or rooms that could be given over to dancing. Even
swimming pools such as Garston Baths, when drained and boarded over, could
be hired for dancing. At least three historical narratives, complementary and
partial, become visible: the Victorian wealth abounding in the area ensured that
urbane luxuriance walked hand-in-hand with abject poverty; the holiday trade at
New Brighton was based on disposable income and largely derived from the mill
towns of the north of England, and the growth of friendly societies such as the
Co-Operative guaranteed parochial venues such as Blair Hall and the Holyoake
Hall, and smaller meeting places attached to shops such as those at Derwent Road,
Stoneycroft and Queens Drive, Norris Green.

Dances were not simply held of an evening. Many aspiring upwardly mobile
Liverpudlians would take an afternoon to go to a Tea Dance. Half Holiday in
Liverpool was a Wednesday afternoon (Thursday afternoon in Birkenhead), and
dances were arranged, accordingly. This dancing activity evidently meant different
things to different people. For some it was 'the only way you could really go up to
a girl legitimately', for others it was 'luxurious compared with the ordinary drab
street' and 'another world for a while' (Jenkins, 1994:4). Inevitably the success of
venues such as the Grafton and the Rialto placed considerable pressure on many
of the smaller dance halls. Many survived but some fell by the wayside. Jack Levy,
a popular MC at the Rialto and Queen Mary's Ballroom (originally Renshaw Hall
but temporarily renamed in honour of Queen Mary's birthday), confirmed many
years later that there was a downside to the opening of the Grafton in that smaller
halls could not compete any longer and were forced to close.

Like cheap-seat cinemas in Liverpool, some dance halls were known as 'flea
pits' and regarded as rather unsavoury places. As one dancer of the time recalled
to IPM researchers in 1994:

> Daulby Hall had a name – a bad name. The wrong sort of girls used to go there.
> I went to Daulby Hall (I didn't know any better) and my uncle saw me from the
> other side of the street. There was a pub on the corner – I didn't see him. When I

got home he had already been around, in the end when I got in, there was bloody hell. My mother battered me all the way up the stairs with a slipper. 'I've found out where you've been going – that's it – no more. I was 18 or 19 [and] I still got battered. I got no supper, no drink, straight to bed. My gran came up: 'here's a cup of cocoa and a biscuit – you won't go no more will you? I said 'no, never to the Daulby Hall'. I was there the next week. (Jenkins, 1994:23-4)

Daulby Hall was brought to mind by some as having a very bad reputation, however throughout the entire 1930s the hall remained open for business. This might suggest that the local clientele were viewed by some as 'different', 'unconventional', 'alien', even. Daulby Hall was situated on Daulby Street, close to the Jewish area of Liverpool; this ran from Moss Street, along Daulby Street, across London Road and into Grove Street (it was on Grove Street, for example, where George Melly's family resided). Liverpool entrepreneur Joe Flannery informed this writer that he was, in turn, told by his father (who had workshops in the adjoining Kempston Street) that when Oswald Mosely organized a rally in Liverpool in the mid-1930s his Black Shirt supporters met at Daulby Hall with the purpose of antagonizing the local populace. Indeed the 'Quickstep' column in the *Liverpool Echo* listed a number of dances across Merseyside each week, and noted that Daulby Hall was a regular venue for fascists. In one such entry it reads: 'Following recent successful dances, the British Union of Fascists is to run fortnightly dances at the Daulby Hall, starting December 15th 1933' ('Quickstep', *Liverpool Echo*, 8th December, 1933).

Playing

Much of the music played in Liverpool dancehalls during the 1930s was based around arrangements of the popular melodies of the day. By the mid-1930s the BBC Light Programme regularly broadcast many of the popular bandleaders such as Ambrose, Henry Hall (who broadcast from Liverpool's Adelphi Hotel on several occasions) and Lew Stone. Gramophone records were also available, but records were beyond the budgets of some (the most expensive costing as much as 3/-). It was the wireless that proved to be the most invaluable source. Bert Jayston learnt 'by ear from radio broadcasts'. Ted Duckworth also admitted to this writer that he used to pretend to be able to read the dots but, instead listened to all of the tunes of the day on the wireless and practised on his grandmother's piano. He was eventually 'caught out', by a local band leader when asked to sight read in rehearsal, but not before he had played (and been paid) for 'at least a couple of years like that'. The wireless was at the centre of the household: Bert Jayston recalled that as a youth he 'hand-made my first one – there were instructions in a magazine or a newspaper, I can't remember now. It had a "cat's whisker" receiver. The sound came out though headphones. After that we graduated onto a second-hand cabinet that my mother bought on Green Lane. When I came home from the

Navy during the war it was still being used' (Jayston and Duckworth to Brocken, 1997).

Some professional bands in Liverpool were known to notate their own arrangements of popular tunes (Mrs Hamer's band at the Grafton, for example), but most of the local bands purchased sheet music with pre-arranged band parts – often from the celebrated Davies' Arcade in Lord Street, or Hessy's, off Whitechapel. All of the musicians interviewed by the IPM in 1994 appeared to have been readers. Some were self taught, using written tutors and magazines such as the *Melody Maker*, whereas others were taught more formally. Local churches provided an opportunity for young people to learn to read music, as choir members (this is how this writer came to be able to read music), or organists. Joe Ankrah of 1960s Chants fame remembers the African Churches Mission where his father played organ in the 1930s:

> My father was originally from the Gold Coast and settled in Liverpool. He was a very experienced musician and a good sight-reader and used to play organ every week at the African Churches Mission. I developed my interest in music and my talent for harmony directly from my father but unlike him I couldn't read a note. I got to know about the rudiments of music as I went along but always thought of it as kind of separate from notation. Even though I didn't really know what it meant technically, I could hear a 7th chord turnaround from 100 yards! (Ankrah to Brocken, 2004)

Many local musicians were able to play 'by ear'. The formularization of dance band music by the 1930s meant that a good self-taught musician could, in local parlance, 'blag it', for most dance tunes were 32-bar songs with run-of-the-mill forms of the AABA or ABABA variety. However, reading music was considered one essential aspect of being *admitted* to a dance band. Although music literacy was not essential (some discussed 'vamping' their way through the more standardized songs), the ability to read was considered of some value.

Many bands also played a similar repertoire and the dancers set the pace. A good band was one viewed as playing for the dancers rather than being self-indulgent. As far as the Liverpool bandleaders were concerned, all but the Adelphi Hotel Band leader H.G. Read claimed to play 'hot' music. However for some, this 'hot' music could be of the more 'tepid' variety. Bert Jayston recalled that:

> They called it 'hot', but it wasn't really; when you heard Armstrong or Goodman; now *that* was 'hot'. The stuff the dancers liked was pretty pedestrian for most of the time and I remember once during 1943 I was on leave and went to the Rialto, and there were Yanks in there. They were pretty disappointed by what was called 'hot jazz', In fact the band were heckled – which I had never seen before. (Jayston to Brocken, 1997)

Clive Garner of BBC Radio Merseyside defined to this writer 'hot' music as 'music that was usually in a jazz or a swing style. It often including trumpet or clarinet solos and had a strong rhythm from a drum kit' whereas in 'sweet' music 'the melody was strong and any solos were performed on the violin or the piano [...] sweet music was the more commercially popular and acceptable to the majority of patrons at dances. In fact the strict tempo of dance music was also very important' (Garner to Brocken, 1997). According to IPM research, many local musicians when interviewed claimed a predilection for hot music, but also stated they were more or less compelled to 'keep it sweet'. Therefore it was not uncommon for musicians to form Rhythm Clubs, listen to recordings, and jam to more 'Hot' styles. These clubs were invocations of complex and articulate discourses concerning oppositions of musical styles: those required for local dances versus the authenticity of New Orleans.

Despite the proliferation of dance halls in 1930s Liverpool, there were also many unemployed musicians. Going back to the 1920s, every local cinema claimed to have an 'orchestra', of sorts (there might only be a quartet, trio or pianist). When 'talkies' arrived in the late-1920s, many musicians were thrown out of work and were reduced, in some instances, to playing on the streets. Ted Duckworth informed this writer in 1997 that in the late-1920s his older brother was a pianist at a local cinema in Kirkdale, but was made redundant when 'talkies' arrived. He was unable to get regular work as a musician so 'scrounged' a piano accordion and worked the area surrounding the Rotunda in Everton for 'at least a couple of years'. Clive Garner further informed this writer that in the early-1930s the busy shopping streets of Liverpool, Wallasey and Birkenhead were alive with music made by good quality busking street musicians. Some restaurants wanting some sort of background music would also have a little orchestra. By 1935 Lewis's department store had two restaurants, the main one being the Tudor restaurant. Here one could find small bands led by Ronnie O'Dell or Harry Rosen. For those who were able to find a position in a working band, the wages became an essential supplement to their (lack of) daytime work.

All wages dropped during the first half of the 1930s, so gigs on Merseyside were vital sources of income. A glance at the dance band information in the *Liverpool Echos* from this first half of the decade shows a great deal of dance-related activity occurring on an almost nightly basis. There were literally dozens of semi-professional bands: some with six pieces, others seven pieces, or more. There were also duos, trios, and quartets calling themselves 'bands' – putting to the sword, perhaps, the oft-considered idea that rock 'n' roll brought about the 'combo' – and they were making at least a part-time living in what could be described as the hardest of economic conditions. From September to April, bands could average five nights playing each week. From 1935 onwards fees per musician were beginning to rise: from 5/- to 10/- per 'man'. That fee was standard if the dance lasted until midnight but if they played on until, say, 1 o'clock, each musician would receive an extra 2/6d. Many musicians were most certainly 'in it for the money', for a standard clerk's wage around this time was in the region of 25/- per week. Dance band fees, therefore could easily double one's weekly wage.

Brass and silver bands were not as prominent in Liverpool as in other cities and towns across the northwest of England; however a few were affiliated to recreational clubs and institutes, such as at Aigburth People's Hall. There were also amateur accordion clubs, mandolin clubs, and ukulele clubs. Gordon Charters (2008) records the existence of the highly active Orrell Mandoliers who began life in Bootle in 1932. This group lasted 65 years and represents only a tip of another partially hidden history of amateur music-making in Liverpool. Furthermore, the musical work of the ever-present Salvation Army and the Liverpool City Mission also goes largely unrecorded, as do various long-standing family music traditions (such as the aforementioned Ankrahs). Elizabeth Blackman remembered her father persuading her in the 1930s to learn to play a musical instrument:

> The only music lessons you had were at a little mission hall at Parkhill Road where the music master put music on the blackboard. It cost a shilling a lesson. My father encouraged me to learn music. He was a very good banjo player and he'd come home and play with me when I was rehearsing in the house. You had to practice before you went out. We'd do an hour. (Jenkins, 1994:64)

Race

The Black population of Liverpool were not always in evidence in local dancehalls, either as musicians or dancers. However, somewhat unknown to many white Liverpudlians, there existed Black music activity in the Toxteth area of Liverpool during the 1930s. This often, but not exclusively, centred on the ubiquitous cellar party or 'shebeen' (also known as 'blues' parties). The styles of music at such events varied considerably and were not always 'hot' in the conventional sense. However, either way, the social attitudes and prejudices that pervaded and segregated Black from white at this time would have been sufficient to prevent a great deal of 'white' knowledge. The IPM in 1994 interviewed Beth Hanning. Beth's father came to Liverpool from Sierra Leone, whereas her mother was from a 'well-to-do' white Liverpool family. They met and married in the late-nineteenth century and this inevitably meant that their social circles were somewhat restricted. Beth recalled her father visiting these cellar parties:

> My father told me about the cellar parties. Apparently the Africans, once a month, would go to a house and they'd all pay 4d each. I've got a photograph of my father in an evening suit. It's the most wonderful suit with a pin tucked shirt and bow tie, because he was the MC for the cellar parties. They'd fill a galvanised baby bath with rice and put that on the gas and cook it, and they would put another one full of bones, pig's tails and ribs and cook that one up and everyone would get fed and sit together. It was taken quite seriously; it

was a social togetherness where they could play their own music. They always
played guitars because only the English played pianos. They played a sort of half
African, half Negro American thing – the beat to it. They make lovely sounds
Africans you know, with drums and things, it made you want to get up and
dance. There's no name to it sometimes, you just play and improvise. (Hanning
in Jenkins, 1994:38)

Mandy Smith's father was originally from Trinidad and a member of the famous
Royal Caribbean Steel Band in the 1950s and 1960s (they discovered the lucrative
opportunity to play in Hamburg), and she recalled to this writer memories of her
father passing on legendary tales of 'blues' parties around the Faulkner Square
area. Mandy remembers her father discussing how some of these parties were wild
affairs with mixes of different kinds of music – some live, some on records. Liquor
could be homemade, and food was plentiful. Grace Wilkie remembered cellar
parties moving from house-to-house. Each family would take turns to present a
'blues'. Sixpence would be collected at the door and probably used to pay the
following week's rent.

Many Liverpudlians were tied in an almost umbilical way to their own localities
– especially under the heinous conditions of racism, so the very act of travelling
across the city brought with it various problems for musicians. Few people could
afford motor cars in Liverpool and private ownership of cars only reached two
million nationwide by the end of the 1930s; in Liverpool a private car was both a
rarity and a luxury. Most local musicians were forced to travel to engagements on
the tram or the bus. A few, such as Peggy Beare's and Margaret Doyle's husbands,
had motorcycles, Peggy's with a sidecar:

> Edward, my husband had an AJS, I think, and it had a sidecar fitted; so we would
> put as much of the drum-kit in the sidecar as possible and do a run to the hall.
> Usually we'd take the bass drum first. I'd ride pillion, he'd drop me off and then
> go back for the snare, shells and hi-hat. One day we had a bit of an accident
> on Queens Drive and ran into the back of a lorry. The drum fell out and rolled
> down the Drive. We weren't worried about ourselves, just the drum. (Beare to
> Brocken, 1998)

Margaret recalled:

> We used to have a motorbike and I used to have my long dress on with two sax
> cases between me and my husband, going down all over the place. I always wore
> a long black dress to play in. You'd hitch your dress up to get on the back of the
> motorbike, bump your knees, and put the two sax cases on the top. (Doyle to
> Jenkins, 1994:61)

All over Merseyside during this period musicians of all kinds would be attempting
to travel between venues of varying descriptions by whatever means of transport

that they had at their disposal. The effect of various music scenes dependent upon a public transport system remains evident; neighbourhood relations revolved around parochial dancehalls like the Co-operative Society's Holyoake Hall, the Green Lane Pavilion, the Aigburth People's Hall, and dances and parties were held at various church, tennis, football and cricket clubs across the city. There were railway social clubs such as the Overhead Railway Social Club, the Cheshire Lines Club, and the BRNESC Club and retail social clubs such as those belonging to Lewis', Littlewoods and George Henry Lee. The Liverpool of the 1920s and 1930s was full of local clubs and organizations, with many linked to the workplace or to political movements and musicians could be in great demand, locally. For example, on one corner of Crawford Avenue in south Liverpool still exists a Conservative Club near to the old Sefton Park Station. In 1935 it was decided that the Young Conservatives should hold a dance there and they proceeded to poach a popular trio from the Liberal Club in Garmoyle Road. There were no political motivations involved whatsoever; there was money to be had at the Conservative Club. Such entrepreneurial histories of Liverpool's musicians are never very far from the surface, and by revealing them we can peel away the veneers of pre-determined narratives.

Summary

This local popularity of equally local bands, trios and duos became a feature of Liverpool music life in the 1930s. Rather like sporting mythologies that surround local footballers who refused to turn professional, fables came to circle not only legendary places, but also musicians on Merseyside who did not achieve national recognition. Bandleaders such as Bill Gregson, Wilf and Mary Hamer, and Walter Richards were mythologized locally, usually in diametric proportion to the apparent blandness of the national music industry – an all-too familiar Liverpool yarn of authenticity. Occasionally a local musician would strike it lucky and join a band in London (e.g. Harry Davis joined Oscar Rabin's band, and was later followed by Ian Hamer; George Dickinson joined Henry Hall's BBC Dance Band), or perhaps someone might record the odd side for cheap record labels such as Piccadilly or Crown. A few such as Mary Hamer were heard on the radio (Mary even made an early broadcast on TV) and some joined what was known as 'Geraldo's Navy' by playing on cruise liners. Most, however were to balance their instruments on their knees on the trams and buses, play their way around the vibrant dancehalls in and around Liverpool and come home with a little money in their pockets. Paid work could be difficult but not impossible to obtain, and once contacts had been made, there was the opportunity to 'make a few bob on the side' as Ted Duckworth informed this writer. During these (some might say) 'halcyon' days of the 'British Dance Band' era, there continued to exist a wide range of dancehalls in the Liverpool area. At one end of this continuum stood the Rialto and the Grafton with their dinner dances and 'Old Tyme' dances. At the other end were the smaller venues such as the Holyoake Hall and the Daulby Hall, existing for different, perhaps marginalized clienteles, and providing a venue for dancing and socialization. In between lay a plethora of dancehalls, church halls, institutes and blues/shebeens, all illustrating that dancing was not simply an alternative to daily life, but part of life, itself.

But as the 1930s drew to a close, and another war loomed on the horizon, changes were to occur. By 1938 attendances at all dancehalls across Merseyside had reduced, for the conflict with Germany did not come as a surprise. Dancing in 1938 and 1939 took place against a backdrop of diplomatic tensions, and while people were encouraged to carry on as usual, life was about to be interrupted. As the 1940s dawned German bombers contributed to the mythology of place by re-shaping entire districts of Liverpool. The war also altered many people's ideas about what dancing, entertainment and the uses of music were all about. Liverpool continued to dance during the war, in fact the Gaumont British Rialto even featured 'blackout waltzes', but there was an increased sense of urgency attached to dancing; personal contact increased, as did a sense of living for today. My own mother informed me that she occasionally went to the Grafton or Rialto when her sister Margaret was home on leave and related that such evenings could be very sad affairs with young servicemen desperate for physical contact of some sort before they disappeared from Liverpool – possibly forever. At these times she felt that she should dance as much as possible and with as many young men as possible. She even told me in one unguarded moment that physical contact for her increased under these circumstances. This was in sharp contrast to the 'other worldliness' of dance halls and ballrooms in the 1930s. The war years also brought American GIs and Airmen to Liverpool, changing people's listening habits as they came. The Black American servicemen from Burtonwood Air Base also began to expose racial tensions, visibly occupying certain Liverpool venues such as the Grafton that had previously been the domain of whites only. Grace Wilkie stated to the IPM researchers in 1994 that Black people were not welcome at the Grafton before the war, but that during the conflict these regulations were relaxed. However, although the Rialto was in the Black area of the city (on the corner of Upper Parliament Street and Princes Boulevard), there remained a colour bar at this venue throughout the war years. Not only that, but many years later Joe Ankrah recalled to this writer a night in the mid-1950s when after visiting the Grafton, he was 'legged' by a group of white youths. Despite its cultural repositioning during the war years of the 1940s, the Grafton would always be situated in what was regarded by some as a 'white' area of the city and Joe duly suffered a beating at the hands of local racists. It has taken a long time for such racist attitudes in Liverpool to subside – and is something that still needs to be continually monitored to this very day.

So what does this information tell us about popular music activity in Liverpool before skiffle, before the Beatles and Merseybeat? Well, in some respects it informs us of what we already know but probably don't really want to hear. That there was indeed plenty of professional and amateur music-making well before rock 'n' roll in the city, that Liverpool had a variety of social, economic, spatial and race-oriented reasons for the existence of popular music activity, that dancing was (as now) a very popular pastime in Liverpool, but came under pressure by the process of hearing new sounds, and that one or two musicians made it to London. It all sounds rather familiar and as Arthur Marwick (1998) advocates it is a mistake for the historian to concentrate upon change; perhaps it is also a mistake to concentrate upon what we see as 'golden ages'. According to Marwick, there are none. We have to, in fact, make 'long-term assessments' (Marwick, 1998:9). It is also essential that the popular music historian does not get carried away with romanticizing and reifying periods of time, be they decades ('the sixties') or even longer periods (the post-war era). We need some degree of periodization, but we also need to contest periodizations as discrete historical entities. Ihab Hassan suggests that any ruptured 'theory of change' could in itself be an 'oxymoron best suited to ideologues intolerant of the ambiguities of time' (Hassan, 1993:150). It is also essential that we do not use the words 'people' and 'places' as a fixed figures of speech in a continuum, for different people with different motivations inhabited different places in Liverpool at different times. Even for those families who remained steadfast to a given area, consciousnesses inevitably changed. It certainly becomes clear via the testimonies of dancers and musicians of the 1930s that structural forces and constraints both promoted and conversely inhibited Liverpool's various popular music actions. Geography, demography, economic and technological forces, were all at play in the 1930s (as at other times) to create landscapes – soundscapes, if you like – within which music could be made and received. There were also ideological issues surrounding this period that made it possible for some but not others to make and dance to music in certain ways.

Such dance band 'scenes' were not exclusively male by any means (take for example the importance of female bandleader Mary Hamer at the Grafton), nor were they exclusively white, but the way in which gender and race issues were conceptualized within that specific period of time need to be presented and considered without recourse to twenty-first-century rhetoric. We must also consider that popular music of the 1930s and early-mid 1940s changed and mutated in correspondence with national taste cultures, and that many of the venues (at least those had had not been destroyed by the Luftwaffe) were still in place as public meeting places for years thereafter, thus contributing to mythologies *of* place. One might argue that these public meeting places had become institutionalized by the 1950s, making the rapid implementation of rock 'n' roll far less difficult than might at first be expected. Although there was resistance to rock 'n' roll, the names of venues such as Garston Baths, Holyoake Hall and Blair Hall are familiar to Beatles historians as strategic suburban spaces for post-1955 local music activity. Indeed this parochial network, resilient but somewhat overrun in the 1930s by the likes of the Grafton and the Rialto, later superseded these more prominent venues as in the 1950s the fortunes of the larger ballrooms declined. Furthermore the institutionalized network of factory and church-based social clubs continued to be of use to those managers such as Joe Flannery of Carlton-Brooke who were able to use politics and religion (in his case the Catholic media network) as apparatus for obtaining bookings.

It should also be noted that many people still do not care for rock music, together with all of its subsets and hybrids, and that there was an era in the history of Liverpool (and popular music) when it literally did not exist. This is a compelling reason for learning from pre-rock and skiffle Liverpool. One such historical inconsistency is that although modern popular music writers claim Liverpool as a strong form of sustenance for its histories, many locals probably do not recognize the Liverpool to which rock journalists cleave. As one year's canonic version builds upon that of a previous year in an almost architectural manner, the people once at the heart of such activities can be left dazed by their own omission. By ignoring pre-rock Liverpool, popular music writers reject whole sets of dominant social patterns that still exist because they do not like what they believe to be the tastes of the silent majority. These writers reject the very heterogeneity of our society that makes the historical writing of popular music relevant in the first place.

It is not that these reminiscences are not without their problems. Obviously we also need to question the status of these memories as fact just as much as we are questioning the rock interpretations of the past. Even though history includes facts, it also involves a contemporary component in the organization and selection of these facts. Therefore if we are to question the memories of these dancers and musicians from the 1930s concerning selectivity and priority, surely we must also, as historians perform exactly the same function about rock historians. History is contemporary thought about the past. And it is this history *as* thought that really requires our examination when we see constructed before us monumental narratives concerning Liverpool, the Beatles, and Merseybeat. One might argue that the facts are in the sources. But they are nothing without interpretation. We cannot slice up the world into the factual and the interpretative. As we disentangle the plural histories we can then revisit the canons and question their status.

Chapter 3
Jazz, the Cavern, and skiffle

John Lennon described us as the old buggers who didn't want the Beatles on stage, which was correct. We lived in different worlds

(John Lawrence of the Merseysippi Jazz Band to Spencer Leigh)

The Liverpool Jazz stereotype is easy to decipher; here is perhaps the latest published version from David Fishel, pianist at the Liverpool Jazz Club:

> The reason why Jazz was put on the map in Liverpool is due to the sailors travelling back from places like Chicago and New Orleans as early as the 1920s with the recordings. People heard Jazz for the first time and went crazy, and soon there were Jazz combos forming all over Bootle. During the 1940s and 50s, we had Jazz venues catering to large audiences. The Merseysippi Jazz Band are the longest serving jazz band in the world. They started in 1949, opened the Cavern in 1959, and still play superb Trad Jazz at the Cricket Club on Aigburth Road. (Fishel, Liverpool.com, accessed 23 January 2009)

Hmmm – not only historically inaccurate (1959?), but pampering once again to hackneyed mythologies. The jazz world in Liverpool, like elsewhere with a society divided by class boundaries, inter-war fringe development, and widely varying income streams, sprang at least partially from the act of listening. Radio, Rhythm Clubs, record recitals, and the famous bands that visited the city all undoubtedly influenced local musicians in Liverpool. For example, it has been variously recorded (Higginson 2005, Jenkins 1994) that the arrival of Louis Armstrong in 1932 had a profound effect upon Liverpool jazz fans.

However, jazz music appreciation in Liverpool cascaded from an even earlier font. Steve Higginson (2005) traces band-leader Gordon Stretton's roots back to 'Afro/Irish parentage' in Liverpool in 1887 and further affirms: 'He [Stretton] first toured with a clog dancing troupe and then took up with a Jamaican choir. He then sang with various Jazz bands before becoming the toast of Paris cafe society with his Orchestra Syncopated Six in 1923' (Higginson 2005:149). In fact, a wide variety of American music had already been popular in Liverpool for many years. Pell's Ethiopian Serenaders appeared in Liverpool in 1848. Vocalist Elizabeth Taylor Greenfield also known as the 'Black Swan' or 'African Nightingale', an ex-slave from Natchez, arrived in Liverpool in April 1853. Hague's Georgia Minstrels toured Britain from 1866 and played at the Theatre Royal on Williamson Square in Liverpool during July of that same year. Higginson (*ibid:*147) also records one section of this troupe apparently putting down roots in Liverpool in the late-1870s. The Original Dixieland Jazz Band disembarked in Liverpool in April 1919, although did not perform in the city. Instead they moved on to London and into a variety show with George Robey, one of the most successful of all British music-hall stars. Like any other major city in Britain, Liverpool had its fair share of theatres and music halls and once the word 'jazz' or 'jass' had filtered through the country in the late-Victorian and Edwardian eras, regional and national tours of such significant creative spaces were quickly established to cater for a growing demand. This demand was further augmented in the 1920s by the growth of radio, the relative drop in the retail price of records, and the significance of a burgeoning popular music press.

Louis Armstrong's visit in 1932 was initially a solo affair. Union regulations deemed that he arrive alone and team up with European musicians (as it turned out, they were French). He too performed at the London Palladium and was extremely well received. However it could be argued that it was Duke Ellington's appearance in the UK the following year 1933 that really advanced the popularity of jazz. Harvey G. Cohen (2008) describes how anticipation was stoked up in England well before Ellington's arrival, inspired by the 'Duke's' recordings together with an editorial about-face from the *Melody Maker*. Cohen states that according to the music journalist Max Jones, *Melody Maker* writers previously argued for the supremacy of white musicians, usually referring to African Americans as 'wogs' and 'blackies'. However, by 1930, journalist Spike Hughes had led a change in policy that began to exalt the African-American jazz musician.

Ellington performed at the Liverpool Empire in 1933 and stuck to a jazz tradition in Liverpool of playing a set at the Empire, followed by a guest appearance at one of the local ballrooms. 'The Duke' played for a week at the Empire, and appeared at the Grafton Rooms on the Friday night. Crowds were so vast for his appearance at the Grafton, that the West Derby Road area surrounding the venue was completely blocked. There are a few surviving memories of that evening among the jazz fans and musicians of the day; first from Grafton band-leader Mary Hamer:

> I wasn't playing when Duke Ellington came [to the Grafton] but I was there. I thought it was the most marvellous band, because they ad-libbed the whole time they were there. They were calling to Duke – he was in his hey-day then – and he played 'Indigo', 'Sophisticated Lady', all those lovely tunes, gorgeous things. (Hamer in Jenkins, 1994:36)

And from Jack Terry:

> Duke Ellington turned up from the Empire at about midnight and carried on until about three o'clock in the morning. It was a most fantastic night. I think it cost us four shillings [4/-], which was one gig with a shilling over. I remember the crowds. Duke Ellington, of course, was well known on records. So when it was mentioned in the *Melody Maker* he was coming to England the whole

country went haywire. He was in London, I think he did a couple of weeks there, and then toured the various cities. You had to book well in advance. It was just impossible to get a seat, and there was always crowds milling around the stage door waiting to see the musicians, and it was quite a thing to see that band on stage. To stand right by them at the Grafton was the biggest thrill of my life, I think. It was superb. (Terry, *ibid*)

After Ellington had returned to the USA, weekly meetings of the 40-strong Liverpool Ellington Society were regularly previewed in *Melody Maker*.

But Ellington's brand of jazz did not appeal to everyone. Spencer Leigh proposes that Ellington was rather 'too loud' (Leigh, 2002:42) for those brought up within the ambience of Light and Palm Court music genres. The story of jazz in Britain therefore is far from straightforward. Indeed it is a confused narrative of musicians trying – somewhat indistinctly at times – to at first come to terms with the different feels and decibel levels of jazz, then to play according to this US matrix, and subsequently (for some) to escape the supremacy of this music that had initially so inspired them. It is also a narrative of a music that despite the occasional blips of popularity has remained part of an underground stream of British non-classical music. We have a chronicle of a British musical environment concerning itself sequentially through time with a (lack of) compromise between art and entertainment, and with the acknowledgement of musical quality surrounding specific selected sounds.

So, despite the usual nautical or 'sailor' stereotype offered at the beginning of this chapter, by the mid-1930s touring bands, record recitals, radio, and theatres had all helped to create a lover of jazz who was interested in the history of the music via a connoisseurship. The more one searched back from Ellington, the more one 'returned' to older and invariably more 'authentic' Black American recordings. So, record recitals, a.k.a. Rhythm Clubs in Liverpool began to take on specific and recognizable forms. At a Rhythm Club there might be a record recital where the music of (say) Duke Ellington, Benny Goodman or Bob Crosby was played on the ever-present gramophone. There would be a master of ceremonies who would also provide information about artists and contextualize the music: discussing the city in which the recording was made, when the song was released, whether it was a cover, in which studio it was recorded and, perhaps most importantly, who played on the track. This would last probably an hour after which refreshments were served. After the break musicians might begin to play.

This would not be a 'performance' *per se* but more like a demonstration leading to a jam session. It could be a version of the music that had just been played, or a prepared piece referencing music presented in a previous week, or even a free-for-all where a blues form might be vamped. This latter alternative appears to have been very popular amongst musicians in Liverpool and probably had something to do with its form. Whereas the dancers in the halls were played familiar 32-bar 'evergreens', many musicians interested in jazz revelled more in the playing of 8, 12, and 16-bar blues forms. These were relatively easy to learn and included spaces and turnarounds in which improvisations could take place. For some these 'blues' shapes historically reflected the origins of jazz; indeed for those who many years later discussed this era with this writer, it was all 'jazz' (rather than 'jazz' and 'blues'). It is little wonder that what became known as 'trad' jazz (the New Orleans music of Louis Armstrong, King Oliver and Kid Ory, amongst others), was a popular form in Liverpool. Via these Rhythm Clubs sessions, actual musical performances of 'New Orleans'-style jazz took place in Liverpool in the decades before and during WWII, and the music came to represent an invented 'tradition' in the city. Even to this day the majority of jazz performed in Liverpool is of this 'trad' variety.

In London this kind of activity led in 1943 to a group of jazz enthusiasts playing on a Monday night at the Red Barn pub in Barnehurst, Kent. This loose aggregation became George Webb's Dixielanders who also avowedly expressed the concept that the most authentic jazz came from New Orleans. It seems that bands such as Webb's were not in it for the money or indeed any fame, they were purists in both a musical and for some a political sense. Indeed Webb's band spearheaded the traditionalist jazz movement in the UK by this avowed purist stance. They believed in a 'belts and braces' approach, allowing the music to speak for itself. There were a few other bands across the UK attempting to forge a similar style. Freddie Randall organized a band of similar devotees in Walthamstowe, East London, as did Ken Smiley in Belfast – but at this stage a band had yet to emerge in Liverpool.

Webb's Dixielanders found a wider following through London concerts promoted by the Young Communist League. These young Marxists found trad to their liking. Trad jazz provided an aural soundtrack that validated what they saw as a richer, fuller, more comprehensive view of society and life in general. If Marxist philosophy explained that the driving force of history was neither the 'Great Men' nor the religiously supernatural, but stemmed from the development of the productive forces (industry, science, technique, etc.) themselves, then jazz, representative of the struggle of an oppressed people in the most advanced capitalist nation in the world, was the most authentic soundtrack of the twentieth century to date. To them, trad jazz aurally reinforced the notion that it was economics that determined the conditions of life, the habits and consciousness of human beings. A great historical contradiction of this politicized stance is that jazz activity remains by no means determined by the economics of the recording industry. Indeed the economic history of British jazz displays to even the most cursory of investigations, a level of subsistence as a distinctly marginal pursuit, made up by necessity of quasi-entrepreneurial networks on the borders of the mainstream music industry.

Organization

In the immediate post-WWII era, organizations rather than freelance networking mostly controlled the jazz scenes in the UK. In 1948 the National Federation of

Jazz Organizations of Great Britain and Northern Ireland (NFJO) was established to further jazz concerns in the UK. The NFJO formed not only to help the job security of British musicians but also to allow Americans to perform in the UK. Such urgings, however, often fell on deaf ears, convincing neither the Musicians Union nor the Ministry of Labour. Some Black US artists had been gaining residencies in London's clubland during the first few years of the 1930s, and it was then that the first rumblings of discontent were raised by the Musicians' Union about 'Negro bands' putting British musicians out of work. The end result of this agitation was that the Department of Employment conceded to the demands of the Musicians' Union and from 1935 until 1956 no American musicians were allowed to play in the UK unless accompanied by British MU musicians, and then, only if a British artist or band could also tour the USA. It is under these archaic circumstances that we see the arrival of Bill Haley in 1955 being somewhat bizarrely counter-balanced by a trip to the United States by the Vic Lewis Orchestra. Soloists were not unwelcome, however, and the likes of Johnny Ray and Frankie Laine became great attractions in the UK owing to their frequent visits, and their agreement to be accompanied by British MU musicians. In 1949 the promoter Bert Wilcox invited Sydney Bechet to play in an unbilled – but widely promoted – appearance with Humphrey Lyttelton and his Band. Spencer Leigh explains:

> Bechet's role in the duplicity is uncertain as he was given a fake work permit from someone who had worked in the Foreign Office. On arrival, he had broken his dentures and had trouble with a stomach ulcer. Possibly there were excuses not to perform, but Wilcox found a dentist and a doctor and ensured that Bechet made the concert. He sat in the audience, Humph introduced him, and the audience begged him to play. Appropriately enough, the first number was 'Weary Blues'. Bechet also recorded illegally with Lyttelton's band while he was here. Bert Wilcox was prosecuted for breaking the law. The defence, and indeed the prosecution highlighted the absurdity of the situation but Wilcox and his Associates had contravened the Aliens Act [...] and were fined £300. (Leigh, 2003:46-7)

Perhaps jazz was for some too American, too alternative, too Black, even. Certainly it appears too much of a threat to mainstream Musician's Union tastes. One might even propose that music was being used to filter an undercurrent of political and and perhaps even racist tendencies. At the very least, such actions surrounding the Bechet incident help us to further contextualize the Anglo-centric, broadcast-influenced popular music genres of the 1950s.

Vague, decentred politics affected trad jazz's profile across the country in a variety of ways. For example, some interests evolved from the grammar schoolboys' curiosity in what could be described as the social anthropology of society's underbelly. Some young jazz fans appear to have been great fantasists and the music of prostitutes and brothels sat well next to an indistinct understanding of Marxist philosophy: the pieces they used to make up this picture were obtained by observing and generalizing their day-to-day experiences, combining philosophical idealism with philosophical materialism. So, by the 1950s reading such volumes as *Really The Blues* by Mezz Mezzrow combined with (say) Alan Lomax's *Mr Jelly Roll* could elicit ideas about dope smoking, whorehouses, and the 'Big Easy' as routes into authenticity. Liverpudlian jazz singer George Melly was to later confess to this writer that that he considered his coterie of jazzers to be 'ambassadors of everything that was considered unholy' in the 'buttoned-up' British society of the 1950s. He also stated that his experiences at Stowe School were part of a jazz and blues journey of discovery and that there were 'little groups of jazz lovers – different sub groups who discussed with each other in hushed terms the music and its history; most of the information turned out to be wildly inaccurate and estimated guesswork, at best, but all of it was part of a romance from which I never really wanted to escape – and never have' (Melly to Brocken 2001). Very bourgeois, yet ironically trad jazz was also encouraged by the hard Left and viewed as somewhat progressive; the Workers' Music Association considered the music to some extent 'educational' and ratified its playing at its well attended summer schools at Albrighton Hall.

For the historian these apparent contradictions, so typical of popular music scenes, are very important to illustrate. Such inconsistencies centre less on how music as an 'authentic' artefact relates with society as a separate entity, but rather how historically the *character* of any such relationship takes shape in a kind of man-made way. Music is a polyglot of diverse influences filtered though stratified societies. Cultural identity is formed though refractions of social place. We exist in fragmented micro-territories that identify authenticities through endless constellations of meanings. One could be a Left wing, jazz loving upper-class Stowe public schoolboy, with a fetish for Bessie Smith as the bisexual Empress of all that is meaningful in music, without the slightest concern over the ambiguities inherent in such a position. Indeed, how such a consummate professional as Bessie Smith is viewed as such a 'natural' and 'organic' icon remains fascinating. These views are not constitutive of one historical instance, but are made up from bits and pieces of preceding and contemporaneous practical and theoretical contexts. In this respect, the appreciation of trad jazz in Britain can be seen as not only a text contingent with contemporary events, but also as culturally convergent.

Liverpool jazz

Probably the most famous of all of the Liverpool 'jazzers' are the Merseysippi Jazz Band (George Melly stated to this writer that he was 'always a blues singer'). The MJB never enjoyed extensive record sales, nor media air time and remain to this day determinedly semi-professional. Yet their enduring image is not only one of a reflection of how a trad jazz scene evolved and survived in Liverpool, but also (and despite the general hostility between the two genres of music) how, without it, the later local rock 'n' roll scene would not have existed in the same way. Indeed one could suggest that Merseybeat as it was later 'known' was never really a distinct period at all, but instead a synchronic construct by popular music writers uninterested in the diachronic threads that were required for it to exist in the first place. Broadcaster Spencer Leigh has spent many years compiling historical material concerning the MJB and his glimpses into the early history of the band (2002) reveal a great deal, not only about the group members themselves, but also about trad jazz on Merseyside.

For example the very presence of trad jazz in the area bears testimony to jazz's grammar school pretensions: MJB trombonist Frank Parr went to Wallasey Grammar School, whereas jazz bandleader Ralph Watmough attended Merchant Taylors' School in Crosby along with bassist Derek Vaux. Leigh shows that trad's non-availability and non-commerciality was regarded as an important authentication: '[…] during the war you only had one jazz 78 rpm issued per month. I got hold of one and liked the sound of it and my interest in jazz started there' (in Leigh, 2002:48). Moreover, his research illustrates how the ubiquitous Rhythm Clubs at first isolated the authentic and then became sites where an emblazoned simulation took place. There was the usual network of Rhythm Clubs where people met in cellars and back rooms, playing jazz and blues records and discussing them. Under these conventions, the Wallasey Rhythm Club (a.k.a. the Wallasey Progressive Movement) prospered and after meeting in members' houses moved to the more salubrious surroundings of the Hotel Victoria in New Brighton. It was as a result of listening to recordings that a few members began to learn to play and a scene began to slowly build. Thus, by Christmas 1948, Merseyside had its first trad jazz bands. Ralph Watmough created the Crosby Rhythm Kings in 1948 and this band evolved from the Crosby Rhythm Club. Watmough and another of the club officials travelled 'over the water' to the Wallasey Rhythm Club at the Hotel Victoria in New Brighton:

> We did the usual thing of seriously listening to all this music and um'ing and ah'ing with profound knowledge, and in the interval a band appeared and it turned out to be the 'Merseys' in the course of its birth pangs. We hadn't got used to hearing amateur bands and we regarded them as a bit of a joke. (Watmough to Leigh, 2002:52)

These events became akin to a way of life. Cornet player John Lawrence even stated to Spencer Leigh that his musical and social life, including his marriage, began when he met the members of the Wallasey Rhythm Club in 1949. At that stage the WRC was a record collectors' club, devoid of musicians, as such, and meeting on a weekly basis, but was something of a lifeblood for those involved. Jazz fan Vincent Attwood also informed this writer that 'being able to hear any form of jazz in Liverpool in the post-war days was quite an achievement so meetings were good fun with people sharing information and tastes – although I don't remember records being loaned or anything like that; they were too precious; it could also get a little heated at times – not just music but politics, too' (Attwood to Brocken, 2007).

The newly formed jazz group from Wallasey played their first engagement supporting Manchester's Smokey City Stompers, as the Wallasey Rhythm Kings at a Valentine's Day Dance in 1949 – promoted as 'Merseyside's First Jazz Band Ball', admission was 3/- and the night resulted in a net profit of £2. 1/9d. Shortly afterwards the band changed their name to the Merseysippi Jazz Band after it was decided that the Wallasey Rhythm Kings moniker had created little impact. By September 1949, The *Wallasey Chronicle* was reporting: 'Another successful evening with the Merseysippi Jazz Band on this occasion being joined by a visitor from London, George Melly, who surprised everybody with his powerful singing of some traditional blues including "Frankie and Johnny". As for influences, the young 'Merseysippis' were undoubtedly initially inspired by Louis Armstrong, however, the Yerba Buena Jazz Band, a two-horn band formed in San Francisco as part of the US West Coast revivalist movement (re-creating the King Oliver/Louis Armstrong sound), has also been cited as a great influence on the style of jazz being played by the MJB.

This was an alternative scene created for musicians with an active interest in the past, but it was much more than that. By the processes of listening at Rhythm Clubs and absorbing this past via a kind of osmosis, the past took on an authenticity, which denied the mainstream music of the present. It also denied the alternative contemporary streams, too, as bop was broadly frowned upon and even the saxophone was considered to be an inauthentic instrument. Don Lydiatt of the MJB stated to Leigh that 'tenor playing was a dirty word with many jazz fans [...] and yet all of the jazz bands in the early '20s had saxophones. They had this limited, narrow view of what the music should be, and the saxophone was definitely out' (Leigh, 2002:56). Founder of the Cavern Club Alan Sytner stated to this writer that trad jazz fans hated anything contemporary and were 'pompous, haughty and smug. They thought that anything other than Armstrong was criminal' (Sytner to Brocken 2003). The reenactment of tradition came to constitute itself as an authentic present as well as past and placed authenticity on the very playing of trad jazz itself. This is a classic popular music contradiction, where the past is authenticated only by playing in the present – enabling and experiencing the past but only by doing so in the here and now.

By 1950 Liverpool jazz aficionados enjoyed the luxury of their own newsletter reporting on all kinds of jazz activities across Liverpool, produced by the Liverpool Jazz Club (ten years, it must be noted, before *Mersey Beat* appeared). Another interesting upshot of this visible musical activity was the emergence of record and tape bootlegging. For those adherents lucky enough to have access to reel-to-reel taping facilities, some found themselves immersed in a not-for-profit bootlegging network where tapes could be exchanged, songs learnt, and contacts established – occasionally even with the US musicians who were being bootlegged. Arthur Critchley, long-time jazz fan from Waterloo in the north of Liverpool, stored and catalogued a reel-to-reel and acetate collection numbering in the hundreds (it is now housed at the Institute of Popular Music at Liverpool University). Jazz fan and studio engineer Ron Clough from Huddersfield had cut the acetates for distribution across the network of jazz fans in the north of England and beyond. According to Arthur, while the manufacturing of illegal acetates was highly unusual, the principle of sharing jazz knowledge was not. Indeed it appeared that there was even a social and intellectual justification for much of this pooling of information and resources – a kind of musical gnosis, as it were. In this way, much of the credit for advancing the case of jazz on Merseyside became the responsibility of connoisseurs and collectors: Harold Culling has been cited by many interviewees as the conduit in Liverpool. For example Dennis Gracey, the first trombone player for the MJB, informed Spencer Leigh:

> Harold Culling did more to bring jazz to Liverpool than anybody else. He used to import records from America and he would get a delivery every month. They would be shellac records packed in sawdust. We never heard music like this. Then he began to get American V-discs, which were like LPs but made exclusively for the American forces over here, and I remember hearing Eddie Condon's New York concerts with all the stars of the day. (Gracey to Leigh, 2002:51)

In January 1950, Liverpool Jazz Club's request to use the Liverpool Philharmonic Hall as a jazz venue was turned down by the city's Finance and General Purposes Committee, apparently on the grounds of the unsuitability of the music to be played. However, Humphrey Lyttelton ventured north on 5 February 1950 to join the Merseysippis at the Tivoli Theatre in New Brighton. Presumably the Tivoli's management was rather more aware of the potential jazz market than Liverpool's elected administrators. Picton Hall on William Brown Street in Liverpool was host to a return visit of Humphrey Lyttelton's Band that November, whereas back in April the 3,600-seater boxing stadium played host to a 'Festival of Jazz'. Kenro Productions (Albert Kinder and Harold Rosen) promoted the MJB playing alongside Ralph Sharon, the Terry Walsh Bop Group, Kathy Stobart's New Music, Tommy Smith's Swing Group, Freddy Randall's Band and Mick Mulligan and his Magnolia Jazz Band. By 1952 the MJB had broadcast for the BBC from the Bluecoat Chambers and were soon to enjoy the beginnings of a long-running second residency at the Temple Restaurant on Victoria Street in Liverpool's city centre.

The Picton Hall, on William Brown Street, is an annex of the Liverpool Central Library and was initially opened as a lecture theatre, but by the early-mid 1950s the MJB attracted so many jazz lovers to the venue (without any perceptible 'trouble') that it came to be regarded as a home for trad jazz and blues in Liverpool. Big Bill Broonzy played Picton Hall in 1952 and returned to Liverpool in 1955 with a gig at the Temple supported by the MJB. This later event was in congruence with the aforementioned Trades Union regulations, whereby US artists were permitted to play provided UK musicians backed them. However, that year of 1952 the MJB were also scheduled to accompany Lonnie Johnson at the Tivoli Theatre in New Brighton, but Trades Union officials apparently barred Johnson from playing with British musicians. The insidious interpretation of rules and regulations concerning live performances by (Black) Americans in this country was never far from the surface of musical life in 1950s Britain. The MJB also welcomed and backed George Melly, Neva Raphaello, and Beryl Bryden and played with just about every jazz band of the day, including Humphrey Lyttelton, Alex Welsh, the Yorkshire Jazz Band, the Saints Jazz Band, Freddy Randall, Mick Mulligan, Sid Phillips, Graeme Bell and his Australian Jazz Band, the Crane River Jazz Band, the Hedley Ward Trio, Chris Barber, Dickie Hawdon, Sandy Brown, Ken Rattenbury, Terry Lightfoot, Eric Silk, Mike Daniels, the Temperance Seven, Cy Laurie, Teddy Foster, the Squadronaires, Ken Colyer, Bobby Mickleburgh, the Christie Brothers Stompers, and Ray Ellington. All these engagements paved the way for the day in 1956 when the band shared the stage with Louis Armstrong at his Liverpool Stadium concert.

As stated in Chapter 1 of this work in 1952, the MJB also recorded the first of many hundreds of tracks and in doing so were the first Liverpool-based jazz band to be recorded. John Lawrence of the MJB informed Spencer Leigh:

> We have never been a big enough name to sell a lot of records through a big company. We worked for a small independent company called Esquire and we made a lot of records for them. Presumably they got their costs back in sales, but it was never a question of getting into the hit parade. The only time we ever made records for a major company was for Decca when we played at the Royal Festival Hall as part of a concert with Chris Barber, Alex Welsh and the Zenith Six, and because Chris Barber's band was on it, it sold very well. (John Lawrence to Spencer Leigh, 2002:69)

The Temple residency of the MJB became legendary around the jazz circles of Liverpool. A young Alan Sytner, future owner of the Cavern was part of this milieu and his recollections now give us a historical link into what was to come. He stated to this writer that other bands also had club nights at the Temple and that the Temple later became a country music venue one night per week. While the Merseysippi Jazz Band had their own West Coast Jazz Club on Sunday nights and sometimes booked out-of-town bands, there was also the Muskrat Jazzmen who had their own club night of a Friday. Sytner further mentioned that the Muskrats were a rather poor band in comparison with the Merseysippis (Mick O'Toole agreed with this) but with trad jazz reaching something of an apogee by the mid-1950s, they still attracted a large following – among them students from the University of Liverpool.

Student jazz in Liverpool

Student jazz is another area that is seldom discussed in a consideration of authenticity around Liverpool, perhaps because in the post-WWII era most students at the University of Liverpool were not ordinarily locals to the area, but more often than not imports from the leafy lanes of middle England. However the importance of student jazz and blues in Liverpool should not be under-estimated. Both the University of Liverpool Rhythm Club and the Guild of Students organized hundreds of jazz dances and concerts during the 1950s and 1960s and all of the famous jazz bands played at one or another of these events. The bands usually hired for Student Union dances were by and large those of the Merseysippi trad jazz variety (indeed the Merseysippis played many times at the various university halls), supported more often than not by the University Rhythm Club Band. But there were also one or two departmental jazz assemblages dotted around the University. Gigs for these bands might include dances at other colleges in and around Liverpool and at halls of residence.

Jazz musician Brian Hudson recalls:

> Most weeks there was a dance at the Students' Union, sometimes two, and our group (the Rhythm Club Band) usually played as a support band. [..] Invariably there were one or two other supporting groups, usually including a top local band together with the University band. The principal band played in the Union's large Stanley Hall, while the University band spent most of its time in the smaller Gilmour Hall. (Hudson, 2006:219)

Most of the University Rhythm Club musicians were interested in forms of jazz beyond trad however. Many were influenced by swing, others by more contemporary jazz, and so spin-off trios and quartets were commonplace. This writer's memory of a late-1960s student quartet performing at Mountford Hall were that the group was based around vibes and guitar and seemingly influenced by the jazz-rock fusions of the day. In the late-1950s there was, in fact, a link between the University Rhythm Club and the Cavern. Members of the Rhythm Club were allowed into the Cavern at reduced rates (occasionally for nothing) on production of their Rhythm Club card, and bands visiting the Cavern often played lunchtime gigs at the Student's Union. Treating them ostensibly as rehearsals, great British jazz performers such as John Surman, Phil Seaman, Tony Kinsey, Tubby Hayes and even Ronnie Scott played these secondary lunchtime gigs at the university. This writer personally recalls a great lunchtime gig at Mountford Hall by British sax player and flautist Dick Morrissey.

Brian Hudson also records that while he was an undergraduate at the University in the late-1950s 'Liverpool University remained relatively resistant to the rise of rock music and the Mersey Sound'. This opinion was confirmed by Liverpool-based R&B musician Les Johnson, who stated that if one of the many bands in which he played performed at college or university gigs, they had to 'watch their ps and qs – half the time we were regarded as a bit of rough for most of them, although the girls were always interested' (Johnson to Brocken, 2009). This attitude was probably concurrent with most universities at the time, which tended to pour scorn on the more plebeian sounds of rock 'n' roll. Despite this generic snobbery, however, these university Rhythm Clubs were probably among the first 'academics' to take at least one or two forms of popular music (i.e. blues and jazz) at all sincerely, and in a 'quasi-academic' manner. Liverpool University's Rhythm Club held frequent talks and record recitals and, at times, members took themselves very earnestly.

Little evidence exists of musical and social interactions between students and local players. Hudson (2006) suggests that, on occasion, some students would sit in with local jazz bands such as in the 1950s those belonging to Dave Lind and Dave Stone. But evidence of such interactivity in the 1960s is scant, at best. By the 1970s, however, the importance of the interface between Liverpool School of Art students and some members of the local populace via certain jazz-related activities in the Hardman Street and Hope Street areas, and at the Bluecoat Chambers, was apparent. Venues such as the Cavern, the Downbeat and the Iron Door were havens for jazz aficionados from both 'student land' and the local communities, despite the oft-repeated mantra circulating among Liverpudlians of an inveterate hatred of all students. From this writer's experiences, the Banyan Tree Club, housed in the Adelphi Hotel was the nearest the two worlds of 'Liverpool' and 'Student' jazz came to colliding in the early-1970s. The 'Banyan Tree' was a genuine jazz club, complete with darkened lighting, affection for trad and blues, and a passion for bebop. Alan Richards recalls 'going through a little door in the Press Club at the Adelphi and wandering into the Banyan Tree where I heard some great Bebop – it was a good venue with a smashing atmosphere' (Richards to Brocken, January 2009).

Bob Hardy, a former pal of Ringo Starr and an accomplished jazz and blues musician, helped to run the Banyan Tree and his tastes tended to ratify the musical programme. This writer not only remembers seeing Sonny Terry and Brownie Magee at the Banyan Tree, but also Ian Carr's Nucleus. However, notwithstanding, while the dominant sub-genre was trad (and this was closely followed by big band and swing) it was increasingly a socially complex issue for modern jazz enthusiasts to build a network on Merseyside. While some jazz support systems existed via the broadcasting of local radio programmes on both BBC and, after 1974, Radio City, these had a tendency to snub modern jazz almost entirely. Also the dominant discourse of modern jazz was one of distance from popular music forms, and although there were plenty of jazz-style singers playing cabaret, they tended to feel that modern jazz was for domestic listening or 'up its own backside'. So there was little in the way of a unitary voice for this broad modern jazz collective. Circle Records on Dale Street was a jazz specialist shop and, while also handling a little progressive rock, soul and funk, did not lend itself to retailing on a broad scale. Subjectivity can be fluid, but this is not always the case when opinions are formed from within an evangelically canonic desire to reconstruct the sensibilities and taste cultures of others. It was always interesting when purchasing a record from Circle to witness looks of either admonishment or approval from the staff.

A little free jazz could be heard at the ever experimental Bluecoat Chambers. Former *Melody Maker* illustrator, the Widnesian Mal Dean played a few events there and the University of Liverpool Guild of Students were known to book jazz-oriented artistes such as the Soft Machine, and Pete Brown, but perhaps like the musical crossover attempts of the early-1970s, modern jazz and rock enthusiasts did not mix especially well. On the one hand some in the jazz scene poured scorn on those involved in 'pop', and the rockers – promoters, musicians, and fans alike – could view the jazz scene as self-indulgent and lacking commercial appeal. Crossover musicians such as the aforementioned Brian Hudson (a student 'jazzer' but also a founder member of Cass and the Casanovas), Alan Peters, and Bob Hardy were a rarity indeed. When UK jazz/rock band If visited the Liverpool Stadium in the early-1970s as part of a rock bill, the majority of the audience were left somewhat bewildered by the group's brass section and odd time signatures.

The Liverpool jazz scene of the early-1950s consisted of independent enthusiasts, musicians, students and venues of varying sizes and influences. It remained motivated more by a devotion to music than by the hope of financial gain, but good money could be earned, too. The division between the fans' loyalty to one style, or opposition to another can be seen as vivid, significant and meaningful. However any perceptible divisions between fans, promoters (pre-1953 Harold Rosen and Albert Kinder) and the mostly semi-professional musicians occupying the generic musical spaces and places were virtually nonexistent. A band (e.g. the MJB) could be fans, a musician could be a promoter, and a fan could be a practising musician or, as in the individual cases of Harold Culling and Arthur Critchley connoisseurs. This situation corresponds to the notion of especially the trad jazz genre being 'authentic' in form and is at odds, at least at this parochial level and at this historical stage in UK jazz history, with any notion of jazz as a thoroughly commercial enterprise. The MJB always remained semi-professional – even after their sometime vocalist Clinton Ford had turned fully professional and gained some national success. But the later jazz scenes in Liverpool were far more difficult to sustain, being fragmented by narratives of musical and social 'difference'. These differences could include issues relating to the role of music in Liverpool, the role of students in the fabric of Liverpool society, the self-indulgence of certain styles of jazz versus the authenticity of New Orleans styles and even the 'difficulties' in cognition of the value of jazz and rock crossovers. After the rise of Merseybeat, the entire social relevance of jazz music in Liverpool was brought into question and as Les Johnson comments jazz was considered by some as either 'old fogies music' (trad) or 'pretentious crap' (bebop). Where such fragmentation occurs, sustaining viable scenes becomes increasingly problematic as new scene-makers become rare. During the 1970s, the more esoteric forms of jazz ceased being performed to any great extent and all jazz activity shrank and imploded.

The experiences of the trad jazz personnel in Liverpool can be seen as an important measure of Liverpool in this immediate post-WWII era. It was spawned to some degree by the inspirational vagueness of the political Left together with an equally vague grammar school polemic about 'real' music. It existed as a kind of judgemental 'movement' with 'goals' linked for some to a cultural pessimism intended to heighten our reception by providing room for interpretation. It also represented to some extent the music of the visiting bourgeoisie studying at the

University of Liverpool. The history of modern jazz, however, is more difficult to pin down – for it appears on first glance not to have a history, as such, or at least not one that can be measured holistically with other forms of jazz music-making. Doing so would create a false sense of the past and would give the impression that Liverpool was, musically speaking, a 'liberal' city. While Liverpool will always have its transient population prepared to promote the unusual, the city is not renowned for its support of alternative modern or free jazz; attendances can run from a few score to the proverbial 'man and his dog'. This remains as true today, despite such experimental bodies as Frakture, FACT (Foundation for Art and Creative Technology) and 10/10 all being based in the city. The decline of modern and free jazz-making in the city suggests that jazz culture in Liverpool cannot be regarded as a singular ethos, indeed even the suggestion that there were links and crossovers might be illusory, for any such links have tended to come from musicians, out-with the city.

Musicians' scenes are structured by networks, identities, demographics (age, race), and by differences in musical styles and levels of performance and professionalism. In the case of modern jazz in the city of Liverpool it can seen to have been both internally and externally marginalized as 'none organic' (not of New Orleans origin) and 'un-presentable' (difficult to listen to). But at the same time even its reduced presence in Liverpool shows us that there is always more than one musical language and one function for a music scene and that, despite such marginalization, music subsets can interlock. Thus the history of jazz in post-WWII Liverpool allows us to reflect on the genealogy of scenes. This discourse can be seen as less natural or organic, and like jazzers themselves: historical, provisional, intransigent and certainly open to further investigation.

Race

As far as Liverpool was concerned, the effects of the Musicians' Union ban, together with the lack of geographical space afforded to Black people in Liverpool turned the Liverpool trad jazz scene into an interesting site of whiteness, despite being largely dependent upon African-American creativity. If an attempt is made to map out the transmission of some of this prodigious music on Merseyside in that 20-year period from 1935 until the partial lifting of the Union ban in 1956, it becomes quite evident that although the Liverpool 8 area of the city might have been home to some jazz-related performances, such as at say, the Pavilion Theatre on Lodge Lane, other local jazz activities were largely hidden from view. As such, Black men and women do not feature to any great extent in the histories of the trad jazz scene because the cultural spaces occupied by that scene were, by and large, white spaces and locations. The extraordinary presence of Black Liverpool music-making is therefore illustrated by its relative absence, through its unbridgeable distance from the trad scene, from the lack of opportunities for a great deal of contact. Such distance therefore calls forth investigations of different creative opportunities, places and cultural spaces. For example, Black servicemen stationed at the segregated Burtonwood Air base were, if not central as transmitters of music into Liverpool, then certainly a significant conduit. They would visit the city and seek out the Black spaces where hopefully a night out could be enjoyed free from racist vitriol. Of course it did not always turn out like that, as there was always the tension and possibility of attack from racist elements active in the city. Despite the US Airmen full of brio and bravura 'liberating' the Grafton Rooms from its position within an essentially white area of Liverpool, the post-WWII era did little to assist Black Liverpudlians in their desires to be citizens of all of Liverpool and the Liverpool 8 district came to accommodate its own music-making where the names of those performing were as important as genres.

For example, a jazz guitar-based scene evolved around the White House pub, on Duke Street. Liverpool-born Black jazz guitarist Odie Taylor was part of this – Odie was an accomplished guitarist who would regularly play at the White House in the early 1960s. Odie recalled to Derek Murray (*Who Put The Beat In Merseybeat*, Granada TV, 1996) how many young white rockers, including the Beatles, would visit the White House and be astounded by the musical complexity of the playing. The Black musicians in the White House at this stage were devotees of the likes of Matt 'Guitar' Murphy and Wes Montgomery and considered rock 'n' roll music rather primitive. Furthermore the white rock scene appeared 'at odds' to some in the Black communities because of the systematic exclusion of elders. Because of the self-contained aspect of Liverpool 8 life, older musicians were treated with respect by all. The youth orientation of rock tended to cut against this important social aspect of music in the area. One Liverpool jazz musician did move on to greater things: Trevor Morais, born in Liverpool on 10 October 1944, began playing drums at 16, a year later turning professional and playing for Merseybeat groups Faron's Flamingos and Rory Storm and the Hurricanes. However he was always more of a jazz fan and left rock music after meeting Roy Phillips and Tab Martin in Manchester and forming the Peddlars, a popular bluesy jazz trio who were signed by Philips Records. The Peddlars went on to enjoy a strong live reputation and, after becoming the first British group to play the Flamingo venue in Las Vegas, a second record deal was negotiated with CBS. The group recorded three albums with CBS, *Freewheelers, Three in a Cell* and *Birthday* and released several singles. After leaving the Peddlars during an Australian tour Morais joined Quantum Jump, opened a studio in Spain, and later drummed with David Essex, Howard Jones and Bjork.

The Cavern

> The Cavern gave us our first focal point for jazz in the city, and it was here that the gifted amateur jazzman first came into contact with the professional dance musicians who played at, say, the Grafton or Reece's for a living, but liked to play jazz for kicks. (Steve Voce in Thompson, 1994:15)

It is well recorded (e.g. Davies, 1968, r1985, r2002; Du Noyer, 2002; Leigh, 2002, 2004; Harry, 1992, 2000, Thompson, 1994, etc.) that the Cavern existed as a jazz club before the arrival of all things 'Merseybeat'. Hunter Davies discussed the club in the original (and some still say best) biography of the Beatles in 1968. But Davies goes no further back in time than 1959. He sees Ray McFall's takeover of the Cavern as significant, while also giving the address as 8 Mathew Street. Bill Harry, on the other hand, in his *Ultimate Beatles Encyclopedia* (1992) gives the address (correctly) as 10 Mathew Street but states that it was in 1958 that Alan Sytner, son of a local doctor, noticed that the premises were empty and took over the lease of the basement in order to imitate a Parisian jazz cellar 'Le Caveau Francais'. These two propositions are attempting to serve two different purposes. Hunter Davies's narrative attempts to create in his readers the illusion of direct experience with the Beatles themselves – evoking an atmosphere, setting a scene. His literary powers are as much to do with his own imaginative writing and an eye for detail. Harry, on the other hand is more source oriented. The justification for his writing an 'ultimate' source book concerning the Beatles lies in the intellectual justification of the original sources, together with his personal vision of his own validity *in* the histories of the Beatles and Merseybeat, as the former instigator and editor of *Mersey Beat*.

But there are also similarities in that they both attempt to create a narrative, for it is via a narrative that the historian garners appeal. Like other forms of story-telling, historical narrative can entertain through the ability to create an emotional response. In Davies's case it is to do with what it felt like to be in the company of the Beatles recalling their own past. For Harry it concerns a logic surrounding source, rather than emotion, orientation. For historians supporting this primary source-based philosophy, the exposure to and listing of original sources emits a power of incontrovertible veracity. Both texts are significant tomes in Beatles historiography, but neither discusses the Cavern in anything resembling its original jazz context, preferring to mark such activity as only pre-history. Actually, Harry's dating is also a little inaccurate, citing (on page 139) 1958 as the year Sytner bought the Cavern lease, when in actual fact the opening night was 16 January 1957; this launch was wholly linked with the jazz scene as it revolved around the Merseysippi Jazz Band.

Alan Sytner had already begun promoting jazz events, principally at number 21 Croxteth Road, in 1956. This was a social club that he had booked on a Friday night for £3 in conjunction with the Ralph Watmough Band. Watmough had asked Sytner to run this promotion as a 'club' and for him to pay the band a fee. Sytner called the night 'the 21 Club' as he was 21 years of age and the club stood at 21 Croxteth Road. This whetted his appetite for jazz promotion and by the time he came across the cellar on Mathew Street, via information provided to him by local estate agent Glyn Evans, he was on the lookout for a permanent jazz venue. It appears, too, that he might have had some knowledge that the MJB were unhappy at the Temple. John Lawrence of the band is on record as suggesting that the licensee of the Temple, realizing that he was onto a good thing, decided to increase the fee that he charged the band for the use of the room. The band, somewhat annoyed, collectively decided upon the move to the Cavern. With the local jazz milieu being small, and subject to the activities of only a few key individuals, both the Cavern and Alan Sytner were already well known to the band.

Spencer Leigh (2002) cites a solicitor's letter dated August 1956, which proposes the transfer of the title 'West Coast Jazz Club' (the name given to the jazz evenings at the Temple) to Alan Sytner. According to Leigh, a separate agreement was drawn up concerning the MJB. This second document stated that on the transfer of the club name to the Cavern, Sytner was legally bound to book the MJB as the resident band on such nights. All of this was taking place prior to the opening of the Cavern and highlights a number of historical points. Firstly it confirms that the MJB were a force on the local jazz scene and that documentation was a necessary part of such agreements: 'Far removed' (as Leigh asserts) 'from the rough and ready world of beat club bookings a few years later.' It also confirms that Sytner was already familiar to the band, and that they saw his club as a way of rescuing their jazz evenings from the overcharging of the Temple licensee. It additionally brings to mind, perhaps, that the city centre of Liverpool was pretty desolate as a home for live music (for jazz fans at least) for most days of the week, so thirsty was Sytner for the reality of live jazz, and they for a residency.

This narrative was in the previous chapter at pains to suggest that the parochialism of Liverpool's venues conditioned the much of the musical activities surrounding what is described as Merseybeat, but it is also worth considering that the jazz scene was more adult than those surrounding both skiffle and rock 'n' roll, and that a journey 'into town' to a licensed premises such as the Temple was the domain of the (over-21) adult. However, intriguingly Sytner did not seek a liquor licence for the Cavern to cater for such a market. This appears to have as much to do with his 1950s sense of propriety, as anything; it also suggests that he set himself up to attract a younger clientele:

> I wasn't anti-booze but my heart wasn't in it and I didn't think that I could meet the requirements for a liquor licence. I was going to get a lot of young people in the place and so it wasn't a good idea to have booze there. They could always get a pass out and go to the White Star or The Grapes, where incidentally they might find me. (in Leigh, 2002:89)

Alan Sytner was an out-and-out jazz fan, but he did actually consider at least a part rock 'n' roll bill for his opening night. According to Sytner, it was mooted by the *Daily Mirror* prior to opening of the Cavern that Bill Haley might play, but nothing came of this. He had actually booked the Earl of Wharncliffe's rock-cum-skiffle combo for the opening night, but they failed to show up, and Sytner claimed no knowledge of any local rock combos in Liverpool. Therefore he realized that the Cavern's lack of a licence was a draw for teenagers. In the 1950s few teenagers openly drank alcohol, and even fewer would be 'seen dead' in a scruffy pub (of which there were many in Liverpool) where a mainly male environment catered for the man who could easily drink ten pints of beer every night. The Cavern, therefore, would have held a certain amount of local mystique for the teenager: effectively a cross between a glorified coffee bar and a nightclub without a licence, in a part of the city that was rather mysterious, yet close enough to the bus stops at Church Street, Dale Street, Lord Street, and the Pier Head.

Phil Thompson (1994:9) suggests that Sytner was taking a 'financial gamble' by opening the Cavern, however whether it was 'huge' (as Thompson also asserts), remains highly debateable. He had to make structural improvements to the floors, but most of the work to make the cellar habitable was completed by a small coterie of volunteers and/or cheap labour ('jazz evangelists with paint brushes', as one interviewee described them to me), and the club was actually set up along guidelines laid down by the National Jazz Union. Despite Sytner's financial impetus, it was all jolly, rather than subversive and more like a scout meeting than a bordello. It showed signs of the bourgeois jazz element in British society that intersected aesthetics somewhere between the nineteenth-century romantic poets and Black authenticity: worthy, if a little dull. I state dull because the jazz scene in Liverpool could not help but reflect a lack of urgency in the UK traditional jazz scene as a whole. Too often it relied on US authenticity, congratulating itself for acting as a kind of crystallizing agent for an iconic music that may or may not have evolved in the way that it was reported to have so done (consider the significance of the great Buddy Bolden myth, for example). Ultimately, perhaps backwards-looking reminiscing of whatever kind does not make for a particularly lively music scene (especially if there is nothing contemporary to counter-balance it).

On his website, artist and jazz musician Robert Percival sheds light on the Liverpool jazz scene from another perspective: that of the opening of the Mardi Gras Jazz Club a little later (1958), similarly without a liquor licence:

> Now in those days there were a lot of empty rooms around Liverpool. So Jim Ireland [a well known Liverpool music entrepreneur] called me again and I went to his Majorca Coffee Bar. He told me I had an excellent opportunity but I told him that I wasn't all that interested in jazz clubs. I was a painter. I liked jazz clubs just as a sideline. He said that we had the Jacaranda and the Majorca Coffee Bar and that we were going to open up this new club and that he needed my help. He said that he wanted me to design the club. He wanted it big time. It was to be large enough to take in 1,500 people. (www.stthomasu.ca/~pmccorm/liverpooljazz2)

Jim Ireland eventually found suitable space in an old movie picture house. The interior was stripped out and rebuilt and Ireland decided to call it the Mardi Gras Jazz Club. There were two (at first) unlicensed bars, and a balcony ran around the main floor of the stage, which was the original stage of the picture house. Ireland booked Ralph Watmough's jazz band which was an immediate success at the 'Mardi'; indeed, all of the original groups at the Mardi Gras were trad jazz-oriented.

Both the Cavern and the Mardi Gras were instant triumphs, but Alan Sytner was soon to note how important demographics were to this formative epoch at the Cavern. Each Thursday he would present an evening of modern jazz, mostly to please himself, and an older, very hip and 'cool' audience arrived. Sytner later remarked that he considered this crowd rather self-indulgent, superior, albeit sophisticated. Demographic differences were immediately apparent: on modern jazz evenings, Mathew Street filled up with cars and so Sytner apparently kept the club open a little longer than usual. Sunday nights belonged to the Merseysippis and also attracted a very middle-class audience, many from the band's previous heartlands of suburban Wirral and Crosby. The Cavern owner was to later admit that 'These people didn't cause any trouble at all, obviously, and as they formed the majority, nobody else did either'. But Friday nights were entirely different: Sytner claimed that the Cavern was full of 'kids from the top end of London Road' (probably meaning the Bull Ring and/or Islington) and he noticed that there were quite a few gangs who used to enjoy making trouble. He later stated to this writer that his preference would have been to have promoted a top flight modern jazz artist for Friday night. A higher admission could have been levied, placing the Cavern out of the gangs' price ranges; but Sytner found this to be practically impossible, at least on a regular basis. Most modern jazzers were London-based, and did not relish a long trip home in the early hours of Saturday morning. Another alternative was to close on Fridays, but takings were just too good.

So the Cavern was patronized by different demographic groups: people with different interests and ideas of how music assisted a 'good night out'. This disparity, according the Cavern boss, also included a young Brian Epstein. According to Sytner the legendary story of Brian Epstein coming down into this murky gloomy place and having his mind blown by the Beatles in 1961 is 'absolute crap'. Apparently Epstein had been to the Cavern on several occasions previously. 'He came down on Sunday nights, he was a very middle-class boy and so were his friends. Brian Epstein asked me to arrange a band for his twenty-first birthday party, and I told him that the Merseysippi Jazz Band would cost about £25. He asked if there was anything cheaper and I said 'yes, I can get you the Blue Genes for £12' (Sytner to Leigh, 2002:93).

National success

There were hundreds of skiffle groups in the country and the Lonnie Donegan factor was so important that Sytner devised a competition for local 'talent'. He would book a couple of more accomplished groups but also (for a fee) encourage young people who were learning to play. Most of these budding musicians played the Lonnie Donegan, Dickie Bishop, and Johnny Duncan songbooks and, according to Sytner, were singularly awful: 'talent night was "no talent" as far as I was concerned, but I wasn't being altruistic, as skiffle was very commercial'. One of Sytner's strategies for the sustainability of the Cavern was to use these (to him) rather alien non-Modern Jazz commodities as financially negotiable. As a modern jazz lover he was personally disinterested in supporting this resurrection of authenticity. It was probably beyond Sytner's imagination that skiffle could offer any meaning other than reconciling the demands of a younger demographic with his needs for paying the bills.

One Cavern regular at this stage was celebrated Merseyside-based jazz critic Steve Voce, who wrote periodically for the *Melody Maker* and later enjoyed a 35-year run of his *Jazz Panorama* programme on BBC local radio. Voce remembers the Cavern catering for all types of jazz-related sounds, including skiffle, but recalls the latter causing considerable rancour among jazz purists – including himself. Voce stated to this writer that despite its jazz roots he and his fellow connoisseurs treated skiffle with almost the same scorn as they did rock 'n' roll and he concurred with Sytner's statement that skiffle was performed at the Cavern for entirely commercial reasons. For Voce the sounds of skiffle were purloined, appropriated, stolen even; the original could not be located and was always compromised. For him, there was nothing to show of originality. In another interview he gave further insight into the almost territorial factionalism of the jazz 'fraternity' in Liverpool by stating:

> The jazz that the Cavern put on covered all the extremes. We had Ronnie Scott and Tubby Hayes, where you needed to use your intelligence a bit more and the rewards were substantially greater, while the Merseys were at the banjo end of jazz, the boozing end where you don't have to use your brain. The fact that they have stuck together demonstrates great loyalty or restricted imagination. (Voce to Leigh, 2002:95)

For Voce, jazz sub-genres represented both intellectual development and levels of retardation, whereas skiffle did not even register on his authenticity metre at all. However, for Mick Groves, later of the significant Liverpool-based folk group the Spinners, skiffle expressed a folk predilection for the self-portrait and the communal:

> [...] skiffle gave me a chance to be creative. I started to make my own music and it gave me the opportunity to be a part of the creative process and not just an onlooker. Donegan definitely gave us the impetus to participate in this creative process. (Groves in Thompson, 1994:20-21)

Externality

Skiffle now exists as a popular music history function myth, an imaginative, yet idealized pre-history, presented as significant only via what came later and an exaggeration of its novel qualities. However, as Alan Sytner suggests ('the Donegan factor was mega'), it is also worth considering its positioning in the real world of the 1950s. For example, contemporary publicity, promotion and exposure (indeed hype) placed skiffle into contemporary discourse. While the Gin Mill and the Ron McKay skiffle groups (note *not* the somewhat inept Quarry Men) were attracting audiences of a hundred-or-so to the Cavern by 1957 it was on the strength of the nationally-mediated popularity of Lonnie Donegan. Alan Sytner promoted this music he so detested because he saw pound signs; for example, he decided to hold a skiffle 'festival' on 27 June 1957 and 20 local groups performed that day: each with their own group (or gang) of fans. This expression of interest should not be attributed to either the management, or members of the Cavern (many of whom only endured this spin-off from trad jazz), but to the *national* popularity of Lonnie Donegan and his recordings and broadcasts – around whom most of the publicity and sense of purpose was centred.

Lonnie was so popular across the nation that he had his own fan club, 'The Lonnie Donegan Club' which produced its own bulletin between 1957 and 1961. A book, *Skiffle: The Story of Folk Song with a Jazz Beat* was written by the Reverend Brian Bird in 1958 concerning the phenomenon of skiffle. It was a big seller and, naturally had a foreword by Donegan and picture of Lonnie and his group on the front cover. By 1960 the editors of *Jazz On Record* were even stating that the Chris Barber Band's skiffle section musically felt the loss of their former banjoist Lonnie Donegan:

> The Barber skiffle group without the ebullient Donegan is a disastrous affair. Copies are never as good as the original and, apart from their thin and callow efforts to sound happy, the tracks on an EP like (18) deserve the censure that would be given to a serious composer who modelled himself on Mozart or a novelist who tried to imitate Dickens today. They are doomed to failure from the start. Young Englishmen cannot sing Negro songs like Negroes, as is amply demonstrated in an EP like (26) where the band accompanies Sonny Terry and Brownie McGhee. (the editors, *Jazz On Record*, 1960:3)

For many, in at least two of the last three years of the 1950s, Lonnie Donegan was the most prominent British *pop* star of the era, and a skilful specialist, to boot. He was certainly identified with the music of young Britain and Donegan's translation of skiffle was a national high watermark, not something to which others could easily subscribe. Mick O'Toole, a Cavern regular (although not a member) in 1957, remembers the local Gin Mill and Ron McKay groups as being rather 'tenth-rate versions of the real thing' and while stating that he enjoyed his times at the Cavern, he also deemed the skiffle bills at Mathew Street somewhat *ersatz*. His interest in skiffle might have been to do with the renowned DIY aesthetic, but it was also because he found Donegan to be a 'consummate professional' in the popular field – hardly the language of somebody who was invited into the genre to be (like Mick Groves) 'part of the creative process'.

Robert Hewison (1981) asserts that the 1950s are a central period in the history of publicity and media in the United Kingdom. Hewison confirms that 1956 was the first full year of commercial television, and in the same year restrictions on newsprint finally came to an end. The addition of a second TV channel, particularly one entirely reliant on advertising revenue, marked a noteworthy alteration in the way ideas were circulated across the country. Music papers benefited from the easing of newsprint restrictions and a small but significant strand of music 'inkies' began to expand their catchments in the marketplace. Without doubt, by the middle of 1957 skiffle was not simply a genre of music, but a catchphrase promoted by aspects of the national press. And, no matter how realistic skiffle was, its reception came to be as a consequence of its relationship with media and publicity. The increasing formalization of the slogan of skiffle brought about a set of definitions through time and space concerning its 'meanings' in society. We have relational logics at play where social identities increase as a consequence of the slogan, but only envisage the slogan with a representational meaning. Previously held referential meanings are subsumed (lost, even).

Mick O'Toole's description of his interests in skiffle could belie Mick Groves's underpinning of the myth of skiffle. Perhaps most of the purchasers of Donegan's recordings had little or no interest in doing 'it' for themselves – they merely liked to hear the sounds. This actually questions a great deal of testimony from musicians about music, for they cannot be in the space of spectators. Musicians have an odd position: vivid yet absent, detailed yet ghostly. If the reception of skiffle involved several complex articulatory practices, then the reasons for its demise were equally multifaceted. One might even contend that, historically, the functions of skiffle have been distorted by its place in the pre-history of Merseybeat, the notable absence of discourses concerning (e.g.) the musical intolerance from a jazz perspective, Donegan as a skiffle 'star', the growth of 1950s publicity and media systems, the development of an (albeit uneven) nationwide interest in skiffle, and a *post facto* inscribed evaluation of the over-importance of local agency. Skiffle was not a process brought to some kind of predetermined end; it was part of contingent struggle with an outcome largely indeterminate. Even the Cavern itself existed in an ambiguous state and Sytner's concept of it as a place for 'insiders' was constantly subverted by a reality external to it. Every identity, every subculture, is relational, and exterior activity cannot but transform identities.

Skiffle was a national phenomenon, centred through the cult of personality surrounding Donegan, but skiffle attendances at the Cavern, while numbering in hundreds, were not a major factor in the profile of the club, itself, especially in comparison with its more recognized jazz activities. Practically every top British jazz musician of the 1950s played the Cavern. Hundreds were often *locked-out* for jazz gigs – one particular occasion being the Springtime Jazz Festival of March 1959. Phil Thompson (1994) quotes Don Smith from the *Daily Herald*, thus:

> It was hot. It was cool. It was cramped. It was gone. It was – man! – it WAS jazz. It went off like a bomb – this city youngster's answer to the strictly-square flickering screen at home. For more than six hundred guys and girls packed into the Cavern Club, Liverpool, for the city's first Springtime Jazz Festival. Yes it was the coolest – and hottest – night of the year, as Humphrey Lyttelton and his

gang vied with Merseyside's own semi-professional jazz band – the Merseysippi outfit. There was little stompin! There just wasn't room, and more than two hundred were turned away when the cellar club got to the stage where fans were trying to listen on the stairway to the street. It was all worth hearing. Humph would be worth listening to even if you were under a foot of water – as one man said. He made the rafters ring with an out-of-this-world version of Duke Ellington's 'Caravan'. Then he followed up with 'Bodega', a saxophone feature which also introduced 'Southern Sunset', a new number by Sydney Bechet, the man who wrote 'Petit Fleur', the jazz number which had swept America and is now heading towards the top of Britain's top ten. Every now and again the Blue Genes skiffle group came on the little concrete stage to give the big boys a rest. Then Humph and his seven merry men went on playing right through the night – long after the club members had left at midnight. They do it just for fun and because they love jazz. With them were the Merseysippi band, and dawn wasn't far off the streets when they finished. It was a great night for cool cats [...] Even if it was a cellar beneath an old cheese warehouse. (Smith in Thompson, 1994:28)

Alan Sytner married in 1958 and moved to London. The Cavern had proved to be such a success that for a while Sytner continued running the club from his London base, before selling to accountant Ray McFall in 1959 for £2750 (McFall's opening night was Saturday 3 October). Thompson implies that the club had not been financially successful by stating 'McFall's experience as an accountant was certainly going to be a crucial factor if he was going to be successful in turning the club into a viable concern' (Thompson, 1994:33). But as long as he lived there was no first-hand evidence from Sytner to suggest that the Cavern *jazz* club was not a success; in fact Sytner's reluctance to sell out implies that even as he investigated the London jazz scene for a venue, the Cavern was producing a useful stream of finance. Thompson's implications, rather, fit into the *a priori* trajectory of the Cavern-into-Beatles story, where the only popular music advancement relates to the historicity of 'the fab four'.

Summary

Every type of identity is relational, relative, and vulnerable to the subversion of any external influence. The combination of events that make up the reality of our uneven lives cannot help but modify the nature, meaning and outputs of local social agencies that enact them. These non-specific influences – from the cultural geography surrounding the class-based development of trad jazz on Merseyside, to Alan Sytner's wish to cash in on national, not solely local, interests in skiffle are clearly part of the stories of jazz, the Cavern, and skiffle in the Liverpool of the 1950s. During this post-WWII era, new mediations of popular cultures existed in Britain. Thus the international, the national, and the popular were highly significant in Liverpool in countless ways. But the national and the popular are curiously excluded from many histories when discussing roots and essences: skiffle, blues and jazz in the UK are positioned as foundational virtues only, and are often viewed as significant only in their regional appeals and activities and how they lead on to something apparently more significant. Eric Burdon of the Animals is on record as stating that he did think that the Animals in Newcastle were part of the only localized blues scene in the country and that this made him feel very special (BBC: *Dancing In The Street* 1997), but he was soon to learn that he was part of a nationally-mediated interest in the blues, rather than a voice crying in the pop music wilderness.

So, jazz and skiffle at the Cavern cannot be explained away as '*ur*-history' with a foundational value only. Both developed their own discursive areas, involved the subsequent emergence of differing entities and categories that, rather than prolong the basic concepts surrounding its formation through a kind of cumulative enrichment, added supplements to it: a two-way opening door to artistic achievement. The withering of initial concepts in popular music activity is inevitable, but has nothing to do with mechanical reproduction in the 'Benjaminian' sense. Supplements (such as skiffle) are such important historical moments because they actually *deconstruct* the family tree myth of origins by their presence and are then deconstructed by further supplementarity. From the outset skiffle was both popular and unpopular, it was recognizable and unrecognizable. It was welcomed by some at the Cavern and disparaged by others; its existence, while giving some kind of shape to further crossover supplements (such as amplification), signified diverse things to discrete demographics. One might even suggest that its very appearance at the Cavern was subject to concerns well beyond its own control. The significant creative space at the Cavern for skiffle was hotly disputed, and owed its existence as much to the pop process, as its roots in trad jazz. Such events do not exist to provide succour to later movements; while we must forever acknowledge indigenous chauvanisms, we must not get carried away by them.

Chapter 4

Oral histories, public and private spaces; the partially-hidden histories of Joe Flannery and Gardner Road, 1961-62*

Joe Flannery was born into a Liverpool Roman Catholic family in 1931, the third of six children, and right up to the present day he has continued to devote a great deal of time and energy to the church, despite prescribing a large part of his working life to fostering and encouraging musical talent in the Liverpool area. As a young man in the immediate post-war era, he was an active vocalist in Liverpool, occasionally working as part of an *ad hoc* duo with comedian Ken Dodd. Following his National Service (1950-52), Joe returned to the family business in Liverpool, and continued his singing activities, contributing to the important 'Sunday Showcases' at Ossie Wades' venue in Everton. This later led to the construction of the important Merseyside Artistes Association – both a venue and a community of artists that developed, promoted and protected local performers in and around Merseyside for several decades.

Flannery's singing talents briefly led him to a vocalist position with the famous Joe Loss Orchestra in the mid-1950s, however when an accident impaired his vocal chords, he subsequently concentrated on retailing and, as a sideline, artist management. A life-long friend of Brian Epstein, for a while Joe ran his agency Carlton-Brooke in tandem with that of Epstein's NEMS Enterprises, handling all of the Beatles' out of town bookings up until 1963. Joe was something of a sounding board for Epstein and the Beatles in the early days of Merseybeat. He was invited by Epstein to merge Carlton-Brooke with NEMS on at least two occasions, and was also invited to join NEMS when offices were opened in Moorfields, Liverpool in 1963 and again in London in 1964, but Joe declined all offers because of both his own self-employed status and loyalty to his brother, singer Lee Curtis. Curtis had also been approached by Epstein to join the NEMS 'stable' but was suspicious of Epstein's motives and gave him the brush-off. Joe was known to all of the Beatles and, to this day remains a friend of Sir Paul McCartney.

Following the live success of his brother Lee Curtis in Germany in 1963, Joe moved to Hamburg, accepting the offer from Manfred Weissleder to become a freelance booking agent for the new Star Club, by then one of the leading popular music venues in Europe. He did this between 1963 and 1967, surviving a closure

---

*   The primary source material used in this chapter is from a series of interviews conducted by this writer with Joe Flannery between 1996 and 1999.

in 1964 brought about by the owner's mismanagement. Joe therefore became an important conduit for many British and American artistes working in Germany at this time and was regarded by some as a 'father figure'. He also helped to develop and promote the Star Club franchise and record label across West Germany. Artists such as Jimi Hendrix, the Hep Stars (later Abba), Paul Nicholas, Gary Glitter and many others were given important performance opportunities by Joe Flannery in Germany on behalf of the Star Club. After this era had ended, Joe returned to Liverpool in 1967 to witness what he describes as 'the implosion of the Beatles' following the death of his close friend Brian Epstein. Disillusioned, Joe moved out of the music business for a while. He did however, launch a local mobile deejay franchise in the early-1970s but concentrated most of his efforts on retailing and charity matters. 'Shopping For the Aged and Handicapped', The Princess Alexandra Homes, Alder Hey Children's Hospital, and various charities for the relief of cancer all benefitted from Joe Flannery's contacts and involvement.

While John Lennon was finishing off his *Double Fantasy* album at the Hit Factory in 1980 Joe Flannery conversed with him at some length on the phone. This was only a matter of a few weeks before Lennon's untimely death. They both enthused about a Lennon tour of the UK in which Joe was to be involved – sadly this was not to be. Lennon's death provoked a period of depression in Flannery and it was only his close contact with the Epstein family that aided Joe through this period in his life. During 1980 Joe had already been persuaded by Clive Epstein to return to management. Clive was regarded by many as a scrupulously fair man and in some people's eyes more reliable than his brother Brian. The partnership lasted no more than three years, but Liverpool band Motion Pictures and singer/songwriter Phil Boardman were part of their stable and did benefit from the partnerships' contacts. It was Boardman who would write the music to one of the best tribute songs to John Lennon: 'Much Missed Man' for Flannery's Mayfield record label in 1982 (MA103). Joe had penned the lyrics to this song following the news of the death of his friend. Clive Epstein sadly died from a heart attack in 1988. Throughout the 1980s Joe continued to sit on various committees in Liverpool and, in 1984, assisted with the immensely successful International Garden Festival, providing his record label, as a *gratis* outlet for the Festival's signature tune sung by comedian Tom O'Connor (see on re Stag Records).

Now in semi-retirement, Joe still takes an active interest in all popular styles. He has been involved in various presentations over the past few years including the re-launching of David Garrick's career in Europe following a surprise hit single in the late-1990s, the promotion of both local and European artistes, and the staging of the Swedish Pitea School of Music's 'Sgt. Pepper Live' show at the Liverpool Empire – one of the first successful attempts to present a live performance of this seminal recorded work. After Joe had assembled boy-band Ecos, this group mutated and found fame as BB Mack. He remains in demand on the conference circuit and is rightly regarded as an elder statesman of the Liverpool scene. This latter point was acknowledged in 1997 when the University of Liverpool honoured Joe with a fellowship. Liverpool City Council also requested that Joe officially acts on their behalf as an emissary and advisor to the City of Liverpool for music and the arts on Merseyside. A well-respected gentleman, Joe Flannery has perhaps done more for Liverpool, especially during its bleakest times, than many more well-known and established figures. He has seldom sought publicity for himself, and has always preferred to be in his own words 'standing in the wings'; however his contributions to the life, art, and cultural profile of Liverpool cannot be ignored and he is truly an example of the entrepreneurial spirit that helped to create his beloved city of Liverpool.

Oral histories

Oral reminiscences – the first-hand memories of people interviewed by a historian – have been increasingly important for history writing since the 1960s. Of course they are problematic: historians are reluctant to sanction any compromise with the fundamental point that contemporaneity is the prime requirement of all historical source material and that oral sources have an inescapable element of hindsight and indeed nostalgia about them. But oral histories do have their uses. They give a voice to those whom history may well have cast aside. Their presence makes a check on canonical history writing that have a tendency to gloss over inconsistency. Furthermore they challenge the historians' preconceptions. This is especially important regarding the more recent past. For example, fragments of the past, given voice by those who would never have dreamed of exalting their own memories, offer vivid challenges to the linear historian who places authority around causes, consequences and centralities. Beatles historiography suffers greatly from given linear narratives of centrality. There appears to be one singular Beatles narrative that all can call upon. There appears, also, to be a posse of 'legitimate' Beatles historians who can be exhumed to give voice to these marshalled facts because they are the ones responsible for placing them in some kind of written order in the first place – this could even be described as the monopoly of professional elite.

In the case of Beatles histories several narratives are visible by their absence. For example, the significance of domestic space and place is usually relegated, for the sources to which most historians turn usually carries the stamp of organizations, venues, listings and group memberships. Yet domestic spaces and specific places (not to mention those occupying such spaces) are spheres that actually give creativity shape. For example, the McCartney family home at Forthlin Road, the country music collection belonging to George Harrison's father, etc. are environments that can rescue a subject and allow them room to consider quality of life. They can also allow the historian to give meaning to chance and opportunity, as so many decisions are contingent to the space in which decisions are made. Tosh suggests that oral histories that contemplate such issues offer 'a role in the production of historical knowledge with important political implications' (Tosh, 1984:177). Oral histories therefore can challenge the conventional historiographies of the aforementioned self-appointed elite. Those concerning early-1960s music activity in Liverpool also provide us with information about self-employment and entrepreneurship. Curiously the Beatles and their cohorts are often written about as 'counter-cultural', when the very systems around them and it must be said, their own ambitions, were classically redolent of Tory entrepreneurship. Cambridge researcher David Fowler, ostensibly dealing with inter-war folk revivalist Rolf Gardiner, was quoted by *Guardian* arts correspondent Mark Brown (2008) describing the Beatles as:

> Young capitalists who, far from developing a youth culture, were exploiting youth culture by promoting fan worship, mindless screaming and nothing more than a passive teenage consumer [...] in effect they were family entertainment, rather than at the cutting edge of youth culture. (Fowler to Brown, *Guardian*, 9 October 2008)

Whatever one thinks of Rolf Gardiner (and despite David Fowler's claims to the contrary Gardiner was *clearly* a Fascist sympathizer), Fowler does have something of a point here; the following oral testimony of Joe Flannery supports the idea that the Beatles were at least during 1962 not only entertainment industry-led but also advised. In fact, after more than ten years of talking to and interviewing not only Joe Flannery, but also a host of other 'Merseybeat (semi) professionals', not one person has ever had anything to say this writer about a 'counter culture' in the Liverpool of the early-1960s.

Tales from Gardner Road

Joe Flannery did not keep a diary. But he did scrupulously keep a set of 'Adcross' account books which further annotated meetings and events. When he came to manage his brother Peter's (Lee Curtis) various bands in 1960 his previous experiences as a temporary replacement vocalist with the Joe Loss Band came in very handy. Not only from a personal point of view in that he was able to deal with agents, venue managers and 'sharks' with a reasonable amount of alacrity, but also because he was viewed as something of a 'guru' for those young musicians who came around to see him at his Gardner Road apartment in the Stoneycroft area of Liverpool. He often thought that he was being miscast in the role of a music pedagogue for, apart from his longer local part-time solo efforts, he was only with Loss for a short period – mostly on the Isle of Man.

However, Joe enjoyed relating anecdotes about his experiences of the music business, if so asked. Before too long, he was holding court to countless young musicians and would-be rock 'n' roll singers, usually after his brother Peter (Lee Curtis) had informed them of his exploits around the various flea pits, pubs and clubs in the Liverpool area, rather than his experiences with Joe Loss. Flannery felt that the young men needed to know who could be trusted and who could not:

Although I was always as diplomatic as I could possibly be, I felt it only right to warn them off some of the more rogue-ish small-time operators in Liverpool. Many groups were already smarting after having suffered, financially, at the hands of 'Battle of the Band' merchants and I felt a degree of responsibility towards them.

It was a good point, well made, for by the early-1960s Liverpool was awash with new entrepreneurs attempting to 'do' an Alan Sytner or a Jim Ireland (see Chapter 3). Questions abounded: who would pay? Who would try to argue their way out of paying? Which venue enjoyed the luxury of P.A. equipment? Which halls had dressing rooms? Which had just toilets? Merseybeat aficionados will recognize names such as Ted Knibbs, Bob Wooler, Alan Williams, Sam Leach, Ray McFall, and Sam Kelly and venues such as Blair Hall, Holyoake Hall, Litherland Town Hall and the Jacaranda. All of these names (and more besides) regularly came under the microscope in one way or another at the Gardner Road address of Joe Flannery. Joe later admitted that several of the names and venues were a mystery to him at the time:

> We were still ploughing our way through our list of Catholic Parochial Clubs and were less reliant on local promoters than many. We did play most of the jive hives at one time or another but the Catholic Church was, by and large, a very good payer!

Beatles (i)

In January 1961 the names of John Lennon and Paul McCartney and their 'combo' the Beatles were dropped into conversations at Gardner Road band meetings. Joe had never previously heard of them, but learnt that these two belonged to what appeared to him a rather nebulous outfit that had been around the Liverpool area for a couple of years. The group had recently returned home from a rather truncated season in Hamburg a changed band ('why Hamburg?' Joe had initially asked). Joe remembers one member of the Detours (Lee's band) informing him of something like 'Of all the people I never expected to make a decent sound, it was Lennon's lot'. Flannery also recalls the conversation continuing along the lines of the group not being very reliable, and turning up without a drummer. 'But, now they're back from Germany, they sound totally different and have a good drummer', continued the comments.

Those present at Joe's apartment that rainy night in 1961 probably thought little more of it as the conversation ebbed and flowed for a few hours more; however this trip to Hamburg in Germany greatly interested Joe, and he recalls making a mental note to check-out the Beatles at the first available opportunity. If a trip to Hamburg had ostensibly produced such dramatic effects on their sound, then he ought to investigate this matter for Lee Curtis' sake. Joe ruminated 'how on earth had they got to Hamburg, in the first place?' But he also remembers thinking that the band's name was a 'most bizarre, yet memorable, moniker for a rock group in the early 1960s. I thought that they were probably students or beatnicks or both with a name like that'. Liverpool in 1961 was still a large, heavily populated city but news did not spread like proverbial 'wild fire'. The parochialism of Liverpool's rock music scene reflected the parochial boundaries of its districts and while Lee Curtis' group the Detours mostly played venues in the north-end of the city, the Beatles were from the south-end and their paths had not, thus far, crossed.

Their name came up again, some weeks later. Joe was informed that they were actually returning to Hamburg 'by demand' and he admitted to being more than a little jealous. He still hadn't learnt anything concrete about this German connection and still hadn't come across the band, first hand. His young informant told him, however, that they were tied to a cafe owner by the name of Allan Williams, and it was he who had organized the trip to Germany:

> I only knew Allan by reputation. I had been told that he had organized the Merseyside leg of the Gene Vincent tour the previous year [3 May] and done quite well out of it, I think. He had something to do with Brian Casser ['Cass' of Cass & the Cassanovas, who were on the Vincent bill]. I knew he ran a greasy spoon in Slater Street called the Jacaranda – that was about it, really – I'd never been near the place and actually Slater Street wasn't really an area I would frequent at that time.

As far as Flannery was aware the Jacaranda was 'a hang-out for Art School beatniks and tramps'. However Williams together with his wife Beryl had also started opening the cellar of the cafe at night for live music: a radical thing to do in those days. The cafe wasn't licensed for alcohol, and so Williams did not necessarily have the vagaries of the Liverpool Police with which to contend. But the Jacaranda was also close to the city centre and Joe presumed Allan might have had protection racketeers to deal with:

> So, I didn't envy him, especially after also being informed that the Beatles were something of a handful, too! The main attraction at the Jacaranda had been a West Indian Steel Band, but I learnt that this was the band that had made the initial contact with a club in Hamburg. They were then followed by Derry and the Seniors [one of Liverpool's top rock 'n' roll bands in which Williams also shared an interest] … curiouser and curiouser, I thought.

As it turned out, the information Joe received early in 1961 was both a little old and inaccurate. Allan Williams had already fallen out not only with his young protégés before they had returned to Liverpool at the end of 1960 but also with the Royal Caribbean Steel Band and, it seems, Derry and the Seniors. So, by the time Flannery came to be discussing the group with his childhood friend Brian Epstein, the Beatles were actually managerless but, in reality, handled by drummer Pete Best's mother, Mona.

Joe Flannery and Brian Epstein benefited from a close and enduring friendship from childhood, which in the case of the latter was sadly very unusual. Their respective parents had met via business dealings in the furniture industry: Flannery's father Chris was a time-served, self-employed joiner and manufactured furniture cabinets in Kempston Street, Harry Epstein purchased these for sale in his shop on Walton Road. The friendship between Joe and Brian persisted despite several separations, brought about by important social and cultural differences. For example, whereas Joe was born into a Catholic working-class entrepreneurial family, Brian was the first born of a small-time Jewish business dynasty. Both families traded in the north-end (NEMS: North End Music Stores) of the city but the Epsteins lived at a south-end address (197 Queens Drive). Joe's father had a tendency to drink away his profits, turning Joe's mother by necessity into an adept business person, whereas the Epsteins were a close-knit family group, interdependent and investing for the future. During WWII Joe's family did briefly move to albeit more salubrious surroundings in Huyton, however the Epsteins were able to evacuate from Liverpool, altogether. Joe's academic education abruptly ended at 14 years of age owing to family problems, whereas Brian was moved from one public school to another in an attempt to resolve his innate restlessness – he finally left Wrekin College in 1950, aged 16.

The two kept intermittent contact in the post-war years but became serious friends once again in 1957 after Brian had returned from RADA (according to Joe) 'very depressed and frustrated'. It was at this time that Brian admitted to Joe that he was gay. By the beginning of the 1960s Flannery had developed business interests in the 'overspill' town of Kirkby and was running mobile shops to and from the town on a daily basis. He also launched a new shop there in 1960 ('regally' opened by his old friend Ken Dodd). Joe also managed his brother's rock 'n' roll band the Teenage Rebels, later re-named the Detours, as a hobby and, following a failed TV audition for the group in 1959, acted on producer Jack Good's advice to cultivate something 'provincial'. Joe Flannery found life exciting and enterprising. Brian Epstein however, while perhaps taking pleasure from managing the record section of NEMS, was frequently disconcerted and despondent.

Joe remembered to this writer the will-o'-the-wisp character of Brian Epstein in 1961 thus:

> I hadn't seen Brian for a few months and then he phoned and turned up on my doorstep. In previous years he had a nasty habit of the latter – usually after getting into some kind of difficulties. As previously stated, my partner Kenny and I were, if not quite an item then certainly 'stable', and Brian, being Brian, had done one of his disappearing acts. To be honest, I just thought that NEMS was taking up most of his time.

By this new decade the musical side of NEMS had outgrown its furniture beginnings and Harry Epstein had opened up two stores in Liverpool city centre – one at an address on Great Charlotte Street, the other on Whitechapel, in order to cater for the growing market for white goods, television and record sales. But Joe recalls that when he met Brian in July of 1961, he could see that the latter was very restless and unhappy at his work. The pair organized an evening at the theatre in Manchester and Brian met Joe at the latter's well-furnished Gardner Road 'pad'. Epstein, according to Flannery, brought with him a copy of a broadsheet that had just been published entitled *Mersey Beat* and Joe recalled that in comparison with his previous demeanour Epstein was very animated about the paper. Joe recalls Brian's envy that Joe managed the Detours and wondered why. 'I remember thinking at that time, well Peter [Lee] was such a pain in the neck – Brian can have them if he liked!'

As they travelled to Manchester down the East Lancashire Road in Epstein's car, Flannery detected that evening that the latter was very, very excited: 'In fact, I vividly remember Brian parking in Oxford Road outside the theatre and he was so excited that he damaged both the car in front and the car behind as he pulled in to park.' On the way home that copy of *Mersey Beat* came up in conversation, once again. Joe had not seen the paper previously, even though he had been informed by a member of the Detours that it had been available since the beginning of the month. For a broadsheet to be published in Liverpool, dealing almost exclusively with musical activity on Merseyside, seemed to indicate to both men that something very important might be happening. Joe claims to have been very impressed: 'Even though I knew nothing of the paper – I wasn't a great reader in those days. It also became obvious to me that Brian had seen something that had galvanized his drifting life.'

This collective information is of interest to scholars of Merseybeat and the Beatles for it becomes quite clear that syncretic popular music activity is disproportionate and that 'significant creative space' is relative. The time it took for news to filter through to these two friends about even such localized music activity was dependent upon their relative positions (and ages). It also shows that the parochial nature of the city of Liverpool in 1961 was important in determining who occupied significant creative spaces. These two men were both at different and similar points of entry – Joe via a concern to help his brother and the relative freedom brought about by his retail entrepreneurship, Brian via a curiosity brought about by his latent frustrations, and his own knowledge of the record retail trade. Yet neither appeared to be completely aware of what was happening around them, musically; there was neither a specific centrality to this setting, nor even a periphery.

Beatles (ii)

The cover of that first edition of *Mersey Beat* referenced the Beatles. Brian Epstein informed Joe that he understood them to be managerless (although, as previously stated, it can be seen in hindsight that Mona Best was effectively overseeing the Beatles). Joe recalls Brian rather disappointed to discover that he (Joe) had no opinion to offer on the young group. He told him that he had heard talk *of* them but that the Detours had not thus far shared a bill with them and that this had something to do with the rather tribal nature of Liverpool's geography:

> I told him that Lee's circuit was still very 'north' Liverpool, Birkenhead and North Wales-based, whereas, the Beatles, I had been informed, were something of a south Liverpool-based group. All I could tell him was that I had heard that they had been a bit of a handful, but that this was only rather third-hand news, and that their names had cropped up in conversations at Gardner Road amongst other musicians, because of they had returned from Germany a very competent band. Brian was evidently smitten. I think it had something to do with their name.

By issue number two of *Mersey Beat* (it was bi-monthly) editor Bill Harry had written that the Beatles had secured a recording contract with Polydor Records in Germany – not strictly true, but great copy for a local music journal. Joe recorded in his accounts a telephone call from Epstein declaring that he had ordered a 'large amount' of copies of *Mersey Beat* for his two NEMS stores and that they had sold out. Joe noted in his books that he might stock the paper in his mobile shops, but then reconsidered, thinking they would be too much trouble to handle. Brian Epstein had been informed by several NEMS shoppers that the Beatles played at the Cavern Club, literally two minutes walk from his office in Whitechapel. Joe put Brian in the picture, however, informing him that he had it on good information that the Beatles were once again bound for Germany, and that 'he would have to wait: I have to admit that I took his enthusiasm with a "pinch of salt". Brian was always thinking of projects in order to bolster what he saw as his rather mundane existence at NEMS. They seldom came to fruition and this seemed to be just another one of those projects'.

By August 1961 however, Joe records Epstein appearing excited by *Mersey Beat* (in particular) and the local rock scene (in general), and that he was reviewing record releases in the paper. Joe recalls that Brian was very proud of his small input into *Mersey Beat*, although he also states that had to keep reminding him that his own tastes were 'rather middle of the road' and that the *Mersey Beat*-buying public preferred 'rock 'n' roll, girl groups, and the like'. This is confirmed by a brief scan of Epstein's 'reviews', for they do appear somewhat incongruous within the bulk of 'copy' in the paper itself. However it was that important contact with Bill Harry and *Mersey Beat*, together with Flannery's direct involvement in the local scene that finally prompted Epstein to (re)visit the Cavern.

Mersey Beat's contribution to the milieu within which the Beatles found meaning and self-expression cannot be over-estimated. In fact, one of the most illuminating Beatles articles of the entire decade came from *Mersey Beat* in 1961. It was not written by editor Bill Harry, but came from the pen of Cavern deejay Bob Wooler. Wooler describes in florid terms how the Beatles had become the toast of the rock scene for 'resurrect[ing] original style rock 'n' roll music [...]

when it had been emasculated by figures like Cliff Richard and sounds like those electronic wonders, the Shadows [...] Here was the excitement – both physical and aural – that symbolised the rebellion of youth in the ennuied mid-1950s [...] Turning back the Rock clock' (Wooler, 1961:12). The article is a wonderful piece of observant, erudite journalism at this decisive early stage in the career of the Beatles. The urban myth about Norman Jones coming into NEMS requesting a copy of 'My Bonnie' and thus introducing Brian to the work of the Beatles can also be at least partially exploded by the fact that *Mersey Beat* would have been sitting on the sales counters at NEMS well before the time of Jones' supposed visit (several 'Norman Joneses' have laid claim to this occurrence in Beatles history, but none can prove incontrovertibly that they were either *the* Norman Jones or indeed ever spoke to Mr Epstein on the day of their visit to NEMS). Joe distinctly recalls that issue one of *Mersey Beat* had been published on 6 July, 1961 and he did so precisely because he had written in his Adcross accounts book that 'NEMS/ BE ordered copies'. One seldom discussed development concerning the impact of *Mersey Beat* to the Liverpool scene is that it also inspired a local imitator. While in 1964 Flannery himself was more-or-less based in West Germany, his partner involved himself in a short-lived competitor entitled *Combo*. This music paper was published for the north-end of Merseyside and championed not only Joe's Carlton-Brooke stable which by this time features artistes such as Beryl Marsden, the Liver Birds, the Nocturns, and the All Stars, but also bands from Crosby, Bootle and Southport. *Combo* was a lively little journal but was destined to fail. It ran from 1963 to 1964, by which time even *Mersey Beat* was struggling somewhat for copy and suffered from being absorbed into a national weekly, perhaps reflecting a slowing of interest in the 'Liverpool Sound'. The music had, indeed, been oversold while remaining relatively static.

Brian Epstein's important decision to visit the Cavern has been somewhat historically muddied. In his biography *Cellarful of Noise* (1964) Epstein states that he 'was not a member [and] regretted my decision to come' (Epstein, 1964:43) and there is an implication that this might have been his first visit. Joe concurs with the above remark by stating that Brian 'would have been very nervous about being seen in such a venue', suggesting not only was it was not the kind of place Epstein would normally visit, but that Brian was also somewhat 'fragile' in such circumstances, and was not naturally drawn to crowded places. However, according to the club's previous manager Alan Sytner (see Chapter 3), Epstein had actually visited the Cavern club on several previous occasions. Sytner claimed to both Spencer Leigh (2002) and this writer that Epstein even spent his 21st birthday there. Nevertheless, by November 1961 the club had changed profile somewhat, and was appealing to a younger demographic interested in rock 'n' roll music, rather than jazz. One suspects the Cavern would not have been considered 'cool' in quite the same sense as it was when trading as a jazz cellar. Epstein records that he was 'apprehensive at the thought of having to march in there among a lot of teenagers' (*ibid*). Maybe his very presence would have been easily identified and scorned by the younger demographic in the club; Joe Flannery recalled: 'I didn't think he would go, to be honest. Bill Harry arranged this and, as all of the usual books will tell you, Brian and his lieutenant Alistair Taylor went to a lunchtime session at the Cavern on the 9th November 1961. At least he wasn't on his own. I couldn't have gone because at that time of day I would have still been in Kirkby. But Brian wouldn't have wanted me there. What the books don't tell you, however, is that he also visited me on a number of occasions that very month.'

Joe recalled November 1961 very well because it was the first time that Lee Curtis and the Detours had been booked into a Liverpool city centre venue (but not the Cavern Club) that year. The week before his visit to the Cavern, Epstein had visited Joe and had told him that he intended to catch the Beatles within seven days and that Bill Harry was arranging everything.

> I informed Brian that Lee Curtis was also booked in town that month for a number of gigs at the old Liverpool Jazz Society, now the Iron Door, which was around the corner on Temple Lane. It was quite evident to me by this time that Brian was entirely hooked on the prospect of management. I must confess, however, that I did wonder whether there was an ulterior motive. I was fully aware that Brian had a taste for younger, working-class men (labourers especially) and, of course, knew full well that he had engaged in a number of disastrous liaisons in the not-too-distant past.

Joe decided, therefore, to keep a relative distance from this new adventure, while at the same time, offer as much practical help that he felt necessary.

> Basically I suggested that if he thought the Beatles were what he was looking for, we would keep in close contact, maybe bringing our artists together, and meet as frequently as possible to debate issues arising from this venture into the world of management. In all honesty, it was all I could do to keep his feet on the ground, and I still hadn't had time to see the Beatles for myself at that juncture, and so I was somewhat reserved about the whole affair, not only from managerial point of view, but also in fear that one of my oldest and closest of friends might be lining himself up to be hurt once again. On both counts of course, I needn't have worried, but at that stage I was not to know what was about to happen.

Epstein agreed, for according to Flannery he was, already 'in his own head', managing the Beatles – which suggests that the visit to the Cavern was merely procedure and that Epstein was determined to manage somebody (anybody?). Before his visit to the Cavern, Joe has record of another, more casual visit from Brian, the previous Thursday late afternoon, whereupon they discussed the Detours, Lee Curtis' appeal, P.R., bookings and publicity and took a trip to *The Musical Box* shop in Rocky Lane for a few records that NEMS did not have (interesting when NEMS were supposed to have 'everything'). Joe recorded spending £1-7/2d that afternoon in *The Musical Box*, approximately the cost of four 45 rpm singles. By the time of Epstein's famous meeting of 10 December 1961 with the Beatles (and although a contract had yet to be signed), he was effectively ensconced as their manager and during December Joe saw very little of him. The Detours were working solidly at the Mecca Birkenhead (and elsewhere), whereas the Beatles continued their residency at the Cavern, while also expanding to hitherto unchartered areas such as Widnes, Runcorn and Ellesmere Port. Brian and Joe finally met up again at the beginning of 1962 at the Liverpool Jazz Society/Iron Door. The Beatles and the Detours were finally sharing the same bill.

The Detours were checking their equipment prior to the gig when they discovered that one of the amps had 'blown'. Although Joe claimed to be roadie as well as manager, he could 'barely change a fuse' and so decided to try to borrow an amp from another band.

> I turned away from the stage area to discover Brian standing in the shadows watching the Detours warm up. Initially I asked him whether he had come to see the show, forgetting that he had now also entered the managerial merry-go-round, but he was quick to remind me that he was now in charge of the Beatles, who were also on the bill that evening. At last our paths had crossed! Seizing my chance, I asked Brian about the amp. He told me it was fine by him, but that I had better ask the band … they're upstairs in the band room. I went up the winding staircase in the decaying warehouse to what were laughingly described as the dressing rooms to see what I could scrounge whereupon I came across the Beatles. Their local profile had risen greatly in the intervening couple of months and they were now sharing the top spot with Lee Curtis and the Detours. But they were still extremely friendly and complementary about Lee, albeit with a sense of irony and a competitive edge. Brian followed me up the winding staircase and promptly introduced me to his 'boys'; they, in turn, having found that I was an old friend of Brian's, greeted me with genuine warmth. Even in the short time that Brian had been with them, he had obviously made a great impression. When it was suggested that the Detours borrow an amp from the Beatles I was delighted to hear John Lennon agree.

This was the beginning of a friendship between Flannery and the Beatles. After the gig they sat around chewing the fat. Brian informed the Beatles that Joe was a good friend, and could be trusted. Joe stated that his flat at Gardner Road was 'open house'. They did not appear at the Gardner Road address immediately, but after learning that Flannery's address was adjacent to the recently-opened Granada Bowling Alley on Green Lane, they began arriving for afternoon tea and toast in between games of Ten-Pin Bowling.

During the month of March 1962, the Beatles spent a fair amount of time at the Flannery residence. Anne, Joe's housekeeper, had married a Scandinavian seaman and their daughter Girda was apparently a big attraction: especially for Paul McCartney. But it seems that John Lennon particularly enjoyed the ambience. He would fall asleep in the chair in front of the fire after endlessly doodling on scraps of paper. Joe remembers getting the impression that there was little at home to inspire him and that he preferred the warmth of Gardner Road. 'John would generally sleep through until late morning, when he would be awoken by the arriving Anne pulling out the ashes from the extinguished fire and lighting the new blaze with the assistance of his doodle-ridden scraps of paper.'

Flannery remembers the Beatles as well-focused individually and collectively 'or at least three of them were. As for Pete Best, I'm not so sure, because I thought he was very shy. But it was very difficult for him because the other three were so incredibly close. It was very difficult talking to any one of them individually, when all three were together. One could only talk seriously to them as individuals when they were on their own'. About this time Joe also recognized a different Brian Epstein from the one that he had previously known so well; he looked as if he was vicariously living his life through his young protégés. Occasionally he would try to impress them with the appearance of a cool, calm businessman. At other times, he would try to make an impact on them by his 'trendiness' and dress in a similar manner to them, causing great hilarity from the group and deep embarrassment from Epstein. Flannery also further noticed that he could be very insecure and 'rather sad'.

Contracts and contacts

The Beatles played the newly-opened Star Club in Hamburg during April 1962. This was an extremely well-paid gig, for the club had been opened by Manfred Weissleder in order to put all of the other clubs out of business and he was prepared to pay the best money. The Star Club had a large capacity, with seating for over one thousand, and Brian and Joe had already viewed the new club at close quarters. During March of 1962 Joe first heard the name of Stuart Sutcliffe: 'The boys explained to me that he was their former bassist. I remember John telling me one evening after a gig that Stuart was his closest friend.'

> And he went on to describe to me the band's previous exploits in Germany at the Indra, the Bambi Kino, the Top Ten Club. All names that I would get to know extremely well over the next few years either by accident or design were coined by the Beatles in that month or so they spent in and out of Gardner Road, eating me out of house and home and being chased out of the way by Anne. Sadly, little did any of us realize that Stuart was already very ill; terminally so, in fact, and the very day before they were to return to the Reeperbahn, Stuart had already died.

While the Beatles were in Germany Joe handled most of the Beatles' bookings outside Liverpool – and they were now coming in thick and fast. Brian Epstein enlightened Joe one evening over dinner that he admired the Larry Parnes style of management, and suggested that a 'stable' of Liverpudlians might be possible, with all of the best local acts under one managerial umbrella of NEMS together with Flannery's newly-named agency of Carlton-Brooke. Brian then asked whether an official combination of NEMS with Carlton-Brooke might be possible. Joe recalls:

> I was a little wary: not because I held any misgivings about Brian's integrity, but because I still thought of him as a dreamer. Also I did consider that if he, like Parnes, had a number of artistes under his mantle, some would suffer at the expense of others. Also, I continually reminded myself of Jack Good's words to me. For Good, Parnes' style of management seemed steeped in the past, and who was I to argue? I declined Brian's offer to formally amalgamate [...] a mistake? Probably.

Joe had only recently given his management activity the working title of Carlton-Brooke and it was merely a case of practicalities. Lee Curtis' local popularity was growing, the money was coming in and there was book-keeping to be done. The receipts and invoices had to be separated from his other business concerns. Joe's partner Kenny suggested that he needed both a company title and an agency licence to increase his professional image. Joe took the name of the cinema (the Carlton) on the corner of Green Lane and Tuebrook, and hyphenated it with the last half of this thoroughfare's name. 'I added an 'e' for 'sophistication'!' Shortly afterwards – perhaps month or two later – NEMS Enterprises was also registered as a theatrical, concert and booking agency and Clive Epstein was appointed Company Secretary. Joe recalls 'Brian had begun to express opinions about other artists by the early summer of 1962'. He was showing particular interest in the Remo Four who had been playing the Cavern since rock 'n' roll had been allowed through its portals. They were good musicians who had been around since 1958. The Remo Four enjoyed their own residency at the Cavern for a while and then became the backing group for Johnny Sandon, former lead singer of the Searchers. Ultimately, rather than signing them as such, the group were hired on several occasions to back NEMS artists. Epstein used the group to back one of his starlets Tommy Quickly in 1963, and they also backed Liverpool's finest vocal group the Chants for a while, and appeared on the Beatles' autumn tour of 1964. They were a fully professional group and went through several personnel changes over the years, eventually in reduced size enjoying a hit record ('Resurrection Shuffle') in 1970 as Ashton, Gardner and Dyke.

However after a few failed singles for Pye, Epstein lost interest in them and it was left to Flannery to help pick up the pieces by booking them into the Star Club in 1965. Epstein also wanted to manage the Four Jays, the Big Three, the aforementioned Chants, and Gerry and the Pacemakers. Gerry Marsden, leader of the Pacemakers was also very popular with the Beatles. In fact the two bands had played part of a gig together in 1961 as an octet. Brian already knew Gerry Marsden a little, via the NEMS shop in Whitechapel. Marsden was quite a record collector and was forever in NEMS. Brian, however, was also very impressed with Gerry's all-round entertainment professionalism and also admired the band for persisting with a piano. Joe recalls Brian remarking on a number of occasions that their dedication to humping a piano around knew no bounds.

Bill Harry (1992) has suggested that Brian's tactics for signing acts were based around earmarking those *Mersey Beat* poll-winners who were not already committed to management. Joe Flannery agreed with this statement; in fact, according to Joe, Epstein was also interested in managing Lee Curtis and wanted what were then conceivably the top two acts in Liverpool both under contract with NEMS. And so, during that summer of 1962 Brian asked Joe for the second time whether they might officially combine their music business interests – 'excluding the shops, of course'. This second offer came on the back of a small coup that Flannery had made by getting the Beatles into north Wales. Lee Curtis had already made some breakthroughs on the north-east Wales coast and into the Welsh Marches. Towns such as Connah's Quay, Flint and Shotton were always good for the Detours, but by spring of '62 one could add Hereford, Malvern, Ludlow and Whitchurch. Having taken over responsibility for bookings on behalf of NEMS away from Liverpool Flannery managed to get a deal with a variety agency entitled 'CANA' which handled dance hall bookings in the Midlands and recalls:

> I was also able to persuade the operators of a small club in Rhyl, quaintly entitled the *Regent Dansette*, to take the Beatles during July that summer. The Beatles' status had undoubtedly grown but, to be honest, it was Lee Curtis' reputation as a live performer that preceded them, not their own. Brian, however, was suitably impressed! He thought that this was really travelling.

The Beatles were also supported on these two 'prestigious occasions' by groups with whom Joe would have a great deal of contact over the forthcoming years. At Stroud, the Rebel Rousers, who would perform for him many times during his work in Hamburg and at Rhyl a group recommended by Bob Wooler – the Strangers. Lead singer for the Strangers was Joe Fagin, who had a couple of solo hits in the 1980s with 'That's Livin' Alright' and 'Back with the Boys Again'.

Flannery recalls being very tempted to formally combine with Brian after this achievement, but held out for two reasons. Firstly the only reason he had taken 'this crazy job on in the first place was to assist my brother'. At this time he had no other acts formally signed with Carlton-Brooke and the entire purpose of his agency was to help Lee gain an outlet for his talent. 'Of course my loyalty to this aim, I realize now, was somewhat misguided. Brian could have done far more for Lee that myself, in the long run.' But, to be fair to Joe, it could also be argued that at this time Epstein was still something of an interloper. Joe had been managing Lee since 1960, whereas Brian had only come into management late-1961. Secondly, even if Joe had agreed to the coalition, his brother would not have gone near Epstein. Lee informed this writer that he could never have envisaged any kind of deal with Epstein. Lee claims that Brian had 'approached' him that summer but was spurned, Lee suspecting that Brian's motives were not exactly 'honourable'. Flannery recalls:

Some have said that he did this with Tommy Quickly, and that Brian simply wanted to bed the young Tommy, but I have always felt that the myth of Brian's homosexuality has outgrown the reality. Primarily Brian wanted success. He was unable to directly gain artistic success for himself and so his ensuing plan was to gain it vicariously through his artistes. Even though he might have 'fancied' myself, Lee and Tommy Quickly perhaps, even John Lennon – although I have always doubted this, I don't believe that he would have compromised this artistic goal for one second. Lee, however, has never agreed with this analysis. For him, Brian was always after something else, and, despite my arguments to the contrary over many years, he still believes this to be true. Another personality, another perspective […] there is no one truth, is there?

The Beatles might have been away in Germany but according to Flannery it was 'pandemonium back in Liverpool' during that spring and early summer of 1962. Epstein was rapidly running out of record company contacts, hawking their demonstration tape from company-to-company, and Flannery was handling increased enquiries for the two groups:

We met every week at either Gardner Road or NEMS in Whitechapel. Usually in the afternoon after my work was done for the day. Invariably Brian was for accepting every offer provided the price appeared right. Both Kenny and I had to keep reminding him, however, that, now that bookings were sometimes six, even nine months in advance, provisos and riders had to be written into contracts demanding payment reviews and get-out clauses in case fees and/or work commitments had expanded so much in the intervening months that contracts were placed in jeopardy.

According to Flannery, Brian didn't even know what Joe was talking about at first and Flannery had to explain to him 'that the Beatles might be bigger than any of us had imagined […] many other local groups were also going to be successful […] and to place his group at rates which seemed equitable in, say, May 1962, for a booking in January, 1963, would not be serving the boys' or NEMS' best interests'. Although Epstein had been astute enough from late-1961 to increase the asking price, locally, for the band, he was floundering when big money needed to be negotiated for advance bookings. It was at this stage that Brian suggested that if Carlton-Brooke and NEMS were not to join forces, then the former should handle all bookings out of Liverpool on behalf of the latter, for an agreed percentage. Flannery: 'Brian, I think, was a good organizer and a superb visionary and, in his own way, he was a fair businessman, but he needed to be a little harder, and think a little more long-term, if he was to make "his boys" any real money – so I agreed to step in for the time being.'

One occasion illustrates this point well. By late-1962 it was evident to those 'in the know' that the Beatles were in their ascendancy and destined for greater things. As Carlton-Brooke partially represented NEMS, Joe had approached the

Prestatyn Royal Lido in August, 1962 attempting to book a variety of Merseyside groups into the venue; at £30 per band the gigs were well paid and the events were well organized. Joe began negotiations by offering them the Beatles. The Beatles played there under the Carlton-Brooke/NEMS alliance on 24 November, 1962, just as 'Love Me Do' was tickling the charts. Back in August '62, Flannery had made an agreement with the Royal Lido which stated that, if the Beatles had expanded their popularity base by the time of the November gig, then, rather than face a re-negotiation of their fee, the Lido should agree to take further NEMS/ Carlton Brooke acts the following weeks. This they agreed to do.

Flannery's reasoning was one of pragmatism: 'If the Beatles were to be the success that Brian, Kenny and I expected, the chances of them ever being able to play the Lido again were very slim. Therefore, rather than hiking up the Beatles fee which Brian would have done and losing our goodwill with the Ballroom, this extra 'Gentleman's Agreement' ensured more work for other NEMS/Carlton-Brooke bands, all of whom paid us a percentage.' Because of this one deal, Flannery developed a strong relationship with the Royal Lido and was able to place as many groups as he wished into the venue, thus making more money for himself, creating more work for the groups, and keeping the management of the Royal Lido happy (even though the Beatles never actually played there again). The Royal Lido proved to be a happy hunting ground for most of the Liverpool bands over the next twelve months or so.

Epstein, it appears, did appreciate that he had to learn fast. Once he had started building up his artist roster, he encouraged artists to visit Flannery at the Gardner Road address. Joe also recorded in his books occasional working breakfasts during 1962, with the pair exchanging money and receipts gathered from bookings, and hypothesizing about their next moves:

> On some of these meetings I would detect that Brian was checking me out regarding my current status with Kenny; on other occasions it was strictly business. He would still be experiencing extremes peaks and troughs of emotion, brought on, I feel, by his loneliness and depression. Brian would say to me that eventually people would find his company boring and would depart, leaving the emptiness that he always felt. I still don't accept that he was infatuated with some of his artists (John Lennon, Tommy Quickly, Michael Haslam, etc.); but I do think that from this very early stage he could envisage a time when they had no further use for him, and this frightened him more than words could say.

Epstein's professionalism did grow, however, and in a short space of time he was not just acting the managerial role, but making 'professional decisions'. For example, one area that troubled him was that the Beatles used to enjoy a drink in between sets wherever they would play. This was fine, up to a point, but they had also grown accustomed to coming out of the band room or dressing room and mixing with the punters. It was often a good excuse to either speak to existing girl friends or 'tap off' with new ones. Previously, this might be considered good

PR; it was also a matter of necessity, for many of the dressing rooms at various venues were little more than toilets (some actually *were* toilets) and it was good to mingle. However, by 1962 as their appeal grew, this mixing with the crowd looked decidedly unprofessional.

There had already been the odd skirmish in the past when a member of the Beatles had attempted to 'eye up' a girl in the audience, only to find during the break that she was attached to a rather grizzly gang member bent on destruction. Flannery had also already witnessed this with Lee Curtis on a number of occasions. Brian and Joe therefore decreed that for all artists being promoted and/or handled by NEMS and Carlton-Brooke this would have to stop. There was enormous resistance to begin with but Joe suggested that it might be a good idea to send drinks into band rooms, accompanied, if necessary, by said girl friends, thus effectively turning the band room into what was described in the business as a 'green room'. This was common practice in the higher echelons of the entertainment industry but had not yet emerged as a strategy around the jive hives of Merseyside and beyond. There were two distinct advantages to this tactic as far as Joe could see. Firstly the unprofessional wanderings would cease. Secondly, and more importantly, an aura of unavailability and distance would be built around any group performing under their banner, thus hopefully increasing their 'aura', appeal and self-esteem. This might all appear rather obvious in the twenty-first century, and did so to the larger stars in the early 1960s, but the Liverpool scene did have its element of accessibility; productive to begin with, but not something that could be perpetuated if appeal was to broaden.

It was at the Queens Hall, Widnes that this plan was first put into practice. Under the auspices of NEMS Enterprises, Brian and Joe promoted a string of Monday night gigs in Widnes, twelve miles outside Liverpool. It was quite a gamble, for the Queen's Hall was a sizeable venue. On 3 and 10 September 1962 the Beatles played the Queen's Hall and were supported by Rory Storm and the Hurricanes. Both bands were kept in their dressing rooms and drinks were sent in. 'Rory enjoyed this, as I remember, because he told me it made him feel like a star, but the rest of the band were not impressed. The Beatles went along with it without much comment, but were a little rattled, I think.' Brian and Joe then eased up on the policy for a few days but insisted that when the Beatles played there again on 16 September they remained, once again, in the dressing rooms.

This time it worked well. Drinks and sandwiches were sent in and the bands were made to feel very special. Brian and Joe then followed throughout October with more promotions at the Queen's Hall, this time with Lee Curtis and his new band the All Stars (who, by this time had their new drummer, Pete Best – of which more later), the Fourmost, and the Merseybeats and all went well. The groups responded well to this concept of 'look but don't touch' especially when, by the end of the evening, a posse of young fans had congregated outside the stage door just as they would to see a national star. Joe still feels that this was the first time that 'an aura' had been created around the bands. It could be argued that something might have been lost by doing this: that an innate democracy of the Merseyside scene was overturned by this show business attitude. But Flannery disagrees. He says that there were ample opportunities for musicians to socialize afterwards and even jam during gigs. He argued to this writer that if one wanted to declare a democratic musical state then there was always the folk scene. According to Joe this show business veneer that was placed over the groups made them more professional and there were immediate results. Subsequently, bands arriving at Gardner Road to get their orders to go on to gigs came prepared both mentally and appearance-wise much more than they had done so previously; there would be less raucous behaviour before gigs, and more responsible behaviour afterwards. As for the Beatles, according to Flannery it was Paul McCartney who led the way, here. He took this new approach very seriously. But, in truth, 'they were all very quick to realize that as Beatles they simply had to distance themselves from their growing army of fans if they were to progress'. Being a 'Beatle' could no longer simply be a musical experience and a 'laugh'. It had become an education for them and increased visits to Gardner Road followed, at least as and when their busy schedules would allow.

The ABC bowling alley just around the corner on Green Lane did tremendous business as groups of all shapes, sizes and talent waited to get into Gardner Road to receive gig information and/or advice. Joe vividly remembers ten-pin bowling matches between the Beatles and Lee Curtis and the All Stars. This interaction between these two groups is another seldom-told story for one is always given the impression that, after the Pete Best affair which shall be discussed shortly the two groups did not speak (Bill Harry alludes to this, 1992). However according to Joe this was not the case. 'The two groups often shared gigs after Brian and I joined forces and got on most of the time. John thought that Lee was a poser (which he was) and Lee thought that John was a beatnick (which he was).'

At this stage Epstein and Flannery was a unique and formidable duo. Both were bright and hungry for success, even though virtual opposites in class, temperament and approach. As an enabler Joe felt he was able to demonstrate the possibilities available in unfolding situations, 'figuring things out, if you will'. According to Joe, Brian, on the other hand, was becoming disciplined. 'He had an attention to detail that was second-to-none and discovered that if all angles were covered to the best of one's ability then a situation would quickly gain momentum.' But, according to Flannery Brian Epstein was ambitious, not only to find the fame that he so desired for his boys, but also to remove himself physically from Liverpool – a city in which he had encountered great difficulties, and for which he had it seems, little affection. For Flannery, the move by NEMS Enterprises from Liverpool to London in March 1964 was inevitable. In *Cellarful of Noise* Epstein claims that he 'regret[ted] this very profoundly' (Epstein, 1964:95), but this, according to Joe, was a whitewash.

Pete Best

Prior to the divergence of NEMS and Carlton-Brooke, however and, historically, of most interest to Beatles scholars throughout the world over the years, has been the dismissal of Pete Best from the Beatles. Flannery was directly involved in that stratagem and explained exactly why and how the dismissal took place – at least from his perspective. When Brian initially began to manage the Beatles, he not only discussed matters with Flannery, but also with Pete Best and his mother Mona. As far as Joe was aware, the relationship between Pete and Brian was amicable enough, but, as he (Joe) became embroiled in the whole Beatles saga during 1962, it became clear to him that Brian's relationship with Mona was rather less than cordial. What perhaps most people tend not to realize about the post-Williams and pre-Epstein Beatles is that the group was effectively managed by Mona Best as a vehicle for her good-looking son, Peter. Further complications arose as a consequence of this relationship.

It is accurately recorded (Harry, 1992) that in August, 1959 the Quarry Men had played the Casbah Coffee Bar's opening night after the Les Stewart Quartet had lost the gig. The Casbah was situated in the cellar of the Best's residence in 8, Hayman's Green, West Derby, a quiet leafy lane just off the main carriageway into West Derby Village. The opening night even attracted the attention of the local *West Derby Reporter* newspaper, no doubt after having been contacted by Mona Best. Mona was the estranged wife of Johnny Best, the main promoter at the Liverpool Boxing Stadium. She, like her husband was one of Liverpool's new self-employed: a real go-getter, full of ideas and a very independent woman in a man's world. The Quarry Men only really got the gig because of Ken Brown, who, along with George Harrison, had left the previously-booked Les Stewart Group and joined up with the, by this time practically defunct, Quarry Men. Brown's tenure with the Quarry Men didn't last long, however, for six weeks later, after a disagreement with John Lennon over money he was sacked and promptly formed a group with Mona's son Peter. This group became known as the Blackjacks and naturally played regularly at the Casbah. Importantly, Mona Best banned the Quarry Men from the Casbah club for a period of time in support of Ken Brown and thereafter relationships would always be strained between Mona and the group, even after the Quarry Men mutated into the Beatles and even when Peter was invited to join the Beatles.

For the Beatles, Pete Best effectively became their drummer by default. The 1961 adventure to Hamburg had been organized ostensibly without a permanent drummer, and Best was only really invited to join because he could play as well as any and had a new drum kit. As far as Joe's sources informed him ('remember, I was not part of the enclave at that time'), Pete's mother Mona did not approve of her son's joining the Beatles. She had little time for John Lennon and still bore a grudge about the dismissal of Ken Brown. So, ironically, during 1961, although Peter and his mother assumed the managerial role for the group, arranging gigs and negotiating fees etc., the 'Quarry Men' element were not well-pleased. Joe recalls that John Lennon informed him that he thought Mona was 'very bossy, like Mimi [Lennon's aunt]' and was using the Beatles 'for her darling son'. Flannery remembers this last comment as revealing:

> One couldn't blame Mona for doing this. She was, presumably, a very ambitious lady, at least for her son, and Pete was very shy. He did have a certain presence on stage which actually assisted the group at times but he wasn't exactly Mr. Personality off the stage. He was quiet and rather broody. In any case, it was very difficult for him to break into the Beatles thought processes. Those remaining three were so close it was practically impossible to separate them at times. So, the oft-touted 'jealousy' theory [i.e. that the three were jealous of the appeal and good looks of the one] simply doesn't go anywhere near the psychological complications of Pete's membership of the group. All because Pete might have appeared to have [at least on the surface] a posse of girls hanging around him does not necessarily create jealousy. Let's face it, Paul had a regular girlfriend – as did John and there were enough girls to go around. From my retrospection, George was always a little more reserved and was into playing his instrument. No, jealousy does not, I feel, come into it at all!

For Flannery, Pete's mother Mona was at the nexus of this crisis, even after Brian Epstein had become the group's manager. 'To begin with, at least from what John, Paul and George had told me during 1962, they had felt rather swamped by Mona during 1961. She had arranged a lot of bookings for them and was the initial impetus behind them getting their residency at the Cavern.' It had actually been Mona, via her son Pete, who had contacted Peter Eckhorn and fixed them up with the Top Ten Club sessions in 1961. Neil Aspinall, their first roadie and close confidante was also a lodger at Hayman's Green and was romantically involved with Mona at the time (a baby was the result: Rogue). Mona had also made approaches to Granada TV in an attempt to get this local independent TV Company interested in the band. Granada did later find the group of some local interest and (co-incidentally or otherwise) recorded the Beatles playing at the Cavern on the very night that Ringo Starr had replaced Pete Best in August 1962. However, all of these apparent plus-points actually worked against the self-motivated Mona Best.

For Paul, John and George, Brian Epstein's taking over the business side of things was perhaps a blessing. Epstein had no initial intentions of removing Best, but made things very clear to everybody concerned that he (and nobody else) was now responsible for not only their living but also their welfare. Epstein had been searching for such an experience as this and he wasn't going to let it all slip through his fingers. According to Flannery Epstein held what Joe describes as a 'very important coffee morning during 1962, to which I was privy'. Epstein invited all of the female companions and relatives of his artists which, by this time also included Gerry and the Pacemakers expressly to inform them that it was he who was in control and that he would look after his protégés:

The vast majority of those present were absolutely delighted that Brian had both involved them and laid down the law. They now knew exactly where they and their loved ones stood. Not so Mona Best, however, who was fuming. She felt that control had been wrested away from her and for the next few days, she apparently made Brian's life a misery, constantly ringing him on the phone, decreeing that she be more closely involved in the group's affairs. Brian informed Joe that he felt that Mona was looking for some kind of ulterior motive for the meeting; that she thought it masked some kind of evil conspiracy; but the meeting was simply held to set the records straight. He gloomily told me at one stage that he was sorry he held it, but I countered by stating that the coffee morning had been very effective and that Mona simply had to back off: Joe recalls Epstein stating categorically 'This is now a professional operation, Joe. It can't stand input from loose cannon such as Mona Best.'

From this perspective, Brian Epstein had motivations but no immediate intentions of removing Pete Best from the Beatles. Epstein informed Joe that he was just going to have to put up with Mona 'from time to time ... as the mood takes her'. This situation put Joe Flannery under a little strain because he had also by this time got to know Mona well:

> I was in something of an invidious position, being gladly received at 8, Hayman's Green, the Best's home. It was only a short drive away from Gardner Road and I was frequently made very welcome, most notably by the Best's dog (either a Great Dane or an Irish Wolf Hound ... I can't remember exactly which!) [...] who enjoyed rubbing itself against my leg! I don't think, however, that Mona saw me as such a threat as she did Brian. She was probably right in that respect.

Flannery had spoken to John Lennon shortly after the coffee morning, however, and Lennon expressed a caustic response to the Mona affair, stating that he was pleased that Brian had laid down the law because he'd just about had enough of her. John and Joe had become close at this stage:

> We would frequently drive down to the Pier Head in my Vauxhall and stand at the railings, eating one of those terrible meat pies that they used to sell there and look out over the narrow expanse of the River Mersey and the more vast margins of the Irish Sea. John was forever dreaming of America. It was as if his 'spiritual home' was across the Atlantic. He would constantly state to me that his greatest desires were involved in crossing the Atlantic; that he ached to play in the USA, the great source of his inspiration. On this occasion he told me that he was not going to let Mona Best 'get in the way'.

Giving Joe the impression that he immediately intended to do something about the Best affair, he informed Flannery that he would speak to 'the other two'. Joe drove

John home, but not before he had been informed that the Beatles were going to 'help sort this thing out for Brian'.

> I could understand John's reaction. Following the new regime of Brian [and myself, to a degree] the relief expressed by the three Beatles was palpable. They were only young men, let us not forget, and Brian was far from being a tyrant, or selective [...] in other words, he was interested in the Beatles as a group, not as a conveyance for one member, that being Pete Best. John's reaction also proved to me that the relationship between the three and Pete was rather tenuous and my impressions of Pete being 'suffered' by the rest were amplified at this time.

Subsequently Joe has pondered that, had circumstances been different (in other words, had the Beatles possessed more time to look for a drummer prior to going to Hamburg) they would not have considered involving themselves yet again with the Bests. He thinks to this day that this would have been the case. However, there remains very little evidence to suggest that Pete Best was inferior as a percussionist. In fact Bill Harry (1992) records that one of the best drummers in the Liverpool rock scene at this time Johnny Hutchinson of the Big Three 'considered Best to be an excellent drummer' (Harry, 1992: 634). Billy J. Kramer was also to comment to Harry that he 'didn't think the Beatles were any better with Ringo Starr. I never doubted his ability as a drummer but I thought they were a lot more raw and raucous with Pete' (ibid). This adds more fuel to the concept of Best being removed for reasons other than his drumming abilities – something with which aforementioned Beatles expert Bill Harry concurs. Joe Flannery still feels that 'to my mind, at least, those encounters during 1962 gave me the lasting impression that they considered Pete's membership of the band to be one of convenience'.

For example, it could be argued that the barriers between the three and Pete had already been erected as early as the Decca recording sessions on New Year's Day 1962. For, when the news finally came through in March that Decca had turned down the group, nobody appeared to inform either Mona or Pete Best. Similarly, when the Parlophone deal went through, nobody bothered to let them know. This might suggest that Best was simply not part of the inner cabal. Although he is on record as having stated that he did not experience any problems during his stint with the group, one man's views of a working relationship can be entirely different from those of another. So from Joe Flanney's particular perspective, the Beatles and not Epstein made the decision to remove Pete Best from the group and the reason? Pete's mother Mona. Joe further remembers: 'The response from Mona Best after Pete was dismissed from the group was very revealing. She immediately phoned everybody – not including myself for I was then attempting to handle Pete's next career move – in a panic. It was as if she had finally realized that the group was no longer her personal play thing.' Joe continued:

> However it has to be stated that it also suited Brian to have Mona out of his hair. Not only was she poking her nose into the running of the band but she had just

had Neil Aspinall's baby. Brian was already concerned about keeping Cynthia's pregnancy out of the news (that was the way it had to be done in those days) and he told me that Mona's liason with Neil was 'very indiscreet – the last straw'; that was something, coming as it did from a man who could be very indiscreet himself, at times!

It was at this crucial stage that Flannery stepped in. Best was, naturally, very hurt and despondent. After unsuccessfully attempting to place Pete with a group under his own managerial scope (at that time – briefly – the Merseybeats), Epstein approached Flannery and asked if he would consider placing Pete with Lee Curtis and the All Stars; then one of Liverpool's premier rock 'n' roll bands. Joe states he was immediately placed in 'a rather difficult position'. The All Stars had been assembled around Lee earlier that year from the pick of the local musicians – hence the name. They were considered a class act and to remove any one of them would have been a great pity, especially at the whim of another manager. However, on the credit side, Best was very popular in Liverpool and enjoyed a personal following. Any group who picked up on the now redundant drummer would also attract his fan-base.

In addition, NEMS and Carlton Brooke were in cahoots and Joe felt pressure from Brian to work as closely as possible with him:

> So, I approached Pete about joining the All Stars and, after a little thought, he readily agreed. Lee and Peter already got on very well and he didn't require any coaxing. After all, it was an easy decision to make. It only appears in retrospect that Pete was the forgotten man because the Beatles were unique and became all conquering, however this was absolutely not the case at the time. We were all aware, by the summer of 1962 that, given a fair crack of the whip, a few Liverpool groups could make something of a 'splash' and that the industry was in need of a change, but that was about it! Nobody could have predicted what was to happen. And so, from my perspective in 1962, Pete Best joining Lee Curtis and the All Stars was a reasonably sound move to make.

Another reason why Best made the move was that he trusted Flannery – practically all of the young musicians with whom Joe came into contact at that stage felt the same. Although at times he was heavily criticized for putting his brother's interests above all others, Joe was considered to be one of the few competent managers around Liverpool at that time. He was certainly one of Liverpool's new breed of self-employed and like Epstein his main source of income did not derive from the booking of bands. He was in effect a recognized entrepreneur – a breed seldom acknowledged and not altogether liked by popular music historians, of course, who it seems feel that these people are trampling on their popular music dreams by reducing creativity to money. Best could see that he was joining a good band, well-managed and earning good money. And, significantly, a possible recording deal between Decca and the All Stars had already been mooted. Decca (then one of the leading British labels – far bigger than Parlophone) had rejected the Beatles, whereas this same company was showing strong interest in (and eventually signed) Lee Curtis and the All Stars. To be a member of a band in the process of signing to Decca in 1962 (Tornadoes, Cruisers, Heinz; the London label) appeared far superior than being one signed to Parlophone (Pinky & Perky and Adam Faith). In hindsight, this might appear ridiculous, for Decca was probably one of the most inept examples of a vertically integrated record industry during the 1960s, but this would not have been obvious in 1962, by any means. 'In simple terms, Decca's Dick Rowe had turned down the group that Pete had left, but had accepted the group he was joining. It's all very well being wise after the event.' Joe continued:

> Brian was very sad about the whole affair and spent a few sleepless nights worrying about it. He absorbed guilt onto the aforementioned pressure, which made him unwell. But I reiterate that it was the Beatles' decision, not Brian's, and that Pete really was the fall guy for his mother's encumbrance. The complicated, and somewhat ironic, twist to the entire Pete Best 'affair' was that although it happened very early in Brian's management and was not of his making, the whole scenario suited him well, because it effectively removed a major thorn from his side, that of Mona Best. Because of this it was not something that could be openly debated. There was a furore in Liverpool over the sacking and hundreds of letters were sent into the local press (*Mersey Beat*, 'the Echo', the *Liverpool Weekly News*, etc). Pete, I feel, has always kept quiet about the matter simply out of loyalty and embarrassment. I think that his career as a Beatle ended because of the lack of judgement of his mother – although Pete would never admit to this.

When the Beatles were due to appear at the aforementioned Cavern engagement with new drummer Ringo Starr on Sunday, 19th August 1962 the Best fans were out in force. Luckily for Flannery, Lee Curtis and the All Stars were not present, having been booked to play in the Mathew Street venue the following Friday with the Big Three, but Epstein rang Flannery on the Monday following the Beatles' gig and was very piqued about the actions of some of the 'Cave-dwellers'. He informed Joe in a most disgruntled way that he had to have a bodyguard, George Harrison had ended up with a black eye and there were shouts of 'we want Pete' from the audience all night. And this was all in front of those Granada TV cameras, to boot. During late-August and September Joe continued to assuage Pete Best's battered ego in preparations for his first gig with Lee Curtis. Best was, according to Flannery 'naturally at times a little low' but it all appeared quite harmonious within the band and the issue was never openly discussed. Pete's drumming suited the group at least as well as the out-going Bernie Rogers, so all seemed well set for Best to make it into the entertainment industry, as his mother wished – but just with another group: 'it happened all the time in Liverpool, in any case' remembers Joe who added: 'Meanwhile, I now had Mona Best to contend with. She never allowed Kenny and I a minute's peace and, by September, her phone calls were driving us insane.'

> The All Stars were due to play with Pete at the end of August '62 but, because I
> wanted the transition to be smooth for Bernie Rogers, the outgoing drummer, I
> scheduled the first date to be 10th September at one of our favourite haunts, the
> Top Rank Majestic in Birkenhead. This didn't suit Mona; she wanted her boy
> thrown right in immediately ('for his fans'), but I had to explain to her that I
> had accommodated Pete in Lee Curtis' band and a home had to be found for the
> displaced drummer, Bernie Rogers. Sadly, Mona couldn't have cared less about
> Bernie and just wanted her boy back 'on the boards' as soon as possible. What
> had I let myself in for?

Pete Best seemed to get on with his role as an All Star for a while and remained with the group after Lee Curtis left to pursue a solo career and concentrate his efforts on the West German market. The All Stars became 'the Pete Best All Stars' and left Carlton-Brooke during the summer of 1963. There are diverse views concerning whether this parting was altogether amicable. Joe Flannery states that it was, however former band member and renowned pop songwriter and producer Wayne Bickerton told this writer some years ago that the band were pleased to leave Flannery's management because they felt he concentrated too much on Lee Curtis' career at the expense of their own. Predictably, Mona Best became their 'new' manager and in retrospect this too can be viewed as something of a misfortune not only for Pete, but also the rest of the All Stars. Nevertheless, perhaps the most significant later development in this saga was the publication of a Beatles' interview in *Playboy* magazine of February 1965 when John Lennon stated that 'Ringo used to fill in sometimes if our drummer was ill, with his periodic illness'. Ringo Starr then somewhat pointlessly added 'he took little pills to make him ill'. It was in all probability this piece of mischievousness and rank bad taste, and less his actual removal from the Beatles in 1962, that depressed Pete Best to such an extent that he attempted to commit suicide. Best sued, and some years later an out-of-court settlement was made.

Summary

The historian experiences several difficulties with oral history: inflation of importance of the recounting figure; centrality of selected discourses; axes to grind, the false premise of attempting to show 'how things actually were', and so on. But it still has its uses. In Joe Flannery's case his interpretations of some of the events that unfolded in 1962 are obviously subject to extraneous factors such as his relationship with Brian Epstein since childhood, his arrival somewhat late on the scene as far as the formative Beatles were concerned, his pivotal role in the Pete Best affair, and his later allegiances to the Star Club in Hamburg together with his subsequent love-hate relationship with his brother 'Lee Curtis' – these latter two issues are not discussed. All of these issues (and more besides) effectively 'colour' what have been presented here.

However these comments at least come relatively free from the patronizing speculations of conventional Beatles historical wisdom and produce a historical narrative that presents components of different consciousnesses for us to consider within the early 1960s popular musical context of Liverpool. For example, homosexuality in the city at this time is still seldom discussed (see Brocken in conversation with Flannery in Inglis, 2000), entrepreneurial histories are still marginalized – oddly, in both cases, for the sake of affirmative class and race-based histories. The status of regionality in broadening the appeal of the Merseyside groups and the fact that money and entertainment systems were at the heart of operations even then are seldom investigated. Moreover, domestic space has never, at least to this writer's knowledge, been even cursorily discussed re the Beatles – and yet the image of John Lennon peering though his bedroom window is called to mind time and time again when one listens to 'Strawberry Fields Forever' or 'Working Class Hero'.

Perhaps one of the most manipulative aspects of our culture is the ways in which the roles of creativity are treated historically. Pop histories often disguise the entrepreneurial, managerial, and domestic modes that exist in all such cultural developments. The fun of the quick buck, the satisfaction of a plate of sandwiches, and the early morning security of a crackling coal fire; these contingencies and convergences – so important if we are to understand cultural activities – are largely ignored. It's all as if everything had a purpose, a direction, a goal. It is indeed naive to suppose that the testimony here represents a pure distillation of past experience but it is important to record how Joe Flannery's concepts of 'aura' surrounding the Queen's Hall Widnes, and his involvement in the 'Pete Best Affair' have both become ghostly palimpsests in the annals of Beatles history.

Chapter 5

I like your hat – country music and Liverpool

What happened was that they [record companies] tried to make everybody else sound like the Beatles. But they were originals, one-offs never to be repeated. In all that kerfuffle, good groups got lost. It killed people's awareness of other music.

(Tony Allen of the Blue Mountain Boys to Kevin McManus, 1994:14)

Scenes

Country music in Liverpool is a passionately contested cultural activity. It is a genre of music that has held sway in the city for many years having emerged both from within and out-with rock 'n' roll, developed cultural resistance to the over arching musical narratives around it but also conceded ground to mainstream tastes and facades. It has coalesced, changed and is now almost at the point at which it is in danger of dying out altogether. The existence of several vibrant interconnected country music 'folkways' (rather than perhaps the usually illustrated key individuals) in Liverpool delivers a classic example of why popular music categories are so important: they are hotly debated, unstable and subject to transformation; they are kinetic, shifting signifiers. But country music in Liverpool is also subject to the attention of those who revel in stability, conformity and stasis. Whereas on the one hand one interviewee described the current music activity at the Melrose pub as almost life-giving, another described it as a 'cabal'. To tackle the full complexity of country music in Liverpool, therefore, one is required to embark upon wide ranging collections of case studies. In the space allotted here this is clearly not possible, however the few insights available should at least point the way and in doing so make a call for more research before the current scene – now (2009) currently residing at a very few venues in the city such as the Melrose pub in Kirkdale, the Bridge pub in Norris Green, and the Derby Lane Conservative Club in Stoneycroft – breathes its last.

Music scenes are developed through a variety of cultural, geographical and personal circumstances. Networks of individuals have to band together in order to create something that lasts longer than a one-off gig or a night in a pub. Music plays an integral role in people's merging processes, developing shared alliances between taste cultures and knowledge. As we now historically look back upon those scenes most vibrant and perhaps most important to popular music sound creation of the past 50 years or so, it becomes clear that networks of like-minded people play an integral part in developing secure yet exciting environments within which creativity can flourish but also be controlled. Scenes consist of people who know or get to know each other, who are certainly prepared to work with each other, perhaps placing the music before the finances, encouraging expressivity. They also consist of those who are able to make money and re-invest in the culture as a product, thus sustaining the activity where those of the more idealistic 'bent' would succumb to financial instability far sooner. Scenes also bolt-on subsidiary activities as they move through time and space. They produce not only sounds but alliances, memberships, journals, recordings, hierarchies and echelons. They develop competitive strains, decode philosophical contexts and authenticities. Scenes surrounding music formulate and then transform, permitting in the process the music to be re-imagined.

Pre-history

While the country music scene in Liverpool was, for many, connected with the arrival of rock and roll in the mid-1950s and carried with it the excitement and 'new-ness' of Americana at that time, it also enveloped a stability and perhaps even a social conformity that was attached to older components of a canon of music to which many Liverpool people have cleaved – those being the idealized traditions surrounding all forms of American music. Sara Cohen recognizes (2007) that all country music is a travelling global culture and implies that the music as a whole tends to set itself down in areas where the sound and sentiment resonate homologically. Cohen also states that music such as country and western (as it came to be known in the Liverpool of the 1950s) also has the ability to 'become' 'local culture' (2007:72). In this respect Cohen is correct for country music appears to have a universality that resonates across disparate communities throughout the world. It is one the most successful popular musical genres of the entire twentieth century, being reformed and rearticulated into myriad different micro-contexts from West to East – the reception of such sounds is both local and global.

However, the significance of the impact of country music in Liverpool post-WWII was that it also represented an imagined reality, a dreamed-of place. Country music acted as a catalyst for perhaps the greatest function myth of all time, containing as it did direct links to the dream world of the United States. Country music in Liverpool existed as an oxymoron: a fragmented narrative where trains, sheriffs, shoot-outs and Mexican bandits existed side by side (or should that be back-to-back) with the Liverpool and Everton Football Clubs, pints of bitter and pans of scouse. As Cohen suggests, country music was a good traveller, but like many of the merchant seamen that left Liverpool periodically to travel to Canada and the USA, its existence in Merseyside should also be attributed to several key components that reflected the ideals surrounding contemporary and historical existences of Liverpudlians during this crucial mid-twentieth-century period, and their affiliations to North America, rather than Europe.

Despite physically bordering the River Mersey, Liverpool's cultural geography extended westward far more than it did eastward into England. There is no doubt that its eastward perimeters remain economically vital to its existence, however for the (migrant-originated) Liverpudlian, there was little value to be gained from extending authenticities back into Lancashire or Yorkshire (from where many had arrived: one reason why rugby league football has never taken a hold in Liverpool – see Brocken, 2008). This westward positioning has always been of economic and cultural significance, for the Irish Sea was a conduit of trade, colonization, and transfer. Viking migrants expelled from Dublin at the beginning of the tenth century set up on the Wirral Peninsula and commerce was established at a very early stage in Liverpool's history between Ireland and the Mersey. When Liverpool came to overtake Chester as the main port of trade, transatlantic exchange followed, and the city's infrastructure came to be based almost exclusively around this westward visage. Liverpool existed as a channel to the rest of England and Wales. So the mythologies of urban life in Liverpool are not simply based around the ethnic origins of Liverpool's migrant populations but also the aspirations, dreams and hopes of all – and the more Liverpool saw of the North American continent, the more it liked. It is from this deep-seated source that the 'Cunard Yanks' stories emerge. The desire to bring home something to Liverpool that represented the new, the different, perhaps even the 'future' was for some a powerful attraction, a function myth.

But the Cunard Yanks were actually serving a need – they were not in and of themselves 'instigators'. They went out on their trips to the US and Canada with shopping lists, for the desire to own or be represented by something that was American was very strong cultural capital in the city. My own father told me that before the war his brother, my Uncle Bert, felt that his identity was 'more American than English'. Over 15 years of conducting research many locals have informed me that they do not really 'feel English' at all. This is common knowledge and is usually credited to Liverpool's 'Irish' factor; however, although the 'Irish-ness' of Liverpool should never be ignored, it certainly did not rule the roost of Liverpool's cultural artefacts (far from it, in fact), for as Liverpudlians during the twentieth century became more and more able to converse with American mass popular products, these items became of great significance. Legendary BBC presenter and deejay Billy Butler (a former deejay at the Cavern) told me that he 'practically learnt to read through American comics and that he was fascinated by anything to do with cowboys'. US comics such as *Batman*, *Detective Comics*, *The Metal Men*, *The Hulk,* and *The League of Super Heroes* were also part of my reading stock-in-trade. I was far less interested in Billy Bunter, Jennings and Just William.

This was not simply a 'Liverpool thing', of course, for all over the country young people were fascinated by the mass media of the United States. Ian Whitcomb recalled a:

> Gleaming future, lure of America – of old musics for new purposes. On TV Johnny Mack Brown, dressed in buckskin, was plagued by the Mystery Riders, who sang as they rode 'we're shadows we come from nowhere' [but] Depression

> hit like a wet kipper in the face as I stepped outside afterwards. Pine trees in
> Surrey looked like cowboy country but weren't. I changed my nationality
> to Canadian, then Red Indian. I told friends to call me Zane. Life improved.
> (Whitcomb, 1972:192)

Musicians are deeply implicated in such processes of cultural identity. Social
dancing brought countless people together, as did the sound of recorded music. The
mass media products such as film and radio intensified imagery and imaginings.
It might even be argued that relatively speaking some repudiated their everyday
life in search of an alternative. However this is perhaps also rather simplistic. In
the case of those interested in the music of the United States, some made it their
destiny. Furthermore, the fascination of this music of the US (of whatever genres)
was intensified by the constant appearance of the contrary; from the moment of its
inception in the early 1920s the BBC held itself up as the great bastion of British
culture and by the 1950s would never play an American record when a British
one would do. Therefore the at times rather dull covering of such US material
only intensified its allure. By submerging oneself almost to the point of ecstasy
and by contrasting this with the monotony of daily life the allure of America was
amplified. This is not to say that a function myth such as this is 'unreal'. Far
from it, in fact: liberation via the mixture of commodity and creativity is absolute
liberation and makes the imagined world a mirror of the subject.

Levels of commodity/creative illusion are numerous but if traced very
illustrative. Echelons of illusion run from those wearing blue jeans on the silver
screen and audiences imitating them to reaching as far as hearing a Hank Williams
record, wearing a big hat and calling oneself 'Hank'. They can even run to a group
performing country rock covers in Merseyside with the Confederate stars and bars
as a backdrop announcing 'The South Shall Rise Again' without truly realizing the
meanings behind such statements. These imitators, these mimeticians, become so
confused and absorbed with cultural extras, so increasing the hyper-reality of it
all, that (say) Hank Snow might pass for a Liverpudlian and Hank Walters might
even pass for a Tennesseean (or in the case of Snow, a Canadian). Oddly, this
combination of sounds and imagined realities can produce an important element
to a music scene: one of relative stability and conformity. This eccentricity is
what helps us to live in a troublesome world – while appearing to express realities
illusion actually protects us from the real. It is precisely this mixture of Americana
and stability that helped to create such an enduring image for the imaginary world
of the Liverpool-American. Add in a reaction to complexity, selective listening and
the perception that musical variety emerges from generic sameness and we have a
different musical order, demanding different modes of reception and experiencing
musical sound – such is (or was) the country scene in post-WWII Liverpool.

So, the country music 'scene' in Liverpool was perhaps unlike the rock 'n'
roll scene in that it tended to combine *pre*-rock 'n' roll genres with contemporary
homespun musical styles in very meaningful ways. While the arrival of rock,
according to popular music historian Ian Whitcomb 'hit us in our sleep, suddenly,

rock 'n' roll came to us fully armed 'like Minerva springing from the head of Jove', as Jack Good put it later. 'Rock 'n' roll came trailing no stormy background' (Whitcomb, 1972:193), it was not quite the same for country music in Liverpool. For example, from this writer's perspective – by this time getting his own musical chops together in the early-1970s – the country scene in Liverpool appeared to be a rather 'straight' collective, somewhat un-flexible, and certainly anti-counter culture. To dislike country music became for some tantamount to being un-Scouse. Local rock musician Joan Bimson agreed stating: 'My first gig was actually playing in a country band and I later came to like the music a great deal but by say 1970 country music belonged to another part of society. Anything that wasn't rock was rubbish as far as I was concerned' (Bimson to Brocken, 2008). Former 'roadie' at the Liverpool Stadium actor Ged McKenna stated that as a 15-year-old in 1970 'country music was older people's music. It seemed that all you heard was bloody Jim Reeves and although that wasn't all there was to it; to my ears at that time it was very conventional' (McKenna to Brocken, 2009). Hatch and Millward (1989) confirm such links between country music and fundamentalist principles:

> For many people country music has come to represent American to the same extent as apple pie and the Constitution. It is only to be expected that any institution that seems to epitomise an ideology [...] will have an in-built resistance to change, including that which might result from adverse criticism. (Hatch & Millward, 1989:128)

R&B and Country musician Les Johnson also told this writer that for him: 'in the '60s and '70s country was seen as more adult and in some ways relevant to those who took an interest in it. It was seen by the close-knit lot surrounding Hank Walters as Liverpool's own music – more so, I would say than rock 'n' roll'. Popular music deejay and researcher Ron Ellis contrasted his interests in country music and doo-wop as being rather like 'having one foot in one camp and one in another', whereas former country rock bass man Les Parry bemoans the fact that as a Hank Williams fan in the 1970s he 'couldn't get it through to other members of the band that Hank was "authentic" – they saw him as representing another style of life not just form of music'. While there was, then, contemporary relevance to country music in Liverpool, for some a perceived root of authenticity surrounding the music and the activity (something perhaps to do with the heart and the home of Roy Acuff and the honky-tonk heroism of Hank Williams), there were also images out-with representing the American establishment at a time when the counter culture was perhaps at its strongest.

Cunard Yanks

Much hot air has been expended concerning the role of Cunard Yanks in the history of Liverpool's musical development; however these merchant seamen certainly did exist and did tend to represent an entrepreneurial Liverpool that saw roots and re-articulations at the heart of its existence. While contemporary American experiences were articulated around mass media products (and were condemned by the likes of Richard Hoggart for being just that) the seamen who left Liverpool for North America reconstituted these representations around their own lived experiences. In fact, rather than the armful of rock records being imported to Merseyside that local myth often records, country and westerns albums and Original Soundtrack albums mixed with a little Sinatra-style jazz was usually the order of the day. Les Johnson confirms that, for him:

> There must have been a market for this stuff – the Cunard Yanks were supplying a real need. Jimmie Rodgers well pre-dates the Cunard Yanks. I can only speak personally: I lived in a pub and a lot of sailors came in; in these pre-jukebox days we had a record player behind the bar. So when they might bring records into the pub they were usually bringing things that were already known but might be a little difficult to get your hands on. In particular Hank Snow's music was popular – it could be heard on AFN and maybe even Luxembourg but it was not always easy to get and so I remember *that* stuff going on the record player. The blues scene never really happened in Liverpool, and it was the blues stuff that was really hard to get hold of, not necessarily country music. (Johnson to Brocken, February 2009)

The point here that is worth reiterating – one that is perhaps seldom made when the Cunard Yanks' voices are heard – is that there already existed a consumers' demand in Liverpool for these recordings, and that, perhaps unlike the blues recordings of (say) Blind Blake, Robert Johnson and Memphis Minnie, many such tracks were actually readily available in this country.

John Belchem (2001:61) claims that Jimmy Rodgers records were brought back to Liverpool from Galveston and New Orleans by sailors working on the Harrison Line. This might be true, however at the Robert Shelton Recorded Music Archive at the Institute of Popular Music, University of Liverpool, there are British releases of such country music stored in the 78 rpm collections. For example, Jimmie Rodgers' material was released on Zonophone prior to its merging with Regal and such 78s, donated to the IPM in their original bags, displayed the names and addresses of local stores such as Strothers, Davies' Arcade, and Lewis'. The rarity of such hillbilly material is perhaps somewhat exaggerated in Liverpool to compensate for the romantic language of the Cunard Yanks. Mick O'Toole confirms that 'one thing you could say about Liverpool was that there was no shortage of record shops (even cycle shops sold records) – and people were well aware of this' (O'Toole to Brocken, 2008).

Albert Connor informed this writer that he was 'listening to Jimmie Rodgers and that kind of thing on AFN (American Forces Network) during WWII'. Country music MC Tony Barnes, interviewed by Kevin McManus in 1994, also confirmed the importance of AFN, a few years later in 1952: 'the show started at five past five [a.m.] until half past [...] Saturday morning was the "American Country Top Seven".' My own father told me that when he came home from WWII he had the sounds of Roy Acuff and Bob Wills ringing in his ears after serving with Americans in Italy. But he already knew this style of music after he had enjoyed watching cowboy films back in Liverpool in the late 1930s (some featuring Gene Autry). Yet another interviewee informed this writer that a Rhythm Club existed in late-1930s Liverpool where country music records were played – although this has yet to be verified. Renowned local broadcaster Clive Garner, a film and dance band specialist, was at pains to point out that the Jimmie Rodgers 'short' film *The Singing Brakeman* from 1929 was a popular feature of local cinemas throughout the 1930s, being shown somewhat randomly when gaps needed to be filled in a programme. Music entrepreneur Joe Flannery also recalled that before he went on his National Service in 1950 he could hear recorded country music regularly in a pub in Liverpool sited near the Liverpool Playhouse Theatre namely, the Duck House.

Even country music 'pioneer' Hank Walters states that he 'heard Hank Williams in 1949 in a place called the Blue Bell Cafe (in Aintree). They had a juke box and on it was "Wedding Bells" [and] "Lovesick Blues"' (McManus, 1994:7). The late Derry Wilkie, lead vocalist with Liverpool's first rock 'n' roll export to Hamburg, the Seniors, also informed this writer that his father, a West African, loved country music; Derry further stated that a great deal of country music was played on records at 'blues parties' in Liverpool 8, probably, he suggested, brought along by Airmen from the US Burtonwood Air Base at Warrington (the word 'blues' is a generic rather than a genre term). Country music is certainly a great and somewhat colourless traveller: Liverpool-based musician and academic Oludele Olasiende recalls that as a child in Nigeria his father greatly respected the music of Jim Reeves: 'he loved it; that gospel/country song 'This World is Not My Home' was a great favourite in our house' (Olasiende to Brocken, 2009).

So, while popular music historians correctly acknowledge key individuals in Liverpool's country music scene such as Hank Walters, Bernie Green, and Phil Brady *et al* we must be careful not to get involved in certain hagiography surrounding country music in Liverpool – it was neither 'created' by Hank Walters nor 'developed' by the Cunard Yanks. Hank would probably be the first to admit that it wasn't all down to himself, yet his position is somewhat elevated as *the* country music instigator, rather than (say) one of a number of key individuals, because popular music historicity thrives on beginnings, middles and ends. But such epistemological presuppositions deny the random co-creative potential of human interaction. Walters appears to have contributed to this mythology by stating to Kevin McManus that he 'started country music off in Liverpool' (Walters to McManus, 1994:5). But in this case Walters is probably referring to the inauguration of *live* country music, for it is clear that the *recorded* sound of country and western, western swing and hillbilly music was not unfamiliar to the ears of many Liverpool people by the immediate post-WWII era. As usual national and international entertainment systems brought this music to the attention of a local populace, rather than a little live music here and there performed by those with a specialist interest in the genre.

It could be argued, then, that the dissemination of country music around Liverpool had begun as early as the latter part of the 1930s and this relationship was to begin with, not of the 'social mores' variety. Instead, country music's 'pre-recorded' face in Liverpool was seen through a very specific refraction – one of myth, and based around the United States as a representation of the real. The close involvement of real Americans in Liverpool life of the WWII and immediately post-WWII era also assisted this image for many Liverpudlians. America was not only a place of myths but close enough to see, to touch (certainly in the form of US Airmen), and something in which one could culturally invest. For most people, perhaps excluding those music specialists such as Walters, Green and Barnes, country music in Liverpool represented less the Deep South and perhaps more the ('Wild') West.

The Wild West

Mick O'Toole was amongst the first batch of Liverpudlians to eagerly seek out country music alongside his existing interests in rock 'n' roll and trad jazz. He was purchasing recordings from Creases, NEMS and other shops in Liverpool as soon as he could earn a little money, and while differentiating between Southern Americans such as Elvis Presley, Buddy Holly and Gene Vincent and those from more northern cities such as Jack Scott it was 'the west' that also appealed to Mick, and the ideas surrounding the west that had been mediated to him by film stars such as John Wayne and British broadcasting personalities such as Big Bill Campbell. During the late-1940s and early-1950s Campbell's programme *Rocky Mountain Rhythm* was broadcast on the Light Programme every Sunday morning. The radio show employed sound effects so that one believed that Campbell and his 'buddies' were sitting around a crackling campfire, with various friends riding in, hitching their horse, dismounting and giving those round the campfire, and the listeners, a song. Although rather corny and stereotyped, for its day it was truly inspired radio and somewhat unusual for the rather anti-American BBC. In actual fact Campbell was another of these 'cod' Americans, being a Canadian by birth and not, of course a cowboy; yet despite this rather salutary discovery, for Mick the show was riveting: 'Later in life you came to realize what a really awful show it was, but as a kid we were all taken-in by it.'

Former Merseysippi Jazz Band vocalist Clinton Ford, who also developed a love of country music in the 1950s after listening to the music of Hank Williams, was much later to inform Spencer Leigh:

> I was only young when I heard Big Bill Campbell on the radio but it seemed
> terribly corny to me. They spoke about the Rocky Mountains and you imagined
> everyone walking round in spurs and check shirts and dancing round bales of

hay. A lot of people listened to it and a lot of people laughed at it. In those days it seemed that country music was for laughing at, but now it's a serious business. (Ford to Leigh, 1996:82)

But Mick and his pals loved everything to do with cowboys:

> In our house, apart from a big old wireless [radio] in the living room, we had a wind-up gramophone in the back bedroom with a pile of 78s. Among these was Jimmie Rodgers singing 'Spring-time in the Rockies' which I absolutely loved and used to play all of the time. Later on I have clear memories of records like Crosby's 'Pistol Packin' Mama' and 'Don't Fence Me In' – hardly pure country but the only thing at the time. There were also the western comics and the movies, the occasional book and even a radio show called 'Riders of the Range'. (O'Toole to Brocken, 2008)

An older brother of an acquaintance of Mick had purchased Hank Williams 78s and they proved to be very popular around the group of friends. The brother was a merchant seaman but it is unclear whether these yellow MGM recordings were American (the UK and US labels were notoriously similar) – but Mick suggests that they were probably of UK origin. The Brocken household also had at least half a dozen of these yellow and black-labelled recordings which were purchased by my father from the deletion bins at Craine's Music House in Liverpool. In fact these UK-pressed MGM recordings of Hank Williams were ubiquitous and cropped-up all over the UK (e.g. Lorne Gibson, Lonnie Donegan, and Tommy Steele all credit Hank Williams 78s as major fomenters of their tastes – see Leigh, 1994:82).

The MGM label was in those days a subsidiary of EMI in the UK and as a rule released songs from Hollywood movies by the likes of Jane Froman and Judy Garland. Hank Williams' recordings however were something of an anomaly to the British arm of MGM and (one suspects) over-pressed. Unlike the recordings made by Williams' more illustrious movie counterparts, his records did not sell in vast quantities and frequently ended-up in deletion bins – a typically British record collecting tale, it seems, whatever the genre. Blackler's Department Store basement in Liverpool was certainly renowned for its 1/- deletions – many remembered as being on the MGM label. Mick O'Toole suggests that music fans became record collectors almost 'by accident' – in other words 'finding' rather than 'searching for' music to which they subsequently became attached. This is an interesting theory based on Mick's own collecting experiences. He stated that, although a rock, trad, and budding country fan, he would search such deletion bins for 'anything of interest'. The over-pressing of Hank Williams 78s might also account for such records cropping up on the afore-quoted jukeboxes of Hank Walters' youth – replenished, one suspects by company-men wishing to dispose of as much over-pressed material as possible.

Mick O'Toole also recalls that once he left school and went into the workplace in 1958, a fellow worker was 'always singing and yodelling country music'; this appealed to the young O'Toole and further supported the ways in which a variety of US music appeared to be ascribed with an almost magical power. As characters came into the life of the young O'Toole they were attributed with significance via their relationship with or relevance to American music. Once the O'Toole household had something other than the aforementioned wind-up gramophone on which to play records Mick's own record collecting expanded exponentially. He also remembers the arrival of country music star Slim Whitman to Liverpool in the late-1950s – note his memories are already using the plural 'we' – the social networking surrounding country music in Liverpool was already growing:

> About that time Slim Whitman came to the Empire: the first country act we'd seen live. He looked marvellous with a full cowboy outfit, black and white, with about seven musos in his band. He would announce each one like 'Sugar Foot Sammy Hodge from Houston in Texas' – this was so new and exciting. All the Yanks liked to do that. He was great for the first couple of years, although strangely his biggest hits 'Rose Marie' and 'Indian Love Call' were both show tunes and not strictly country songs. He got too 'Vegas' and lost his appeal for me. (O'Toole to Brocken, 2008)

As Mick came out of his teens, lyrics became important to him and he felt that country music lyrics resonated more than those of rock songs. This appears to have occurred with many country fans throughout Liverpool during the post rock 'n' roll years of the very early-1960s and is perhaps a marker that sets the country music network apart from the younger rock 'n' roll scene. Those a little older than the battalions of young teenagers attempting to turn the clock back to the more authentic days of the mid-1950s had become a critical community. They did not rush to embrace the Beatles with the fervour of their younger brothers and sisters (after all they had literally heard it all before, first time around) and were not necessarily motivated by theoretical concerns put forward by the more pessimistic folkies. So the meanings attached to country music became increasingly more complex – in fact there were many kinds of meaning in Liverpool's country music scene and many ways of making meaning, too. The very eschewing of certain styles of music was in itself a kind of creative expression. Mick recalls:

> Folk clubs I tended to avoid. The music was OK but the groups and the patrons were all far too po-faced and serious. The Merseybeat boom came ten years too late for me. They were mostly covering all my 'fave' numbers of which I had all the originals so the idea of watching local lads copying them held little appeal. (*ibid*)

Pubs, or is that Honky-Tonks?

In the Rediffusion TV documentary of December 1963, *Beat City* reporter Daniel Farson records the significance of music in the public houses of Liverpool. He features two singer/guitarists entertaining the locals with rather 'beery' renditions of 'We are the Brothers Malone' an Irish drinking song and 'Welcome to My World' – a piece of 'countrypolitan' music recorded by 'Gentleman' Jim Reeves. This rather inept duo proceeds to lose its way in the second of these two songs, but it makes little difference to those singing along and the point that Farson attempts to make is that such live music was a feature of many pubs across Liverpool by this time. This is both correct and incorrect. For many people residing in Liverpool in the early-1960s diverse pubs took on different cultural associations and music was not always a feature of perhaps the more 'up market' suburban pubs. Furthermore different breweries had different ideas about whether live music was acceptable. A duo might be able to perform in a free house, but not necessarily in (say) a managed Higson's Brewery pub.

These restrictions – and others such as the punitive licensing regulations which also required licenses for 'live music' – meant that various pubs had different images. Along the Dock Road, for example, say from South to North Liverpool there were a variety of free houses that entertained their public with live musicians. In the suburbs there were mostly managed road houses many of which did not use music at all and only latterly agreed to jukeboxes when breweries made agreements with copyright agencies *en bloc* and jukeboxes came to be served by teams of national agents. So the aesthetic of performance was not present in every pub in Liverpool, by any means and was linked more to the pub's locality, its ties to a local brewery (or not) and its shape and size. Many pubs in Liverpool were simply not big enough to engage in live music, others might have had a back room or a lounge where only a duo could perform. There was not a 'hard and fast' rule and the contingencies of finance and local geography certainly played their part.

Nevertheless, as Farson asserts, in certain pubs across the city music was featured throughout the 1950s and 1960s and, excluding the formalities of folk clubs, which were set up with strict guidelines and were far more prescribed experiences, by and large the live music that was encouraged strongly resembled country music. The Lighthouse and the Blue Ball were among the first to feature two guitarists singing all night for a couple of pounds and a few pints of beer. It has been related to this writer on more than one occasion that the country fan tended to prefer pubs to clubs. One interviewee stated that there was a 'basic honesty' to them; another discussed the 'principal of the thing', disliking being asked for entrance money to a club: this seldom occurred in a pub. One area of activity Farson misses entirely in his documentary is that of the Liverpool social club network, which was well established by the time of his documentary (1963). There were many trade and business house venues (e.g. 'Dunlops' 'Littlewoods', BRNESC, Crawfords'), sports clubs (e.g. the Dockers' Sports Club, Marine F.C., South Liverpool Members' Club, etc), and Labour Clubs and British Legions that all served Liverpool's parochial needs extremely well; indeed throughout the 1960s and 1970s memberships of such clubs grew at an astounding rate. Literally all of these venues became country music bastions over the next 20 years.

The sound of local country music was also subject to change and mutation and many variations took place across this loose performance network. Some singers such as Hank Walters might incorporate a folk song or two – especially if its subject matter happened to refer to Liverpool; others such as Phil Brady had an Irish tinge to their performances, reflecting the great interest in country music across the Irish Sea. Others such as the Hillsiders were also immersed in rock 'n' roll and Kenny Johnson's later band Northwind and (from Warrington) Poacher also wrote their own material and incorporated this into their live sets. Indeed Poacher enjoyed a major worldwide hit when blues-rocker Frankie Miller recorded their song 'Darlin' in 1978. Country rock of the West Coast variety was a late and rather reluctant appendage to the Liverpool country scene. It was, in fact frowned upon by many as being rather too 'clever' for its own good. My own experiences as a country rock band member on Merseyside are mixed. Sometimes we were welcomed, at other times scorned and our brand of country rock tended to be judged not simply by our (probably amateurish) performances but also by the in-authenticity of our musical heroes such as the Eagles and Poco. By the mid-1970s aspects of the Liverpool country music scene were solidifying into a community, and as a consequence became reluctant to change. It was only when Willie Nelson and Waylon Jennings bit the 'alternative' bullet with their 'Outlaws' compilation in 1976 that the Liverpool scene saw some validity in 'rocking out'.

The Black Cat

Re-installing the vitality of rock 'n' roll via covers – the Merseybeat 'matrix', as it were – did not have the required effect for all Merseysiders. Mick O'Toole represented a portion of the Liverpool record-buying public that undoubtedly warmed to the sounds of (say) Elvis Presley and even Johnny Restivo the first time around, but was not enamoured of a bunch of youngsters attempting to turn back the clock. Despite the unorthodox nature of Merseybeat when compared with, say, the works of Cliff Richard and Adam Faith, some local country music fans viewed the sounds of Merseybeat as somewhat unadventurous, tiresome and even incompetent. The Merseybeat groups could be a little younger than those plying their trade in country music, so it was also, of course, a demographic issue. Tony Allen recalled to Kevin McManus that:

> Country music had done very well in Liverpool at that time. There were that many groups that I can't remember them all. But then it became THE Beatles Era and we started to get lost a little. We weren't getting much work. (Allen to McManus, 1994:14)

Instead Mick, Tony, and others like them had already 'discovered' Hank Walters in The Black Cat Club in London Road in 1957 – seeking musical content external to what we historically view as an alternative scene. The club had opened that same year and Walters was to later claim:

> The Black Cat Club kicked country music off as such in Liverpool. See, before that we were doing a few working men's clubs but there was nothing regular anywhere until the Black Cat took off. You won't find any country music clubs anywhere in Britain as long ago as that. (Walters to McManus, 1994:9)

Hank Walters was a good performer, known to be able to work an audience in an almost 'Music Hall' style and had a repertoire that in those days suited the punters ('lots of Hank Williams and Jimmie Rodgers'). Walters also invited guests to the evenings and was known to help develop talent. Walters' band – known as the Dusty Road Ramblers – was very traditional to the roots of country: they were, according to some, 'almost old timey' in their musical approach and sound. Hank was always there, singing and organizing the evening. He was not simply in front of the crowd, he had extraordinary charisma. If one considers the importance of such a performer as Hank Walters in this way, we can see him as a lynch-pin in the development of a real, active scene. As Walters began to bring other musicians through and allow guests to perform, it became clear that some of the other artists were more up to date in their tastes. So a generic line was drawn between the music purveyed by Walters and that performed by the likes of Tony Allen, Jerry Devine and others. As a consequence Allen and Devine formed a new group The Blue Mountain Boys and found a residency at the Temple in Dale Street (in the city centre) in order to perform this more contemporary material.

Walters' claim of the Black Cat being the first country music club in Liverpool has been challenged over the years, not the least by fellow country music originator Bernie Green who at various times has suggested that via an advert in the local *Liverpool Echo* a certain Carl Noviski inaugurated a rhythm club style of evening in the early 1950s. Diane Caine of the Musical Box shop was present at these events that in due course developed into a live country music evening at a Labour Club in Dean Road. Apparently, Noviski later deserted country for Liverpool's other emblematic sound: soul music, but it was he, not Walters (claims Green) who established some kind of working scene for the genre. Nevertheless Walters soon established himself as, for some, the 'Godfather' of country music in Liverpool. The Black Cat was apparently a difficult club to negotiate one's way out of, especially if a little inebriated – being up a tall flight of stairs. Mick O'Toole remembers how much of a logistic nightmare it was, with bands forced to plot a route to and from this upstairs room. Mick recalled it as a 'nuisance for the bands because they had to carry their gear up'. So, for some this 'discovery' of the Black Cat was also followed by visits to the perhaps more accessible Temple off Dale Street, Blair Hall on Walton Road, The 21 Club on Croxteth Road (owned by George Bolt) where every Thursday Gordon Fleming and the Miller Brothers performed, and other such venues. The 21 Club incidentally was also the home of Alan Sytner's jazz evenings prior to his opening of the Cavern Club on Mathew Street.

Naturally, several venues came and went during the 1960s but a few became renowned for their support for country music. One was the 'Blue House' (not the pub's real title). This was adjacent to Everton F.C.'s Goodison Park ground and was packed most weekend nights and Sunday dinner times with nothing but country music. Mick O'Toole remembers 'It was a properly run pub in those days and as for Sunday nights: if you didn't get in by 7.30pm you didn't get a seat and had to sit on beer crates ... but it was worth it!' Ossie Wade's Club, on the corners of Spellow Lane and Walton Lane in Everton mostly featured variety-style acts, mainstream popular music turns, comedians and the like but also opened its doors to country music. It was here among other local North Liverpool venues that actor Ricky Tomlinson – as 'Hobo Rick' – cut his proverbial entertainment teeth. Sunday night country events at Wade's were promoted by country music aficionados Carl and Joan Goldby. These were financially successful and so became regular events throughout the 1960s. According to Carl and Joan, the Hillsiders were given their first chance at Wade's. The later 1970s Locarno 'Outlaws' nights (where the Liverpool stars would emulate the great Jennings and Nelson 'Outlaws' songs of the mid-1970s), were also Goldby promotions. Carl Goldby had been a member of the Blue Mountain Boys and on an engagement at Butlin's in Filey met and married Joan. They subsequently performed as a duo in and around the northwest of England for many years as 'Carl and Joan Goldie'. Carl was also a member of the Tradewinds, the leader of Carl Goldie's Country Sounds, and later Country Gold.

Throughout the 1970s there were at least six pubs on the Dock Road all featuring live bands on Friday evenings. Each of these pubs was within a short walk of each other and the only problem for the country music lover was the order in which one should visit. The Union, the Bramley Moore, the Goat, O'Gorman's, the Langton, the Atlantic and Sherlock's all catered for the country music lover and such was the popularity of the music that some even ran mid-week nights. Certainly, by the mid-1970s the appeal and location of country appeared to be very geographical. One might find it difficult to locate country evenings on a regular basis in the South end of the city – although the South Liverpool Members Club, the Victoria Club, various Royal British Legion and Labour clubs, and the Garston Woodcutters Social Club were known to promote the genre irregularly, but country music was far easier to find in the north of the city – ubiquitous, in fact. This geographical split is interesting for it has some links to the make-up of Liverpool as a city about to venture on a journey of (for some in the north end), long decline and (for others in the south end), the erection of growing fortresses of semi-detachment.

Auras

For this writer, the authentic presence of country music in late-1970s Liverpool seemed to be quite reverse of what was on offer at Roger Eagle's now famous Eric's Club from 1976-onward. A language of criticism was certainly inherent in both scenes, so too the notion of aura surrounding peripheral music. But the aura within the country music scene had little or nothing to do with the physical presence of the authentic American original and was more centred around a dialectic mixture of immanence and musical canons. This appeared distinct from both the live and recorded music played at Eric's, which placed certain rock, R&B, and reggae material in contradistinction to the pomposity of 'progressive' musical ideas, still abounding at that time.

Auras of authenticity could be secured at Eric's by deejay Norman Killon simply playing (for example) a Love or Damned 45 rpm record on his decks: it did not need the transposition of recorded-into-live sound to achieve this aura (far from it in fact). In fact Eric's released a compilation album in 1981 *Jukebox at Eric's* (Eric's 008) consisting of tracks purloined from their jukebox and re-mastered at S.O.S. Studios in Liverpool – this disc has now become a great collector's item in its own right. Once again in popular music history in Liverpool the attentive listener was acknowledged and while Eric's was noted for its live performances, it is often the work of deejay Norman Killon that is most fondly remembered by ex-patrons of the club. However, the aura surrounding the likes of (say) the excellent Joey Rodgers Band was about their (or perhaps even his) presence in a particular pub at a given moment in time. My own experience of watching a Joey Rodgers Sunday afternoon gig after having spent time in Eric's the previous Saturday evening is forever etched in my mind. I was literally amazed at the authenticity of it all and found it difficult to work out exactly from which direction this aura was emanating. In fact it seemed to emerge from all apparent directions: the place, the sound, the crowd, the booze, and of course Rodgers himself. Here, there appeared to be a decentred space. Here, were peripheral music activities facing Liverpudlian crises of identity; these communities were witnessing marginalization and decay, alongside the very Dock Road that carried this activity. Parts of 'their' city were being destroyed and both sounds and venues were homological and resistant-giving. The afternoon therefore was adorned with ciphers of identity and refined images of cultural awareness. The importance that was placed on the geographical specificity of place and locality were extraordinary. One got the feeling that these Liverpool country conformists were in some way social minorities and that this music was part of a political project: local in scope, part of surviving traditions, and involving suppressed forms of popular culture. This remarkable yet ramshackle work of art was probably in the place where it always should have been.

It was that aspect of the entire Sunday afternoon I spent on the Liverpool Dock Road that survived the acid test of authenticity for me as a young fan of both punk and country music. Joey Rodgers made as much sense in the Union pub as the Clash made in Eric's (more, perhaps). It was the very authenticity of the *presence* of country music, by prevailing throughout time that made it valid. It was only the declining population of the North end of Liverpool with all of the inherent problems that the areas of Kirkdale, Everton, Anfield, Walton and Bootle had to face that finally diminished this aura – certainly not the proliferation of copies. In fact those copying were those around whom the aura survived the most. Walter Benjamin had stated that the uniqueness of a piece of art is 'inseparable from its being embedded in the fabric of tradition'. Benjamin went on to state that 'The conventional is uncritically enjoyed, and the truly new is criticised with aversion' (Benjamin in Brooker [ed.], 1992:46, 47).

But neither of these two statements – oft-repeated by cultural critics – comes close to explaining the re-integrated framework that is erected by those who might have slipped from the centre to the periphery to create a forum for re-articulation. The aura surrounding these re-articulation processes were not 'mechanical' as Walter Benjamin perhaps thought, but deeply historical. It would be incorrect even to describe these covers as 'copies'. The interpretations of these songs under these specific circumstances were intense commentaries on the relationship of people with their surroundings. Country music's fascination with jealousy, pain, fears and loves was caught up in the locality of North Liverpool at a very transient time in its residents' existences. Perhaps not unlike the Honky-Tonks and road houses that gave post-WWII country music some kind of authentic meaning, the Dock Road pubs created an aura of reality. Mick O'Toole now takes into account:

> Those Sunday dinner-time gigs were keystones of the scene with the same pubs putting on bands. The Rodgers Band was always known as the band that the others went to see. This was particularly obvious during their residency in the Union. On a Sunday night the bar would be thronged and every third guy was out of a band and if nothing else we all knew that we were in for a cracker second half. There were usually that many musicians that they couldn't all get up to do a number. (O'Toole to Brocken, 2008)

Perhaps rather incongruously, however, award-winning British country music deejay Kenny Johnson of Sonny Webb and the Cascades, the Hillsiders and Northwind did not get involved in this scene at all. He thought it more of a 'pub thing' and the Hillsiders and then Northwind were 'better than that'. Thus we also have evidence of distinct hierarchies within the country music scene in Liverpool. Mick O'Toole confirms this by stating that 'Kenny and his various bands were a little above this activity, in a musical sense and also through their position on the UK country scene – which was pretty high for most of the time.' Kenny added 'But I can understand the whole presence thing about it all – it was a case of being there, in that scene, at that time: that was the important thing for those involved. When Joey Rogers recently died and I did a tribute on my radio show I had to admit that our paths seldom if ever crossed'. (Kenny Johnson to Brocken, 2009)

Clubs and networks

For Johnson, it wasn't all about the pubs on the Dock Road. By the late-1960s 'Club-land' in Liverpool had begun to embrace country music and several cabaret venues such as the Coconut Grove aka The Annabel Suite on Green Lane in Stoneycroft, The Shakespeare Theatre Club in the city centre, The Wooky Hollow in Anfield and even the Philharmonic Hall began to embrace local country acts. The 'Phil' promoted the 'Country Meets Folk' evenings where the likes of Phil Brady and the Ranchers would perform alongside Jacquie and Bridie and the Spinners from the folk scene. Indeed, by the mid-1970s country music was so successful in Liverpool and its environs that a very successful country music festival was held at Skelmersdale in 1974. This was followed by local promoters the Denton Brothers staging the first Liverpool country festival at the famous Shakespeare Theatre Club in March of that year. It was so well attended that the Shakespeare then promoted a monthly country music show at the venue for the rest of the year. The first show consisted of a powerful list of artists: the Abilenes, Hartford West, Gold and Silver, The Tennessee Five, and Hank Walters. There was also a guest appearance from Phil Brady who, by this time was living and working in Spain for most of the year. Having obviously understood the authenticity paradigms of both soul and country music in Liverpool, former Cavern deejay and renowned BBC Radio Merseyside presenter Billy Butler was the M.C. for the entire occasion. Yorkshire country magazine *Okie* was especially pleased by these events stating that the Skelmersdale festival had been a 'resounding success' and that the reporter was 'very impressed' (the editors, *Okie*, 1974:9).

On 25 November 1976 the first *Merseyside Country Music Awards Show* took place at the Annabel Suite. Although the Country Music Association of Great Britain had been presenting their national awards for some years these were the first regional honours in the UK. The event was promoted by Pat and Gerry Allen's country music record shop, and an independent group of judges was appointed. It was presided over by Billy Butler and Eddie Hemmings of BBC Radio Merseyside and awards went to Hartford West, Kellie, Kenny Johnson, and Little Ginny amongst others. One decoration of note was the 'Pioneer Award' which was presented to Hank Walters. The columnist for the new local country music magazine *Country Music Spotlight* was to state:

> Hank has been a familiar figure in the clubs and pubs for many a year and his unique and forceful personality has livened up many a dull evening. The Hillsiders may have popularised the Merseyside sound but, without a doubt, Hank started it all and takes his rightful place up there with the rest of the award winners. (the editors, *Country Music Spotlight* 1/1, 1977:23)

By the late-1970s, then, there were literally dozens of venues and scores of artists one could see performing music that fell within the country music spectrum. There were pub venues in the North end of Liverpool, Labour Clubs all over the

Merseyside area and new venues in overspill areas such as Runcorn (The Moorings) and Kirkby (Royal Naval Club) playing host to professional and amateur country singers of a variety of styles and ages. Artistes such as Carol Weston, Paddy Kelly, Moe Silver, Hartford West, Northwind, Cash & Co, the Everglades, Phil Brady, and many more besides were performing regularly to packed houses. In one *Social Sounds* magazine from February 1980, 19 paid adverts for different social clubs can be found – most of whom promoted at least one country music night each week. But this was to gradually change during the 1980s. As the financial downturn of the late-1970s fed through to the grass roots entertainment industry and the existing licensing laws came under pressure to be repealed, drinking establishments began to adopt themes such as the ubiquitous 'Irish' pubs and also sell food. Viable and successful social clubs (such as the Montrose) were increasingly exceptional. This recession had such an effect on both the country music and cabaret scenes that, in his research for the Institute of Popular Music 14 years on from the *Social Sounds* publication, Kevin McManus was to find only a skeletal circuit still in operation:

> The lack of venues also bodes ill for the future prospect of country in the city. Many of the Dock Road pubs where country music was once so popular have now closed down and [...] there are few clubs left which still have a regular country night. (McManus, 1994:35)

And even though Tony Allen ex-of The Blue Mountain Boys was to open his *Hank's Place* country music club on Green Lane in Stoneycroft in 1994, this dream venue was to last a little over a year before closing-down and being replaced by a supermarket.

Broadcasting, records and retailing

The mention of Pat and Gerry Allen's record shop on Lodge Lane (of which more later) and Radio Merseyside's Billy Butler highlights other important links in the Liverpool country music chain. In some respects, by the 1970s country music in Liverpool was a conformist musical language. Many popular music artists of the 1960s regularly raided Nashville songwriters for material. Ken Dodd's 'Happiness', 'Still', and 'Eight By Ten' were all Bill Anderson songs, jazz singer Cleo Laine scored a hit single with the country song 'You'll Answer to Me', Tom Jones recorded the Porter Wagoner and Bobby Bare hit 'The Green, Green Grass of Home' and the likes of Miki and Griff ('A Little Bitty Tear') and Karl Denver ('Mexicali Rose') were persistently demystifying country and western music for British audiences on TV, radio, and in theatres all over the country. By the mid-1960s the BBC had even agreed to broadcast a regular weekly country music show on the Light Programme and while still filtering the music through its usual cultural refractions, this show kept many of the local Liverpool country music fraternity relatively happy. This writer well remembers rushing home from a morning at the

ABC Minors at the Carlton Cinema in Tuebrook and listening to Murray Kash presenting a selection of the more popular country music items of the day. By 1966 the pirate station Radio Caroline North, being moored off the coast of the Isle of Man, had a strong Irish following and country music was *de rigueur* for one particular deejay 'Daffy' Don Allen.

His shows were also well-received in Liverpool at least until the pirate's demise in 1967, by which time BBC local radio had commenced broadcasting and BBC Radio Merseyside presenters such as Bob Azurdia were playing country music in what little needle-time they had available. The BBC on Merseyside evidently recognized not only the international popularity of country music by 1967 but also how country music symbiotically expressed for some 'traditional values', locally. Former Radio Caroline deejay Don Allen was given the first all-country music show on Radio Merseyside in the early 1970s, and he was followed by Billy Butler, exchanging his beloved soul music for country; the baton was finally picked up by former Hillsider Kenny Johnson – originally brought in as a guest on Butler's twice-weekly show – and it has been that way ever since. By the mid-1970s Johnson in fact had a battle on his hands, for after commercial station Radio City had begun broadcasting in 1974 he had to compete for an audience with fellow Hillsider Joe Butler. Former Radio Merseyside producer Bill Holt remembers the excitement of it all:

> As far as I know the history of Local Radio country was [that] we were first in the country at Radio Leeds [Don Allen was living in Leeds at this time]. Stan Laundon visited us and started the second show somewhere in the North East (perhaps Cleveland?). Some Merseyside people visited us, but nothing came of this. I then came to [Radio] Merseyside and started the programme with Don Allen, then with Billy. Then for about one or two shows this man from Huyton who had been helping. He was bad. Then Kenny. I'm racking my brains trying to remember that Huyton man's name. He won the pools and his wife ran off and left him taking the money. He was one of the Merseyside conspirators who ruined the career of Pat Campbell on the Radio 2 country show with a vicious hate campaign. Those were the days. (Holt, email correspondence, February 2009)

Major record labels RCA Victor and CBS had plenty of country music product by the mid-1960s but tended to release it in a somewhat 'scatter gun' approach. Artists such as Hank Snow, Jim Reeves and Patsy Cline were also by this time on budget labels such as Allegro and RCA Camden and such 'rack-fillers' were selling for less than £1 in newsagents and larger stores such as Woolworth's. Mick O'Toole remembers that the international record labels – especially RCA Victor – stumbled along somewhat, experimenting with formats and themes:

> There was a series of EPs in those days called 'Country Guitar' – perhaps 14 titles in all and at one time I had about ten or so of them. Talking to BBC's

Country presenter Kenny Johnson one time, he mentioned that he was only two short of a full set of them as well. There was some good stuff on these EPs and we were all pretty much buying the same stuff. They say that blues records were scarce – which they were – but it could be the same for all kinds of music. Finding this stuff on record was part of the fun, I suppose. But without record shops like the Musical Box and Pat and Gerry Allen's we'd have been sunk. In some respects I think this is another reason why the Cunard Yanks myth evolved. It sounds more romantic than searching through dusty deletion bins! (O'Toole to Brocken, 2008)

By the 1960s the burgeoning Liverpool scene even came under inspection from national record labels and several artists were recorded. This was not simply because of the attraction of Merseybeat for the first to be recorded, the Blue Mountain Boys, brought interest from the independent Oriole label in 1962 – around the same time that the Beatles' first single was released by Parlophone. 'Drop Me Gently' (coupled with 'One Small Photo of You') was recorded and released in 1962 but without any degree of success, although it was enthusiastically purchased locally. Tony Allen of the band informed Kevin McManus in 1994 'It caused quite a stir because we were actually the first country band to do a recording. At the same time the Beatles' 'Love Me Do' came out and we just got lost. As good as we were we were just too old' (McManus, 1994:13). But of course there was more to it than this. The Oriole label, one of Britain's small posse of independents in the early-1960s, enjoyed neither the financial clout nor the distribution networks to make anything but a few of their recordings hits. The company was known to be a shambles: undercapitalized and inefficient. Most importantly they could not afford to purchase air time from Radio Luxembourg and only made money from subcontracting pressings from other companies and running Woolworth's Embassy label. Sadly the Blue Mountain Boys didn't really stand a chance – whatever their chosen genre or demographic. Clinton Ford recalls this ineptitude:

Oriole wasn't a very good label: they had nice people there but they didn't have a clue. I wanted to go into country music in 1958 but they didn't understand. I'd discovered Hank Williams and wanted to sing country but they wouldn't let me. They said 'You sing rock 'n' roll and go along with the trend'. (Ford to Leigh, 1996:82)

Hank Walters, the Hillsiders, Phil Brady (and the Miller Brothers) were all recorded by Rex in 1965. This Rex label was unrelated to the earlier Crystalate-owned dance band imprint. Decca had purchased Rex in the 1930s but then made the name obsolete in the late-1940s. As an imprint aimed directly at the Irish market, Rex re-emerged as a subsidiary of Decca in 1965 to serve Decca's record distribution arm 'Irish Record Factors'. An album *Liverpool Goes Country* was released that same year. Actually another L.P., this time by the Liverpool Ceilidh Band was also recorded by Rex and released in 1965 principally because they had recently become All-Ireland Ceilidh champions. While Rex's marketplace was British-based and records were advertised across the UK music press, the label was seen as being aimed at the Irish customer and it was not especially renowned for any promotional machinery directed at the UK market. Rex was eventually replaced as a Decca subsidiary by the perhaps more authentic sounding Emerald Records, which went on to record a further two Liverpool country music artists in the 1970s: The Ranchers (without Phil Brady), and George C. Smith.

Four Hank Walter tracks were taken from the LP and an EP resulted. The *Liverpool Goes Country* EP was well-received by those who sought it out. No singles were extracted, which was probably a good move, for there was very little chance of a Liverpool country band scoring a hit on the singles charts by 1965. Instead, the *Liverpool Goes Country* EP remained undeleted until the Rex imprint ceased trading; it was a consistent seller, although not always easy to find. A Hillsiders' single ('Hello Trouble') was released by Rex in 1965 and Phil Brady and the Ranchers also released a single for Rex the same year. This was 'Little Rosa' a popular country ballad around the Liverpool scene; both failed to trouble the British chart compilers. In all probability these deals (Walters, Ceilidh Band, Hillsiders, Brady) may well have been linked. Chester-based country music collector John Speake:

> Yes I've wondered about that one from time to time. I do think that the three deals were probably linked in some way. It strikes me that Rex were probably looking for something to sell in Ireland, and some bright spark marketed it accordingly, with some idea about Liverpool as the centre of all kinds of music activity – something like that. Now obviously the success of country music in Liverpool would be appealing to the Irish fan because of the popularity of a few Liverpool country bands in Ireland and vice versa in those days because of the size of the Irish community in Liverpool. These Liverpool country bands could sometimes sound like an Irish Show-band in any case because the material that say Hank would play did vary into that kind of, well, rather mawkish, sentimental stuff that goes down well over there. Phil Brady, I think did play Ireland quite a bit. As for the Liverpool Celidh Band, that seems a bit like selling coals to Newcastle to me. (Speake to Brocken, 2008)

But Kenny Johnson remarked that the first port of call for Rex was actually the Hillsiders and that it was *they* who gave Rex 'the nod' to record Brady and Walters. Certainly, soon after the Cascades were re-named the Hillsiders in 1964 they had attracted enough attention for Decca to show more than a passing interest. So, two singles came out of their recording sessions: the aforementioned Rex release and another on Decca, a cover of the Everly Brothers' 'I Wonder if I Care as Much'. This in turn this led to Lionel Segal's Strike label recording some material with the Hillsiders. Gordon Smith was the producer responsible for these recordings – as he was for a great deal of British country music recordings over the next few years (although few of the artists recorded ever felt that he accurately captured their sound). A Hillsiders' single 'Almost Persuaded' coupled with 'Wastin' My Time' (Strike JH322) emerged in 1966. Although the single received a little airplay on Radio Caroline North via Don Allen's *Country and Western Jamboree* programme, it did not trouble the charts. Strike seldom ever joined the ranks of the big boys, enjoying only one hit single with Neil Christian in 1966 ('That's Nice') and struggled against inadequate funding and poor distribution – in all probability the track was licensed to Strike, for Kenny Johnson has no recall of ever dealing with the label first-hand.

The Hillsiders (and Phil Brady and the Ranchers) also released product for Pye records in the late-1960s. There were two Pye singles for the Hillsiders: 'Children's Song' and 'Please Be My Love' and subsequently both groups were placed on a short-lived Pye subsidiary Lucky Records. Lucky was the brainchild of producer Gordon Smith and was set in motion with the intention of promoting British and Irish country music. Several titles emerged between the years 1969 and 1972. One budget-priced Strike compilation of British country artists featuring both the Miller Brothers and the Hillsiders was re-released by Lucky, and the 'Hillies' also released an eponymous album for the label in 1969 (LUS3002). Kenny Johnson now thinks that this album was probably material previously recorded by Smith when still licensing tracks to Strike. By 1970 the album *No.1 In The Country* by Phil Brady and the Ranchers was released (LUS3007) and this sold moderately well across Britain and Ireland, but the Lucky experiment was not so lucky, sales wise, and the project did not continue beyond 1972. It seems that the inescapable problem of British country fans not being willing to purchase recorded British country music in sufficient quantities forever dogged Gordon Smith's hard work.

By 1967 the Hillsiders had already become the most prominent British country band in the UK and, following a tour backing Bobby Bare in Germany, followed by a successful gig with Bare at the Grafton in Liverpool, were invited by RCA Victor to record in Nashville. While working with Bare and producer Chet Atkins in Nashville in August 1967 the Hillsiders played the Grand Ol' Opry. *The English Country Side* (RCA Victor RD7918) still stands to this day as a well-crafted example of Liverpool-recorded country music. While in the USA the band met and performed with George Hamilton IV and this was to prove a fruitful liaison as they became firm friends and later toured Europe, performed together on Hamilton's BBC TV series and recorded an album together in 1971 *Heritage* for RCA Victor (LDP4609). RCA also released two Hillsiders singles in 1969 and these stand as a testament to the high quality of this fine group. Kris Kristofferson's 'Sunday Morning Coming Down' and Neil Diamond's 'Kentucky Woman' were both taken from the *Leaving of Liverpool* album and released that year. In 1971 the Hillsiders signed a two album deal with Polydor and the albums *By Request* (1972) and *Our Country* (1973) appeared; however neither really captured the group at its best and, given the albeit later propensity for Kenny Johnson to pen a pretty good song, both records now sound rather un-ambitious. However it must also be stated that as one of British country music's leading draws the Hillsiders were constantly on the road, so exactly how much time they had to record any LP remains a moot point.

There is little further evidence of Liverpool's country music artists being recorded in the 1960s. It was still at this time a very expensive business, of course, and appeal was limited. The concept of point-of-sale (i.e. direct sales at gigs) marketing had to yet arrive in the shape of Alan Richards and Stag Music (of which more later). As previously stated local singer 'Georgie Cash', later known as George C. Smith, made a name for himself around Merseyside and Ireland and signed a contract with Decca but these recordings (two albums) did not appear until the next decade. Lee Brennan also recorded an album's worth of Johnny Cash covers for Decca in the 1970s. Several bands and artistes used the facilities at the local CAM Studios in Moorfields for demo discs and tapes. One such disc surviving at the IPM Vinyl Archive is that of the Foggy Mountain Ramblers, an obscure Merseyside outfit about which little is known. This recording was on the CAM 'Unichord' label which was reserved for demonstration discs (there also exists a Unichord single by the Liverpool R&B group, the Almost Blues). Alan Richards' Stag Music label recorded several country artists on his 'Stag Country' compilation from the mid-1970s but according to Alan the album was not a good seller – perhaps reflecting the usual lack of interest by British fans in local country product. Alan also recorded Lee Brennan in the mid-1970s by which time Brennan had ceased to imitate Johnny Cash and was penning most of his own material.

After Kenny Johnson left the Hillsiders in the 1975 to form his own band Northwind, he signed a singles deal with EMI International. One single emerged from this arrangement in 1977 entitled 'City Lights' (INT545). This disc probably remains the nearest that any of the Liverpool country acts came to a genuine hit single. The original single was a gradual seller, gathering momentum over a period of months and eventually selling thousands of copies (sadly, not enough to break into the national charts in any one week). Johnson then re-released the song for OBM Records – an imprint partially belonging to Poacher's manager Robert Kingston – in 1980 (OBM1004) and this version crept into the Top 100 in 1980. An excellent song, 'City Lights' certainly became a local (indeed regional) 'radio hit' and is still popular on the British country music network to this very day. Johnson also recorded an album for OBM in 1980. One of Liverpool's finest country bands of the mid-late 1970s was West Virginia. They formed in 1976 and by 1978 the band was appearing at the National Country Music Festival at Wembley, touring with Marty Robbins, and guesting with Don Everly on BBC TV. But they too were only recorded by a local label – Dave Crosby's Wirral-based Rox Records – an offshoot of Crosby's independent retail 'Rox' empire which covered both east and west Wirral. One album, *Country Dreamer* (Rox LP002), turned-out to be a rather hurried affair and did not truly reflect their virtuosity – a pity, for they were an inventive group.

British and Irish country music groups seldom ever 'made it big' partly because the British country music fans were a seriously critical community. The usual criticism proposed that these groups were entertaining but derivative

– inevitably comparisons with the American original, usually unfavourable, were often made. However, nationally, singers such as Kelvin Henderson and Raymond Froggatt had far more to offer than imitation and, locally, even when groups were covering US material they always added something of their own traditions to the music. In all, very few of the Liverpool country musicians were ever recorded to a thoroughly professional level and of those that were recorded even fewer were allowed time to work up their own material. Even when an artist such as Kenny Johnson was writing good original country songs, it was feared that the country music conformist would simply not purchase an album of material that he/she didn't already know – a circular argument, indeed. Derek Wakefield, editor of the Ellesmere Port-based *Country Music Spotlight* complained in 1977:

> Another reason the British country artist can't make it big is because the so called fans won't give him a chance. I hear good groups constantly being knocked, with the comment 'Oh they're just an imitation of so and so [...] If we want originality from our own groups we have to give them a chance with their own material.' (Wakefield, 1977:3)

Renowned Scottish country artist Lorne Gibson confirmed this anomaly to Spencer Leigh by stating that he 'knew at the outset that country music was a "minority" music and that British country fans don't buy British country records. I was the only country singer on Decca although they didn't have a category for it at the time' [1950s] (Gibson to Leigh, 1996:83).

Perhaps the one local artist to eventually break through to the *popular music* big time is singer/songwriter Charlie Landsborough – although it is questionable for some whether his brand of composition could be described as country music *per se*. Born in Birkenhead, Charlie – a committed Christian – was well known as a pleasant, but only adequate pub singer on the local country and folk scenes for some years. But he began to blossom in the early-1980s penning a sub-genre of country music that had both an Irish tinge and a Christian emphasis – very influenced by Foster and Allen and George Hamilton IV, respectively. However, Landsborough's big break came not initially in the UK, but in Ireland. His first recordings were made for the oddly-titled Pastafont label in 1982 and 1983. It was the latter of these two discs 'I Will Love You All My Life' that received heavy airplay in Ireland and following this he began touring and writing his own material in this very distinctive style. By the early 1990s Charlie's lugubrious deliveries of his own songs had awarded him such a reputation that in 1994 the Irish-owned Ritz label signed him. One song, in particular, was to transform his career. Charlie's 'What Colour is the Wind' tells the story of a young blind child's attempts to picture the world about her. As a result of deejay Gerry Anderson playing the track on radio in Northern Ireland, the song came to the notice of chat show host Pat Kenny in Dublin, who invited Landsborough to perform on his popular *Kenny Show Live* (RTE, January 1995). A week later, Charlie's album, also entitled *What Colour is the Wind*, toppled Garth Brooks from the summit of the Irish album charts. His recordings have now sold in their hundreds of thousands and he is truly a national and international artist; however it would have to be stated that his success was a very individualistic process, only tenuously connected with Liverpool's country music circuits.

Local female artiste 'Little Ginny' also cut a single for the Pastafont label in 1981. Indeed there was something of a slew of recordings in the 1980s with the likes of Lee Brennan, Joe and Gerry Clarke, Jerry Devine, Northwind, Poacher (signed briefly to Ritz), Val Summers, Carole Weston, Whiskey River and others all releasing product. Some were vanity products, others country music network releases on Crow Records, others were released on the Kirkby-based Amazon Studios 'Jungle' imprint, but all by this time were point-of-sale items – seldom stocked in anything other than specialist retail shops and in a real sense 'merchandise', rather than music releases, *per se*. These recordings were by and large for sale at gigs and festivals around the local clubs and on the national country music circuit. Some were advertised in the British country music press, for by the mid-1980s national gigs were replacing local venues as a main source of income for those still ploughing their country music furrow; for others the prospect of semi-retirement loomed large.

Pat and Gerry Allen

For a popular music scene to develop, several important entities must be in place: there needs to be a network of interconnectivity with like-minded people being able to communicate ideas across space and time. There needs to be the aforementioned critical community that decodes certain sounds as authentic and others as inauthentic – with the absence of that other sound demarcating the peripheries of acceptable material. There needs to be the presence of leaders in their field who might have virtuosic tendencies or be confident, entertaining and knowledgeable about the music of their choice. Venues that signify difference from other venues and also representing access, warmth and communality are vital. Communication between fans and supporters is also paramount and, here, one record shop based originally on Lodge Lane in the Toxteth district of Liverpool was such a supporter of country music that for players and listeners, alike, it became central to the entire scene. This was the store belonging to Pat and Gerry Allen. Originally located ostensibly in the 'Black' area of the city, Pat and Gerry initially served the local community with all forms of popular music, even specializing for a time in ska and reggae. However, little by little, their personal musical interests over-ruled and by 1970 the shop was almost entirely (but not exclusively) country music-based. This was based, not simply on enquiries from white Liverpool for country music but as a response to the musical interests of the Black element of the local population. Pat and Gerry soon discovered that both the West African and Caribbean communities also enjoyed a strong interest in country music.

Allen's shop served as a drop-in centre for all country music fans and musicians. Gigs were arranged, even promoted by the Allens; coaches to country shows in London organized. Saturday mornings at Allen's shop were feasts of music and information. Rare import records were regularly sourced from America and networks of collectors developed and maintained. There were no second-hand sales at this stage, for interest sustained a new sales market – although this later changed. Without Allen's shop the country scene in Liverpool would have been far less focused, far less dynamic. The Musical Box record shops in Tuebrook and Old Swan also served the country community well. Proprietor Diane Caine remains to this day a solid country music fan but her shops did not specialize in the way that Gerry and Pat Allen's did. Allen's became a force in the city that was difficult to ignore – all at a time when the original boom of Merseybeat had subsided, and musical tastes were fracturing into niche markets. From personal experience Allen's shop had an odd quality: that of an utter understanding of its chosen genre, but a total lack of knowledge of other styles. Such was this the case that the deletion bins in Allen's were wondrous places, full of material in which they had little or no interest, but were of great value to a budding record entrepreneur such as myself. I vividly remember in the late-1970s raiding their deletion bins on a regular basis, forever finding obscure and long-deleted Island albums by Jackie Edwards, Millie Small, Rico and the Rudies and Bama Winds; purchased, no doubt for the local communities but ignored and unsold.

The Allens' shop made such an impact that by the 1980s they had moved to the more salubrious surroundings of Aigburth Road – further into the South end of the city than their previous premises on Lodge Lane. But it is arguable whether this move was a successful one. In Liverpool there is a noted lack of success for those that move and/or change premises. Edwards' tried it, the Musical Box expanded to another site and Penny Lane Records even opened-up a shop in Chester – all with mixed results. In all cases, one might argue that these moves were abreast of a curious withering of interest. The local country music scene undoubtedly declined in the 1980s and within a short space of time local country fans were noting that Pat and Gerry had started to trade in second-hand albums. So, although an atmosphere still surrounded what was now titled '*Pat & Gerry Allen Country Music Shop*' on Aigburth Road, this had changed into one of decline. The foot fall was noticeably less – perhaps an inevitable fact of that time.

The increasing second-hand nature of the shop, the lack of new stock and the shop's relocation to a more suburban locality did not render the enthusiast with ideas of sustainability. Mick O'Toole recalls a conversation concerning a second-hand dealer named Mike Howell. He had purchased a vast collection of country material and was putting it up for sale in one fell swoop and enthusiastic punters reported this to Pat expecting her to show interest in the collection. She replied that, at that moment in time 'if I could get into anything else, I would', and the subject was dropped. One could certainly see that her heart was no longer in it, that new LP records were being sold off cheaply, and that the perhaps inevitable wilt was coming to its culmination. My last call at the shop was after Gerry had died and

Pat had the unenviable task of continuing, while also managing local country artist Paddy Kelly. On this last visit, I purchased a Robert Earl Kean album and never returned. No degree of effort on Pat's behalf could restore the past's uniqueness.

Summary

The Liverpool country music scene that developed throughout post-WWII era was not only a music genre culture with idealized images of a function myth, it was a culture based around traditional values and ideals. It drew upon existing ideas about the function of American music both in Liverpool and as part of a national and international canon. It is therefore a perhaps perfect example of how popular music activity forms around sound, the images of sound, historical dynamics of the uses of that sound and then the generic parameter within which that sound is formalized. The emergence of country music as a practical as well as an idealized state of representation can be seen as one element in a complex course of events by which tradition is supported, but then mutated by social and technological processes. It shows how historical narratives can be simplified to a few reductive yet symbolic elements and how enthusiasts can live their lives according to deep-seated strategies surrounding their musical activity. This activity continues to be a challenge to historians because such discursive, diachronic elements become so redacted that they are presented as linear myth-stories containing 'beginnings' and 'endings' – this is clearly not the case for country music in Liverpool; it continues to change but despite appearing to be at an end, will simply further mutate.

This is perhaps why it is the historian's responsibility to convey these other meanings and other complexities as integral to the popular music histories of the UK. Music is encountered in conditions that both root and uproot, perhaps in the process even forcing people to re-negotiate their own strategies for survival in any given era. If we research and then confront these scenes we see that music categorizations are both informative and misleading. Informative in that people respond to idealized nostalgia in very productive ways; but misleading in that scenes create internal discourses among those interested, and so become elevated to such an extent that those involved feel neglected by other narratives (to which they also behave perhaps in a rather 'Luddite' fashion). However, whatever confusions arise, it also becomes clear, that engagements with idealized myths of place and fundamental ideas concerning roots ultimately lead to pro-active reconfiguration, not Walter Benjamin's passive absorption-based 'mechanical copy' culture.

Within Liverpool's country scenes, the music is lifted out of its actual historical and cultural contexts (whatever they might have been) and appropriated into new environments (and also technological mediations). Although this has been deeply authentic for those involved, in the UK at large, this activity has been barely acknowledged because the very concept of a British imitation of such a US cultural product is still frequently derided. An opposition that was once an integral part of the 'British Blues Boom' discourse – whether white men can sing the blues

– has now been reformulated as part of a rather ham-fisted binary opposition for the UK country music scene. Indeed even today British country music fans will still not purchase in the required quantities any British country music product on record; as a consequence there remains to this day only a small, localized, and under-representative discography bearing witness to the existence of country music in the UK, never mind Liverpool.

So although by 1980 country music was a genre of great national significance with large sales figures in the UK, it was mostly sustained by the mass media systems that actually brought the music to Britain in the first place, and its visages included mass voyeurism and specialization, rather than participation. Any upsurge of interest in country music appeared less to do with how this previously somewhat 'un-presentable' music had assumed a variety of uses and could now be authentically re-presented by British artists in a variety of interesting ways, but (more alarmingly) how the American original had grown in authenticity compared to its British 'imitator'. For some on the Liverpool country scene the arrival of the New Country artistes such as Lyle Lovett, Steve Earle and Nancy Griffith on the international country music scene during the 1980s only served to propound detachment and difference, rather than sincerity and similarity.

There was also, by the 1980s, a discernible split between those country music artists such as Northwind and Poacher who could afford to 'go national' and play in the 'first world' of the national country music network (which, like Nashville itself inexorably moved towards the west coast country rock model of the 1970s), and those who felt unable so to do. For these latter artists of the Liverpool scene of the late-1970s such as Paddy Kelly, West Virginia, Saratoga, Terry Fletcher, Gus Travis and the Midnighters, and the inimitable Joe Rodgers, they retreated back into their manuscripts and became experienced insiders with knowledge of the hegemonic discourse in which their music continued to be involved, albeit on a decreasing circuit. These days, George Nield's music at the Melrose in 2009 continues to deal with similar re-imaginings of music, place, and space as it had done for Hank Walters in 1949, Mick O'Toole in the mid-1950s and Paddy Kelly in the 1980s. Much of the value of what little country music performance remains in Liverpool today still derives its meaning from country's function myth status and is physically represented by old and stable components of a long-established canon of music.

Chapter 6
Some Other Guys – R&B in Liverpool

They were playing the stuff we'd stopped playing. We were doing Cliff stuff and the Beatles were still doing the old stuff.

(Faron of Faron's Flamingos to Brocken, 1996:23)

Covering

Despite the fact that, as listeners, we often ascribe in-authenticity to cover versions, it could be argued that all popular music activity has been built on a tradition of 'covering'. To perform a cover version is to execute a song or tune written, performed and/or made famous by another. This process of covering has been fundamental to the popular music performer who, in the first instance, often models his/her own performance and repertoire on that of another more illustrious or authentic artist. One might argue, in fact, that despite an apparent obsession with the present, popular music continues to be inter-textual in this way and is always at some stage immersed in one past genre or another. For example, the expression 'evergreen' evolved from the pre-WWII era when many bands would play their own arrangements of the same song; by the time Frank Sinatra was making his seminal recordings with Nelson Riddle (beginning in 1953), he was re-working and re-articulating many of these 1930s 'evergreens' to serve different purposes.

In the immediate post-WWII era, covering gained cultural, as well as musical, capital. By the early-1950s the record industry was re-inventing itself and vertically-integrated companies were faced with increased challenges from independent record labels such as Atlantic, which primarily catered for a Black audience. Recorded sound became a site in which different, rather than past, genres of music – some considered acutely authentic, others less so – were exposed to debate and tension. For example, country artist Hank Williams found his songs covered on record by artists such as Tony Bennett and Joni James, whereas artists from the R&B (or 'race') genres such as Big Joe Turner or Laverne Baker were covered by white mainstream artists such as Bill Haley and Georgia Gibbs respectively. Most popular music historians appear to accept that Tony Bennett assisted in 'breaking' Hank Williams to a larger audience whereas it is commonly argued that white covers of R&B were tantamount to cultural as well as financial theft. However, while the (say) freelance production work of Tom Dowd is evidence of cultural transference (Dowd replicated his Atlantic backing tracks for major labels), there was little realistic chance of an original Atlantic 45 rpm breaking its way out of the 'Race' charts and crossing-over into the mid-1950s American mainstream. So, in point of fact, it could be argued these 'bleached' versions made a very useful contribution to raising the profile of R&B in the United States (and elsewhere) at this time.

Meanwhile, in Britain, there was a proliferation of UK 'cover versions' of US songs. By the mid-1950s, music radio had come to dominate the outputs of both the BBC Light Programme and Radio Luxembourg. At the BBC issues surrounding needle-time initially restricted the playing of records to a minimum; however, disinclined to broadcast any song of US origin when a UK cover could exist, the BBC encouraged their own house bands such as the Northern Dance Orchestra to 'Anglicize' US songs. On record, it was a similar story and British covers of American recordings tended to flood both the airwaves and the marketplace. The careers of two Liverpool-born singers, Michael Holliday and Frankie Vaughan, were advanced by such covering (e.g. 'The Story of My Life' and 'Green Door', respectively) and following the advent of rock 'n' roll, the British record market was further saturated with UK cover versions. Partially because of unwritten policies at the BBC, culturally, the word 'version' signified at least as much as 'cover'. UK record and song publishers, although not averse to promoting US records, collectively felt that these American originals should be made to compete with British adaptations, therefore many such UK cover versions appeared (for example, Tommy Steele's cover of Guy Mitchell's 'Singing The Blues') and battles developed where several versions of the same song vied for the highest chart position on the UK Top Twenty. As a consequence many US originals, poorly distributed and inadequately promoted, were lost in the rush. Retrospectively regarded by some popular music authenticists as rather bland ('poor', even), these UK covers can now be seen as revealing, contextual examples of popular music 'Britishness' attempting to rival a product those such as Richard Hoggart (1957) might have considered constitutive of American cultural colonization.

The appearance of the London American (Decca) label in the UK introduced to British youth a great font of cover versions. Young rock and proto-rock skiffle groups accordingly attempted to musically emulate their US idols via listening to and replicating records. This label was regarded as a distributor of authentic US material and in cities all over the UK groups covered and rearticulated material for live performance – thus reversing the traditional model established by the music industries of performance being followed by recording. It was an important reversal of listening practices, for such popular music record connoisseurship now complimented jazz's collectability and both sets of collectors soon developed an increased relationship with musical obscurity. In Liverpool the rock 'n' roll scene of the early-1960s was almost exclusively built upon the act of listening and covering; it was even in part a 'retro' movement based for some upon an earlier, more 'primal' rock 'n' roll sound of the mid-1950s and was literally fuelled by the 45 rpm record. For at least three years (say 1959-62), little or no self-penned material emerged as groups such as Cass and the Casanovas, Derry and the Seniors, Rory Storm and the Hurricanes, the Beatles *et al* gained local reputations not simply via their performances but via their selection of appropriate material. In the London-based R&B movement similar concepts of authenticity abounded around blues and R&B 'tracks' (rather than 'songs' *per se*) and, based upon knowledge and virtuosity of a canon, this covering of authentic material was a fomenter of the later British rock meritocracy.

So the Beatles were effectively a 'covers band' and throughout their brief performing career they remained, at least partially, a 'covers band'. Their 'last' gig at Candlestick Park in San Francisco on Monday 29 August 1966 began with a (partially inaudible) rendition of Chuck Berry's 'Rock and Roll Music' and their very last recording session in 1970 ended rather poignantly on 3 January 1970 with a version of Buddy Holly's 'Peggy Sue Got Married'. They were undoubtedly great fans of rock 'n' roll but perhaps less aware of (or maybe less engaged by) more esoteric forms of Black rhythm and blues, folk blues and country blues. However before getting any further into this dichotomy it is worth stating that the differences signifying limitations of genre would not have be altogether clear to many at that time. For example Chuck Berry and Bo Diddley were both classified for the British market as rock 'n' roll singers; so too Clyde McPhatter, the Drifters and even the Platters. As we look back 50 years genre labels appear to some extent unambiguous, but they would have been far less crystal at the time. Different people in Liverpool listened to a variety of different things, and if one liked and was able to find (say) a Jackie Wilson single, it could be purchased without too much contemplation concerning the genre of music from which it emanated – for many, such analysis was not embraced; for others it was constitutive of one's demographics, upbringing and education. Mick O'Toole:

> If I came across something I liked, say if I had been listening to Radio Luxembourg or if I fancied something advertised in the NME, I often bought it first and asked questions second. It's not that I didn't recognize what I liked, but in a funny kind of way I liked lots of things – up to a point. It just depended on where that point was. I could like Mario Lanza up to one point, but Elvis or Lonnie Donegan up to another, and I didn't like Lonnie because he was expressing some musical 'truth', I liked him as a performer. But some did closely scrutinize music; I went to grammar school and recognized it as a grammar school thing to do. (O'Toole to Brocken, 2009)

School

Throughout the 1950s the differences in Liverpool between secondary modern schools, technical high schools and grammar schools were distinct. There were structural and cultural disparities between a grammar or secondary modern school education in the late-1950s, for some possibly not marked, but disparities nonetheless (for example without exception, *all* grammar schools within the districts of Liverpool were single-sex schools, *all* were better-funded than secondary modern schools and *all*, at least up until the arrival of comprehensive education in the mid-1960s, were able to retain staff), and these could be reflected by and through music taste cultures. Les Johnson attended Birkenhead Institute for Boys and confirms that:

> There was a very small coterie of [blues] people [in Liverpool] and it was a very grammar school thing. At grammar school you tend to be a little more analytical. I moved to Liverpool but carried on at Birkenhead Institute, rather than getting a transfer – I used to cycle all the way from Old Swan to Whetstone Lane. I listened to Ken Colyer, Dickie Bishop, Barber. I knew it through my brothers and sisters – my family was mainly trad jazz and we used to go and see it; I went but preferred skiffle.
>
> We had an art teacher at school and she was interested in music. We started a skiffle group at school – also a very grammar school thing to do. I do think we thought of ourselves as a bit middle-class – But I lived in a pub, so I don't know how middle-class that actually was – but the schooling was definitely very middle-class. We could afford records – that says something in its own right – and we would read the record labels and our art teacher would fill us in with the details – she was a real 1950s middle-class intellectual if you like. She pushed us towards Seeger and Guthrie and we came to see that Donegan was ripping these people off. So I switched from Donegan to the originals – with the direct help of the art teacher. I reckon it could be a bit like that in all Grammar Schools. She was also very left-wing and pulled us, politically towards that kind of thing. So in some respects this might have been similar to Quarry Bank, The Institute, The Bluecoat – all of those kinds of schools across Merseyside. (Johnson to Brocken, 2009)

The inner schoolboy sanctum of the Liverpool Institute-based Beatles (McCartney and Harrison plus assorted friends) was most certainly grammar school-established and helped form a 'world view'. Although not 'officially' musicians at school (neither of the above, for example sat either music 'O' Level or 'A' Level examinations), their approaches to popular music were affected by attendance at school (for better or worse) in addition to their interests away from that institution. A temperate form of elitism existed at such places, where masters might tolerate and even occasionally encourage a level of self-expression concerning issues surrounding 'art'. Mick O'Toole remembers an afternoon in 1957, at De La Salle Grammar School for Boys when he was allowed to deliver a discussion on popular music to the rest of the 'Music Appreciation' class. Although Mick also brings to mind the teacher's disparaging remarks concerning pop tastes, the event was not altogether atypical, at least within the realms of such liberalist elitism.

However, by the time John Lennon met Paul McCartney at the Woolton Parish Church Fete on 6 July 1957 Lennon was about to enrol at Liverpool College of Art: his grammar school education was behind him and so too perhaps any musical ties (brought about by skiffle) that demarcated a folk blues, rather than a rock 'n' roll, route. The Quarry Men formed ostensibly as a grammar school skiffle group – with all that involves generically concerning the 'folk' music of the US, but Lennon was not slow to include some of his favourite rock numbers into the band's limited repertoire as soon as he could. This dichotomy in tastes might be one reason why the Quarry Men gelled only briefly, as the authenticities of Lennon and (say) Rod Davis diverged. Banjo player Rod Davis was a 'hardened skiffle purist and there appears to have been a great amount of friction over […] change of direction. Eventually, by February, 1958, Davis had left the group' (Brocken, 1996:109). Although Lennon was a lover of Lonnie Donegan's music (at least to begin with), Presley was his idol. In his renowned interview with Jann Wenner (1971) Lennon name-checked the blues singer Sleepy John Estes but also stated 'there's a self-consciousness about suddenly singing blues. I mean we were all listening to Sleepy John Estes and all that in art school, like everybody else. But to sing it was something else'. When asked in the same interview about his personal tastes Lennon commented that he:

> always liked simple rock and nothing else […] I like rock and roll and I express myself best in rock […] Wop bop a loo bop. I like rock and roll, man, I don't like much else […] That's the music that inspired me to play music. There is nothing conceptually better than rock and roll. No group, be it Beatles, Dylan or Stones has ever improved on 'A Whole Lot A Shakin'' for my money. Or maybe I'm like our parents, you know, that's my period and I dig it, and I'll never leave it. (Lennon to Wenner, 1971:30, 34, 42-3)

This evidence presents an interesting inconsistency between the fun and perhaps working-class associations of rock with the alternative and serious nature of grammar school folk and blues. Perhaps Lennon was somewhat unlike his middle-class Liverpool R&B contemporaries such as Mike Evans, Alan Peters, John Donaldson, Bob Hardy, and Les Johnson – maybe even his Liverpool Institute musical compatriots in the Beatles (George Harrison reportedly claimed 'no Leadbelly, no Beatles'). Perhaps at an early stage Lennon saw through the quasi-elitist posturing of musical authenticity created within the domain of the British grammar school system. Paul McCartney also admits to a rock 'n' roll epiphany, brought about by the 1956 US movie *The Girl Can't Help It*. In the Beatles' *Anthology* he recalls with great relish the moment the star of the film Tom Ewell 'widens' the screen, introduces colour, and then cuts to Jane Mansfield walking up the steps of a New York apartment block to the accompaniment of Little Richard. McCartney regards this as a seminal moment in his life – a moment perhaps when the authenticity of US popular culture moved some young fans away from the overt seriousness of folk blues and into the realms of the here and now.

Bob Hardy, for a while a close friend of the young Ringo Starr, and a member of several prominent blues, soul and jazz line-ups over the years also alluded to this cultural-cum-musical division. Although Ringo was from a decidedly working-class background, he did spend a great deal of time away from it as a boy

– in hospital – and later went to Riversdale Technical College to get his seaman's ticket. Bob told this writer:

> I left the Institute [grammar school] after being allowed to take my 'O' Levels. I had been threatened with expulsion during the final spring term but was able to hang on, as it were. I went to Riversdale Technical College to obtain my ticket as a 'sparks' in the Merchant Navy. During my time at Riversdale, I hung around with Rory's drummer, Richie Starkey, who enjoyed the stage name of Ringo Starr. We became good friends, so much so that we decided to migrate to the USA – Texas to be exact. Ringo remains very important to me because it was he who gave me my first blues LP – a sampler. He had got it from Gerry Marsden when, apparently, the latter was in Hamburg – I was hooked! And why did I want to go to Texas? Because that was where Lightnin' Hopkins lived. The only reply to that statement in the Liverpool of circa 1960 would have been 'Lightnin' who?'
>
> You must understand that there was absolutely no information available on the blues and rhythm and blues at this time. Although some have made the most extraordinary claims for certain radio (e.g. Alexis Korner's, to which I didn't listen) and TV shows (e.g. Josh White's which I watched and loved), there was literally no body of work to which any budding Liverpudlian blues fan could refer. I eventually did, however, purchase Samuel Charters' *The Country Blues* the day it arrived in Phillip, Son and Nephew in Whitechapel. This book became my Bible and, with it, I introduced Lance Railton to African American blues musicians. There were now two of us […] *the rest appeared to be Buddy Holly fans* [my emphasis]. (Hardy to Brocken, merseybeat.org)

Lennon and McCartney were indeed great Buddy Holly fans, as too were, at least after 1960, the young dancers at the Cavern and a structural resonance developed between the Beatles and these dancers over the forthcoming 24 months.

While Lennon some years later freely admitted in song that 'a working class hero [was] 'something to be' ' this comment, was especially ironic for a young man relatively disconnected from the 'fucking peasants' by the inter-war fringe development area of Menlove Avenue, but sharing their tastes and performing their favourite songs. Lennon appears to have engaged with the working-class authenticity into which he was actually born, but he did so via a rather bourgeois angry young man-style of 'reverse social authenticity'. My experiences at West Derby High School in Liverpool in the late-1960s also bear testimony to this. A melange of somewhat confused Marxist polemics, rock 'n' roll authenticities, British motorcycles, and even Belstaff jackets created among a small elite in our 'A-stream' a self-conscious inverted snobbery that condemned middle-class cosiness. Of course, the irony of this artificial and rather patronizing position was that the people to whom this group attempted to cleave immediately recognized the bourgeois aesthetics that put such ideas into place, rejecting them as expressions of phony concern: somewhat frustrating for aspiring middle-class teenage Marxists, but nevertheless hilarious to observe.

This information certainly suggests that any examination of the popularity of rock 'n' roll, skiffle, folk and/or blues music in the Liverpool of the late-1950s and early-1960s should be considered from a variety of disparate diachronic angles – in particular from the perspective of records as the centre of the listening and learning experience, class-based erudition concerning musical and social value, and the significance of an audience-based sound quotient that approved some pieces of music, but not others. The Beatles mostly covered 'old' rock and there were indeed connoisseurs who preferred the 1950s sounds of say Buddy Holly and Carl Perkins to those of Cliff Richard and Adam Faith. But there were other reasons why this music prevailed in Liverpool. For example, this early rock era actually produced some very danceable and sexy music, which it could be said was not always the case with the Norrie Paramour, John Barry-led BBC-approved British pop of the early-1960s. Early-era rock was also relatively easy to learn and play moderately well, especially on the hoof, whereas a John Barry pizzicato on an Adam Faith record had to remain just there – on the record. So, while there might have been a taste culture surrounding the connoisseurship of authenticity, there was also one contiguous of the practicalities of dancing to a live group on a Saturday night: a little record collecting evidence bears this out.

The Beatles fan club began in Liverpool before the band had even recorded for Parlophone and early fan club member Val Davies informed Gareth Palowski (1989) that she regularly purchased the original 45 rpm recordings of material featured in the Beatles' live set. But she did so in order to obtain approximations of 'Beatles' performances, rather than owning 'authentic originals'. The authenticity of this small collection of records lay within the Beatles' repertoire; the Beatles provided a homological framework within which she could invest. This investment included dancing and the Beatles were so adept at re-articulating this material that, for Val, their versions 'came first', so to speak. This suggests three linked areas of further investigation: one, that the group were playing a repertoire of conformity constructed out of localized alternativity; secondly that they were an excellent covers band, and thirdly that the significance of audience reception, particularly one might suggest, in the Cavern, was paramount.

There is no evidence that the Beatles 'practised' (say) 'Smokestack Lightin'' but then played (say) 'Some Other Guy' ostensibly for 'the punters'. In fact, the group's different sets appeared to reflect not only their own musical interests but those also of their fans. They frequently performed requests, they responded positively to musical suggestions from their fan base, they were even involved in helping to organize fan club evenings. So their responses to audience reception were direct and affirmative. Ian Hoare wrote in 1974 'John Lennon's work has always implied a recognition that rock is a communal music, a music whose power derives largely from the proximity of the performer to the audience' (Hoare, 1974:27). Their version of Richie Barrett's 'Some Other Guy' was sadly never recorded for Parlophone, but was regarded as a prime mode of communication between band and devotees. This song was in fact, not only representative of a Beatles canon of music, but of more widespread tastes on Merseyside; Former Cavern deejay Billy Butler remembered:

> Some Other Guy everybody played […] my own band [the Tuxedos] did it. It was a song that everybody knew would go down well. Gerry Marsden told me that he'd gone into NEMS to buy a copy of the original to learn, and was told by the assistant that Lennon had just been in and bought it. He was mad because he knew that it would be instantly added to the Beatles act before the Pacemakers' […] he also knew that the Beatles would do a really good job on it. (Butler to Brocken, 1996:61)

I have written elsewhere (1996) that the ubiquity of 'Some Other Guy' in Liverpool asks whether the song represented an 'alternative canon' of music ('i.e. alternative to the record charts') and whether the Beatles actually used that canon. The question here however is of a different kind: whether 'Some Other Guy' was canonical in a genre-sense and whether there was a rhythm and blues 'line in the sand' that some groups did not wish to cross. Was 'Some Other Guy' locally conformist rather than transformist? Were groups, such as the Roadrunners and the Clayton Squares who crossed beyond 'Some Other Guy' labelled differently? The kinship and competitiveness surrounding 'Some Other Guy' suggests that some Merseybeat groups fell over themselves to perform the song, so perhaps this does not represent any 'alternative' culture at all, but rather an outer perimeter of taste culture encapsulating a canon. Billy Butler informed this writer when asked whether he thought that a Merseybeat music canon existed:

> Definitely, yes; there were songs that always went down well in Liverpool. Yes, there was a kind of agreed repertoire. Bands would argue with each other when they were on larger bills […] 'we do that one, not you' and 'this is part of our act'. Many were easy to play, I think, as well as being good to dance to. It was what people wanted and what bands wanted. If they went down well they could earn £6 a night. Two nights of gigs would mean £2 each. Many of these young lads were only earning two pounds a week at this time, so it was good money. Some bands showed their signs of success through their gear, they would improve their equipment. Other bands would try to emulate them. All of them would be into the same sort of sounds; heavy bass, rhythm, and it would produce results with the same batch of numbers. And it was alternative too; [in the sense of] not the sort of stuff that was coming out of London. (Butler to Brocken, 1996:63)

However of myriad assorted ex-R&B band members questioned by this writer over the years, 'Some Other Guy' appeared less popular. Bob Hardy stated that his various R&B groups did not perform the song. Frank Connor also admitted that the Hideaways did not perform it: 'we learnt it, but it didn't suit our style, so we didn't play it'. Les Johnson performed 'Some Other Guy' in several different bands, but not, usually, in the more R&B-inclined outfits. Alan Peters of Almost Blues stated that they did perform the song, but for very specific reasons, and not in its original style:

> The 'Almost' Blues did perform 'Some Other Guy' after we purchased a Wurlitzer Electic Piano from the Mississippi via Frank Hessy.
>
> The reason we chose that particular number is that it had that 'Wurlitzer' piano reed sound, a sound we wanted after hearing Ray Charles's 'What Did I Say' that eventually replaced 'Some Other Guy' in our set.
>
> I must add that we emulated the more laid back southern beat rather than the up tempo Mersey Beat as most bands did with particular reference to The Big Three.
>
> The Beatles Cavern version has a more original feel even though there was no electric piano. This was the early 'Almost' Blues, the five piece that performed blues classics like 'Hoochie Coochie Man', 'Dust My Broom', 'Big Leg Woman', 'Scratch My Back' etc, before we were advised to become more commercial. (Peters to Brocken, February 2009)

From the Quarry Men era through to 1962, the Beatles did not cover any Muddy Waters or Lightnin' Hopkins songs (see appendix), nor did they move into the 'folkier' territory occupied by Les Johnson's favourites Sonny Terry and Brownie Magee (or indeed Leadbelly). This, one must assume, was not solely an issue of personal preference, but one concerning the relative unpopularity of these US artists in Liverpool at that time. The pre-1963 repertoire of the Beatles does not include *any* songs that hint at perhaps deeper investigations into playing the blues. While Little Richard, Chuck Berry and Arthur Alexander songs are present, for others more closely associated with the R&B genre, these artists tended to represent only an 'introductory level'. Billy Butler once informed this writer that, despite his fascination with Black music he 'didn't really like the blues'. He found it 'boring and couldn't understand the appeal'. Frankie Connor also stated to this writer that in the 1960s Billy had little time for Alexis Korner and his authenticities. Billy did admit to playing Pye International singles 'by the dozen', but was 'very selective; I would play say Sugar Pie Desanto but not Muddy Waters; Billy Stewart but not Little Walter, if you see what I mean'. Butler, then, was fully aware of just how far he could take a dancing audience's interests in Black music: perhaps as far as (say) Bobbie Parker's 'Watch Your Step' or Richie Barrett's 'Some Other Guy', but no further – perhaps so, too, were the Beatles.

Although John Lennon later admitted to Jann Wenner that 'it was black music we dug', his own interests in such musical areas did not follow the pathways of those such as Ringo's college pal Bob Hardy, or Alan Peters. This difference between what the audiences in the Cavern or the Mardi Gras clubs actually wanted and what some of the R&B bands wanted to play supports Les Johnson's opinion that these bands 'listened to one thing and played something else'. It also might suggest that the tastes of the Beatles were more in-line with a populist discourse. It might even indicate that Chicago blues of the variety that led to a rock meritocracy surrounding bands such as Led Zeppelin, Free, and Deep Purple (who it could be argued contributed to the ousting of the Beatles in 1969) was not *at all* popular in Liverpool. Bob Hardy alludes to this when he states: 'Perhaps unfortunately for me, I presumed that everybody else in the world must also be affected by this music in the same way. Of course, they were not; a position I failed to appreciate until I was well into my thirties' (Hardy to Brocken, merseybeat.org). These comments make a great deal of sense, for by 1965 deejay culture was pressurizing live music in Liverpool. Billy Butler was garnering a reputation for knowing what people wanted ('the platters that matter') while groups could only provide what they able to, within their sometimes limited musical abilities. This dichotomy was a substantial motivation for the rapid growth in popularity of dancing to pre-recorded soul and Motown music in Liverpool during the mid-1960s.

R&B after the Beatles

The Beatles were long gone from both the Cavern and from Liverpool by 1964. In their wake a few latter-day beat groups such as the Dennisons, the Escorts, the Kirkbys and the Masterminds were tipped for great things, but although each of these groups earned a living from their music for a couple of years they did not effectively 'make it' in their own right. The Kirkbys actually scored singles success in Finland, but only Terry Sylvester from the Escorts and Joey Molland from the Masterminds went on to enjoy higher profiles in the music business (by joining the Hollies and Badfinger, respectively). The Black five-man vocal group the Chants also established for themselves long-term careers on the cabaret club circuit before mutating into Ofanchi and the Real Thing in the mid-1970s. But Jim Ireland, who owned the Mardi Gras and Downbeat clubs, and managed several of these 'later' beat groups, such as the Kinsleys, informed this writer some years ago that, by 1965 he had already noticed that listening practices were changing. Recorded music: portable, repeatable, and relatively affordable was beginning to make inroads into live music in Liverpool. Jim stated that records requests became increasingly important in his clubs, and the cult of personality began to embrace not only the groups, but the deejays spinning the discs in between sets. I was even informed by one Cavern member that by the mid-1960s she:

> found live music a bit of a mess; I remember one night in the mid-60s the Clayton Squares were on; we thought it was too loud and didn't know a lot of the stuff that was being performed. So we waited until the band came off and then asked Billy Butler for requests. He was only too pleased to play things we wanted because we would dance. Once we were dancing everybody else got up too. Live music was dead for me after that. I know it sounds a bit daft but I think that the importance of live music in the Cavern is exaggerated. (Sandra Smith to Brocken, 1999)

The aforementioned beat groups were by 1964 rubbing shoulders with a few R&B groups of the 'Rolling Stones' variety. The initial popularity for these latter groups tended to be with the student audience in Liverpool, for example, from circa-1962 the Roadrunners had a residency at Hope Hall, a short distance away from the University of Liverpool and the Liverpool College of Art. For about 12 months the Roadrunners were Liverpool's only R&B group, but this began to change when rhythm and blues music became relatively popular, nationally. One of the first groups to join the Roadrunners was the Almost Blues. Alan Peters recalls:

> My band the Almost Blues played their first of many gigs at Hope Hall starting on Saturday 22nd August 1964 including supporting blues legend Alexis Korner under the heading 'London Comes to Liverpool'. His band included guests such as Long John Baldry, Reg Dwight, Rod Stewart and Dick Heckstall-Smith. The reputation of the Almost Blues along with that of the Roadrunners appealed to the art fraternity especially as they were the only bands at that time dedicated to the less well-known black American bluesmen. Mike Hart [Roadrunners] and myself were Ray Charles fanatics at that time, so much so that I used to sag off from Art School on Wednesday afternoons to listen to the new R&B releases that Brian Epstein and Pete Brown of NEMS had put aside for me. (Peters, groovin'. com)

The Bistro in the cellar of Hope Hall became an important meeting place for like-minded young people – geographically close to, but culturally some distance from, the usual watering holes across Liverpool's city centre. For some the Bistro was even more select than Ye Cracke pub (a favourite of John Lennon's), O'Connor's Tavern on Hardman Street, or even the Philharmonic pub on Hope Street. Alan Peters describes the Bistro as ' a place to discuss, digest and plan the more avant-garde and anti-establishment projects in all subjects [...] It was during this time that I met Adrian Henri [...] and started working on combining the spoken word with the rhythmic beat of R&B' (ibid). Peters' band did not have a 'Merseybeat' sound as such, and were enjoyed by student aficionados for precisely that reason. The Almost Blues merged interests in blues, jazz and spoken word and this tended to reflect the way that some music-loving students moved in and out of genre-located discourses of authenticity. Such paradigms of authenticity were also geographical in that they reflected physical boundaries between students and residents. Therefore, for locals, experiencing this 'scene' involved physically moving into the places where such genre discourses took place. The social ramifications for R&B in Liverpool, therefore are historically illuminating in that places such as Hope Hall, being linked with student activity, were not altogether constitutive of the cultural imaginations of Liverpool everyday life. Hope Hall, Hope Street and the surrounding area became regarded as 'student-land', not simply because students frequented the area, but because other subject positions, other discursive boundaries, and other imaginations took place and became part of another social reality – it was probably geographically and socially the closest

Liverpool ever really came to having a counter culture. Alan Peter's impressions of his group's fan-base at this time make for interesting reading:

> The Art School Students during the 1960s had a very distinctive dress-style that stood out from the 'normal' teenage dress code of the time. You could easily spot an Art School student as they stood out from the crowd and inevitably the people that followed the Almost Blues and the Roadrunners usually comprised of the 'arty' set. *Even to this day and probably due to my involvement with the combination of music and the spoken word, there has been a slight distance between us and the Merseybeat bands* [my emphasis]. The Art School influence was far more prominent in our approach to this less popular form of Afro-American music and our inclusion of a horn section to accentuate a more political vocal stance moved us even further from the popular mainstream of the guitar-based bands. (Peters, *ibid*)

This comment was also supported by Frankie Connor of the Hideaways who stated that 'The Hope Hall area was probably the centre of the more arty and folky crowd, and at the same time did not attract a lot of the Cavern crowd. The Hideaways played at the Sink [club], just around the corner from Hope Hall and it could be a different crowd in there, especially Wednesdays, from the one at Hope Hall – fans of the group as much as of the music, if you see what I mean' (Connor to Brocken, 2009). Evidently, blues and jazz on record continued to support cultural and historical imaginations creating discerning listeners who might distance themselves from the crowd, pass binary judgements upon the music related to issues about authenticity, and also make judgements about the rather 'plebeian' taste cultures of the masses. Because jazz and blues were learnt primarily via recordings those involved considered themselves reflecting a pedagogy, with the record a tool for distilling sound and dividing listeners into categories.

The Hideaways included Ozzie Yue, one of the very few rock musicians to come out of Liverpool's Chinese community (now a well-known actor), and Judd Lander, recognized at the time as Liverpool's foremost harmonica player in the Cyril Davies style. It was many years later when Lander would add his harmonica sound to Culture Club's 'Karma Chameleon' in 1983. Grammar school friends Ozzie Yue, John Shell and John Donaldson formed the group in 1964; Frank Connor was added a little later and the line-up was then completed in early 1964 by the arrival of aforesaid harmonica player Judd Lander. During the spring of 1965 they met two music lovers from the Netherlands who were putting together a book to be titled 'Beat in Liverpool'. The main purpose of the book was to pursue two local Liverpool groups the Clayton Squares and the Hideaways. The two writers visited several Hideaway gigs around the city, namely the Cavern, the Iron Door, the Way Down, the Mardi Gras, and the Sink Club. Frank stated 'I can't recall if they recorded us at all of the clubs mentioned (I seem to remember the equipment being a tape recorder over the shoulder and a hand held microphone thrust into the air in the middle of the audience!) – but I think not' (Connor, mayfield-records.co.uk). The Hideaways were recorded at the Sink, however, and these recordings were made available on a 45 rpm vinyl disc accompanying the book. These tracks were also commercially released some years later by Mayfield Records (MACD201A).

The Hideaways are widely remembered these days as the group that played the Cavern more times than any other (in the region of 400 appearances), although Les Johnson stated that following the departure of the first wave of Merseybeat groups, Cavern gigs could be rather chaotic affairs, often subject to great variation, with group members playing in perhaps one or two bands in one evening. According to Les, truly accurate statistics are impossible to compile. The Hideaways almost certainly appeared on TV more than any other group of the period because they were featured playing at the Cavern in an advertisement for Timex watches. By 1966 the Hideaways, with the exception of John Donaldson, turned professional, and found themselves playing further away from their Merseyside home base, looking for work in an ever-changing '60s scene; by all accounts it was very hard going. They were often incorrectly associated with the (by this time) 'old' Liverpool sound and found themselves often misrepresented by booking agents labelling them 'Merseybeat', rather than 'R&B'. Additionally the record industry, according to Frank Connor, seemed to presume all Liverpool groups sounded more or less the same and so paid little attention to Hideaways' demos.

Alan Peters of Almost Blues recalls resorting to recording a demo at CAM studios in 1965. It was called 'Just Won't Do Right' with 'Jerk' on the other side and was on CAM's Unicord label [UP655A]. Personnel included Black Liverpool singer Eddie Williams a.k.a. 'Jerkin George Paul' (vocals), Al Peters (trumpet), Mike Haralambos (guitar), Ray Fowlis (alto sax), John Beesley (bass), and Ronnie Wilson (drums). Note the two-tone line-up and the presence of a horn: Alan recalls 'it was a job done in a hurry, but was good quality; but the problem was that people didn't want R&B groups from Liverpool – it didn't fit the stereotype!' (Peters, mayfield-records.co.uk). However this demo eventually brought the Almost Blues to the attention of EMI and the group recorded further demo material at their Abbey Road Studios in London. Alan remembers:

> This session was recorded in Studio 2 at Abbey Road, apparently sandwiched in-between the Beatles and Englebert Humperdink. The reason I remember this session in particular is due to having to move Ringo's drums and John's amp to one side so that we could set up! This was our second visit to Abbey Road Studios, the first being with Liverpool soul vocalist Colin Areety. We recorded four tracks with Colin but he absconded with them immediately after the session – I have never heard, or heard of them since! (Peters, *ibid*)

Unfortunately, the Hideaways did not get to Abbey Road, but they did travel from being a somewhat rudimentary teenage musical covers band to an accomplished Chicago-style rhythm and blues group. Their repertoire included songs by Muddy Waters, Howling Wolf and Sonny Boy Williamson and the group played alongside

Howlin' Wolf, Hubert Sumlin, Jimmy Witherspoon, John Lee Hooker, Little Walter and they actually backed the great 'Sonny Boy' at the Cavern on 10 November 1964. The Hideaways also appeared on the same Cavern bill as Wilson Pickett (21 November 1965), bearing witness to the shifting tastes cultures in Liverpool (from R&B to soul music).

It was during 1965 that Billy Butler tentatively began deejay sessions without any live music back-up. These sessions proved so popular at the Cavern that, once the club re-opened in July 1966 Butler began to dominate proceedings, effectively ousting several aspiring young bands in the process – but it appears to have been what the dancers wanted. Frank Connor recalls:

> The Hideaways officially re-opened the Cavern, but Judd had left us for London by this point and so we had lost our harmonica-style of blues playing – which made a difference to our sound. The first song we played was the Temptations' 'The Way You Do The Things You Do' – looking back now that's quite an interesting choice, as far as moving away from R&B was concerned. (Connor to Brocken, 2009)
>
> The club was now licensed (in 1967) and to me it had lost its innocence. The Hideaways were a teenage group, but when the club re-opened it seemed more grown-up. It was now similar to other Liverpool night clubs such as the Mardi Gras or the Downbeat Club. Most of the same kids were still coming, but the club had definitely lost something. It was now much bigger with the improvements and more hygienic. Joe Davey was a more friendly man to deal with than Ray McFall [the previous owner]. Ray was always polite, but very aloof – he was never a friendly man. Joe and Alf [Geoghegan] were different people altogether (Connor in Thompson, 1994:88). [...] We were involved in Bob Wooler's management and so became a regular act at The Cavern; we eventually signed with RCA Records in 1969 and released our only single 'The Brandenburg Concerto' under our new moniker of Confucious. Locally, the record sold very well, but sank nationally (Connor to Brocken, mayfield-records.co.uk).

Once the Netherlands-based book/record of the Hideaways and Clayton Squares emerged, of particular poignancy were the shots of Hideaways bass player John Shell in the group's favourite meeting place, the Kardomah Café in Whitechapel. John could be seen with his then girlfriend Elaine Curtis. They were, in fact, married shortly after these photographs were taken. However, sadly (tragically, in fact), John Shell was to lose his life in the Vietnam War (he was born in Dallas in 1947), leaving Elaine a teenage widow.

In truth, the Cavern management never embraced R&B from a cultural perspective and although they did see money in it, the Cavern was never an 'R&B club', as such. The ever-attentive, articulate Bob Wooler was Billy Butler's predecessor at the Cavern, but like Butler was not a fan of blues music; he stated to this writer in the 1990s that R&B was too 'vernacular an idiom to be thoroughly successful [and that it was] soul music that locals really came to love' (Wooler to Brocken, 1997). However Bob Wooler cultivated his own stable of R&B groups which included the Hideaways, the St Louis Checks, the Almost Blues, TL's Bluesicians, The Fix, the Richmond Group, the Michael Allen Group and the Clayton Squares. Although Wooler recognized a market for this material, by 1965 that market was very confused and the Cavern not long for this world, losing money hand-over-fist after unsuccessfully attempting to start its own recording studio. The Cavern closed its doors with hefty debts in February 1966. Following its reopening it had, by the following February, effectively become a soul music club with far fewer groups being booked. By August 1967 the Cavern was licensed for the sale of alcohol and became a somewhat dingy version of any other club in Liverpool of the mid-late 1960s – ironically a rather 'soulless' watering hole. It did later become an important venue for the local hippie community when the club turned into a split-level venue: soul music and skinheads on one floor, and rock music and 'troggs' in the basement (not an ideal situation, by any means, especially in Mathew Street, at 2am).

Several other schoolboy or post-schoolboy R&B groups formed in Liverpool during 1964 and 1965. The Cordes (mentioned in the introductory chapter) wore little cord jackets and also featured a harmonica player, the diminutive Dave Dover: later of Colonel Bagshot's Incredible Bucket Band (sampled by DJ Shadow in the twenty-first century). The Cordes were also typical of the nascent grammar school breed of R&B group in mid-sixties Liverpool. They hailed from suburban south Liverpool (Childwall) and colonized the circuit established by the older beat groups, most of whom had left the city for one reason or another. Others followed the Cordes out of these middle-class suburbs including, from the Allerton area, the Calderstones (including Tom Evans later of Badfinger), from Crosby the Music Students and the Anzacs, the Valkyries from Birkenhead, Les Johnson's band the Detonators, Dave Crosby's Tabs, and Southport's Rhythm and Blues Incorporated which included Barry Womersley later of Jasmin-T and a young Ollie Halsall, soon after of Timebox and Patto.

These above-mentioned groups found that they were not always to the liking of the dancers who found some rhythm and blues rather dull ('how many verses of 'Got My Mojo Working' did we need?'). So certain bands, perhaps seeing the proverbial writing on the wall, began to adopt the styles of the popular touring soul groups of the day such as Geno Washington and the Ram Jam Band and Jimmy James and the Vagabonds. These British-based 'soul revue' bands incorporated horns and, despite most mods usually preferring to dance to recordings rather than live groups, proved very popular on the 'mod' scene by unashamedly replicating the sounds of Motown and Stax. The Clayton Squares were one such Liverpool group who attempted to clone such sounds. From 1964 they featured two sax players, and were probably the first to embrace a more commercial soul repertoire. By 1965 their material reflected the growing interest in Stax/Volt soul and the Clayton Squares were one of the first groups to incorporate Wilson Pickett's 'In The Midnight Hour' into their set. They seemed ready for great things after appearing on TV's *Ready Steady Go!* but a premature move to London condemned them to obscurity.

The Terry Hines Sextet formed when Hines left the Clayton Squares in early 1965. This sextet comprised at various times Hines, Albie Donnelly and Bob Hardy (sax), Terry Kennaugh (guitar), Geoff Workman (organ), Pete Newton (bass) and Dave Irving (drums). The repertoire of the Terry Hines Sextet was initially very catholic. The band drew their musical range from forties big city blues such as Eddie 'Cleanhead' Vinson, jump blues artists such as Louis Jordan, through to more contemporary sax specialists such as Junior Walker. They even played Horace Silver material and were including James Brown numbers when few people in Liverpool had even heard of him. When Terry Hines was replaced by Eddie Cave, former vocalist with the Richmond Group early in 1966, the group became the Fix. Success continued to elude them, however, and Donnelly increasingly involved himself in rather bewildering and sometimes incestuous permutations of musicians until the more well-known Supercharge line-up emerged in 1973. The first Supercharge consisted of the aforementioned Albie Donnelly, Ozzie Yue (lead guitar, vocals), Bob Robertson (tenor, baritone, guitar, vocals), Alan Peters (trumpet, flugelhorn, vocals), Tony Dunmore (bass), and Dave Irving (drums) and were a kind of Liverpool 'supergroup', of sorts. When they weren't messing about (which was a rarity), this group was possibly one of the most exciting and adventurous performing in Liverpool since the days of the Beatles.

Gender and R&B: the Liver Birds

One relatively unsung and noticeably unusual group to emerge from the post-Beatles Liverpool R&B scene were the Liver Birds. By late-1963 the Liver Birds, formerly a folk group in Liverpool were making ready to travel to Hamburg courtesy of Joe Flannery's booking agency, Carlton-Brooke. Following the success of Lee Curtis at the Star Club, Carlton-Brooke had become Manfred Weissleder's freelance agents for UK bands wishing to play in Hamburg, and Joe was constantly on the look-out for new or unusual trends to take to the Star Club; in the case of the Liver Birds, he had both. Visually, the Liver Birds were probably years ahead of their time for they were a female four-piece R&B group, not (as one might expect in those days), a female vocal group. They wore their hair in a cross between a Beatle cut and a mod bob and sported leather jerkins, tight fitting slacks and winkle picker shoes – quite a shock for the male-orientated scene in Liverpool.

Predictably, the group had found things chauvinistic back in Liverpool and it had taken a successful support gig with German band the Rattles to bring them to the attention of Carlton-Brooke. The Rattles had spent most of December 1963 in Liverpool and had become quite a draw at the Cavern. They returned to Germany just before Christmas to promote their recording 'The Stomp', which was a hit on the Continent. There were simply no female group role models and few precedents for the Liver Birds back in the UK. To compete, any new girl group not only had to contend with well-established images of female singers such as Dusty Springfield and Kathy Kirby but also the seemingly unassailable brigade of male groups. When Joe Flannery decided to manage the group his thoughts were that the Liver Birds should target West Germany: 'The Germans were no-less misogynist than the British, but we knew that the group would – by association – be described by the West German press as "female Beatles".' The word 'Beatle' had become such an encryption in Germany by 1964, that any person – male or female – associated with Liverpool, the appropriate sound, and hairstyles would be called 'Beatle'. Joe thought that tapping into this etymology would be superb publicity for the group before even playing a note. Prior to the Liver Birds leaving the UK Joe duly contacted the German music press, in order to hype the arrival of the group in Hamburg.

Between the New Year 1964 and their departure for Hamburg mid-February the Liver Birds were heavily booked throughout Liverpool. Carlton-Brooke placed them in as many local venues as possible in order to expand their skills and repertoire. With the help of Cavern deejay Bob Wooler they were able to get regular gigs at the Cavern alongside the likes of Chick Graham, the Kubas, the Riot Squad, and the Remo Four. Their most successful gig, however, was supporting Alexis Korner's Blues Incorporated on Sunday 26 January 1964. Flannery recalls: 'They were up against a very knowledgeable blues crowd that evening – all duffle coats and beards – but they handled the gig well and were commended by Alexis. The hype certainly worked in Germany for there was a large posse of pop press and male fans at the airport on their arrival with Lee Curtis and the All Stars Mk 2 during late-February, 1964' (Flannery to Brocken, 1997).

The band was led by Pam Birch, who according to Joe was something of an eccentric, 'but she was totally her own person and I admired her for that. I'd brought Pam into the group myself at a late stage after a fellow Liver Bird – Mary McGlory's sister – had decided that the beat group life was not for her' (*ibid*). Pam Birch had been attempting to make a name for herself on the folk scene in Liverpool during 1963 but has found it equally misogynistic and intransigent. She was apparently a little unpredictable as a performer, but always willing to take musical risks moved into R&B. Pam was fully aware of trends, for she had worked in the NEMS record department, buying imports. The aforementioned Mary McGlory was the bass guitarist and Joe recalls Mary as:

> A very quiet individual and religious; she married Frank Dostill in Germany. I shall never forget Mary's first sight of the Reeperbahn. Our taxi dropped us off near the Catholic Church around the corner and Mary remarked that her parents would be very pleased. We then walked around that corner to view all of the strip clubs and prostitutes! She nearly fainted! (*ibid*)

Val Gell played rhythm guitar; Val eventually married a young fan by the name of Stefan who, having met the band at the Big Apple club in Munich, attempted to drive to Hamburg to see the group again. Sadly, Stefan was involved in one of those all-too-common 1960s car accidents, leaving him paralysed. Sylvia Saunders played drums. Joe recalls that 'Syl was the mothering type but also quite bossy and independent. She ultimately met and married a drummer from the Bobby Patrick Big 6, came back to Britain but then subsequently spent some time in Spain. I believe she has returned to the UK' (ibid). Once in Hamburg, the Liver Birds were given a slot at the Star Club supporting Lee Curtis. On this occasion, they were not officially booked in under their own name, being part of the Lee Curtis 'show'. This was similar to the arrangement that Joe had made for Lee Curtis the March of the previous year. Joe remembers Lee Curtis not particularly enamoured of the Liver Birds, he thought them a bunch of female amateurs. Also by playing R&B, rather than the increasingly-dated rock 'n' roll, the Liver Birds appeared to be challenging the All Stars. Joe felt that 'their novelty value, alone, would fill the Star Club for at least a week and the musical ability stuff could take care of itself'.

Manfred Weissleder was duly impressed and retained the Liver Birds for the rest of the month. After the Star Club booking had been successfully completed, Flannery sent the girls home to rest and recuperate. They returned to Liverpool full of hope and with money in their pockets. Once back home, however, they retreated into relative anonymity and played only a handful of rather uninspiring gigs – including one at the Cavern with the Kubas once again, and another at the Peppermint Lounge with the Hideaways. They desperately wished to return to Hamburg, away from a scene in Liverpool that did not appear to be going anywhere. Indeed, Manfred Weissleder was so keen to have them back that he offered the Liver Birds a recording contract with his newly formed Star Club record label. At this time, recording deals in Germany were not as in Britain, being mostly on-off deals with a performance fee, however Flannery was able to negotiate royalties for the group:

> I can never work out whether I caught Manfred in one of his rare weaker moments or whether he really loved the band. Either way, they recorded regularly for Star Club Records over the next couple of years and sold plenty of records in West Germany.
>
> Which leads me to their repertoire: one of the things that attracted me to the group in the first place was their repertoire. The Liver Birds' set had moved one step beyond most of the Merseybeat groups in 1964, playing R&B numbers that would not have been out of place in the Marquee or the Crawdaddy. I distinctly remember storming versions of 'Got My Mojo Working', 'Too Much Monkey Business', 'Diddly Daddy' and 'Roadrunner' – odd, if you think about it! One could argue that the very term 'Mersey Beat' is a rather over-used narrative. It has certainly deflected attention away from groups such as the Liver Birds, the Hideaways and the Clayton Squares – all because they did not sound like they were about to burst into a rendition of 'Some Other Guy' – what a pity! (*ibid*)

Eventually the Liver Birds settled in West Germany and they are still fondly regarded by German R&B fans of '60s R&B to this very day. But also there remains a rather 'snotty' attitude to this group from those male mid-'60s R&B musicians still living on Merseyside. Expressions range from 'a Flannery cash-in' to 'crap girls who couldn't play' to 'better-off in Germany'. The chauvinism associated with the later rock meritocracy certainly had its gestation in Liverpool's R&B 'scene' and draws our attention to the way that women were regarded, even within the so-called counter culture. For example Alan Peters remembers Hope Hall as a place to pick-up members of the opposite sex often 'referred to as "chicks" in the vocabulary of the time' (Peters, groovin'.co.uk).

The Kirkbys

One final small case study concerns the Kirkbys, a group which was not strictly R&B-oriented, but one which perhaps exemplified the confusing and sometimes disappointing conditions for Liverpool groups in the aftermath of the Beatles. The group was formed by Jimmy Campbell, a brilliant and offbeat songwriter. According to many authorities on British psychedelia, his composition 'Michael Angelo' (sic) is one of the greatest examples of the genre. The group that recorded this marvellous piece of English pastoralism was named the 23rd Turnoff and appeared to be, on the face of it, one of those Deram one-offs that were part of that particular label. This was not the case, however, for this group was previously known as the Kirkbys and the history of Jimmy Campbell (and that of his group) can be traced back to the early days of Merseybeat. The Kirkbys recorded an excellent single for Decca ('It's a Crime') but it was Campbell's song writing skills that began to attract attention. The Escorts, for example, recorded his 'You'll Get No Lovin' That Way' as the flip side to their 'C'mon Home Baby'.

The Kirkbys became a popular attraction in Finland – where they scored two hits – and also spent some time backing the Merseys after their hit 'Sorrow', under the management of Kit Lambert. Broadcaster Spencer Leigh informed this writer that 'Campbell was far too talented a songwriter to languish in just a backing band' (Leigh to Brocken, 2007) and, re-naming the group the 23rd Turnoff (the slip road from the M6 onto the East Lancashire Road) Campbell embraced psychedelia. The aforementioned 'Michael Angelo' was the group's only release (Deram DM 150) and its incomprehensible failure to chart eventually contributed to the demise of the group. Jimmy Campbell then briefly quit music but began, in 1969, a truly fascinating but unsuccessful solo career. He was signed by Billy Fury's manager Hal Carter (Fury, during his Parlophone 'era' recorded Jimmy Campbell songs) and, between that time and 1973 Campbell made three solo albums for Polygram (Fontana, Vertigo, Philips respectively). During this time, he also became a mainstay of Rockin' Horse alongside former Merseybeat and Mersey, Billy Kinsley. This high-quality band backed several rock 'n' roll artists in addition to recording their own material for Philips (equally worthwhile). Anybody lucky enough to find any Jimmy Campbell recording is in for a rare treat. A lost prophet, indeed, Jimmy died in 2007.

The late Albie Power was the bass player with the Kirkbys and latterly became firm friends with this writer; he was able to talk about the post-Beatles era in Liverpool with some distance and detachment, describing it to me as 'a slump' and remembering not being surprised when the Cavern closed in 1966. He suggested that a changing national scene was so rapid that the traditional rock fraternity in Liverpool found it hard to adapt, and that younger (R&B) bands were simply not good enough to compete on a national level. Albie commented:

> They were good enough for an hour in a local club but couldn't compete with some of the giants we had come across on our travels. We played a lot with groups from the Midlands – like the Spencer Davis Group and they were outstanding. They came to the Cavern once, as I remember, and wiped the floor with everybody – it could be embarrassing. (Power to Brocken, 2003)

Albie proposed another reason for the decline in the Liverpool scene. He described to me the Liverpool of 1966 as saturated with 'third-rate bands'. Billy Butler also saw this coming and recalls: 'The whole thing had got so big that anyone with a guitar formed a group, so good groups were being financially undercut by groups willing to play for nothing' (Butler to Brocken, 1996). Albie further stated that even as one of the better groups in the city the Kirkbys would receive only £15 per night in Liverpool; they were able to achieve four times that amount elsewhere, particularly abroad. In March 2009, Frank Connor also brought to mind this diminutive figure with some degree of horror.

So Albie Power bore witness to an 'old guard which was breaking apart, playing soul covers, or leaving for London or the Continent' (Power to Brocken, 2003). There is some evidence to support this statement: as we have already seen, several Liverpool groups disbanded in London, and the Roadrunners ended their days spending more time in Germany than at home, before finally splitting. Howie Casey stayed in Germany, as did the Liver Birds and Lee Curtis. The Kirkbys toured Scandinavia and Finland before returning home to witness club life in Liverpool moving over to alcohol and discotheques. Alcohol licenses turned such venues into members' clubs with expensive bar prices. Albie recalled that many stopped turning up for the groups because (for him) 'a lot of the groups were rubbish', and 'a club with a Motown or Stax disco was reliable' in a sound sense. Unlike in the early-1960s when 45 rpm records were stored by Val Davies as a reflection of the Beatles' repertoire, soul records were now deemed far more authentic in their own right. Albie considered: 'People look back now and think that it was 1967 and flower power and all that that killed off Liverpool's music scene. But for me it was 1966. The clubs collapsed and there was a polarization between good bands and bad bands; discos slipped in between before anyone had noticed' (*ibid*).

Even the local music newspaper that had helped to hold matters together – *Mersey Beat* – was by 1964 renamed *Music Echo* by new owner Brian Epstein, turned into a carbon copy of a London-based weekly and then amalgamated with the national 'inkie' *Disc*. In a rather meagre quarter-page 'Mersey News' column in *Disc and Music Echo* of 28 May 1966 the item read: 'Liverpool cafe owner Joe Davey, who recently bought the Cavern, is expected to plough about £12,000 into it by the time the world-famous landmark re-opens in July. Such is his optimism that the Mersey pop scene will continue to thrive.' But this was followed by the salutary comment: 'On the other hand Liverpool agent/promoter Chris Wharton pronounces: "The scene is as dead as a dodo. There are too many tenth-rate Liverpool groups."' Albie Power agreed with this last comment: 'I drifted out of the music business by the end of the sixties. I got married, moved to Winsford in Cheshire, and got a proper job! Jimmy Campbell also tried his hand at a proper job but drifted back into the business and recorded those albums, but I never thought he was very happy. It was as if all of the work was for nothing. Great times, of course but we ended up being a little empty inside – Jimmy more than most, I feel.'

Summary

The gramophone allowed people to analyse what they were hearing and this helped some to reconsider music as 'just' music. Gramophone records established attentive listening to jazz, folk, blues and popular music in the UK to such an extent that connoisseurship emerged from record collecting. It seems incredible now to think that a great deal of British post-WWII music composition came from the convergence of society with functional artefacts such as record players, plastic records, and radio sets (not to mention film and TV) – but, of course, it did.

But were these specialists representative of broader taste cultures? Not all of us enjoy deliberate or measured listening and one form of listening cannot be 'superior' to other forms. Records bring music into the everyday but their role as pro-active arbiters of taste can actually be over-emphasized at the expense of other equally legitimate listening experiences. The experiences of Les Johnson's left-thinking art teacher in the 1950s propose to us that there will always exist a minority of people who are very interested in talking about and attentively listening to music, discussing sound, history, artefact, affect. But perhaps those dancers at the Cavern also suggest to us that at least as many do not wish to deepen examinations of (obscure) sounds. To be sure, the mythology of recorded sound provided this writer with a more vivid conception of his own life-experiences: popular music allowed me to feel less anxious and more in control of life. But, for some, looking more closely at the workings of musical processes and genres can be less reassuring. It can in fact alarm those who do not wish to take music so earnestly, for it questions the way in which the world is ordered. Music might be a traditional part of life – but is popular music analysis part of everyday experience?

Both Les Johnson and Bob Hardy propose that blues didn't take off to any great extent in Liverpool. But why should it have done? Liverpool, like any major city, was musically conventional, and such interests in African-American authenticity emanated from cultural sources that placed binary oppositions such as convention and 'other' into the cultural arena in the first place; in their own way both oppositions are equally conventional and linked though discourse. The possibility that the Beatles (or perhaps John Lennon) embraced a different kind of musical tradition – one of rock 'n' roll convention – only really permits us to consider one form of imagined middle-class liberal elitism being partially rejected in favour of an equally imagined working-class immanence: both were streams of the same cultural font. Could it be that the Beatles were popular locally because they did *not* take chances with the tastes of their fans? Most of us would be mortified to learn that we have made elementary *a priori* mistakes in constructing deterministic meanings from an earlier period, but it should be possible to reclaim some of the indifferent. In a positive sense this embarrassment recognizes that there are many co-equal claims to meaning and significance.

This more open-ended historical narrative suggests new perspectives for looking at the so-called 'culture' of Merseybeat (and its aftermath). For example that cover versions could be both liberative *and* conformative, that live music could be exciting *and* unadventurous, that listening to records could creatively focus around not only live music (in the case of Val Davies) but also dancing to recordings (Sandra Smith), and that, post-Beatles, music identity fragmented in a sea of oppositions concerning the musical 'next step' (maybe it was always this way). Further, one might theorize a new proposition: that perhaps the Beatles attempted to compose their way out of such conformity, that their own compositions, initially derivative of covers, removed them from the cultural glue that had, on the one hand, sustained them, but on the other set them in position: Various early fan club members jealously informed Granada TV in August 1993:

> They were ours. They were Liverpool's they belonged to us […] they were there one minute and gone the next […] Bob Wooler gave it out that they were going to London, expecting everybody to be pleased, but […] for ordinary fans, we felt a bit deserted […] why did they have to go and leave us? […] we lost them to the world. After they'd gone, after they made it, I didn't go to any of their concerts (at the Empire and so on), and I didn't buy any of their records. (Granada TV, 'Celebration', 1993)

There are also other possible avenues of historical investigation. For example, that class-based schooling was at least partially responsible for genre conventions; that the cultural geography of Liverpool University and Art School students and the gender relationships within R&B in Liverpool created distinct interpretations of what it meant to be a Liverpudlian musician in the mid-1960s. One might also put forward that, in Liverpool popular music finance capital was far too small and slow off the mark in exploiting any post-Beatles market. Ray McFall's interests lay perhaps in preservation rather than development, and so failed. Thus, following the Cavern's re-opening in July 1966 a kind of mutual agreement between records and live music took place. This involved the Liverpool groups playing a junior partner role and then eventually acceding to the record's domination.

We might wonder whether it is fair to ask so many questions and propose so many theories concerning narratives of music in Liverpool – after all, pre-existing accounts have been accepted over a long period of time. But the reception of recorded sound had such a radical affect on people that the popular music historian has to acknowledge that several narratives accompany the emanation of every musical sound. For some in the Cavern between 1964 and 1966, live music was dull, bands boring and their sounds amateurish or too loud. Records, on the other hand became models of conformity, with sound levels appealing because of correspondence to each other. An older brother of a teenage friend of mine, Val Smith, was in 1969 an avid collector of Tamla Motown singles. He purchased every single release and kept them in a box in his bedroom. One evening he 'allowed' me to view, but not to touch them, and was horrified when I stated that, to my ears they all sounded the same; he replied, rather piqued: 'but that's the point!' In Liverpool, such modes of authenticity came to surround the 45 rpm record – little wonder that by the early-1970s via the 'Northern Soul' subset, venues surrounding the city (such as Wigan Casino) were exploiting such record connoisseurship.

I also recall a girl I dated back in 1971 asking me whether I liked music to which I replied 'yes'. She then asked 'who' and I told her – but the list seemed to go on forever, it became a litany and my enthusiasm ran away with me in front of her. I could see I was in trouble. She stared at me rather blankly and said 'you're a bit up your own arse, aren't you?' and I replied that I *really* liked music. She replied she liked Motown, and we left it at that – I can't remember her name now but I can remember that's what she said. From that moment we understood each other. For me music was part of my identity: attentive, serious; for her it just 'was'. It struck me then that there were people who did not enthuse about music as I did. My feelings are that the Beatles understood this dichotomy. They appreciated not only the power of music, but also its demarcations. Who would deny the communal character of popular music, but who would also deny that popular music enthusiasts construct worlds around favoured images that can also marginalize?

Chapter 7

'Mist over the Mersey' – folk scenes on Merseyside

At times it was like East and West Berlin!

(Geoff Speed to Brocken, February 2009)

In recent years scholars have recognized the need to address issues associated with popular music and its relationship with time, place, locality, scenes and mediations. This interest has stemmed in part from an attempt to understand how music reflects and responds to socio-cultural issues – something that also lies at the heart of folk music discourse. All popular music scenes exist in a relationship with their immediate and immediately preceding contexts. Folk scenes are not altogether different, but do not always respond positively to an affirmative sense of immediacy. Sarah Cohen (1991, 1997) views popular music scenes in Liverpool as productive and contradictory assemblages constructed via associations with, and counter-balances to, differing interpretations of locality. Barry Shank (1998) describes the musical use of place in Austin, Texas as both historically and musically organic and correlative. Will Straw, in his study of popular music scenes, suggests that popular music scenes are created by overlapping alliances valuing the 'redirective and the novel over the stable and the canonical' (1991:386). But Straw also expresses a level of scepticism about the enshrinement, thus veracity of wholly backwards-looking 'scenes', because he notes no scene is devoid of contact with contemporary movements and mechanisms.

This contemporary exchange actually proposes that traditions are subject to modern life, thus invented and, of course, that modern traditions are as valid as those apparently deemed under threat: '[…] each emerged within international, industrial and cultural contexts which shaped the conditions of existence and certain of the "meanings" of music localism throughout Western countries' (Straw, 1991:369-70). So while the very presence of folk music might be interpreted by an insider as a reaction to popular music conformity, according to Straw, folk as a 'scene' has to remain typically characteristic of all popular music activity. It is certainly true that different forms of folk music are listened to by a variety of different people at different times, in different places, eliciting many diverse contemporary responses. Folk music, like all forms of popular culture, is also dependent upon media and communication systems. One might describe this as a 'popular music perspective' on folk activity, but it is not a perspective to which most folk aficionados cleave.

My own work *The British Folk Revival* (2003) received much criticism from within folk circles both for its popular music studies approach, and for its apparent 'misunderstanding' of the greatest authenticity paradigm (or should that be 'function myth'?) of all: 'tradition'. But, of course, a questioning of the exclusivity of one 'tradition' was central to the point being made. All popular music has many traditions deriving from the preceding past, however there has not and will not transpire one specific language to deal with such issues. Instead, there have emerged a variety of discourses to deal with variable sounds. So, rather than adopting the idea that one universal language can explain musical meaning, a popular music studies approach takes in a more 'nomadic' viewpoint in which alliances are seen to express and convey mythologies that can be replicated in all aspects of all scenes connected with music. 'Tradition' (an over-used word), therefore is not, in itself singular, but eclectic, kinetic and transmutable. The inevitable result is that folk music is also eclectic – whether folkies like it or not! Validating art from a popular music perspective does not only identify sounds with a 'deep' past, but also acknowledges the ability to pick and choose from the surfaces of the present. For example, a consideration of the power of local radio post-1967 is paramount for our understanding of Merseyside's folk scenes. This writer, therefore, maintains the conviction that in a society in transition towards an indefinable end, the only option open to those who study all popular music is one afforded by a nomadic and transitory mentality.

Indeed, it is this transitory state rather than the usual fixed static states that actually comes to at least partially explain multifarious folk music activity on Merseyside in the '60s and '70s. However if we use this 'nomadic' approach in a discussion with folkies about their 'scene' and place that scene within a construction of interactivity, many would regard such motifs as forms of subtle destruction, not only from traditional cultures but also the creative nucleus of all cultures. In their view, folk clubs in particular reflect a continuance of the parochial, rather than an expanding cultural web as represented by 'the popular'. The folk scene is viewed from within as representing an almost architectural halt to the spreading of mediocrity brought about by musical melting pots. This 'block' thus empowers the folk scene with an authority to acknowledge a form of musical history and a 'natural engagement'-style function myth. This is obviously valuable, for folk clubs in particular can serve as reminders to the popular music industry that it is unnecessary to jettison the old cultural past. During the 1960s, for example, the power and presence of folk clubs on Merseyside and elsewhere convinced the music industry and media that it could be both modern and hang on to sources, that it could revive dormant cultures and take part in new forms (after all, there was money in it). However, the discovery of a pre-existing all but lost 'tradition' (rather than the contemporary mediation of the same) tends to be fore-grounded in folk circles and this creates a particular 'folk' discourse where the media is only reluctantly acknowledged as an integral part of the folk music milieu. Recently Peter Cox in his excellent work *Set Into Song* (2008) has illustrated how the BBC

Radio Ballads series was one of the most convincing series of radio programmes ever made:

> Before these programmes were made, radio and TV in Britain rarely featured real people talking about their own lives. The Radio Ballads creators made listener and programme-maker alike realise that 'ordinary' people can tell extraordinary stories.[...] Woven into the stories are carefully crafted songs [...] Their words are literally 'Set into Song', as the preamble to each programme announces. (Cox, 2008:iv)

This extremely positive acknowledgement of the validity of media systems in the dissemination of folk music is not universal within the folk scene, where word-of-mouth is still prioritized, and a dualism of traditional versus commercial production, mass versus folk culture, and authentic versus manufactured art is still prominent. These ideas are concomitant with concepts surrounding the musical forms and practices that emanate from a shared culture and community, the 'true' expression of an artist, and the freedom from commercial contamination and/or determination in cultural production.

On Merseyside, the 'folk scene' appears retrospectively to have been something of a monolith and has been described by some writers (including myself see *English Dance & Song*, autumn 2004) as the largest such 'scene' outside London. However this can be seen as a rather homogenizing concept. How music is expressed socially, with regard to locality, how such issues both restrict and release musical expression, and how activities are effectively 'tied' together as 'scenes' by social echelons, politics, and even communication systems (disguising their enigmatic cultural geographies), remains fascinating. Scenes variegate and are problematic to record; indeed discourse-related investigations usually break down idealized concepts of 'scenes'. Because of such socio-cultural variables and akin to any popular music activity, the folk 'scene' on Merseyside was contextually moderated. Objective though they strived to be, folk revivalists on Merseyside became shaped – perhaps even distorted – by not only their own views concerning which musical customs and histories should or should not be designated authentic, but also by an ever-changing contemporary cultural geography, demographics of their own region, their own era, and their own financial circumstances (not to mention the power of the BBC).

Merseyside folk

Despite the propaganda expressed by Ewan MacColl who announced in 1957 that there were over one thousand clubs in the UK, the 'What's On and Who's Singing' column of September 1959 *Sing* magazine could only identify nine English folk clubs and only one was in Liverpool. So, the folk scene as it came to be known in Liverpool really developed in the 1960s, rather than in the 1950s. Certain pubs were selected for folk club 'births' not only for their ambience and convenience, but also because they were located in physical, stirring and ultimately meaningful spaces and localities. There were sometimes visibly noticeable associations between music and the locality of a venue. It was as if the respective members received a level of cultural and political sustenance from a 'working class' area, rather than one in the suburbs, from whence most of them came (although this tended to change by the later 1960s as many moved to fringe development areas and new clubs were accordingly opened). This cultural visage, then, contributed to the significance of a continual, 'organic' musical interactivity which further aided a historical manifestation of musical authenticity – being both geographically and historically significant.

Not unlike the aforementioned documentary-maker Daniel Farson, the first folk club that this writer came across in Liverpool in the 1960s was that of the Spinners Club, located at Gregson's Well pub in Low Hill. By the mid-1960s this area of Liverpool was somewhat run-down. On the immediate outskirts of the city, Low Hill had most certainly seen better days and by the mid-'60s was de-populating. There was still a sizeable local population around the Boaler Street and Islington areas but the latter of these two districts was scheduled for partial demolition so that Brunswick Road could be widened. On the opposite corner of Low Hill stood, oddly, another pub of the same name, which itself was adjacent to a building that had also seen its time come, and go: The Royal Hippodrome, a cinema that had in a previous incarnation existed as the Hippodrome Theatre and 'Hengler's Circus'. The area was predominantly known in local folklore for the presence of Brougham Terrace, the city registry office for births, marriages and deaths (a.k.a. 'Saint Broughams'), which itself was only a two minute walk away from the Grafton Rooms and the Olympia (by this time known as the Locarno). Generally speaking, the area was transitory and on the verge of partial destruction.

By the time this writer visited the Gregson's Well pub, there were actually two folk clubs operating on different nights at the location, and it soon became clear that they purveyed different styles of folk music. The second of these two clubs was the Calton Club and it alternated with the Spinners' Club. On the surface there might have appeared little difference between the two, for example both clubs included a couple of floor singers and a guest, together with a set by the residents, but the music policy at the Calton was far less eclectic. The resident group were the Calton Three which included the renowned Stan Ambrose and the material chosen reflected far more 'earthy' subjects than those sung by the Spinners. Ambrose for example was known for his interest in Music Hall and anarchist song and would attempt to make several political and cultural points via the presentation and performance of selected material. The Calton Three essentially held a 'come all ye' where bothy-style songs, Irish material and political songs that were of a more active historical bent were presented. The Spinners, on the other hand, were undoubtedly popularizers in the Pete Seeger mould in that they wished to broaden the appeal of folk music by any means possible. Their musical specialisms tended to be based around nautical songs: sea shanties, halyard songs, and the like, and they owed a debt of gratitude to Stan Hugill, one of the last remaining shanty-men in the country, who lived in Hoylake and occasionally performed as a guest. Geoff Speed:

> There was a difference, that's for sure and it was very evident in Liverpool. Some ideologies were influenced by Ewan MacColl at the time. This was of great importance and affected the great divide: in fact at some clubs you weren't welcome with a guitar – it was as stiff as that: very much frowned-upon. Stanley [Ambrose] had an anarchist reputation he was very proud of. He came to Liverpool as a social worker and loved it immediately. He was a political animal – he was a councillor in the south of England as a young man. He was born within the sound of Bow Bells and was more interested in the traditional music than many of us were. Some of us had a love for Burl Ives and his ilk, but for Stanley there was a great divide. (Speed to Brocken, February, 2009)

So the sounds within the Calton Club attempted to bear testimony to tradition as struggle. It also validated its existence via a collective critical consciousness, a historical awareness that today was different from yesterday. This is not to say that the Spinners' Club did not also consider these political issues, but rather that the Spinners tended to put the music first (they were extremely good performers) and a rather wistful invocation of place concerning Liverpool's (often nautical) past was evoked: it was all far less conspicuous that the polemics proposed by the Calton Three. Geoff Speed also recalls:

> That issue about clubs beginning in the '60s is true; my club [the Howff] started in 1963 and ran for about four years and I don't recall much of anything else around before this club – there might have been but I don't recall. It was John Kanneen. There was the Calton Three with John, Jim Peadon and Shirley his wife. But basically there were two clubs. Stan Ambrose and the Spinners were never altogether friendly towards each other, as I remember. Stan later became involved at the Cattle Market in Liverpool and then the Bothy in Southport. (*ibid*)

Only one member of the Spinners, Hughie Jones, was born in the city of Liverpool and despite their line-up including Cuban-born Cliff Hall, folk music in Liverpool tended to be a site of white activity, with many such activists even hailing from out-with the city. Notwithstanding the revivalists' obvious sympathies for music as a racially unified expression, it remained largely whitened on Merseyside by large proportions of non-Merseysiders. This can possibly be explained by three somewhat underdeveloped discussions during this time: firstly of how racialized folk music categories did not essentially give Black people a voice unless they were prepared to connect with authenticity stereotypes of slavery and acoustic blues. Secondly, how the political Left failed to consciously address their own presentations of cultural mediation – blithely discussing issues such as 'national music' 'lost cultures and jobs' and (say) English 'heritage' in the face of inward migration, and thirdly how the cultural momentum of folk music as the music of the 'other' failed to deal with the realities of Black British experience, i.e. that the bourgeois middle-classes rejection of systems to which Black British youth aspired appeared, for the latter, deeply patronizing and redolent of the class system it seemed to oppose.

Activity

Concurrent with the establishment of both the Spinners and the Calton clubs was the Howff in Widnes town centre – a short bus or train ride away from Liverpool. This club was also visited by this writer and for him it became a watermark by which others were judged. The Howff was run by Geoff Speed, a middle-class ex-grammar schoolboy from one of Widnes' leading families involved in the electrical engineering business. This latter expertise tended to mean that one could find better technology at the Howff. Some performances were even recorded on Geoff Speed's precious portable reel-to-reel. There is, in fact, still a splendid recording of Hedy West at the Howff in 1965; sadly one does not exist of Paul Simon's performance a year previously (Simon wrote 'Homeward Bound' at the time of his Widnes appearance).

The music at the Howff tended to be different again. Geoff Speed was and remains a great connoisseur of American music and so there was a distinct, identifiable strand of US folk and even at times a little blues and jazz music in the Howff that was not always reflected elsewhere. In this case the presence of the club involved on-going explorations and they were not rooted within specific geographical/historical inheritances. Furthermore, unlike at some other clubs there did not appear to be a strict hierarchical structure. There were few, if any, connections with the Critic's Group and Singers' Club in London therefore 'music policy', as dictated by this self-appointed clique, was not strictly adhered to. It was generally agreed that the cultural space occupied by the Howff could include a wide range of musical practices, co-existing and interacting across diverse pathways. This contrasted strongly with a club I also visited on several occasions in Liverpool city centre at the Criterion pub. This club was, I think, run by Frank McCall and was strictly demarcated and disciplined, at least in a 'folk' way. It was certainly not considered to be mainstream entertainment and was more akin to an educational experience – albeit an enjoyable one. Singers were often unaccompanied, and material was frequently based around Irish and Scottish traditional music. In this case, support of the Criterion equated with a perception of involvement with a different, possibly older form of communality so that the 'carrying of a tradition', rather than a performance *per se* constituted the realistic historical continuity. This was not something (as I remember) that was outspokenly articulated at the Criterion although as Ruth Finnegan suggests in her work on the folk worlds of Milton Keynes (1989) ideas such as these can be largely implicit rather than a fully formed articulated ideology and rather vague soundbites such as 'pastoral' or 'traditional' and whether a song has passed into 'oral tradition' are frequently used.

In the Criterion the search for a folk culture was a predetermined and fixed act. Unlike perhaps at the Howff the rediscovery of this identity involved a mythical, backwards-looking return to sources. This certainly ran the risk of producing a static view of origins and acted as a spur to separatism and although the evenings were largely fun, they were also intrinsically ritualistic. This direction, of course held some force, for music interpreters still need reminding that the here and now is not always of primary importance to the music adherent. While a signifying community does need to expand its horizons, it also needs to recall previous contexts, musical and social struggles and the like. It undoubtedly remains important to have a sense of perpetuity in eras of change. Even if the sense of a music 'being old' is in itself a reconstruction, this can add a value of longevity. However, one might suggest that this was an 'activity' at the Criterion (and that those involved were 'activists') rather than a 'scene', *per se*. So, folk clubs such as the Criterion provided visible attestations that society can learn from musical substrata. For this writer, who was in his late teens at the time the Criterion was being run, the club provided an enduring image and presence; but, to repeat, it was merely one manifestation of folk music on Merseyside among many others.

Clubs were not the only visible attestation of interest in musical traditions across Merseyside. There were several folk events in the 1960s that spoke of the importance of regional and national networking. One of these was the Liverpool Folk Festival of 1964, a unique British folk event – one of the very first British folk festivals held away from Cecil Sharp House (and a full eight months before the first Cambridge Festival). On 31 October 1964 the historic Bluecoat Chambers in Liverpool was host to an event co-organized by the English Folk Dance and Song Society. It was an all-day affair and those appearing were an eclectic mix. Firstly the Black Diamonds Folk Group (they were partly based in Liverpool but hosted an important club in Chester), and their young fiddler Gerry Pugh (from St Helens), were well-respected for their club nights and were at the populist end of the folk revival. Andy Kenner was also a local folk club luminary at the singer/songwriter end of the folk continuum, and the Liverpool Ceili Band were about to become recording artists in their own right, signed by Rex later that year. They were already reigning All-Ireland Ceili champions and featured at least two virtuosos in Sean McNamara and Eamon Coyne. There were others, too (mostly floor singers from around the various clubs in Liverpool), and the entire concert was recorded on behalf of the EFDSS by Lynsound, a local one-man recording outfit from Wallasey. So successful was the day that the EFDSS issued an LP 'The Liverpool Folk Festival' available from Cecil Sharp House, their headquarters in London. Over 40 years later the sound of this music remains fascinating.

Most of the album consists of genuinely entertaining pieces of music history and each track represents folk music in action at a crucial time in the history of both the British folk revival itself and the Liverpool of the 1960s. Furthermore, as representations of folk music performance from the mid-60s, they remain stylistically intriguing. The singing and playing styles from the festival are a little incongruous and in the vocalizing (in phrasing if not in accuracy) an element of Peter Peers can even be detected. The lack of 'Travis' or 'clawhammer' guitar styles are highly noticeable (instead we have 'Spanish' or classically-orientated ripple playing), and a pounding piano accompanies the Liverpool Ceili band. Of course, the piano featured for years in many ceili bands – yet these days such bands are considered to be string bands in the conventional sense and seldom use a piano. Geoff Speed brings to mind:

> the event well – the EFDSS had an office in the Bluecoat Chambers and it was at the Bluecoat that it took place. There were workshops during the day and a concert at night. It was recorded and an LP came out. The piano didn't make a great deal of difference to people then, but yes it does sound odd these days. There were two LPs for Rex – probably aimed at the Irish market as much as anything, but good albums. As for the guitar playing, I don't think the American influence had penetrated by that time too much, so guitar styles were different and perhaps even a bit classical or Spanish. Not what you would expect to hear at all, these days. (Speed to Brocken, February 2009)

Another significant event – on this occasion attended by this writer – was the Merseyside Folk Meet at Wallasey Civic Hall in early 1969. This was an odd mixture of renowned folkies such as the Yetties from Dorset and Hector Gilchrist (the 'Cornish Nightingale') being joined by a few local and regional folk bands such as the Black Diamonds and Union Folk. The day consisted of performances, workshops and lectures, and represented an important phase of regional and national networking. It was, as I remember, a far from perfect day, being somewhat generically bound via the maintenance of a rather politicized musical demarcation (perhaps a little dull for a teenager) and this tended to create an uncalled-for tension between tradition and entertainment. But the Yetties, in particular were well-received as markers of both. The day stood as a signifier of musical co-operation, something from which all popular music can benefit. It was also a day that displayed folk music's capacity to draw attention to what Sara Cohen describes as 'Music's peculiar ability to affect or articulate mood, atmosphere, emotion etc and to consequently trigger the imagination'. This, she continues 'contributes to people's experiences of places and attitudes towards them, and this occurs in a multitude of different ways and contexts […] Music thus constitutes a focus or frame for social practice, and it establishes, maintains, transforms social relations, playing a role in the social construction of place' (Cohen, 1997:10-11).

Although now somewhat hidden as a musical force by the ravages of time itself, these contact points of the folk scene on Merseyside in the late-1960s displayed the potential to articulate and problematize the apparent oppositions of musical artifice versus musical veracity. This debate still has important consequences for any musical criticism concerned with how to position musical texts as forces for change. One might suggest that such activity constituted a 'scene', for debates of this kind are vital (and noticeable by their absence in the twenty-first century). However whether such activists are also scene-makers is another issue. In some cases, musical activism has nothing to do with scenes, but rather tries to persuade people to directly change their listening practices. Therefore if a given historical manifestation of musical authenticity is postulated, then a broadening of creative space required by a scene is effectively denied (perhaps growth and development follows the establishment of a critical consciousness).

There were other such events: folk days were established at St George's Hall (Fred Jordan sang at one), another was held at the Adelphi Hotel. There were educational sessions here and there concerning dance and song supported by the EFDSS which (as Geoff Speed states) held offices at the Bluecoat Chambers in School Lane. John Kanneen taught weekly folk music classes at the Roscommon Institute, and a Merseyside Traditional Music Club opened at Forbes House. There is no doubt that such folk music-related activity in Liverpool epitomized the bourgeois aesthetics of the day, but it did not, to paraphrase Bourdieu, have 'nothing to say'. Folk's appeal was that it was not morally agnostic. Geoff Speed recalls that for him:

> There was a social awareness. When I came into folk music I was pleased to see that the people were opinionated, worried about what was happening with industry in the UK, others involved with the unions: things that you could put your teeth into. It drew people in. I include myself in that even though I was working in a commercial family company – a 'pricklish' position, probably. Maybe that's part of the secret: those who are in a relatively privileged position have the time to think about it. So the revolution would never have happened because it would have had to have come from the middle classes – and that was never going to happen. So I was drawn to the scene because it had opinions about things – not all of which I subscribed to but most of the time opinions were important in the folk scene. So that music was linked to issues about America and its treatment of Black people, or issues to do with the rather unbridled technological advances of society. There were many such issues that the folk scene faced head on, as it were, and I liked that very much. (Speed to Brocken, February, 2009)

BBC Radio Merseyside's 'Folk Scene'

By 1968 BBC Radio Merseyside's *Folk Scene* programme had become a major agent for the dissemination of folk music on Merseyside. In fact one might state that this local programme codified all of the disparate activities into a recognizable entity. Stan Ambrose was selected as 'the voice of local folk music' and his drawing together of these incongruent diachronic musical and social strands immediately gave voice to the concept that there existed one singular scene. It was an illusion, but one that had an important social function. Together with Geoff

Speed, Ambrose brought together performers for broadcasting purposes, rather than simply featuring folkclubs *in situ*. For example, at 'Le Masque' on Clarence Street, Geoff Speed and Stan Ambrose organized eclectic sessions representing both blues and folk music. Jim James and Raphael Callaghan, a blues duo from the Sefton area of Merseyside and regulars at the Bothy Club, played alongside Jim Peadon and John Kanneen of the Calton Three and Harry Boardman from Manchester – the latter said to have started one of the very first folk clubs in the country. Geoff Speed:

> I suppose it shows how important the *Folk Scene* progamme was. Jim James and Raphael Callaghan were very blues-based. Solidly blues, in fact, but I don't think they ever had a blues club as such. It wasn't popular enough for a club to exist just for blues. They were on a compilation album of British blues called *Gasoline* that was recorded by Liberty. I think it was at the time that Alexis Korner was on Liberty [*A New Generation of Blues,* Liberty LBL83147, 1968] and he was involved. It was a one-off album. R&B never seemed to take off in Liverpool and although the duo had 'soul', I never saw them with an electric guitar. We set up those events at the Masque for broadcasting – a splendid place to record in and we invited an audience. It was a BBC job and worked really well. (*ibid*)

Ambrose and Speed also visited clubs in Kirkby and Runcorn run by Willy Russell (who briefly had a group called the Kirkby Four). At the Tuning Fork club in Chester, Martin Carthy and Dave Swarbrick, before their respective ventures into folk-rock, were recorded in-session by Speed and Ambrose for *Folk Scene* in 1968. A raucously live ceili at the Traveller's Rest in St Helens featuring Florrie Brennan and Cahil McConnell was also recorded and broadcast. At the Hare & Hounds pub in Commutation Row in Liverpool Irish music sessions featuring Sean McCarthy (who had enjoyed an Irish hit record with 'Step It Out Mary'), Bruce Scott and Frank Coran were also broadcast in 1969. Ambrose and Speed set up a special Boxing Day edition of Folk Scene in 1968 where the King's Shilling, clog dancer Rosemary Davies, Andy Kenner and Willie Russell were all recorded performing (in the case of Russell, a self-penned Christmas monologue 'Sam O'Shanker').

Goings-on at the Irish Centre on Mount Pleasant, began to catch the attention of those interested in learning instrumental tuition and playing sessions. Geoff Speed remembers recording Bruce Scott there on several occasions: 'he sang at the Irish Centre. There was a strong Irish thing going on, and it was much more relaxed than some clubs, of course sessions would take place'. Indeed the 'Oily Joe's' club in Oil Street regularly featured Irish material and here an Irish penny whistler who worked on the ferries would, after a shift, entertain the members. This 'tradition' was frequently interspersed by a wide variety of music, humorous poems, and monologues. Renowned author Brian Jacques, who began his performing life as a member of the Liverpool Fishermen shanty group, would frequently perform spoken-word material at Oily Joe's. Geoff Speed also recorded a monumental evening at the Irish Centre in May 1971 featuring stalwarts of the centre's traditional music experience such as Ann McPartlan, Billy O'Reagan, Andy O'Hanlan, Bridget Hayden and Sean Macnamara. Speed's recordings remain of great historical value to the history of Liverpool's performance-past. The *Folk Scene* programme was truly a landmark programme and undoubtedly united disparate entities into a perceptible whole – perhaps not as a 'scene' as such, but certainly as a 'reading' of a scene. As a consequence of *Folk Scene*'s impact on the airwaves of Merseyside in the late-1960s innumerable young Liverpudlians, such as myself, were attracted towards folk music. Currently folk music exists in a state of radio semi-exile, mostly 'confined' to BBC local radio. But in the era shortly after BBC local radio began (1967), these very same systems, so popular prior to the advent of ILR in 1973, helped to facilitate a boom in folk music participation. It is not co-incidental that the peak period for folk music in this country (between, say, the late-1960s and the mid-1970s) was concurrent with peak listening figures for BBC local radio. So popular was folk music on Merseyside, that when Radio City began in 1974, this station immediately established a folk music programme in their schedules – presented by Bob Buckle.

Leesiders

At the Central Hotel, Birkenhead the Leesiders held court for those interested in hearing visiting guests, a little bluegrass banjo, and old-timey guitar *a la* Doc Watson (the famous blind guitarist actually appeared at Jacquie and Bridie's club at the Mill Street Mission in Liverpool). The Leesiders were a Wirral-based ('across the water') duo, and probably opened the first folk club on the Wirral in 1963. By 1966 they were already recording and had become fully professional. Bob Buckle and Pete Douglas were regular contributors to several BBC Radio shows such as 'Night Ride', usually broadcasting from the Oxford Road, Manchester studios. The Leesider's sound was very accessible and they were popular in-concert attractions. Indeed, Bob Buckle later went solo and enjoyed sell-out concerts at the Little Theatres across Birkenhead and Wallasey for several years. By 1970 the Leesiders were recording for Birmingham-based Ash Records and selling copious amounts of albums on their travels. This writer was fortunate enough to have been taught guitar styles by Bob Buckle, and Bob's methodical approach to US fingerpicking methods still looms large to this day. Buckle's folk clubs across Wirral became traditions in their own right and unlike the quasi poeticizing at the Criterion were more akin to what Niall MacKinnon (1993) describes as linking to a cohesive and coherent aura of 'cosiness'. Buckle's folk clubs were able to revive and cultivate a resistant, identity-giving culture, but also existed within MacKinnon's culturally secluded comfort zone.

This aura of comfort reflected the suburban fringes of Merseyside in the early-1970s and this cultural and geographic topography changed the acceptable musical parameters of folk clubs. As a regular folkie at this time, and also moving with my family from Liverpool to Birkenhead in 1971, it was immediately apparent to me that many of the folk music adherents were somewhat semi-detached. Many came from new development areas and were in jobs such as teachers, council officers with a few predictable social workers. On the Wirral this manifested itself though the music. The folk ideology that I came across resembled Ruth Finnegan's idea of 'the intellectual perceptions of certain scholars and collectors' being filtered through an educated refraction. Finnegan stated re her findings in Milton Keynes that 'If any of the local music worlds could be regarded as "middle class" it would be that of folk music […] those operating mainly on the folk club and folk festival circuit [were] often well educated, professional and middle-aged with few teenage adherents' (Finnegan, 1989:68). This was never more apparent than in folk clubs in West Kirkby, Parkgate, Neston, New Ferry and Chester, but it would be wrong to think that the music in each of these towns was similar. The clubs were established along specific musical lines (after all, who would want to visit a variety of clubs to hear ostensibly the same stuff?) and most invited guests from across the UK. But it would be accurate to state that the *ambience* in each club resembled each other and that this, in turn, affected the sound of the music. Geoff Speed agrees with both MacKinnon and Finnegan:

> Demographics did play a part – new suburban estates often led to folk clubs appearing on the outskirts of Liverpool. The ambience was similar, a bit comfy – yes that's true. A very high percentage of those involved were either teachers or social workers. Clubs would close for the summer break in the way schools would break up for the summer break – it was linked to their status in society. It's true of the folk scene. (Speed to Brocken, February, 2009)

Most clubs were also united by an anti-amplification policy and universally decreed what styles could and could not be performed. In this way, Finnegan's (1989) idea of using 'worlds' rather than 'scenes' to describe folk music activity in Milton Keynes in 1989 also appears accurate for Merseyside in the early-1970s by suggesting an encapsulating, exclusive and rather isolated environment. Geoff Speed concurred, stating: 'Yes, looking back this appears to be a good way of describing matters. I still use the word "scene" to this day, but perhaps "world" is better because it also suggests that these places were self-contained, as it were; which many of them were, as I recall. I think Ruth Finnegan is correct when she talks of "worlds".' However, while Finnegan also suggested that Milton Keynes folkies were a small and select minority, there were substantial amounts of people involved on the Wirral: far greater, one suspects than the current folk happenings in the same areas.

In fact one might even argue that the folk music 'worlds' on Merseyside and Deeside were of great importance and highly influential because they attracted several thousand people. Geoff Speed speaks of these days with great pride and affection:

All of the time clubs were popping-up. I was looking at the local folk directory for 1972 the other day which was co-published by the EFDDS and the clubs listed in it are those registered within the Merseyside and Deeside Branch. Just listen to this:

On a Sunday there were 11 clubs, Mon 16, Tues 11, Wed 9, Thurs 9, Friday 4, and Saturday 4: somewhere around 64 clubs all-together. This was around the peak of things in the early 1970s. A lot of these clubs would be very different. The Golden Lion in Rainford, the Bothy in Southport, Bull and Stirrup in Chester, the Toplock run by Willy Russell and John Kannean, with Jim Peadon in Runcorn. Then there was the Pez Espada in Temple Street – where the 'Merseysippis' previously played. There was one 'offshore' club based in Laxy, there was a club at the 'Poly' in Tithebarn Street, also each one in Wrexham and Warrington; one in Ellesmere Port – the 'Penny Farthing' – and then the 'Oldest Profession' in Wigan. And these were just EFDSS clubs; many others came and went and there were also sessions at places like the Irish Centre. But to say that they were part of one scene would be misleading. They were largely different clubs run by different people some interested in different sounds. There were identifiable strands but even the heavier clubs still weren't really part of the Singers Club-style of club; that seemed to be more in Lancashire.

Clubs always existed on a shoestring. If you were getting bums on seat then you could get guests. They would cost £15-20 – Paul Simon cost me £12. (Speed to Brocken, February, 2009)

Perhaps one might argue that by the late-1960s, there were broadly two folk music camps on Merseyside. To begin with, one based around the populist aesthetics of the Spinners, who were by this time also achieving national prominence and were increasingly spending more time away from the locality. They even produced their own 'what's on' magazine, entitled *Spin*. The aforementioned Leesiders, featuring Bob Buckle were the Spinners' successors and when not performing all over the country, they tended to concentrate their club activities on the Wirral. The Leesiders also toured the UK and Europe and regularly took part in song competitions in East Germany. In the other camp were organizers of such clubs as the Bothy. The Bothy club is still based just outside Southport and became one of the leading folk club venues in the 1970s and did so by presenting itself as the bastion of authentic folk culture. But in addition were myriad small ventures that served very specific musical, ideological and geographical needs – from Irish sessions, to unaccompanied singing, to drama-style monologues and all points in between. One's engagement with these folk 'scenes' demanded great commitment: not only to the music, but also to the structural hierarchies and ideological functions surrounding the uses of that music. Ultimately any music 'scene' comes to be shaped not simply from within, but by the musical, ideological and social perimeter ropes under strain from both sides. Popular music perspectives tend to acknowledge these tensions as positive, but this is not always the case from a folk music perspective; thus music at the borders tends to get lost if it does not have a powerful discourse.

The Bothy

The Bothy Club effectively began in Liverpool in 1964. Four people: Tony Wilson, Stan Ambrose, Dave Boardman and Christine Jones (the original Bothy Folk Group) came together in order to run a folk club locally – but with a difference. Ambrose, in particular, had been around the Liverpool folk scene for some time and was rather dismayed that floor singing was being overlooked by the increasing amount of guests being imported into the clubs – an ideological issue, to be sure. So the original idea was to make it a club where solo singers got a fair chance to showcase their talents. *Liverpool Daily Post*'s David Charters recorded in 2007: 'Strangely, the idea for the Bothy Folk Club arose in The Cavern, Mathew Street, Liverpool, in the early 1960s, the zenith of the beat boom. But some "Cave-dwellers" fondly remembered how, in its early days, the cellar was home to jazz and skiffle (really just folk music speeded-up).' Stan Ambrose also recalled in the above interview with Charters:

> I suppose The Cavern was our womb really, The Spinners were on when we were plotting our own folk club. We were all individual singers, doing our own thing at folk clubs. We weren't getting a very good deal at folk clubs because they tended to be run by groups. So we had the idea of running a club for individual singers. Eventually, people started to see us as a group anyway, so we abandoned the idea of being individuals and became a group. (Ambrose to Charters, 2007)

The Cattle Market Folk Club on Prescot Road, Liverpool was therefore inaugurated and the informal 'bothy' concept, one that had featured at the Calton sessions, was further developed. By the time the decision was made to open a Southport club the group had already gained a good reputation for their club nights at the Cattle Market. A hunt for premises in Southport followed and the club ran for several weeks at the now-demolished Railway Hotel on Chapel Street and then settled at the Blundell Arms. It was eventually decided that running two clubs, in addition to performing at other venues, was too difficult for the residents, so the Cattle Market club was abandoned. By this time Liverpool had many clubs, but Southport none.

Changes occurred when Christine Jones left the group to concentrate on raising her young family, and Dave Boardman left for Jamaica. The King's Shilling became the resident group but after a promising opening spell audiences dropped off. Thus, in September 1969 local Sefton and Southport-based artists were given the opportunity to come in: Kevin Littlewood, Jim and Raphael, The Dalesmen, Frank Sellors, plus a returning Stan Ambrose formed among others a strong band of residents. Lifetime member and singer Frank Sellors recalled on the club website his first night at the Bothy:

> I arrived early on the opening night only to find a huge crowd all waiting to be 'processed' by Godfrey, who was seated at a table outside the room where the club was held. I had been waiting to sign-in for what seemed like ages when the soon to become familiar strains of 'Barnyards' started up. I already knew the song via a recording by Alex Campbell but I was most impressed with Tony Wilson's version, even through the closed door. When I got into the club it was packed. It was the first time that I had been to a folk club and I sat with some friends who had persuaded me to join their Peter, Paul and Mary style folk group. At the interval I asked Stan Ambrose if our group, The Everglades could do a floor spot but he said that the Bothy Singers wanted to do the whole evening as a way of introducing themselves to the Southport folkies. Even though my all-consuming passion in those days was for the contemporary folk songs of Bob Dylan, I was enchanted by the Bothy Singers' performance. I loved Tony Wilson's virile shanties, Stan's wonderful music-hall songs, Dave Boardman's ballads and Chris Jones' banjo work. That first evening was somewhat of a magical experience for me and I looked forward to the following week's session. (Sellors, www.bothy.co.uk, accessed 28 December 2008)

The Bothy Folk Club became so significant across the region that by August 1968 it was also running late-evening folk concerts at the Everyman Theatre in Liverpool and contributing personnel to the aforementioned evenings at the Masque. In the process, Stan Ambrose had become the voice of folk music radio on BBC Radio Merseyside – a position he still holds to this day, sharing the ether with the redoubtable Geoff Speed.

Records

As with the country music scene, however, very few of these artists were ever recorded to any great extent. While probably all of them were recorded for broadcasting purposes by Geoff Speed and Stan Ambrose at one stage or another (and this music is archived) with the notable exception of the Spinners not one major record label ever came calling. The Spinners recorded for Topic and HMV before signing a lucrative deal with Philips and appearing on their Fontana subsidiary for many years. However others were not so fortunate and of all of the Merseyside-based folk musicians only Bob Buckle and Jacquie and Bridie recorded with any enduring regularity – and Buckle's albums were point-of sale items and not easy to find in shops. Both as a Leesider and on his own Buckle recorded several albums and an EP for the Birmingham-based Ash label, which also handled Indian music under the moniker of Zella. Recordings were mostly made in Birmingham and then pressed on demand. The Black Diamonds Folk Group was recorded by

Geoff Speed and one Studio Republic album resulted (Studio Republic specialized in one-off albums). Speed also recorded the Bs Band from Parkgate (Bryan and Barbara Bonnett) and the King's Shilling from the Bothy Club. The Bs Band recordings also resulted in a Studio Republic LP, but nothing came of the King's Shilling sessions. Jim James and Raphael Callaghan were included on the aforesaid UK Blues compilation released by Liberty, and several live recordings were made at the Bothy club, but not commercially released.

Jacqueline Macdonald, originally hailing from the northeast of England, began her folk life as female singer with the Spinners, staying with the group for three years, before leaving in 1963. She made several recordings over the years with her singing partner Wrexham-born Bridie O'Donnell. They recorded one single for Fontana in 1964 ('Roses'/'Roving Jack') and another single 'Come Me Little Son' and 'We Only Needed Time' was recorded for Irish-owned Major Minor in 1968, but their peak period of sales came in the late-1960s when two albums *The Perfect Round* GAL4009 and *Next Time Round* GAL4010 (the latter a live recording) were recorded for the Norfolk-based Galliard label. A single to celebrate the opening of the Metropolitan Cathedral was also released: 'Cathedral in Our Time' and 'Lord of the Dance'. Galliard was a small independent label and after an advertising campaign in the folk press (*English Dance and Song*, *Folk News* and the *Folk Scene* etc.) brisk sales ensued on the expanding folk network. Jacquie and Bridie, like all folkies in the late-1960s, sold albums wherever they happened to play, but so high was their profile on Merseyside that most local record shops also stocked the two Galliard albums, thus their recorded work was never difficult to find locally. Another album (*Hello Friend*) was cut for the Scotland-based Nevis label in the mid-1970s but, following this they tended to record sporadically before Bridie's untimely death. Musically they were renowned for their performance of Stan Kelly's 'Liverpool Lullaby', a song made famous by Cilla Black on the b-side of her 1969 hit single 'Conversations'.

At her clubs at various venues across Liverpool, Jacqueline provided performance opportunities for such varied performers as Fred Jordan, Doc Watson, Ewan MacColl and Peggy Seeger, Martin Carthy, Barbara Dixon, Peter Bellamy, The Corries, The Johnsons, Don Partridge, Tim Hart and Maddie Prior, and even Phil Ochs. This writer remembers the Coffee House in Wavertree as perhaps the best of these venues, having a large, friendly concert room with ample space for a few hundred folkies. However Jacquie and Bridie are probably best-remembered, locally, for their many concerts at the Liverpool Philharmonic Hall. Some were exclusively folk concerts, whereas others were mixtures of genres such as folk and country music. Along with Bridie, Jacqueline also hosted a live chat show on BBC Radio Merseyside for seven years and it was during this time that her material came to reflect the more eclectic folk-meets-country traditions well established in Liverpool by artists such as Billy Maher, Hank Walters and Don Woods.

Billy Maher seldom if ever played folk clubs, preferring instead what he saw as 'less pretentious' working men's clubs and cabaret lounges, and Walters and Woods were effectively country singers, but all three, on different occasions, tended to include 'folk-style' material in their acts. Maher in particular, as a member of the popular Jacksons group tended to write and play interesting commercial and comedic variations of folk music that enjoyed far greater levels of local popularity than those demarcated by the somewhat musically uncompromising folk clubs. Thus, while he never considered himself to be 'authentic' in the more purist folk sense, he did succeed in drawing people who would not be 'seen dead' in a folk club towards Liverpool's older forms of popular music. Maher's group the Jacksons recorded for Alan Richards' Stag Music (see on) and also released EPs under their own point-of-sale imprint 'Flowerpot Records'.

This mingling of folk (in this case mostly Irish) traditions with local popular traditions is an area of interest for popular music historians for it occurs in most major cities across the UK and also tends to manifest itself in narratives of nostalgia. Billy Maher's repertoire included a song entitled 'Double Thick Marmalade Butty' which was celebrated locally and the Jacksons' routine also included a medley of old-time children's street songs. The late Pete McGovern, host of the Wash House folk club at Sampson and Barlow's had loved Marty Robbins' country record 'Strawberry Roan' and, in the best folk music tradition, he purloined the melody for perhaps one of Liverpool's most renowned anthems 'In My Liverpool Home' in 1961. Glyn Hughes' song 'Whiskey on a Sunday' was also a feature of both the Jacksons' and Bob Buckle's acts. Buckle also included a little folk-comedy and nostalgia material. Lee Brennan ostensibly from the country music scene created several such narratives of nostalgia and released an album's worth in the mid-'70s. Comedian Tom O'Connor worked with ace guitarist Brendan McCormick as comedic folk duo: 'Tom and Brennie', and performed several such songs: to begin with on the folk circuit and later in cabaret. Bob Pride, resident at the Mons Hotel 'Hainault' folk club, would also regularly perform folk-comedy numbers. We could conceivably compare this musical phenomenon with other growing nostalgia quotients of the 1960s and 1970s such as the popularity of family history: it was part of a search for a more personal tradition via remembrances of idealized childhoods and nostalgia for long-dead relatives and work patterns.

Crofters

By the late-1960s, and in the absence of both the Spinners and the Leesiders, the Crofters were probably the most popular Liverpool folk group working locally. The group were previously members of the Liverpool Anglican Cathedral Choir and, as such, their harmonies were conspicuously exact. They held court at several clubs throughout the 1960s and 1970s but are perhaps best well-known for their residency at the 'Clubship Landfall', a rather decrepit former Royal Navy vessel that had previously landed on the beaches of Normandy on D-Day. 'Landfall' was originally moored at the Canning Half-Tide dock but was then moved to one of the north-end docks: the Collingwood on Regent Road. It was a club largely notable during its lifetime for its 'over-25s' policy and sported three different well-appointed bars. Here the Crofters tended to convey a good-natured and relaxed atmosphere. The Crofters performed a lot of contemporary material which at times contrasted with more overtly 'traditional' material one might find in the more traditional clubs based in the pubs of Liverpool's city centre. From this writer's experience it was noticeable that there sometimes appeared more women in the club than one might usually find in a folk club elsewhere. Even as late as 1974 Bradley and Fenwick found that 90 per cent of women interviewed stated that they would not enter a pub on their own. In the Liverpool of the late-1960s and early-1970s females did not tend to regularly attend folk clubs on their own and were often accompanied by a male. At the 'Clubship Landfall', however – which also operated as a night club – the atmosphere did not replicate those of the inner city pubs and so a different gender balance was palpable. This might have been as a consequence of the musical material and the ambience of the venue – both somewhat 'at odds' with the historically masculine character of a city centre pub backroom and the traditional nature of the folk material performed.

The Crofters cut a number of tracks for the CAM record company and two moderate selling EPs: *Four From The Crofters* and *Four More From The Crofters* (CAM 21/22) emerged. These tracks on both EPs also featured on their one CAM point-of-sale LP. The Crofters were not outwardly Christian in that they did not evangelize via their music, but as former choir boys of the Anglican Cathedral, they did tend to be associated with the Christian ethics that converged with the moral tone of the folk revival and they regularly sang Sydney Carter and Jeremy Taylor songs. Several folk evenings, some involving the Crofters, took place in the Metropolitan Cathedral crypt in the late-1960s and early-1970s. Due to all of these factors (and more), for a brief period of time they were perhaps one of the most well-known folk groups on Merseyside. They continued to perform well into the next decade and were also occasionally captured in session by BBC Radio Merseyside's Geoff Speed.

Summary

The multitude of soundtracks that came to represent Liverpool's folk music 'scene' cannot all be recorded. But they were certainly not all bound by the social and musical definitions that were laid down at the more prescriptive folk clubs, or indeed by the dictums passed down by the EFDSS. From the work of the Spinners on the one hand, to Jim James and even to Tom O'Connor on the other, myriad interchangeable forms came to develop, and the strength of this musical activity on Merseyside eventually came to support the continued existence of folk clubs, while at the same time question continuation. Many folk club audiences in Liverpool during the peak time for folk music in the late-1960s and early-1970s tended to project into their clubs particular needs, wants and desires, often the kinds of musical fantasies that gratified their 'folk' senses. This of course happened across the wide spectrum of popular music activity, but in the case of folk music it did perhaps become problematic when such projections were regarded as genuine authorizations. The past was made more vivid, but by doing so it was re-presented, re-written and probably polished-up. On the Wirral Peninsula, it tended to be domesticated and semi-detached, made safe as it was rescued, removed, restored and rearranged to suit people's contemporary lifestyles as well as their function myths.

In Liverpool and Southport representations of identity and ideology via authenticity were overt; in some cases 'pure' culture was mythologized, and made intrinsic with the clubs themselves. Some clubs represented musical, social and political fundamentalism, others even a benign Christian ethic. In all cases folk networks were structures of mythologized resistance. Dave Harker points out that the very title of Lloyd's 1944 work *The Singing Englishman* was 'redolent of the Anglo-centred and masculine attitudes still common on the British left' and such gender issues were evident as a rather patriarchal attitude subsumed some clubs. But these attitudes were also part of institutional and collective practices established within the post-war era and had a great deal to do with the relationships between many living issues, such as suburban growth, the upward mobility of the middle-classes, and the development of a left-thinking, largely male-dominated, educated bourgeoisie. Certainly the dynamic 'embryonic signifying community' that Barry Shank qualifies as a scene in his work does not appear to be attributable to the folk network in and around the Merseyside of the 1960s and 1970s and, although there were many dimensions to folk signification, it is questionable whether these necessarily fused into a recognizable scene. As a consequence folk music on Merseyside has been somewhat lost in time and exists as a partially-hidden history because it did not essentially 'hang together'.

There are still folk clubs on Merseyside and for some the club has been a hugely successful invention. Lovers of tradition have their proof beyond objective validation that the folk club works and creates a scene. But the job of the folk club has also been one of a pedagogic force, a moral force, a cultural force. Perhaps the 'cosy' environment is a step towards an equally cosy netherworld where instead of actually representing a community, the club is curled in on itself rather like a fossil. Within the short period of time between the opening of the first folk clubs in Liverpool and the end of the decade, considerable changes in musical definitions had taken place and the inter-relationship of different musical spaces became productive for both hybrids and 'traditions'. But this fluidity between generic differences did not as a rule happen in Liverpool's folk clubs and folk music activists expected popular music-lovers to come over to the folk oeuvre, as if 'enlightened'. This chapter has used the word 'activist' on several occasions, but not the expression 'transformational activism'. This expression suggests that people are required to change on the inside in order to create any meaningful change in the outside world. Concerns for personal rights, and willingness to become involved in risky actions is one thing; but a willingness to reconstruct one's *a priori* ideas of authenticity is something else, entirely.

The very presence of BBC Radio Merseyside's *Folk Scene* programme as a conduit and a codifier certainly requires greater historical acknowledgement, for it represented difference and drew together distinct musical entities of folk music practice on Merseyside. Perhaps we should actually award more importance to all forms of broadcast media, but particularly radio, in the annals of folk music history. Geoff Speed:

> I think a lot of it has to do with radio and radio producers. Maybe the 'blame' for all this should lie more squarely with the radio. It's amazing when I think back to an interview I had with Lonnie: Guthrie and Leadbelly always get mentioned. Perhaps people did hear it on the radio at times. I tend not to subscribe to the idea of not giving the BBC credit. Where would you find a Leadbelly album in the 1950s? Would not people have heard this material on the radio though Donegan or Lomax? It is difficult to contemplate that people would just 'come cross' the work of Leadbelly in the UK without being directed to it. (Speed to Brocken, February, 2009)

Growing to adulthood under a BBC 'Light Music' umbrella created value systems that pervaded even within a framework of so-called non-conformity. The sounds offered up by (e.g.) the BBC in the mid-part of the twentieth century are difficult (nay impossible) to ignore. According to Geoff Speed's analysis of folk music reception, like any other form of popular music, folk was different only within the realms of similarity. On Merseyside folk music gathered sustenance from societal 'norms' and class-based values, including those surrounding and created within specific cultural geographies. Folk's inventions and its imaginings were actually integral to a number of British society's most certified manifestations. There is no such thing as impermeable music and no one 'world' (whether that be folk, rock, country, etc.) is any more authentic than another.

Chapter 8
Cabaret – reality amid the fake

I think that scholars could devote more time and published space to studying music constructed as 'bad' – or good. Why does the music industry champion one music rather than another? One kind of sound rather than another? One producer rather than another?

(Timothy D. Taylor, 2004:99)

Within the academic field of popular music studies the cabaret scene is seldom, if ever, discussed. The reasons for this are probably legion but might include a discourse that expresses disapproval of all forms of cabaret-style engagement as inauthentic. For example, a scene that is based around middle-of-the-road musical material, containing a lack of critical self-consciousness in performance, and displaying a willingness to bend to the requirements of a music policy determined by a venue or an agency has not readily attracted scholarship. Maybe the historical evidence to support cabaret's lack of popular music 'grace' does appear persuasive: not one artist having emerged from the UK cabaret scene, has ever been hailed as an album-oriented singer/songwriter, few have been considered virtuosos in a rock sense, and not one cabaret singer has joined the 'club' of rock, pop or folk meritocracy. Indeed a reverse process i.e. that when a popular singer falls from this 'grace' he or she 'ends-up' on the cabaret circuit (usually for the want of more authentic work) is usually the chosen linear narrative. This lack of attention might also suggest that political impulses still guide many popular music studies academics in that they feel less comfortable when confronted by the apparent bedrock realities of cabaret (entertainment, hard work = pleasure = money), rather than the poetic and altogether philosophical approaches of popular music as art for 'everyman'. Popular music studies academic Mike Jones states 'that's the point: cabaret's unexplored because it falls outside the canon. A chunk of popular music is censored by academics because it's not cool enough – in fact it's too popular – liked by people whom academics don't like!' (Jones to Brocken, 2009).

While popular music scholarship continues to write-off this area of activity as 'conformist', it has remained insufficiently attentive to the theoretical prerequisites of dealing with such issues of musical diversity and/or conformity. Popular music academic scholarship should be a continuous widening of spaces, with an ever-increasing quantity of interest topics. The demystification of cabaret cultures logically leads to the search for different perspectives outside the hegemonic space of popular music studies' 'first world' – rock music. Popular music studies pioneer David Horn agrees:

> It's evident that whilst admissible topics and areas have widened a lot in PMS, that process has not been wide enough to embrace cabaret. Plenty of reasons, no doubt, I think it may partly be an age thing – or rather an anti-middle-age thing – as well as an obvious preference for the 'cutting edge' in one field or another. There may even, God help us, be a class thing at work – lower middle class activities as opposed to the working men's clubs so beloved of Hoggart? The odd thing is that, in its way, cabaret could be seen as *anti*-establishment – if the establishment in this case is multi-national corporations, large venues, global tours, record contracts, format radio, even nowadays downloading. (David Horn, email correspondence, February 2009)

Although the acknowledgement of minority subcultures was a very important stepping stone for popular music studies in the 1970s (Stuart Hall, Dick Hebdige *et al*), the apparent eternalness of this cultural studies material as a place from which criticism, rather than investigation begins has tended to posit certain music scenes as lingering problems, rather than interesting discourses. This is a pity, for Stuart Hall in particular became one of the main proponents of reception theory. This focused on the scope for negotiation as well as opposition on the part of the audience, suggesting that an audience does not simply passively accept a text, and that an element of pro-activity occurs: each person negotiates the meaning of each text, with the meaning dependent upon the complex cultural background of each individual. Hall developed these ideas further in his model of encoding and decoding of media discourses. The meaning of any text lies somewhere between the producer and the reader and even though the producer encodes a text in a particular way, the reader may decode it with a slightly different approach, creating, to paraphrase Hall, a margin of understanding.

However in popular music studies, an illusion of academic durability via sub-cultural analysis has developed and, rather than recognizing Hall's theories as relatively inclusive, this illusion has succeeded only in condemning certain musical activities via a concentration upon 'authentic' social models of cultural capital (punk, dance, reggae, hip-hop, etc.). So the possibilities for cabaret club music being, as David Horn suggests, a critique of other forms of musical expression, is thus refuted. Large blocks of linear historical narratives and historically-situated social theories (such as the above) are delivered as indispensable, but this is surely not a robust enough paradigm by which to judge or ignore entire tracts of trustworthy popular music activity. Any discussion on cabaret venues or cabaret performers simply has to acknowledge, not only a continued popularity, but also a manifestation of multifaceted musical and social experience. For example, the cabaret 'scene' is not even a popular music scene in the 'PMS' conventional sense at all – it is (or was) frequently described by those involved as a 'circuit' and, as such, should attract far more attention from the popular music academic with an interest in understanding the pathways of commercial music.

Developed by those who made their livings booking and touring, music in a cabaret setting has always been produced and distributed within a contemporary context, whether that context be local or national. The progress of cabaret clubs in Liverpool was therefore measured and constructed though the work of agents, club-owners, concert secretaries and artists, who attempted to produce a commercial form of music that could reach and relate to a growing audience. Thus, any claims of in-authenticity for cabaret are already false in the sense that cabaret was a commercial re-articulation of musical elements already in circulation. Commerce was not imposed, but integral to both the commercial goals of the organizers and the artistic goals of artists, and the entire notion of a successful cabaret circuit in Liverpool rested on *bona fide* cultural and economic conditions existing at any given moment in time; these are substantive traditions indeed. Furthermore, cabaret activity in the post-WWII era in the UK became increasingly layered with alliances around universally-shared interests and identities. The cabaret circuit recognized the diversity of people's entertainment needs and experiences and was an authentic response to new and expanding ideas surrounding post-WWII city life and suburbia. This ought to attract from historians investigations surrounding convergence, contingency, social mobility, lifestyles and class positions. Cabaret in Liverpool is a distinctive signifier for consumption and social conventions – how could we have ignored this significant creative space for so long?

So, conducting research into not only the existence, but also the connotations of cabaret activity in Liverpool is vital for the popular music historian, for such enquiries help us to measure the authentic cultural pulse of a city such as Liverpool at key moments in its history. During the 1960s and 1970s, a number of popular music genres came to be recognized as intrinisic to noteworthy cultural discourses. But these were by and large rock and folk acknowledgements. Sadly, cabaret activity (and its accompanying networks), has seldom been identified as contributing to such collective meaning. Despite the authority of agency in the day-to-day running of the cabaret circuit, no single opinion or identity, no singular musical genre, no sound or instrumentation (despite the pervading 'keyboard' stereotypes), can be associated with cabaret. We can only gauge the success of cabaret by its immanence (it has not left us with much recorded material – and even this is largely unrepresentative). One underlying premise of understanding a cabaret circuit should be that while cabaret clubs did share common interests, facing, in the process common musical goals and enemies, such commonalities were by no means universal. Rather, the profile of each venue, each agent, performer, MC or concert secretary etc. was interlaced with differences, even with conflicts. Cabaret in Liverpool was most certainly made up from a *bricolage* of overlapping alliances, and was not one circumscribable by a singular essentialist definition or tradition. One might best speak of cabaret in the plural sense. Popular music historians need to begin to understand the political differences between ideologically-loaded expressions such as 'variety' and/or 'similarity' before inflicting them upon activities that, by falling outside of pre-existing canons, they do not fully understand.

This chapter principally deals with one key individual – Alan Richards – and his Liverpool-based record label Stag Music as an expression of the hybrid nature of the cabaret circuit. Unlike record labels such as folk's Topic, or jazz's Tempo, the existence of Stag Music did not encompass any grand social theories. It was localized, was not specifically issues-related or genre exclusive (recording disparate material such as comedian Tom O'Connor, the funk/rock of Supercharge, the progressive rock of Pinnacle and the local vernacular 'folk' music of the Jacksons), and did not engage in any particular musical function myth. Stag Music was explicitly fallible and, as such, was continually modified to the vagaries of contingency.

Origins

The word 'cabaret' is of French origin and in France the word initially referred to any business serving alcohol. But the history of French cabaret *culture* is far more complex. One history of cabaret culture appears to have begun in 1881 with the opening of *Le Chat Noir* in the Montmartre district of Paris. This was an informal saloon where composers, poets, and artists of all kinds could share ideas. Performers were able to test new material, audiences enjoyed a stimulating evening for the price of a few drinks, and owners could count on a steady flow of regular customers. It was a good deal all round and as it grew in stature as a cultural meeting place *Le Chat Noir* attracted such notables as Maupassant, Debussy, and Satie. By 1900 similar establishments appeared in several French and German cities. As time went by, many of these rooms featured scheduled entertainment, ranging in size from a few musicians to full floorshows. Such cabarets brought a new intimacy and informal spirit to public performances. Audiences sat at tables and consumed food and drink while performers worked right in their midst. Inevitably, audience members became part of the show, interacting with performers.

Following the end of WWI, cabaret enjoyed even greater popularity across Europe, predominantly in Germany, where the Weimar government essentially ended all forms of censorship. London's cabaret clubs such as at the Savoy Hotel, and the Monseigneur and Kit Kat Clubs were somewhat different from those in Germany being less anarchistic and far more restricted by the class system. These venues were often full of debutantes dancing to key dance bands of the day such as those led by Carroll Gibbons, Lew Stone, Roy Fox, and Geraldo. In the US, however, cabarets were at least 'officially' forced out of business when the Volstead Act made the sale of alcohol illegal in 1918. However, Prohibition, as it came to be known, did not wipe out America's taste for alcoholic refreshment, and there was an immediate demand for secretive, intimate places where people could consume alcohol. This kind of ambience also required a soundtrack and so the stage was set for cabaret to continue in America, albeit in an illegal condition.

Most of these 'speakeasies' were controlled by the gangsters who supplied the alcohol. Live entertainment made things look more legitimate, and owners found that women singing jazz or ballads worked wonders for drinks sales. These saloon singers became a regular part of American nightlife for decades to come, with future Show Boat star Helen Morgan the first in an endless line of ballad-singing females. Large floorshows were also popular in the larger clubs. The Cotton Club in New York, taken over in 1923 by gangster and bootleg queen Owney Madden, launched the careers of Fletcher Henderson, Duke Ellington, Jimmy Lunceford, Lena Horne amongst many others on the strength of revues with floorshows. Future Warner Brothers star Ruby Keeler got her start in a speakeasy, working for the outrageous hostess Texas Guinan. Upon the introduction of Prohibition, Guinan opened a cabaret called the 300 Club in New York City. The club became famous for its troupe of 40 scantily-clad fan dancers. Arrested several times for serving alcohol and providing entertainment, she always claimed that the patrons had brought the alcohol with them, and that the club was so small the girls had to dance in close proximity to the customers. Guinan even maintained that she had never sold an alcoholic drink in her life. Women were not only present as performers, but as a key part of the audience:

> Miss Morgan, Tex Guinan, Belle Livingston were among the more notable women who dominated the nightclubs and other rendezvous of revelry in the twenties. But the pattern persisted all over the country – speakeasies and 'intimate' spots featured women torch singers and piano players. That is what the night-life public wanted. And in the Lawless Decade the nightlife public was no longer predominantly male. The women wanted their fun too, their share of the whoopee – a word that's almost obsolete probably because the wild, hectic and abandoned sort of gaiety it described is also almost obsolete now. (Sann, 1957:190)

By the mid-1920s, a general resentment of Prohibition laws in the US was so widespread in New York that residents voted to suspend enforcement by local officials. This left only a meagre federal force attempting to shut down the city's speakeasies. While some states and cities did cling tenaciously to Prohibition cities such as New York capitulated to the inevitable.

Prohibition ended in December 1933, and although the Great Depression was at its worst, these larger nightclubs became the order of the day. Venues such as *The Copacabana*, *The Cotillion Room*, and *The Diamond Horseshoe* featured former vaudeville stars such as Jimmy Durante and Sophie Tucker. Candlelight and a formal dress code added to a sense of luxury. These elegant showplaces held hundreds of high-paying customers at a time, and were more like Las Vegas showrooms than the previously mentioned French cabarets. However, the material and performance style were still in the cabaret tradition – singers, dancers, MC comedians and dance music played at full throttle by a professional jazz-oriented band was usually the order of the day.

However, by the late-1930s, smaller, more intimate rooms had become fashionable in most large American cities and because New York law required establishments serving alcoholic drinks to provide food, out of convenience these rooms called themselves 'supper clubs' – even if there was nothing more than a token sandwich kept in a glass fronted refrigerator to earn the title. Since many of these supper clubs were rather poorly furnished, they were often reliant upon low lighting, cigarette smoke and strong performers for ambience. Tables were small, jamming 50 or more people into a space meant for perhaps only half that number. A singer might be perched on a tiny stage with one piano, a single spotlight and a microphone. The music was mostly jazz and Broadway-sourced and comedians spouted rather adult material for late night audiences.

In the 1940s and 50s, New York was home to several clubs that achieved legendary status: *Tony's* had Italian food and the legendary songster Mabel Mercer. *Cafe Society* was a very Left wing, politicized venue and the first club to welcome integrated audiences for performers like Billie Holiday – it was here that Holiday first heard the song 'Strange Fruit'. *Spivy's Roof* had the outrageous lesbian headliner and owner Spivy. *The Blue Angel* featured future stars Pearl Bailey, Eartha Kitt, Bobby Short, and guitar-strumming Russian folksinger Yul Brynner. It was this latter New York style of club, rather than the original French model, that initially inspired a small coterie of music entrepreneurs to bring such cabaret club 'culture' to Liverpool.

Cabaret in Liverpool

In the late-1950s Liverpool enjoyed the dubious privilege of having only one 'real' cabaret club. It was called, fittingly, The Cabaret Club and was situated on 28 Duke Street, in what is now known as the 'Ropewalks' area of the city. Bill Harry cites it as 'one of the main Merseyside cabaret night spots in its time' (1992:128) but if one excludes the social club circuit, the Lyceum Gentleman's Club, and the Olympia Theatre (the latter of which could be given over to cabaret), it was probably the only such venue in the city. The Cabaret Club, it appears, catered for an older demographic audience, and booked performers such as Liverpool-born Lita Roza, who might normally appear at cabaret lounges in and around London and the Home Counties. The Beatles played The Cabaret Club on 25 July 1962 and it was, by Bill Harry's account, 'a total disaster' (*ibid*).

On 22 March, 1962 Allan Williams opened the Blue Angel Cub at 108, Seel Street, Liverpool. Williams named it after the Marlene Dietrich film of the same name and erected a large blow-up photograph of Dietrich in a scene from the film on the club wall. On the opening night cabaret artiste Alma Warren (or Williams depending on the source) appeared, backed by the Terry Francis Quartet. The club lasted for a year or two but its initial intentions of being a cabaret lounge were somewhat overtaken by Williams' need for cash flow and the popularity of rock 'n' roll, so becoming a late night watering hole for many local beat groups. Although the Beatles did not play at the Blue Angel they did frequent the club and celebrities from all over the world such as Bob Dylan, Allen Ginsberg and Judy Garland (who was apparently thrown out by Williams) visited the club. There was also a club based on Upper Parliament Street entitled the New Cabaret Artistes Club (later known as the Gladray), but this was basically a cellar strip club and has only gained some historical value as being a place where the Silver Beatles backed a stripper – Janice – in 1960, despite Liverpool's Watch Committee declaring strip clubs illegal.

So, by the early days of Merseybeat Liverpool was not exactly 'swimming' in cabaret lounges. By the following decade however, the region could boast several significant cabaret clubs such as Rumford's Coach House, Russell's, The Shakespeare Theatre Club, The Wooky Hollow, The Coconut Grove, Allinson's, and The Hamilton Club. These clubs were established directly upon the popularity of the most visible and audible forms of popular music, but were less concerned with beat music, and more a response to the growing divide between an older, more upwardly-mobile population and the teenage market interested in dancing to (at first live) music and (then) discotheques. These cabaret clubs resembled the supper clubs of the American model and booked performers who could aid this ambience. These would generally include a comedian, who might double as a master of ceremonies, a group who would be able to rattle their way through a selection of chart material, mixed with (say) a little country music, Motown or evergreens, plus, in the larger venues, either a well-known cabaret star such as Bruce Forsyth, Shirley Bassey, Lovelace Watkins, or Bob Monkhouse, a recording artist who might also be local, such as Colin Areety, or a visiting US artiste or group. In the latter case, by the late-1960s, there were several 'rogue' groups appearing in the UK, under the monikers of the Drifters, or the Coasters. There was also a battalion of pop groups who having made a stab at, or even a brief name in, the pop charts of the mid-'60s, re-made their reputations as comedy-pop groups. These were numerous, but included the Barron Knights, the Black Abbots, the Rockin' Berries, Freddie and the Dreamers and the Grumbleweeds. By the early-1970s several mid-60s pop stars had decided to tread the more lucrative cabaret path. Artists such as Gene Pitney, Cilla Black, Georgie Fame, the Searchers, Vanity Fare, the Fortunes, and many more besides discovered touring the cabaret circuit was a financially-secure manoeuvre. One might be able to work across the country via the cabaret club network, rather than rely upon the aging provincial theatre circuit. Many theatres were under the threat of closure, or in the case of the Royalty Theatre in Chester being turned into Theatre Clubs.

As live music venues closed across the country, cabaret came to serve relatively new purposes. Here were venues for 'twenty-somethings' who might wish to eat, dance, and enjoy an evening's entertainment away from (but associated with) the entertainment systems that TV had made so popular, and linked-with but not subsumed-by, late-'60s discotheques (many clubs also had a disco 'round'). They were venues for those who might like to dress in a perhaps less trendy, but more 'sophisticated' manner, so in most clubs there were 'collar and tie' policies. They were also venues for the growing generations of senior citizens who carried sets of values, attitudes, beliefs and expectations that were vastly different from, not only younger, but also previous generations of elderly people. Cabaret lounges that were added to Social and Labour Clubs were also renowned for cheap alcohol, whereas more high-profile clubs, such as the Wooky Hollow, charged 'club prices', which tended to boost already excessive pub 'lounge' tariffs. All such venues were considered refuges from the excesses of the counter culture, and places where one could hear 'good' popular music of all varieties.

Although when one turns to the popular music of the late-1960s the counter culture fittingly gets exposure, it cannot be over-emphasized that a musical revolution was also taking place around the cabaret circuits of the UK. For the most part, patrons of the cabaret circuit had not experienced deprivation for many years (some not at all), and were not reinforcing their identities via album-oriented rock music or motifs of anti-commercialism. Their upward mobility and levels of self assurance were reflected in their consumption patterns, and due to sheer weight of numbers, their demands were quickly identified and met. The success of cabaret in Liverpool was therefore couched within the framework of the city's changing demographics and power structures, and in the (incorrect) assumption that there would be few significant changes in the UK economy. It was this latter assumption that eventually forced many clubs to close, for the downturn in the economy, post-OPEC (1973-74) hit the very entertainment market that presumed unending post-industrial affluence.

Agents

Agents and agencies were intrinsic to this burgeoning tertiary production circuit and within Liverpool there were several very important artiste agencies. Ricky McCabe's agency handled many of the local comedians and pop groups, The Billy 'Uke' Scott agency based in Southport controlled the rest. The Wilmington Agency owned by Joe Wilmington also co-owned with Harold Collins of Industrial Marine Liverpool's only 'real' recording studio: CAM Records at 44 Moorfields. The Mike Hughes Agency, based in the Liver Buildings, controlled groups such as the Black Abbots – from which comedian and actor Russ Abbot emerged, and overall there was an association of agents going under the umbrella term of the MAA – the Merseyside Artistes Association. Originating from Ossie Wade's venue in Everton, by the early 1970s the MAA had established itself in premises on Sheil Road, Kensington and it was here that a cartel of bookers, agents, concert secretaries, and performers worked closely together in order to guarantee bookings, earnings, and fair conditions for all of the social club and cabaret venues across the area, and also to provide showcases for aspiring new talent. The social impact of such actions was that cabaret encompassed several manifest functions even when, by the mid-1970s, Liverpool was beginning to suffer from economic decline.

The cabaret circuit supported and created regular work for budding musicians, it stimulated the sale of goods and services within the licensed trade, and protected several areas of employment such as bar and technical staff. It was, if not quite a 'scene', then certainly a complex web of post-industrial integrated business concerns, based around popular music and entertainment. Unlike other scenes in

Liverpool, however, it was openly money-led, well-organized and dependent upon resolute business behaviour. When this did not occur, artists or agents could be black-legged or placed into difficulty by their intransigence or amateurism. There was undoubtedly an ethical majority working in Liverpool for the benefit of all, and club managers were collectively advised on deals with breweries and outside agents, just as much as artists were advised with whom to deal. Club-owners such as Terry Philips of the Wooky Hollow were held in great esteem because of their 'fairness'. However Phillips also regarded himself as an arbiter of acceptable taste and it soon became clear to an up-and-coming group or artist what kind of musical menus were on offer.

By 1970 many former Merseybeat 'luminaries' had joined the cabaret circuit. Some quite evidently made more money than had previously been the case, and were not required to extend themselves, musically. While music was supposed to be progressing between the years of 1969 and 1976, those bands such as Yes, Caravan and Van Der Graaf Generator (all of whom were popular in Liverpool at this time) were hardly known to keep an audience on the dance floor. The Fourmost, the Searchers (both sporting changed line-ups), Gerry and the Pacemakers (after Marsden's return from a spell on the West End stage in *Charlie Girl*), the Chants, the Swinging Blue Jeans, and others played the cabaret circuit locally, nationally and internationally, for several years. By the mid-1970s, the local cabaret circuit was full of names from the beat boom. One-time Undertaker sax player Brian Jones turned his musical attention to cabaret performances, as did Lance Railton of the T.T.s, who held a residency at the Wooky Hollow which for a while was also managed by the late Paddy Chambers, formerly of Faron's Flamingos, Paddy, Klaus and Gibson and others (one of the few local players to attempt a jazz/rock fusion – in Germany with Lewis Collins). Billy Kinsley of Merseybeats fame enjoyed a distinguished popular music career and in the late-1960s became a session player at Apple, but this did not prevent Kinsley from occasionally working the cabaret circuit or even recording anonymous cover versions for the Pickwick 'Top of the Pops' series of albums. These former beat music players were among the first to realize that a portfolio career beckoned.

Surprisingly, and despite the usual historical stereotypes of gangsterism surrounding Liverpool's clubland (perhaps exemplified in Roy Adams' text *Hard Nights* of 2004), there were few areas of conflict between cabaret clubs. Adams certainly rubbed shoulders with notorious Liverpool gangsters, but he owned a city-centre club (The New Cavern) which was a different experience from owning a club in the suburbs. There could be problems: such as when one agent might attempt to poach another's artist, or when, in the case of Stag Music, a recording or publishing contract might financially exclude an agent. However, there was such a vast potential market that most club owners considered that there was enough business to go around – at least until the mid-1970s – and the financial fates of individual owners tended to reflect the financial fates of their organizations. When clubs thrived, individuals thrived, when clubs did not, the individuals did not. To view cabaret clubs as a kind of subterranean society and economy would be incorrect. These entrepreneurs offered strategies for survival in a highly complex music business, and their contribution to the entertainment industry was not only self-fulfilling and self-contained, but also contributory to the creative image of the city (perhaps far more than the galleries and museums of the city, which had a tendency to lock away creativity). This was a breed of entrepreneurs, still seldom considered by the writers of the histories of the city of Liverpool.

However there were many instances of local language games which involved artists or agents having to decipher what some considered the natural science of clubland, with its moral traditions, social cultures, networks and generic conventions. This language deeply affected the musical output of each club. For example, a dress code was essential, long hair, although acceptable, had to be coiffured. It was recommended that artists' repertoires should pass the master of ceremonies scrutiny before each engagement, in case (by the early 1970s) anything 'heavy' – therefore inappropriate – might slip though unnoticed. Stage gestures were seen to reflect upon the performer and so some MCs were permitted to pass judgement on particular moves and/or gestures. Perhaps the most striking feature of playing cabaret in the 1970s was that there was an established set of rules that seemed to explicitly validate its existence. But this is perhaps less surprising when we consider that as a cash-based business, all artists were required to abide by rules. As in all forms of cash-based enterprise the prospect of almost immediate reward re-evaluates concerns about creativity. Liverpool's cabaret 'scene' was viewed as a healthy tradition somewhat in opposition to the excesses of the counter culture and it was seen to sustain via its own internal arguments, conflicts and rules of engagement. The historical significance of cabaret in Liverpool does not revolve around the simplistic notion of whether marketing did or did not affect musical authenticity, but concerns, instead, cabaret's contextual meanings and identifications, as these were understood by those within and out-with the milieu. It was into this ever-changing, vibrant, yet heavily-structured environment that Alan Richards was dropped in 1969.

Alan Richards

West Derby-born Alan Richards was born into a musical house. His father Wally was a jazz fan but his two brothers and his sister were not especially interested in music.

> It was anything jazz, I was brought up with Ellington and Basie – Dad's God was Art Tatum – this was serious jazz. He liked Dizzy as well but from an early age I remember he used to *collect* records. Collecting was important to him and wherever he might be he would bring home albums. When we would go to NEMS I would search through the jazz for him and by the late-'60s I would go to supermarkets to pick this stuff up for 99p or £1 on labels like Music For Pleasure so, now he's no longer with us, I now have this huge collection of jazz

on vinyl. Because I showed an interest we used to listen to jazz together and I knew the names of the players on the tracks. He encouraged me and we could play duets together – our favourites were 'Sweet Georgia Brown' and 'Caravan' – that type of thing. We went to see Basie twice, Ellington twice, once with Sarah Vaughan, we saw Dizzy on the Phil, Oscar Peterson Trio. So we used to go together and even when we went to the States in 1970 we found that Buddy Rich was appearing in Boston and so we went: wonderful. I didn't have any classical training: it was all jazz.

In the Banyan Tree it was like a goldmine in the Adelphi but it never lasted for a long time. Trad jazz seemed to rule the roost in Liverpool so you felt a bit special. But I absolutely had mainstream tastes too – I loved to listen to all sorts of stuff: Beatles, Searchers, slightly too young to be in the actual scene, but I came in just afterwards – I played the Cavern and all of that, but not until 1967. It was a licensed club by that time and things had changed, but it was still a great buzz. I got into song writing and wrote simple songs and made my friends listen to them. I never taped anything as a kid but I did show off a bit at parties such as with 'Ain't She Sweet'. Dad told me it would impress the girls – and it worked. Whenever you played the piano it would attract the girls. (Richards to Brocken, January 2009)

Alan began song-writing at an early stage and then went through the usual Liverpool schooling via groups. He started at his local youth club with a group by the name of the Corner Set. This group, perhaps typically for Liverpool, shaped itself into a soul band performing mostly Stax material. Gigs were forthcoming and Alan discovered he could earn pocket money. He then joined the group Deep South and while working with this group brought in two singers, one of whom was a protégé of local opera singer Rita Hunter. Belsize Productions got in touch with the group: 'around the time of "Love Grows" era [January 1970] and came up to Liverpool and said they wanted to sign-up the band to a deal. They took us to Wolverhampton, of all places and recorded us there. We signed our life away for about four years for publishing and song writing but it probably didn't mean anything. I think the guys were probably shysters really'. By the summer of 1970 Alan was on holiday in the US and when he returned, found that the band had moved in another direction – attempting to 'go heavy'. So, without a working band he proceeded to write to as many publishers as possible in an attempt to obtain a publishing deal:

I would read the publisher's name on the records and I would then try to find their address, and also write to the artist on the record. I wrote to Tom Jones! 'Dear Tom, I have a song for you', that kind of thing. I found out Jones lived in Weybridge and I sent the letter registered. Nothing happened for a fortnight and then I got a letter from Ronnie Scott of Valley Music and got an appointment.

I also knew Bobby Shack the compere at the Wooky Hollow and he arranged it so I could meet Vince Hill and, in turn, he said to go and see his record producer at EMI: Bobby Barrett. So I did; Bobby Barrett was such a gentleman and listened to my song even though he had stacks of tapes on his desk. He was very polite. He played some Leonard Cohen – pure poetry – and I sort of got the gist of what he was talking about – mine, no doubt, was rubbish. (*ibid*)

Back home in Liverpool there were plenty of gigs around the mainstream circuit of social clubs and cabaret lounges and being a keyboard player was an advantage. Alan owned a Farfisa organ that he had purchased with a little insurance money following a road accident, and his keyboard skills helped him to obtain work. Working solo Alan had no egos to assuage, no problems with transport, and few difficulties picking-up his money. In fact he did not recall to this writer a single cancelled engagement, or being short of work at any stage of his young career; it all 'worked liked clockwork – it was fun and easy, I couldn't have asked for anything more'. Practically all of this work came through agents such as Ernie Mac, Mary Wells, and Billie 'Uke' Scott. Alan also went to the Merseyside Artists' Association 'but I didn't do the showcases, myself – I didn't need to: there was plenty of work'. Alan was not a full-time entertainer at this stage, being a trainee quantity surveyor at Roneo Vickers in Kirkby during the day, but his life truly centred around performing, writing and recording. He did not only view himself as a songwriter, as such, but also a performer: 'There were lots of good musicians after the Beatles had left Liverpool and I enjoyed the performing side of things, it was a great buzz.' He was paid in the region of £8 as an organist but was spending most of this money making demos and 'potential' Eurovision Song Contest entries:

I'd written a song 'On My Own' and demo-ed it at CAM – the engineer Charlie Weston loved it. Valley Music liked it too and wanted to do something with it. But Dad spotted a competition for the Duke of Edinburgh's Award scheme and sent in a tape of the song and I discovered I'd got to the second heat in London. So I went; I had a wonderful day, came home and then a letter came to say I'd got through to the final. I went to the finals at Elstree Studios live on TV – an incredible experience. They picked me up by limo and all my family came to see the show live. (*ibid*)

From the highs of live independent TV broadcasting Alan returned to Liverpool and recommenced his live work around the Liverpool clubs. It was arduous and the music policies somewhat conservative, but Richards found that he could integrate his own material into his live sets without great difficulty, for it all had that 'pop tinge' of the day. Other than holding an aversion to music of the 'heavy' variety, patrons were not especially judgemental, and with Alan's name being mentioned in the local press after finally coming third in the Duke of Edinburgh competition, he was never short of an engagement. He even decided to create his own small revue, 'The Alan Richards Show', and along with a local comedian and a couple of dancers, toured Liverpool's clubland with some degree of success.

By 1971 Richards was successfully placing his songs with London publishers, and working directly with Valley Music. He was finally persuaded to go full-time into the music business when offered a position of A&R at the Liverpool Sound Studio in Kirkby. This enterprise had evolved out of CAM Records in Moorfields, Liverpool which had effectively ceased to function via a combination of mismanagement and the news of the imminent arrival of a new Moorfields underground railway station. Co-owners Harold Collins and Joe Wilmington ran the diminutive studio as something of a plaything. Harold Collins was co-proprietor of the Industrial Marine Security Company and Joe Wilmington was proprietor of the Wilmington Agency. Collins purchased Wilmington's share of the studio and moved it lock, stock and barrel to the industrial estate in Kirkby next to his business premises. The idea was to upgrade facilities with a new eight-track recording desk. The eight-track recorder had been promised to Collins and business partner Eddie Hunt by a local boffin who had bits and pieces of equipment from, of all places NASA, but the desk failed to materialize. However the studio, upon employing Alan for £30 per week, advertised in both the *Melody Maker* and the local press for local songwriters to contact them. For a fee of £3 Liverpool Sound would record a demo, consider its merits and then, if suitable, Richards would take on the job of hauling it around his publishing house connections in London – it sounded like a good deal all round. The *Liverpool Echo* was to report:

Launching pad for a new Mersey sound

Two former policemen hope to make Simonswood, Kirkby a place that will start a new Mersey sound. Harold Collins and his friend Eddie Hunt formed the studio with the intention of recording and promoting local talent.

'We honestly believe that there is going to be a new Mersey Beat era very soon. There is so much local talent coming to the surface that it just has to be tapped' said Harold

They both left the police force six years ago to form their own security company which is now one of the largest in the North West. 'I have always been interested in music and when we were in the position to be able to go ahead with a studio there was no question of our not doing so. It is our intention to give as much local talent as possible the break they need to put them on the road to success' said Harold.

They have called their new company Liverpool Sound Enterprises. From the outset the studio, which adjoins their security company in Stopgate Lane, looks like an ordinary office, but it's a world of microphones, speakers and technical equipment inside. The studio, using an eight-track recorder offers all the facilities of a London studio 'for too long people have been drawn to London by a myth' said Harold.

Helping out is local songwriter 20-year-old Alan Richards, who produces the sessions. 'Like Harold, I really believe that it is all going to happen again. I

also believe that this studio is going to be the place where it will all start from'
said Alan. (*Liverpool Echo*)

The £3 demo fee immediately brought in revenue of several hundred pounds in a
very short space of time and gave Alan the opportunity of continuing his contacts
in London via those publishers he had already canvassed. Although none of the
music being demo-ed at Liverpool Sound ever made it into the charts, several
songs were recorded by leading artists of the day and the name 'Liverpool Sound'
became respected in London among those publishers who dealt with more
mainstream tastes, such as Ronnie Scott and Bobby Barrett. Alan 'knew who
would be interested and who wouldn't depending upon the genre of each song –
although I never really took anything "heavy" down there – this would be the age
of Tony Macaulay and his songs [such as "Baby Make it Soon", "Love Grows",
"Build Me Up Buttercup", etc.] ruled. I was looking for that kind of material as
well as writing my own in those styles'. This demo activity led Liverpool Sound
into, not only a prominent position locally, but also one of modest significance in
London.

The word was out and several Liverpool cabaret acts visited the Liverpool
Sound studio with ideas of recording their own demos. As a consequence,
Alan Richards and engineer Charlie Weston – the latter of whom had also moved
to the Kirkby studio when CAM ceased to exist – considered the idea of forming
a record label to cater not only for the incoming demo material, but also as a
label that might attract point-of-sale business in its own right. The cabaret circuit
was by 1972, Liverpool's most prominent music business activity and so Alan
thought that, given the correct financial approaches to recording and pressing,
it might support its own label. So it proved to be – at least for five years, and
Stag ('*S*ongwriters and Ar*t*ist M*a*nagement') Music came into being. The idea was
to provide local artists with a limited-run product that could be retailed at gigs.
A Stag recording would also provide the artist with a product to tout to agents for
further engagements and/or production and publishing companies.

In effect this was Liverpool's first proper record label. Despite previous efforts
such as Phillips' Sound Recording Services at 38 Kensington, where between the
years of 1955 and 1969, Percy Phillips recorded numerous tapes and acetate discs,
and CAM Studios in Moorfield which had the largely one-off CAM and Unichord
imprints, this was the first label that would seriously provide local artists with a
product backed by publicity. Stag Music would promote their product at venues
and events across Liverpool, advertise in the local and national music press, and
generally assist the artist in reaping the benefits from the product. Alan informed
Melody Maker in July 1974 that 'The idea of basing disc sales at the actual venues
where an artist performs was first tried by a company in the Isle of Man about
ten years ago, but it didn't last long. We started just before Christmas [1973], and
I think we're the only ones doing it in the country' (Richards to Evans, *Melody
Maker*, 1974:17). However there were a few financial caveats Richards put into
place before undertaking the project ('profit was sanity, turnover vanity'). Firstly,

pressing plants were hired on the strength of their low-costs. Richards understood that many point-of-sale purchases were not enduring, as such, and so vinyl quality was not a great issue. Also, sleeves were not made from the best quality card. Alan attempted to outsource the sleeve-making to local companies, but few printers in Liverpool at that time were able to produce LP sleeves of the required standard and so most Stag sleeves remained un-laminated and spineless, thus creating a product similar to that of rack-jobbers Studio Republic. Most of the Stag Music sleeves were made by CBM Advertising in Bold Place, Liverpool and duly reflected a rather *ad hoc* arrangement. It was therefore relatively easy to detect that these were not major label releases, contrasting the matrixes developed by labels such as Harvest, Island and Transatlantic in the early-1970s, which were gatefold-sleeved product of the highest quality. Even more cautiously than this, Richards decided on two financial paths for Stag releases and he developed a catalogue system of 'SG' and 'HP' to reflect these paths.

The SG releases were financed by Stag Music itself, and Richards would receive a royalty 'if the potential was there', whereas the HP prefix indicated that Alan would arrange a hire purchase agreement between artist and a local finance company, thus limiting any losses. The finance company would supply Stag with the money upfront so that the funds would be in place for the project. This arrangement was based on common retail practice of the day where companies such as Paybonds and Provident effectively reduced retailers' risks by taking full responsibility for repayments. So, the money would come to Stag as a straight sum for their services, and the artist would arrange to re-pay the finance company over a period of six or twelve months. The initial pressing of 1,000 albums would cost Stag a little under £900 and their profit margin would be in the region of 20 per cent. The artist would receive all of the gross sales income and pay Stag their fixed percentage. On subsequent pressings the cost price would be far less for there would be no recording or master costs. So both Stag Music and the artist would reap further profits.

The first Stag Music releases – by country music artists Duo Mikenos (SG1001) and cabaret group Silver Set (SG1002) notched up sales of almost 2,000 apiece in the first months of release in 1973 and 1974. This was measuring popularity in a totally different way, via grass roots support at live gigs, and cash flow was certainly speeded-up immensely. For performers such as Silver Set these sales and increased cash flow came as a great career boost, enabling them to turn fully professional. For many local cabaret performers, the status of being locally recognized artists was not matched by their incomes, and they remained semi-professional. But with the aid of record sales, some were able to turn their attention fully to their cabaret careers. Richards was recorded by Mike Evans in 1974 in a fiercely partisan mood stating 'we've got the talent here, as we always have had. I felt more of it should get released on record without having to move down south first' (*ibid*). Richards, of course, also carried on his usual 'bread-and-butter' functions of demo recording throughout this era; in fact these sessions increased as the Stag Music label was naturally associated with the Liverpool Sound Studio and attracted even more budding songwriters to the Kirkby premises.

By 1974 the cabaret circuit in Liverpool had reached something of a zenith. The Shakespeare and the Wooky Hollow clubs were enjoying national prominence; locally with the assistance of brewery loans, even the Garston Woodcutter's club and the NUR club on Dean Road had constructed very popular cabaret lounges. The list of Stag Music recording artists, therefore grew exponentially. Cabaret artists such as New Image and comedian Tom O'Connor were recorded, with the latter providing Stag Music with an enormously successful album *Alright Mouth* (SG1006). By this time, O'Connor, a former teacher from Bootle, had developed a folk/comedy crossover act that adapted songs, replacing lyrics with humorous couplets and combining them with 'off the cuff' stories. Alongside similar comedians such as Mickie Finn, George Roper, and Al Dean, O'Connor's fame on the Liverpool cabaret circuit grew. He later appeared on the Granada TV show *The Comedians* and by the early-1980s had risen to a position of national prominence, in the process turning into a genial game show host. When he recorded *Alright Mouth* for Stag Music his popularity in Liverpool was escalating after he had become particularly renowned for his performances at Russell's Club in Liverpool's city centre (a venue later part of the 1990s Cream dance music club). Richards decided to replicate the atmosphere of a night at Russell's and with the exception of one track ('Jimmy Mack') O'Connor was recorded in front of a live audience in a simulated 'club setting' at the Abbot Sound Studios in Chester. Apart from a little editing, the entire album was recorded in one take and upon release immediately recovered its costs. Alan Richard's father decided to contact Woolworth's about this local success and Woolworth's 'Record Merchandise' wholesaling department agreed to stock the album. Alan was invited to send at least one copy to every Woolworth's store in the country on sale-or-return terms. This he did:

> But we were never sent a record back, so apart from the strong local sales we just kept on supplying 'Woolies'. It was amazing – we were constantly parcelling-up LPs and posting them out. Eventually we sold 44,000 copies of *Alright Mouth*. There was a Record Merchandise contact in Swansea for us – a Mr Egerton – and he knew that although we agreed to sale-or-return, his shops would just place unsold records in the deletion bins and nor be bothered about sending them back. So we were probably supplying shops with new product after they had already put unsold copies in the deletion bin. We never received any returns. It was mad, but that wasn't the only reason we sold so many. Tom was by the mid-'70s growing in popularity and everywhere he went he took LPs with him. (Richards to Brocken, 2009)

The sleeve for the album was typically Stag in that it was un-laminated and without a spine. This meant that as time has gone by, it is very difficult to find a copy of the LP in good condition. The sleeve was designed and illustrated by another previously unexposed local talent, John Cornelius and this helped to boost his artistic and commercial profile. As Alan informed Mike Evans in 1974, 'all along the line we're utilizing local artists who otherwise might not get a look in' (Richards to Evans, *Melody Maker*, 1974:17). Alan's concept proved to be highly successful; it helped to resolve the problem of providing a sustainable professional product representative of Liverpool's cabaret circuit. It allowed artists to consider a professional career by giving them an added revenue stream, and also a marketing tool in one. Stag Music was also able to represent an identity-giving culture recognizable to, not only many Liverpudlians, but to others across the UK.

The success of the Tom O'Connor album proved to be a substantial event and marked a sea change in cabaret marketing. Previously celebrated cabaret artists in Liverpool such as the Jacksons, Al Dean and Mickey Finn and O'Connor himself were known only as 'live' performers. But via these recordings, these local artistes received far greater local exposure. The Stag Label also emerged at a time when local radio was in its ascendancy and many of these point-of-sale records found their way onto the turntables of Bob Azurdia, Pete Price, Billy Butler and Monty Lister, presenters at BBC Radio Merseyside (and for Price and Butler, also Radio City). They were all non-copyright productions and, with BBC Radio Merseyside allocated only a very limited needle-time, any recordings not subject to PPL regulations were exploited. Once aired, they further reconfigured and re-contextualized these artists in the imaginations of the local public; according to Alan 'for two years it was an almost perfect situation'. One might even suggest that these recordings are now of great historical interest, for they capture very different examples of popular music entertainment at an important moment in Liverpool's history. By the late-1970s that moment had passed, as the downward spiral of the UK economy devastated this cash-based entertainment industry.

However these days, record collectors typically attach greater significance to two other albums, predictably from the rock field. The first is the *Between Music and Madness* album (Stag SG1008S) by Supercharge. Supercharge was a local 'super group' formed by the best of Liverpool's late-'60s R&B musicians. The band later signed to Virgin, but at this stage (1973) enjoyed a large local fan base, based upon their appearances at the Sportsman (St John's Precinct) and Dove and Olive (Speke) pubs. Supercharge arranged a one-off album deal with Stag, and it was recorded at Abbot Sound Studios in Chester over only a few days. Alan was made aware of the group's growing status and financed the project himself. *Between Music and Madness* certainly ranks as the finest of all of Stag's productions. The initial run of 1,000 copies sold out in a very short space of time but the LP was not re-pressed; the band was already beginning to fragment (Alan Peters left immediately after the release of the LP) and the album is now hard to find, although a CD reissue appeared on the German JJ Records in the late-1990s. It was another three years before Virgin Records signed Supercharge but it could be argued that not one of the subsequent Virgin products was as representative or inventive as that first Stag Music album. Another highly collectable Stag album, also recorded in Chester, was by Liverpool-based heavy rock group Pinnacle. *Assasin* [sic] (HP125S) is a somewhat primitive recording in comparison to the Supercharge LP, perhaps representing the HP rather than SG prefix, but nevertheless has some interesting 'progressive' moments. Local singer Bobby Sox later augmented the group and this more pop-oriented band 'Bobby Sox and the Prize Guys' was a familiar draw for many years across the region.

Stag Music continued releasing SG and HP product for another two years. The label diversified into singles, maxi-singles and EPs and several were strong sellers locally such as those recorded by Abbey Road, Lee Brennan, Kellie, and Mickey Finn, and received continued airplay from BBC Radio Merseyside. But there were occasional 'turkeys': an LP by comedian Steve Faye was the weakest, sales-wise, of all Stag products. There were also a couple of items released under the Liverpool Sound subsidiary label, the most successful being another Tom O'Connor product *The Tom O'Connor Show* (LS1750) released in late-1973 (later re-issued on DJM). However, by 1976 Alan Richards was also spreading his wings, having moved into management firstly with his young protégés Buster, a Merseyside pop group who were signed by RCA and enjoyed considerable success in Japan, and then with Bonnie Tyler, who cut her first successful singles with Richards at the helm, also for RCA. Richards also commenced a business relationship with Renee Franz, a local publishing and advertising agent who produced *Nite Out*, a social and cabaret club 'what's on' guide. This mutated into *Social Sounds*, a short-lived magazine that similarly exploited Liverpool's club circuit – but neither of these editions was altogether successful, financially, although highly regarded by social club secretaries.

As for Liverpool Sound Studios, Charles Weston retired, the owners lost interest and the last Stag Music release came out in 1977. Gerry Lewis then purchased the business, it was re-named Amazon Studios, and their 'Jungle' imprint carried on a policy of releasing occasional 'paid-for' product for local artists such as Terry Fletcher, and the Blue Magnolia Jazz Band. Amazon also recorded some of the most interesting pop music of the following decade with groups such as China Crisis and producers Dave Roylance and Steve Wright, who also wrote the Channel 4 *Brookside* TV theme. Roylance, who died in 2006 enjoyed a long career, and was involved in writing television themes, over 400 advertisements, corporate and training films as well as musicals and theatrical productions, He wrote the music for the Shake and Vac carpet cleaner TV advert: one of the most enduring in advertising history. But Roylance was also involved in a long-term dispute over royalties he claimed were owed for the 'Brookside' theme tune. The *Wirral Globe* was to record on his death:

> The former China Crisis producer believed he was owed repeat fees in relation to the long-running series, and was also claiming royalties for Brookside video off-shoots and overseas sales of the Channel 4 series that ran for 23 years. In 1988, in a statement that went before the High Court, he declared: 'I have received virtually no benefit from composing the theme tune to a popular series which

has been on air for over eleven years, and has attracted millions of viewers week after week in that time.' (Dunn, *Wirral Globe*, 2006:1)

Amazon Studios were to eventually relocate to Liverpool's city centre. From its humble beginnings as CAM, followed by an exciting journey up the East Lancashire Road to Kirkby, manifesting at first as Liverpool Sound and Stag Music, Amazon's wheels finally came to a halt on Parr Street. The new Amazon Studios were but a short walk across town from its former home at Moorfields.

Summary

When attempting to map cabaret's local history in Liverpool we immediately become aware of why discussions concerning this circuit and its associated music genres are so contentious. The problems appear to begin with the split between its designated market and the youth-orientation of rock music at the time that cabaret grew in popularity. Cabaret seems, in effect, to exist in a state of opposition to rock, so much so that definitions and style delineations tend to run the rule over all cabaret music socially, culturally, and economically. But cabaret first emerges fully formed in Liverpool in the late-1960s as a separate and recognizable world and to fully understand its components, it is important to examine the historical factors that spurred this social formation. With the advent of rock 'n' roll, followed by a growing demographic of 'twenty-somethings', the commercial appeal of Merseybeat was narrowed. As Merseybeat groups split, evolved or mutated into either soul or rock bands a popular music need existed among those who were unconcerned with the idea of personalized artistic expression supposedly superseding the function of entertainment. The pre-existing social club circuit, together with a dinner-dance style of club, catered for this 'new' audience. This dramatically changed the direction of popular music on Merseyside as many artists refocused their endeavours along the lines of this altered reality. Professional and amateur musicians alike, were challenged by the presence of a musical world unconcerned by contentions of musical progress – at least along the pathway suggested by the rock narrative.

For artists such as Alan Richards it all made perfect sense, for his long-term relationship with jazz music had not exposed him to the binary oppositions between rock and pop. One need look no further than his own song writing and publishing aspirations to realize that rock's authenticity paradigms simply did not apply to his popular music objectives. For the historian, one outgrowth of the cabaret scene in Liverpool is that it emphasizes the significance of autobiography in the real sense of the word: writing oneself into history despite over-arching narratives constructed to question the validity of one's very presence. Alan Richards created a small but significant challenge to, not only the recording industry of the day (which was not his initial intention), but also to the systems that place certain modes of performance into legitimacy-based echelon systems.

Any historicization must be concerned with both continuity and discontinuity. After all, these two perspectives are both complimentary and partial. A view that discusses only disjuncture cannot, without parallel conjuncture, reflect the world as we have come to know it. The cabaret circuit represented shared common values, norms, and attitudes, not only towards music but towards life in general. As a result, cabaret people spent a great deal of time with others of a similar mindset. Thus cabaret became a subculture in its own right because it helped shape attitudes, beliefs, and actions. This could be described as leisure-based encapsulation. Simply sharing leisure experiences helps to create important social bonds. So the 'world' of cabaret music in Liverpool and the existence of Alan Richards' Stag Music label invokes two historical narratives at one and the same time. It engages a double or dual perspective of 'con-and-disjuncture'. If we truly seek to understand popular music popularity in its entirety, warts and all, we simply have to examine a wide variety of experiences and countless manifestations. Studies of the world of cabaret in Liverpool might, in fact, reveal much more about contemporary society than a focus on (say) the Cavern because, in the first place it was such a world that partially put the Cavern to the sword, and this new world then became a backdrop to the development of Liverpool as a modern city. Sameness and difference, unity and rupture must all be historicized if we are to deal with Popular (with a capital P) music history.

Chapter 9
Taste-makers, reception, word-of-mouth

It seems most of the air breathers who can walk fairly upright and were born in the last thirty years, have wires in their ears [..] They will never know the joy of flicking through a rack of records, being captivated by cover artwork and reading the sleeve notes [or] Of getting a record home, sliding it reverentially out of its cover and then out of its inner sleeve, marvelling at the lustre of the grooves.

(Lashmar to Pettit, 2008:61)

Taste-making – the introduction, development, and fostering of taste is seldom discussed in great detail in popular music discourses, being somewhat partially hidden from view. The massive improvements for many in the twentieth century in their material life, partly brought about by the financial and cultural investment in consumer goods, does tend to be ignored by those researchers following a path designed to support predetermined theories about popular music as an agent of bourgeois hegemony. Furthermore, the above-quoted personal narrative of a 'journey of discovery' into the 'world of vinyl' often excludes (or takes for granted) the existence of traditional broadcasting and retail systems, despite people physically going to record stores to purchase songs that they heard on the radio. Historically, it was relatively easy and convenient to purchase a record, but more difficult to purchase a record of choice, therefore the agency of the retailer or broadcasting system can be neglected and forgotten, or viewed as 'passive' in an instrumental sense: almost suggesting such presence was somehow accidental.

Yet record retailing, micro labels, local radio, and niche venues are perhaps one of the most complex and most direct contact points for most fans of popular music activity. The history of these multifaceted and often interconnecting pathways involves tracing the convoluted routes by which music comes into being, gains a market and is heard. Key individuals, places, spaces and technologies all play their part in making music audible. But the diffusion of such communications technology over the past one hundred years, and its relationships with taste cultures has been something of a hit-and-miss affair. Retailing of music is especially fraught as it emerged not through the dictates of the technology alone, but in fascinating ways which were entirely contingent to the actions, needs and desires of the consumer as well as the marketer. Indeed one might say that unlike the music industry model so commonly offered by those academics who gloomily see a mature executive working out the 'next big thing', it become clear that the market aids consumption at practically every level: purchasing, aesthetics, value, authenticity, indeed helping to communicate with like-minded people – especially via the provision of a platform for taste construction. The journey of listening, then, is never carried out alone. The cash might have flowed from fans to the stores and on to artists, writers, and producers of music, but culturally it was always two-way traffic. People truly enjoyed the experience of hearing what was to their mind, 'free' music on the radio and in return enjoying the financial and cultural investment of purchasing a record at the record shop. One record collector from the mid-1970s informed this writer:

> You would go to a shop that was at the very least neutral and hopefully positively drawn towards your tastes. At the Musical Box I would wait outside until Diane's dad had left the shop and then go in. I knew I'd get the 'bum's rush' from him, but that Diane would be genuinely interested in anything I had to say – or at least show an interest. It was her business and she appreciated all custom. Later I found Jon Weaver at Skeleton in Birkenhead to be the same. In fact Jon would recommend things. I have Jon to thank for introducing me to Gene Clark's 'No Other' and Paul Butterfield's 'East-West'. This was so different from the record department at, say, Beatties – they couldn't have cared less. Somebody I knew worked there and began to, let us say, 'remove' certain items from their stock. They never even noticed. (Ellis to Brocken, 2007)

In Liverpool and Birkenhead these acts of facilitation and encouragement were so obvious as to make the aforesaid dark predictive mythologies redundant. Indeed the common perception of there being one industry for music is quite clearly dispatched on a local level when a coterie of those who recorded sound, others who retailed sound, and still more who allowed sound to be heard comes into view. There were also those who co-created this resourceful universe by culturally investing in the products to such an extent that a vernacular authenticity was fashioned. Despite taste cultures ranging from the obscure to the eclectic, this co-creativity should be seen as an aesthetically unpretentious act, with images created by grass-roots tastes aiding and abetting everyday purposes. In 1997 Bryan Biggs and Colin Fallows mounted an exhibition at the (re-named) Bluecoat Arts Centre in Liverpool that combined both sonic art and LP-sleeve artwork under the title 'Live From The Vinyl Junkyard' to express how ingenious the act of cultural investment in mass-production could really be. A monograph under the same title appeared a year later. In the introduction to the monograph Biggs described record-buying as a 'reciprocal relationship' with 'the pop industry itself becoming the subject of fine art [...] where the very material of pop – vinyl, audiotape, record sleeves – is fashioned into new objects' (Biggs, 1998:3). He went on to discuss that there were 'hundreds of [...] LP designs worthy of our attention lurking in the Vinyl Junkyard [...] in revisiting them we can fully appreciate their worth as cultural artefacts' (*ibid*:9). One might also contend that even the often-maligned broadcasting systems helped develop profiles of authenticity and that radio personalities acted as taste-makers on a creative level. Once seeded and well-tended such cultural taste reflectors were not only extremely profitable, but also culturally influential.

There is far more to taste-making than simply directing people towards music, getting them to listen to it, and then persuading them to purchase a so-called 'functional artefact'.

Sound

Throughout the twentieth century recorded sound has not only been a tool for the preservation of music, but also a vehicle: in other words, the technology itself became an agent in the very 'sound' of music. Recorded sound initially existed as a record of 'live' sound. This concept was based around the impression that the sound one heard on a gramophone was at least a record of a live repertoire; the existence of the gramophone was supposed to recreate the natural acoustic balance of the concert hall. This, of course, was a miserable failure for both the reproduction and dissemination formats were woefully inadequate. However, the function of the carrier changed dramatically during the course of the twentieth century, especially in the early–mid 1950s when a new audio culture emerged and technology actually became a catalyst. From the moment Ampex tape was used in the studio in the late-1940s 'hi-fidelity' became an achievable goal and a culture of composers, sonic artists and listeners emerged. On a purely practical level surface sound was a thing of the past, tapes could be cut and spliced, and multi-track recordings could create sound images previously only imagined. The works of Les Paul and Mary Ford and the production techniques of Mitch Miller are but two popular music examples of how sound could be manipulated in the studio of the 1940s and 1950s. However *avant garde* experimenters such as Cage, Schaeffer and Henri also noted that the tape recorder opened-up music to an entire world of lived sound:

> Schaeffer came to represent the new breed of musician: an amateur explorer working directly ('concretely', as he put it) with sound material rather than going through the detours of musical notation, conductors, and performers. (Cox and Warner, 2004: xiii)

In reality, the vocals of Louis Jordan could never have been heard above the honking saxophones of his band without the available technology of the day. By the 1940s performances, let alone records were not 'real' in the organic sense, for the microphone had matured from a device used for 'public-address' into a means of completely remodelling both vocal grain and the balance between instruments. A sound picture existed over a terrain of a new sonic landscape, so significant that by the early-1950s, sound recording was beginning to make inroads into peoples' everyday lives. By the late-1950s recording technology was encouraging a sound 'illusion', people could imagine that the 'lush moods' recordings by Jackie Gleason, Martin Denny, Esquivel, and Mantovani (in actual fact made-up from different 'takes' and including unusual sound balances and effects) were 'real'. Such sonic architecture was redolent of new ways of listening to music, led performers to change the way they performed, and allowed entirely new hybrid genres of music to come into existence. After his shock retirement from public performance, former classical pianist Glenn Gould stated in 1966: 'In an unguarded moment some months ago I predicted that the public concert as we know it today would no longer exist a century hence, that its functions would have been entirely taken over by electronic media' (Gould in Cox and Warner, 2004:115).

The Beatles were among an important battalion of popular music artists to recognize the creative potential of sound manipulation. As their careers developed, they layered take with take, performance with performance, onto an ever-increasing number of tracks. The recording producer, the engineer and indeed the recording desk all effectively became 'members' of the group. The recording studio was no longer simply a transmitter, and the word 'fidelity' was linked less with the art of capturing the artist as faithfully as possible and more to do with the purity and possibilities offered by sound enhancement. The studio was not simply a laboratory, but freed from the subservience of reproduction, a veritable maze of sonic possibilities. By the mid-1960s many popular music records had a sonic autograph: Motown records were easily-identifiable via their 'high hat' or tambourine sound. Phil Spector's recordings had unique multi-tracking, echo, and reverb. A Dusty Springfield or Scott Walker recording could be equally recognized for the 'depth' of sound offered by Ivor Raymonde, Wally Stott or John Franz. These days, we can even 'date' such disembodied voices by their studio sounds awarding such works a kind of sonic literacy and acousmatic, non-linear history. For example, recordings made by several Merseyside artists in the 1980s such as Kirkby-based China Crisis and their 1983 major hit recording 'Christian' would simply not have be possible in either preceding or ensuing decades, thus presenting the music as non-linear and the studio as repository for sonic alliances.

Collecting

We have already seen how in Liverpool, record collecting created important social networks surrounding the consumption and production of music, and listening to records was central to new ways of learning to play music and in understanding different taste cultures. Such networks provided Liverpool with different ways of introducing and celebrating new sounds. Record collectors became important people in and around Liverpool. For example, in the immediate post-WWII era jazz collector Harold Culling became a focal point for the trad jazz scene. In 1961 record collector Bill Harry was to start his own local music newspaper *Mersey Beat* in July 1961. Five thousand copies were distributed through Liverpool wholesalers, 28 newsagents, venues such as the Cavern and the Mardi Gras and to all record and instrument shops in the city centre. Record collector Billy Butler, deejay at the Cavern, the Mardi Gras, and the Back of the Moon clubs passed on his knowledge of soul music like a form of gnosis to fellow soul fans. Later, as a broadcaster he helped to 'break' hit records for both Kate Bush and Jennifer Rush by his insistence that these recordings were of the highest quality; people listened. So much was Butler considered an arbiter of taste on Merseyside that his constant playing of Rush's 'The Power of Love' when others had removed it from their playlists, greatly contributed to the record's UK success.

By 1970 record collector and celebrated deejay Roger Eagle was passing on his esoteric knowledge to myriad young people at the Liverpool Boxing Stadium, and later at Eric's Club. In 1975, towards the end of the Liverpool Stadium rock venue era 'The Last Trumpet' a free music newspaper-cum-fanzine was distributed at appropriate venues, shops and cafés across the city centre in order not only to promote Eagle's promotions at the Liverpool Boxing Stadium, but also to spread the word about what Roger might consider 'good taste'. Norman Killon was an avid record collector and as deejay at Eric's and a retailer at Silly Billie's and Probe Norman imparted good judgement to collectors, so too Jon Weaver at Skeleton and Dave Crosby at Rox Records on the Wirral. By the late-1970s second-hand record fairs were established at the Bluecoat Chambers in School Lane to cater specifically for the growing legions of second-hand record collectors and it was here that this writer first came to know such tastemakers as Billy Butler, Bryan Biggs, Steve Hardstaff, Trevor Hughes and others who were utterly absorbed in this way of life.

Record Collector magazine started trading at this time (1979). The first standalone issue of *Record Collector* was published in March 1980, however the magazine's history stretches back further and is directly connected with the fan base of the Beatles. In 1963, publisher Sean O'Mahony ('Johnny Dean') launched the official Beatles magazine, *The Beatles Book*. This had links with Frieda Kelly's Official Beatles Fan Club and the magazine became an important mouthpiece for the club. When the Beatles imploded in 1969, the magazine also honorably 'fell on its sword', but owing to continued popular demand for Beatles historical material following the continued successes of the former Beatles throughout the 1970s, *The Beatles Book* reappeared in 1976 in its original pocket-size form. *The Beatles Book* included several pages of 1960s reprinted material, together with some contemporary articles. Throughout the late-1970s, the 'small ads' section of *The Beatles Book* became an increasingly popular conduit through which collectors could make contact and buy, sell, or trade Beatles rarities. However, in a reflection of burgeoning record collecting activity, the adverts became dominated by traders interested in rare vinyl out-with the world of the Beatles fan. In September 1979, *The Beatles Book* came with a record collecting supplement, and the response was so encouraging that in March 1980 O'Mahony decided to launch *Record Collector* as a separate title. Throughout the 1980s, several style magazines rather 'sniffily' condemned the journal for its appeal to what were often seen as fixated neurotics, yet *Record Collector* has long outlived most of these titles and continues to thrive in the digital age.

Retail

The history of record retailing is linked not only to profit and loss accounting, but also to significant creative communities. Indeed record shops were a visible indication of an audio culture, both supporting and eradicating the distinctions between high art and low art, contributing a place where taste alliances could be formed and then crossed, and vividly illustrating that such audio culture was a discourse, a loose collection not only of products, but ideas and statements gathered together from the broadest of cultural fields – music. In this way, record retailing reached-out to people interested in arbitrating their world through sound. In the twenty-first century, for better or worse, this world has been changed by chain stores, on-line shopping and internet downloads. Such incursions into the domain of the record retailer raises questions concerning the ways in which sound locates us in particular social and cultural contexts, hence Emma Pettit's recent work *Old Rare New* (2008) that portrays the significance of second-hand record collectors' emporiums. This used to be one end of a record shop continuum, a valued outlet for musical obsession, but that continuum is now almost completely broken, for new sales are diminishing and the record industry is in tatters. Pettit does not discuss new-record retailers and therefore disregards a distinctive part of Britain's cultural landscape, as if the selling of new records was somehow less important than the trading in old ones. For some this might be true as an aura builds up around a hard-to-obtain disc, but it seems a pity that the exhilaration of purchasing a pristine recording is not given its due place in the pantheon of popular music experience.

In Liverpool record retailing has an interesting history for it was here in 1909 that the first Woolworth's Store at 25-25a Church Street began trading. Within a short space of time Woolworth's was selling both sheet music and records and by 1921 were selling their own 5" Mimosa records, pressed by the Crystalate Company, for 6d a time. Mimosa was superseded by the 'Victory' 7" 78 rpm records which in turn were replaced by the 8" Eclipse and then the 9" Crown imprints. These records were of surprisingly high musical and production quality and often featuring the work of, amongst others Jay Wilbur and his many pseudonyms, Jay Whidden, Harry Leader, Bertini and Billy Merrin. Davis' Arcade also opened in Lord Street only a brief walk away from Woolworth's and here records, record players, instruments and band parts could be purchased relatively cheaply. By the late-1920s there were several such record shops and retailers in Liverpool's city centre, ranging from a record department in Lewis Department store (who also briefly had their own budget label) to independent music and record shops in nearby Moorfields and Victoria Street. But Woolworth's and Davies' made perhaps the greatest impact in Liverpool's city centre prior to the onset of WWII, owing to their locations, cheap prices, and the opportunities to eat: in the case of the Woolworth's a lunch counter and Davies' the Edinburgh Cafe, where people could linger and talk about music.

As Liverpool expanded, district shopping areas such as those at Walton Road, Old Swan, and Tuebrook grew in significance. Here the retailing of popular music also played its part: but record shops were not always immediately identifiable, as many cycle shops retailed records (Gerry Howard's on Green Lane, Stoneycroft for example) and furniture shops also opened record departments to compliment their furniture-based gramophone players. So identifying record retailing in Liverpool's outskirts in the inter-war period is more problematic that one might, at first, presume. Nevertheless by the late-1930s several shops had become synonymous with the buying and selling of records. For example both Robert Crease and NEMS on Walton Road gave innumerable locals the opportunity to hear new sounds. So the processes involved in hearing new sounds throughout both the twentieth and twenty-first centuries are complex and contingent with the actions of ordinary people.

But the major recording companies were not always helpful to retailers; while handling most of the distribution, they ensured that independent record companies such as Topic (folk), Tempo, and Esquire (jazz) were forced to find their own ways of reaching the public. In the early days of the post-WWII era such small companies usually resorted to running their own record clubs and mail-order services to furnish their customers, advertising with flyers at gigs and on the back pages of the music 'inkies' such as *Melody Maker* and *Jazz Journal*. Alan Peters even brings to mind that:

> Myself and Mike Haralambos (Almost Blues) used to send to the States for many recordings. We paid one guinea for three 12" LPs i.e. B.B. King, Elmore James, and Pee Wee Clayton; I still have the B.B. King and Elmore James LPs on the US Crown label. These American recordings were noticeably different by their weight and thickness of the vinyl and cardboard outer sleeves. We used to wait in anticipation for these recordings and the only other place I recall we could get hold of early blues was in Circle Records in Dale Street and sometimes Edwards' in Kensington. (Peters to Brocken, March 2009)

As for the broadcasting of 'other' music such as blues, folk, hillbilly, and even rock 'n' roll, this was often left to the discretion of a self-appointed connoisseur (usually a producer) at the BBC who knew little about popular culture. So the record shop became for many an emporium of discovery in which the specialized nature of the value chain surrounding recorded sound was regarded as an important feature of the buying and selling process. Certain shops and record departments in Liverpool, as elsewhere, became renowned for their active participation in the process of endowing a public with the sounds that it came to know and enjoy. This was by no means representative of any quasi-Adornian concept of passive engagement with a pre-digested product masquerading as culture. Far from it in fact, for the potential to 'create' art via its vernacular use-value was intrinsic to the very act of walking into a record store.

Record shops: The true art form of taste-making

The Musical Box

By the 1950s there were a handful of Liverpool-based record shops that 'bucked the trend' of some local record retailers selling only major label product. Two examples would be the Musical Box on Rocky Lane (and also later of Prescot Road in Old Swan) and NEMS in Great Charlotte Street (and also later of Whitechapel). The Musical Box is still a family run business and Liverpool's longest running independent record shop. It was established shortly after WWII by the Caine family and gradually became a beacon for all record collectors in Liverpool. Indeed one might argue that without this important popular music conduit in Liverpool, the history of Liverpool popular music would be very different. Liverpool music entrepreneur Joe Flannery recalls:

> Without the Musical Box I don't think I would have been able to have kept up with the music that other groups were playing. My brother's stage name Lee Curtis (and the All Stars) was derived from Curtis Lee and that was because we had bought Lee's 'Upstairs at Daddy Gee's' single from Diane – she kept us all on top of what was happening. (Flannery to Brocken, 1999)

As suggested previously by one interviewee Mr and Mrs Caine were not always 'obliging' or altogether accommodating to record purchasers with tastes that they did not immediately identify, but daughter Diane became and remains legendary in her willingness to find an obscure track, or to order rare and hard to find recordings. Indeed, because of this enthusiastic attitude (and unlike other independent retailers) Diane was able to order large quantities of records, knowing that they would sell. It would not be uncommon, during the peak of singles sales in the mid–late 1960s, for the Musical Box (at this stage with two branches) to order as many copies of a new single as the major Liverpool city centre record shops such as Rushworth and Dreaper's, Beaver Radio and NEMS. This meant that Diane's margins were greater: consequently sale-or-return recordings were not always returned to the wholesale distributors. Collector and, later, record dealer Bill Hinds admitted:

> Musical Box has to loom large in my legend as it's the place (the one on Prescot Rd) I bought my first ever 45 ('The Boxer' – not too bad to own-up to) but even before that, before we had a record player (!) their window acted as a kind of news board as to what was out/available (i.e. what I was missing out on!). A great shop – always worth asking for old deleted stuff right into the 70s; I can remember buying 'House of the Rising Sun' there in about 1969 – and getting the original Columbia release, proper sleeve and all. Now there was one place I wouldn't have minded being locked-in overnight for a good rummage. (Hinds, email correspondence, 2009)

This attention to detail and general over-stocking also meant that the Musical Box later became a 'landfall' for the growing squads of 'serious' record collectors in the late-1970s and 1980s. Diane 'controlled' (if that is the correct word) her singles stock by the re-use of the boxes in which 7" records were sent. She would write the name of each artist on the front of each box and place it on her expansive shelving – in such a small shop this was a sight to behold. This writer recalls revisiting the Musical Box in the mid-1980s on several occasions and asking to see what Diane might still have in stock on the 'pink' Island label. She would reach for various boxes on which she had scribed names such as 'If', 'Nirvana', 'Blodwyn Pig' and 'Spooky Tooth' and then open up a cornucopia of record delights – pristine, un-played singles within. It was like having several birthdays all at once.

Diane's lack of attention to out-and-out profit-making in the 1960s (by not returning records, or placing them in a deletion bin) had worked wonders, for it lengthened the life of the Musical Box perhaps literally by decades. Once these Island singles became acknowledged, not only as collectibles, but also as objects of art, Diane was then able to use the *Record Collector* price guides in order to demand fair prices. So her active interest in all forms of popular music and direct involvement with the needs of customers meant that the shop continued to exist where others had already failed years previously. One brave shop attempting to offer-up competition to the Rocky Lane branch of the Musical Box was the Golden Disc, in Tuebrook. This turned out to be possibly the worst of all record shops in Liverpool by an almost irreligious adherence to chart material (specifically Tamla Motown), and a determined returns policy that travelling reps must have hated. One record collector also recalled:

> The Golden Disc was the only record shop in Liverpool I remember NOT having a deletion bin! But the Musical Box towered above even the major city stores in my opinion. Nothing was too much trouble. Sometimes you had to wait for Diane to be in the shop, though! But when she was there, it was brilliant. Diane opened a branch near Greenberg's in Old Swan, so I followed her there. When I walked in with my long hair and trogg-like clothes she probably knew I was after something a bit more unusual, but by and large she had it and if not, she'd always order it. (Parry to Brocken, 2008)

All record shops should be judged on one criterion – customer service. There is nothing like a record shop proprietor or member of staff getting to know the customer and their musical tastes, and recommending music on repeated visits. Diane Caine's position in the specialist value chain is one that should always be associated with record retailing at its very best; her value to the history of the city of Liverpool is thus assured.

NEMS

Despite its internationally known brand name being directly associated with the Beatles, NEMS initially fulfilled a similar function to that offered by the Musical Box. The North End Music Stores was originally the name of an annexe to the Epstein furniture store, selling pianos and sheet music in the Walton area of Liverpool. When Brian Epstein's father decided to expand his business into the centre of Liverpool, he opened a branch in Great Charlotte Street. Brian and his brother Clive (1936-88) were placed in charge of this new outlet. Brian handled the ground floor record section, while Clive ran the white goods and furniture-based electrical goods department on the first floor.

Like Diane Caine, Brian Epstein was fascinated by the record retailing industry and soon became an expert at tracing hard to find recordings. NEMS was renowned for being the first in the city to stock OST (original soundtracks) and West End and Broadway Cast albums. Epstein often walked across the road to the Lewis's department store (which also had a music section) where Peter Brown was employed. He watched Brown's sales technique and was impressed enough to lure Brown to work for NEMS with the offer of a higher salary and a commission on sales. On 3 August 1961, Epstein started a regular music column in *Mersey Beat*, called, 'Record Releases, by Brian Epstein of NEMS'. He was known to be very obliging and helpful. Rock and skiffle fan Mick O'Toole remembers purchasing records from Epstein most Saturday evenings after hours. For example, Mick recalls working at the adjacent St John's Market until well after six o'clock and spotting Brian behind the counter of the (by that time closed) NEMS store. Mick would knock on the shop door and Epstein would let him into the shop informing him to 'always give a knock on the door – if I am there doing the books, I will open up'.

> Mr Epstein, as everyone knew him, would always be helpful – it wasn't like other shops where the record racks might be just an add-on to a TV shop and you were considered to be a bit of a nuisance. He genuinely cared about music and would not hesitate to order something for you. (O'Toole to Brocken, 2007)

Alan Peters also recalls the joys of NEMS:

> Mr Brown, Epstein and Sheila at NEMS used to compile any new Blues and R&B records that they could get their hands on for me to listen to on Wednesday afternoons when I used to 'sag-off' from Liverpool Art School sports at Calderstones Park (I disliked having to play football with being an asthmatic). (Peters to Brocken, 2009)

A second store was opened at 12-14 Whitechapel, and Brian Epstein oversaw the entire operation. He placed Pete Brown in charge of the Great Charlotte Street branch and personally managed the Whitechapel shop until his NEMS Enterprises agency took him to Moorfields, thence to London. The record department in this later NEMS was in a basement, the journey to which became in itself an exciting trek down a dozen or so steps into an inner sanctum, an 'Aladdin's Cave'. Brian Epstein had covered the entire ceiling with album sleeves and it all appeared very exciting and exclusive. NEMS had an interesting lay-out with listening booths by the entrance and the entire shop floor being taken up by racks of record sleeves. So, from personal memory, this basement of NEMS became a good place to 'hang out' – one could ask for records to be played (without any intention of purchasing) for some considerable time before the staff became irritated, then it was a mere skip up the stairs to street level. One might then walk across Whitechapel to the Kardomah Cafe and make a cup of coffee last an hour, or else annoy the staff in Newmart Electronics by endlessly leafing through their odd selection of deleted obscurities, such as the endless copies of Stuart 'Champion' Damon's eponymous solo LP:

> I used to sag-off school pretty regularly in the late-1960s and would wander into town. But in those days if you were seen in the city centre on your own people would ask why you weren't at school. One of the best places to go was NEMS. You were off the street and could listen to a few singles in the booths before the staff got fed up and chucked you out. I heard a lot of new stuff like that. (Scott to Brocken, 1997)

Edwards', Kensington

By the 1960s one of the easiest of ways for a budding record enthusiast to get on the record collecting ladder was by spending a little time and money at Edwards' second-hand record shop in Kensington. Here one could examine the plyboard lists of singles hanging by the entrance to the shop: on sale for half retail price, or less, or one might scrutinize the shop window for secondhand recent releases which, full-priced, might be out of financial reach. It was in this window that the rock/pop dichotomy came to be visibly evident via Mr Edwards' stock control. By the late-1960s one could almost guarantee that a successful single from a group such as, say, The Crazy World of Arthur Brown would also attract interested album purchasers. But singles by such artists were, by definition, the most commercial tracks and such 'heavy' albums considered by some a 'let down'. It was here that Edwards' came in useful, for if a 'heavy' single charted, within a short space of time the respective album would accordingly appear, as if by magic, in Edwards' shop window. The average singles purchaser might be able to enjoy (say) three minutes of Brown's 'Fire', but not, one suspects, his 'Prelude – Nightmare' from the same album.

The shop appeared, initially to be a trading-post for those interested in jazz and blues, for there were many such albums on display and collectors of all ages could be seen there. By the late-1960s one could also find several hundred country music albums, a good selection of folk material, and the ubiquitous soul music singles pinned-up in the diminutive shop. It was truly host to a profusion of delights and many people were to be found at the Edwards' shop – once it had opened, of course. The opening times could certainly vary. Indeed Mr Edwards would often not open at all and on other occasions would wait until the schools let out at 4pm. Then an after-school walk to Kensington from the surrounding areas became *de rigueur* for those bitten by the popular music bug.

Mr Edwards' back room was out-of-bounds to all but the most trusted. It was in this inner chamber that items were rather cursorily examined for defects, and priced accordingly. The risk of buying a defective album from Edwards was relatively high, but this was not the fault of the shop. By the late-1960s vinyl faults such as white lining and impurities, not always visible to the naked eye, were an increasing problem for all record collectors. Several UK pressing plants such as Philips had taken to recycling vinyl and so there was a risk of purchasing what on the surface looked like an unmarked record, but in fact contained jumps or clicks. I recall purchasing second-hand a badly-pressed John Martyn album (*The Tumbler*) from Edwards' and being too embarrassed to loan it to school friends, thinking I had been a fool to buy it there in the first place. But I returned to Edwards' shop and managed to smuggle the rogue record past Mr Edwards' eagle eye, alongside a Marble Arch-labelled Foundations LP (good) and a cheap Ember 'early' Scott Walker album (terrible). One might view a rarity being inspected from the boundaries of the outer shop, and then be forced to wait for days until it appeared in the home-made racking in the shop proper. I well-remember observing Mr Edwards inspecting a copy of the first Bert Jansch album in the backroom. I returned to the shop several times thereafter, only to disappointedly see it in the hands of another collector before I was able to part with my 25/-.

For a teenager, trading with Mr Edwards was a rather frightening experience. In order to supplement one's growing interest in all things musical, singles and albums were often surrendered back to the shop in order to purchase something more up-to-date or of greater interest. But when the aforementioned 'heavy' or 'underground' music became the 'rule of thumb' for those such as myself in the late-1960s, Mr Edwards was not always keen to restock that (e.g.) Van Der Graaf Generator or Deep Purple album after having already disposed of it once (or twice). Comments such as 'We can't use this' or 'We haven't got a market for this' would ring out across the shop as yet another disappointed would-be trader was forced to rethink his/her strategy. Bill Hinds:

> First discovered Edwards' when walking home from some 'school do' in town aged about 15 (to save the bus tickets!) and being amazed by looking in the window and noting that here was somewhere you could buy records that were no longer available in the normal shops (even The Musical Box). Brilliant! At that time of course there was no concept of 'rare' or 'collectable' pop stuff. Having come quite late to record buying, there was much to catch up on from the preceding 5 years-or-so, so the first Saturday after that I was up there with my paper-round money scoring old singles – I distinctly remember getting 'Alone

Again Or' on my first visit. I remember scanning the lists with pencil-in-hand, writing down the numbers and hoping-against-hope that they wouldn't be gone by the time we'd got to the counter. Being just a written list, you never quite knew what you'd be getting – I can recall asking for 'My Mind's Eye' – always my favourite Small Faces track – for 3 bob and getting a stunning French EP complete with really cool glossy picture sleeve.

My memories of the place are all good, really. They were always fair and respectful when buying stuff from you and they paid – what was it? – 15/- or even £1 an album, which they then sold-on for 28/-? 30/-? You can't say fairer than that, really. Those rejected were rejected reasonably politely – usually with 'I've got thousands of these', which, to be fair, he usually did. Pricing was rigid – no haggling, buying or selling. All this allowed more experimentation with things as you knew you could usually take it back next week if it turned out to be crap.

I can remember an occasion of us being allowed into the back room – I can't recall why, maybe you had asked for something he was searching for – and almost salivated at the rack of vinyl within, itching to just dive-in and flick through the lot! But that would have been a step too far, alas. (Hinds, email correspondence with Brocken, 2009)

By the late-1970s Edwards' had moved from Kensington to the Daulby Street-end of London Road on the fringes of Liverpool's city centre. This turned-out to be a very bad move as rents and rates, coupled with record company over-production and the newly introduced record fairs at the Bluecoat crippled the already fragile and limited second-hand record shop trade. Edwards' never recovered from this unsustainable move and sadly closed its doors in the early-1980s.

Skeleton Records, Argyle Street, Birkenhead

Jon Weaver began Skeleton Records in 1969 as 'Phineas Fogg's Picture Emporium' – a dark and rather cramped basement address on Argyle Street, close to the Central Hotel. It was a shop typical of the independent 'head-cum-record shop' of its day. It did not cater to any great extent for the singles market and concentrated more fully on mostly second-hand 'underground', folk and, significantly, *bootleg* albums. The first bootleg is now legendary, a collection of Bob Dylan recordings dating from 1961, plus miscellaneous studio out-takes, and seven tracks from the Basement Tapes sessions, all under the unofficial name of 'The Great White Wonder' due to the fact that the sleeve was plain white. The tapes that made up this release had been circulating amongst collectors for some time, but it was for some the disappointment of Dylan's album *Nashville Skyline* with fans knowing that the Basement Tapes contained the musical missing links between *Blonde On Blonde* and *John Wesley Harding* that created enough interest for an enterprising pair of Californian record plant workers to produce bootleg vinyl copies. A lucrative but highly illegal business was born and, in the UK, enterprising bootleggers, similarly employed at record pressing plants across the UK, soon followed suit with (at first) live recordings of Jimi Hendrix.

The bootleg industry, therefore, was growing apace by the early-1970s. Bootlegs at first featured usually very poorly recorded live sets from famous artists, but underground fans clamoured for these 'new sounds' and 'Fogg's' tended to specialize in such new and used rock bootlegs. The shop became a focal exchange point in Birkenhead for a growing legion of rock fans. Record purchasers would trade their albums, bringing in unwanted LPs and part-exchanging them for new items. Trade in hard rock LPs (rather than the psychedelia and country rock more popular in Liverpool) appeared at times to hold more sway in Birkenhead. When the 'Picture Emporium' outgrew its modest basement premises, it moved at first to the Hamilton Square end of Argyle Street and then finally took over the former Gas Board premises on the same street. By this time Weaver was also selling new albums and as punk began to take a grip of the independent shop network, Skeleton (as it was now known) embraced this new subculture. Former manager of the Cherry Boys Graham Jones recalled to *Liverpool Daily Post* writer Jade Wright his 'favourite shop was Skeleton in Birkenhead. It was dark and dingy, but had a great atmosphere' (Wright, 2009:22). Weaver was another obliging, knowledgeable retailer who also tried his hand in the independent record label market by launching 'Skeleton Records'. This was a far from prolific label but did produce an excellent sampler EP in 1978 containing local new wave artists such as the Geisha Girls and the Zorkie Twins. Eventually Skeleton was to struggle, but like the Stairways Rock Club in the same row of buildings, certainly made its mark on the cultural landscape of Birkenhead. There is still a Skeleton Records trading in Birkenhead, on Oxton Road, not far from its original incarnation at Argyle Street.

Probe Records

By the early-1970s Probe Records had arrived in Liverpool like a breath of fresh air. Probe began trading in 1970 in Clarence Street, catering for a mixture of 'Liverpool Stadium rock fans' and students, and by the mid-'70s had built up a clientele interested in a variety of 'new' genres such as progressive rock, west coast rock and psychedelia, jazz-rock, and funk. Proprietor Geoff Davies claims to have merely ordered the kinds of records that he would have purchased. As such, Probe appealed to a specific group of fans with little interest in 45 rpm recordings. Probe did sell a few singles but in their first few years their main interest lay in album sales. Like Skeleton, this shop was similar to an American 'head' shop where other products such as copies of the underground press, joss sticks, etc could be purchased. Probe added another 'branch' in 1974 when they placed a small record department at the rear of Silly Billy's boutique in Whitechapel – only a few hundred yards from the larger record shops on that road – this was manned by future Eric's deejay Norman Killon.

The 'Silly Billy's' experiment was followed by the more renowned Probe store in Button Street in October 1976, where punk, new wave, and reggae recordings increasingly sat alongside their previous progressive and west coast catalogues. Probe's record stock came to physically reflect the changing profiles of popular music in 1976. Probe was not only a record shop, but a meeting place for a variety of like-minded popular music fans drawn to the Mathew Street area by both the presence of the Eric's venue and the growing historical interest in all things 'Merseybeat'. Saturdays at Probe could be amazing affairs. Young people would gather on the corners of Button Street and Mathew Street simply to hear the records that were being played on the turntables by those working at the shop. Records were purchased, of course but in the late-1970s Probe also became the centre of many young people's musical universe. All of the Probe employees were regarded as arbiters of 'good taste'. So much so that one Saturday I went in to buy a country rock album: Poco's *Rose of Cimarron*. Pete Burns, later of Dead or Alive fame was working behind the counter and he was the only one in the shop at the time. I picked up the sleeve and took it to him and he wouldn't let me have the record. He said I could pick something else, but he wasn't going to soil his hands with a f*****g Poco record.

These above discussed record shops (and others such as Penny Lane Records, Virgin Records in Bold Street, and on the Wirral, Rox) were more than just retailers. They were audiophiles, cultural practitioners, taste-makers: important links in the chains of popular music reception. They were advice centres for people looking for specific recordings, agents of change: recommending other recordings, other artists and other styles of music. As generations of young people came to find their voice in the Merseyside of the post-war era, such shops as the Musical Box, NEMS, Probe, and Skeleton were facilitating the discovery of new ways of hearing music. They smoothed the processes of accessing music, supplementing the concert hall and the radio, and in helping people to discover 'new' sounds for themselves, these shops gave people an expression of autonomy within an industry often accused of manipulation. Artist Trevor Jackson confirms this important supplementarity:

> I owe a huge part of my musical interests to people who have served me, and people I have met whilst shopping. Record shops are more than just a place to buy product, the best are cultural landmarks, social places to converse and debate, a retreat from the mundane, an escape. Music is one of the most powerful and enjoyable forms of communication and deserves to be delivered in an environment that fully panders to every music-lovers desire. (Jackson to Pettit, 2008:89)

Labels, studios

Before music can have any kind of impact, the artist who creates it needs an audience. The audience must hear the music, either in recorded form or in performance. One might imagine that given the success of many Merseyside-based artists throughout the latter half of the twentieth century Liverpool was home to several independent record labels finding a paying audience for records. However this was not the case. By the general definition of the term 'independent label' there were historically few record labels in Liverpool, and those that did exist were initially part of micro-studios dealing directly with the public.

Phillips Recording Studio, 38, Kensington

Eventually, Liverpool did emerge with a handful of record labels of its own but these took a long period of time to develop and most were successful in only limited ways. The first recording *studio* of any note was that of Percy Phillips in Kensington, Liverpool. Country music fan Percy Phillips had originally run an electrical goods shop in Liverpool and decided in 1955 (at the age of 60) to buy a portable tape recorder and a portable disc-cutter. He also added microphones and a four-way mixer. This studio was no more than a recording booth set up in the front room of Phillips' own home: a large terraced house in Kensington. One-off discs were produced, however: spoken word messages to relatives, birthday recordings and occasional contract work for choral societies and church choirs. Percy Phillips would first commit the performance to tape and then transfer this to a shellac disc, wiping the tape in readiness for the next customer. The only historical traces of these recordings, therefore, reside with those for whom the records were cut. The studio's name did appear on the mustard coloured record labels but each label contained only hand-written details of the recording. There were no catalogue numbers as such, although it is probable that Phillips kept a logbook of work completed. The world's most expensive and collectable recording – the Quarry Men's 'That'll Be the Day' c/w 'In Spite of All the Danger' was recorded by Phillips in Kensington. Various dates in 1958 are given for this event but none can be verified, although ex-band members recall arriving wearing coats, which could place the season as winter.

The records could be either double or single-sided and although basic, Phillips' studio was something of a novelty. Word spread among young local musicians in the 1950s that there was an easy way of cutting a record at his studio and it has been claimed that several local artists – including the aforementioned Quarry Men – made their 'one take' recordings there. They were eager to record for the sake of allowing them to say they possessed their own record. Sadly, Phillip's so-called mobile equipment was seldom if ever used away from the Kensington address and so many opportunities for remote recordings of some of the burgeoning sounds in and around Liverpool were lost.

CAM, Moorfields

CAM Studios in Liverpool has already come under the spotlight in discussions concerning the country music, R&B and cabaret scenes. CAM was run by electrical engineer Charles Weston, and the studios were co-owned by the Wilmington

Agency and Industrial Marine. The technology at CAM was more sophisticated than that at Percy Philips' studio and CAM began life as a genuine demonstration studio. Weston also provided a vinyl 45 rpm service for those wishing to have a single recording to tout around publishers and record companies. This service had both a matrix (i.e. pressing) and a catalogue number and was named 'Unichord'. All artists who received their Unichord disc/s from CAM had to guarantee payment for the entire process, which included studio time and microphone use in addition to final pressing (the latter of which was out-sourced). Artists therefore could find themselves in debt to CAM for extra studio time used in event of a problem with a 'take'. By the mid-1960s a few local artists such as the Almost Blues, the Perfumed Garden, and the Foggy Mountain Ramblers had recorded for this 'label', but it could be an expensive and rather frustrating business; Barry Cohen recalls:

> After a failed recording test at CBS we [Perfumed Garden] decided to pay for a recording session ourselves. Then it was to decide where do we go? Considering Liverpool was the birth place of the Beatles, the city even then had the most famous club in the world. But when it came to recording studios, there simply was no choice in Liverpool other than CAM. So we did our demo at CAM. We all chipped-in our share to pay for it, and one week-day evening we booked about three hours or so, and put our two tracks down.
>
> The playback sounded really good. That evening we left feeling confident the acetate would be good for us. As we were packing up to go, the engineer said 'what about echo, do we want some added?' We made the major mistake of leaving it to him to play about with adding echo. Only 25 copies were pressed. Neither song on that record ever got played outside the group. The whole thing, including studio-time and acetate pressings, cost us about £35. This was a *small fortune* in those days. You could buy a second-hand car taxed-and-tested for anything between £10 and £30, so in comparison a good chunk of money. I know, because my first car a Ford Anglia cost just £30. After all these years, still having my copy of the CAM recording, I have recently listened to it again. Compared with what else was around at the time and considering the restrictions on money, therefore the limited studio time, the record is actually not too bad. The Perfumed Garden for me sadly came to end towards the end of '69 after a disagreement. (Barry Cohen, email correspondence, 2009)

CAM did strike out a little and by 1966 had introduced its own 'CAM' label. Jim McCulloch, a local club owner attempted to bail out the failing CAM studio by starting a record label. The deal was an extension of the Unichord idea: artists or their management would not only pay for the recording, but also multiple pressings and packaging. Charles Weston would engineer the tracks but also provide the artists with a product that could be retailed. However persuading Liverpool's larger record retailers to stock CAM material was very difficult. The argument from the shops during this boom time for record sales was that local material would take the space of recordings of national interest. In truth, the larger shops just couldn't be bothered and matters were left, once again, with retailers such as the Musical Box to stock these now rare local 45s and EPs (no evidence has come to light to suggest that CAM records sold elsewhere in the country). Perhaps the most significant CAM record was the Klubs' 1968 classically psychedelic 'I Found the Sun'/'Ever Needed Someone' (CAM682). Jim McCulloch cut several tracks with the group in the summer of 1968 and this single was issued by CAM in December of that year, but only being for sale in local shops (despite advertised nationally in the *New Musical Express*), few copies were sold.

The renowned ex-Anglican Cathedral choirboys-turned-folkies the Crofters also recorded an excellent LP for CAM from which two picture-sleeved EPs were extracted in 1967. This album contained a beautiful version of the little-heard Cyril Tawney song 'Sally Free and Easy'. CAM-labelled recordings did not sell in any great quantities but they remain good representations of, firstly Liverpool's one truly psychedelic group and, secondly one of the leading lights of Liverpool's late-1960s folk scene. In all there were few CAM releases, for pressing and packaging was an expensive affair; somebody (either Jim McCulloch, CAM or the artists) probably lost a lot of money.

Amazon Studios and Jungle Records, Kirkby

As we have seen, when the financially unstable CAM Studios closed its doors in the early 1970s some of the equipment went to the 'new' Liverpool Sound Studios in Kirkby. There is a probably apocryphal story that Kingsize (Ted) Taylor's infamous Star Club Beatles reel-to-reel tapes were actually found at the old Moorfields studios when the equipment was being cleared. Liverpool Sound lasted a few years but eventually closed its doors. A new outfit, Amazon, took over and became a very professional company recording over the subsequent years several local and nationally renowned bands and artists at their well-appointed studios. But they also launched a record label – appropriately entitled 'Jungle' which served a similar purpose to Alan Richards' Stag enterprise. Jungle did not always use their own catalogue numbers, preferring on occasion to use those of the well-known independent pressing plant SRM ('Studio Republic'). Over the course of a few years in the late 1970s and early 1980s several Jungle singles and EPs were issued (such as those by the Blue Magnolia Jass Orchestra, Cy Tucker, Terry Fletcher, and Whiskey River) – but none, sadly, were of any great distinction.

Problems began to beset this kind of freelance single production by the late-1970s. The likes of the wholesale Rough Trade Cartel could guarantee good distribution for local labels provided the group/artist fitted into the punk or new wave genres. However for those artists working in other fields such as cabaret, country, or trad jazz (all still very popular music genres in Liverpool at this time), distribution was practically non-existent. There was little likelihood of locally made recordings receiving anything other than occasional local radio airplay, and a smattering of sales via gigs. Evidently, this independent wholesale cartel was just as fussy about what they considered to be 'acceptable' genres of music, as were the 'majors'!

Probe-Plus

Geoff Davies, co-owner of Probe Records, latterly of Button Street, Liverpool branched out from retailing into record production, establishing Probe-Plus Records in 1980. Geoff did so with the knowledge that the independent record distribution service was in full flow and that he could produce music from the above-mentioned 'acceptable genres'. Independent record charts were being featured in the weekly music press such as the *NME* and *Sounds* and both Probe and Penny Lane Records in Liverpool (and Skeleton and Rox in Wirral) were doing a roaring trade in punk and reggae singles. Eric's Club proprietors Roger Eagle and Peter Fulwell had already experimented with an Eric's record label prior to the closure of this famous nightclub (e.g. the Pink Military album), but Davies saw great potential in the 'indie' network and developed Probe-Plus along these lines. Probe-Plus has represented several important local and national artists and groups of the 1980s and 1990s such as Mr Amir, Attila the Stockbroker, Gone to Earth, Half Man Half Biscuit, Marlowe, and others. Geoff Davies still believes in handling all aspects of a record's development and this hands-on approach has garnered for him a great reputation among all those musicians who have fallen under his influence.

Throughout the 1980s many local recording labels have come and gone on Merseyside. Most of these were one-off labels but one or two have weathered the storm and still survive to this day. These include 'indie' labels Probe-Plus, Viper, and Audio-Visual; reissue label Mayfield (which was started in 1983 by music entrepreneur Joe Flannery and is still releasing product), distributors Pink Moon and several dance music labels. However the music industry is now changing so rapidly and so dramatically that what was once a people-based manufacturing industry is now moving (albeit unsteadily) towards being a technologically based service provider. The chances of any independent record label existing in the ways that they have previously done is extremely doubtful. This is a great pity when according to Joe Flannery of Mayfield 'the technology should still be seen as secondary. It's only a *way* of making music, not the "be all and end all". Most music producers now are computer programmers' (Flannery to Brocken, 2007).

Radio

The BBC is excellent at self-promotion; the Corporation would have us believe that it was always a supporter of popular music. Barnard (1989) suggests that this was not the case and that until the 1960s the bulk of pro-active popular music broadcasting in the UK was from land-based pirates in Europe. In practical terms alone, the BBC's very monopoly of radio lasted for only a short period of time.

Radio Paris actually began broadcasting an English language programme as early as 1925 and the following year Radio Normandy began to broadcast to the south of England. By 1930 there were five million radio sets in Britain but most British listeners had little alternative but to tune in to the BBC. Demand, however, existed for more popular styles of programming – especially from the dance band and hot jazz genres. To exploit this, a private company, the International Broadcasting Company (IBC) was set up. It hired 'air-time' from overseas stations and transmitted popular programmes aimed at the UK market. While these programmes were perfectly legal, and while BBC transmissions were covering the continent just as readily as the continental stations were reaching the UK, the attitude of the BBC and the government towards the IBC was continuously hostile, especially when the British population tuned to Radios Lyon and Normandy, Radios Athlone, Mediterranee and Radio Luxembourg in increasing numbers.

In the early months of 1933 Radio Luxembourg commenced its Europe-wide broadcasts on 1250 LW and within a short space of time those listeners who could pick up the transmissions began to reject the formality of the 'Beeb' for a night time schedule that included the likes of the 'Kraft Cheese Music Hall of Fame', the 'Bile Beans Concert', the 'Andrew's Liver Salts Concert', and the 'Ovaltinies Club' – the latter of which by 1938 enjoyed a membership of one million UK listeners. It has been recorded (Preedy, 2004:8) that in 1938 Radio Luxembourg held an 80 per cent market share of all UK listeners of an evening time. The BBC was to complain to the government, which in turn put pressure on British newspapers not to print programme schedules of the overseas stations. Royalty organizations were also persuaded to overcharge for permission to play pre-recorded material. The BBC even discouraged employing any artist or presenter who had worked previously on a 'continental station'. The government were anxious to suppress mass communication over which they did not have control, yet still, the overseas stations flourished and by 1938 Radio Luxembourg had 45 per cent of the Sunday listening audience against the BBC's 35 per cent and advertisers were spending £1.7 million per annum – a substantial sum.

At the outbreak of WWII in 1939 all such commercial broadcasting into the UK ceased. Radio Luxembourg was taken over by the Nazis and used for propaganda purposes and the station only returned to English broadcasting in 1945 initially on long wave and then in 1951 on 208 metres on the medium wave. It became so successful that by the mid-1950s all of its airtime was being block-booked by British record companies. For many years thereafter the BBC continued its daytime monopoly and delivered a style of programming that was often either homogenizing or patronizing. The BBC's comedy programmes were adventurous, but musically lost the evening broadcasting battle with Radio Luxembourg. Opportunities for hearing youth-based music on BBC radio were limited to one Saturday morning programme, 'Saturday Skiffle Club' (later 'Saturday Club' after the skiffle craze had ended), one Sunday pop ballad-style programme 'Easy Beat' and a Sunday afternoon review of the current charts. These shows were hosted by established BBC presenters and failed to capture the youthful essence of rock 'n' roll. In fact, as in any other city across the country, popular music lovers in Liverpool were largely taken for granted by the Corporation and force-fed a diet of Light Programme blandness.

The only real alternative was to tune to Radio Luxembourg, the only cross-border, land-based 'pirate' broadcaster to the UK that had been able to restart operations after the war. The Luxembourg signal could only reach the UK after dark when propagation conditions changed. Even then, the signal tended to fade in and out for long periods. Notwithstanding, Radio Luxembourg was hugely popular. By the late-1950s many young people tended to listen to Radio Luxembourg for new sounds rather than the admittedly popular BBC programmes such as 'Easy Beat' or 'Saturday Club'. So important had Radio Luxembourg become to the youth of Britain by the 1960s that it effectively forced the BBC to investigate its own activities in 1963. This report eventually led to the arrival of both Radio 1 and local radio in 1967. Liverpool band manager and good friend of Brian Epstein Joe Flannery remarked to this writer that when the Beatles' first recording 'Love Me do' was released 'Brian and myself were desperate to listen to it on Radio Luxembourg first, certainly not the BBC'.

Music Radio in Liverpool

Liverpool did have a BBC relay station (6LV). This was opened in 1924 and initially operated from a small room in Lord Street above Davies' Arcade. Various light entertainment programmes were broadcast mostly of an evening from Liverpool to the local population. Liverpool's first regular radio announcer was Freddie Stabback – he read the evening news and introduced programmes, but Mary Hamer of the Grafton also broadcast from Lord Street. The transmitter existed above a disused paint shop, near Smithdown Road, in the Wavertree district of the city. It has also been recorded that a local pirate radio station existed before WWII in the Merseyside area: 'The station, 6NI, used to broadcast gramophone records from a house in Merton Road, Bootle, after 6LV stopped transmitting in the evening' (Young and Hunt, 1997:9). 6LV closed down broadcasting when the North Region transmitter at Moorside Edge opened in 1931. After this the Lord Street location was bombed during the WWII and following the end of the conflict, the BBC were only lukewarm as far as broadcasting from Liverpool was concerned. In 1950 Liverpool Corporation agreed that a room at the council-owned Rylands Buildings in Lime Street could be leased to the BBC and this was used as a 'talk studio'. The studio was later moved to Castle Chambers. It was not until 22 November 1967 that Liverpool finally received its own BBC local radio station at Sir Thomas Street.

However, by the mid-1960s offshore pirate stations such as Radio Caroline North were of some significance to music activity in Liverpool. Radio Caroline had offices on Prescot Street, near to the Majestic Picture House, and one could, at least in theory, send a request to the station from this address. However in reality things were rather more chaotic than this and, although Caroline North is remembered fondly by some in Liverpool, others remember that the 1967 Marine Offences Bill put paid to a rather shambolic radio station that was rather overly inclined to have Don Allen present country music for listeners in Ireland rather than the pop for which they were renowned. As this writer recalls, it was fun listening most of the time but they used to plug Major Minor Records incessantly, play country music a lot and *not* bother much with actual requests. I remember putting a request into their office one week, listening in, and being very disappointed not to hear it read out. I also recall going past their offices on the number 10 bus thinking that the postcard was probably still sitting there, uncollected. Perhaps predictably, the Major Minor record company was owned by Radio Caroline co-proprietor Philip Solomon who bought into Radio Caroline in 1966 with the intention of creating a 'Caroline' record company. Instead, he formed Major Minor and, via a mixture of Irish releases and licensed US product, created quite a splash for around three years. Solomon openly exploited Radio Caroline as a 'plug' vehicle for his record label.

When Radio Merseyside first appeared in Liverpool in 1967 listeners were pleased to have local representation but programming was decidedly uninspiring and the playing of records kept to a minimum by the 'dictat' of 'needle-time'. To begin with Radio Merseyside was allowed only eight hours per week of recorded music and although this improved over the years it severely hampered opportunities to get directly involved in new sounds. However by 1968 Radio Merseyside began its long running *Folk Scene* programmes – hosted by the aforementioned Stan Ambrose and later Geoff Speed, and this weekly look at the folk scene of Liverpool was (as we have seen) an important conduit for both the committed and the curious. Ambrose and Speed have over the years dedicated thousands of hours to local folk talent and have helped to keep folk and traditional music alive in Liverpool where in other cities it has all but disappeared.

Radio Merseyside also re-launched Kenny Everett's career after Radio 1 had unceremoniously dumped him in the early-1970s and the station later took a great interest in the growing scene at Eric's club on Mathew Street. Innovative programmes such as the now-famous 'X-Ray Dolls' (an investigation into the 'goings-on' at Eric's) highlighted this new musical undercurrent across the region. Janis Long was to take this concept further by incorporating new local artists into her popular music programme. Perhaps the most effective campaigner for new music across the North West, Roger Hill, still presents his PMS 'Pure Musical Sensations' programme for those interested in non-mainstream music. Roger has racked-up hundreds of sessions and interviews with local, regional and national musicians, many of which are kept and catalogued at the Institute of Popular Music at the University of Liverpool. Up until very recently Steve Voce's jazz show was also a feature of Sunday evenings on BBC Radio Merseyside. For a while the commercial station (1974) Radio City also introduced listeners to several new musical styles. By 1975 Radio City were organizing concerts at the Royal Court Theatre. In the process they introduced new artists such as the Ozark Mountain Daredevils to Liverpool music fans. But these concerts were not to last.

Well known local folkie Bob Buckle presented a folk programme, rock fan Phil Easton a rock show, and choral specialist Philip Duffy a classical programme, but as advertising dictated more mainstream programming these shows sadly fell by the wayside.

Venues

Of course, music venues play a vital part in the ability to hear new sounds. However, the history of all concert halls is complex and asks us to consider attitudes about the status of popular music. Several styles of music were not heard in certain concert venues because of that venue's position on 'culture'. For example, in Liverpool the Royal Liverpool Philharmonic Hall was for a time home only to classical music, whereas the Liverpool Empire promoted only what it considered mainstream popular forms. It is interesting to note that only after rock acquired an 'intellectual' connotation was it featured at the University of Liverpool on a regular basis – all though the years of Merseybeat and the R&B boom, groups hardly got a look in at Mountford Hall. In different ways all of these venues had to be 'persuaded' to promote more youth-orientated and niche styles of popular music. When other styles of music emerged, such conventional venues were often to miss out on the important 'developmental' stage of music scenes. In the case of the highly significant trad jazz and folk music scenes in Liverpool, major venues did not at first get on board and it was left to smaller venues such as Alexandra Hall, Knotty Ash Village Hall, Picton Hall, the Liverpool Stadium, Blair Hall, etc, and various pubs across the city, to encourage people to hear these 'new' sounds. In this way, word-of-mouth became increasingly important. Joan Bimson recalls matter from the perspective a of a female teenage rock fan in the early–mid 1970s:

> Discotheques were unwelcoming places for the average rock fan of the early to mid-1970s. Females could at least get in without compromising their sense of identity too much. For male rockers the strict dress codes were a massive deterrent. The ban on jeans and trainers was there to keep them out. But why on earth would anyone want to go there in the first place?
>
> The 'straight' club scene was rigidly conventional. The girls were on display, dancing round their handbags. The men would eventually move in. The 'slowy' at the end of the night was your last chance to cop-off (the club's *raison d'etre*). And the music. oh dear God – the DJ was the arbiter of average taste, whose job was to keep them dancing. Even a moderately rocky pop song would be rejected as too 'heavy' (the cardinal sin was to clear the dance floor). After suffering the likes of 'the Locomotion' and 'Love Train' for several hours, some drunken pig reeking of *Brut* would try and stick his beery, nicotine-stained tongue down your throat. *That* was the dominant culture. *That* was what people looked forward to on a Saturday night; but not me.

The rock scene – being more focused on music – seemed refreshing and honest in comparison, though not without its hazards. Nightclubs, chippies, and taxi-ranks may have been swarming with thugs in cheap suits, but a long-haired hippy or freak was more likely to be harassed by the police (as well as by the thugs in cheap suits). Liverpool Stadium was a safe-haven for rock music fans, but many recall a heavy police presence on a concert night. According to other accounts, an eccentrically-dressed individual wandering abroad could expect to attract unwelcome police attention. Being different in Liverpool could be dangerous in those intolerant times. (Bimson, email correspondence March 2009)

The Moonstone

Part of the Ravenseft development of the St John's Market area in the late-1960s included a shopping precinct, which, in turn, housed a few pubs. One of these pubs was The Moonstone and its somewhat 'gothic' décor and ease of entry for young people soon attracted a subculture loosely based around the hippie movement. In the Liverpool of the early 1970s hippies were something of a minority with the all-pervading mod and then skinhead subcultures being more visible. However The Moonstone, in catering for a more alternative crowd, soon gained a reputation within the hippie or 'trogg' (as it was called locally) subculture as a venue that was friendly towards this group of young people. Not since the days of trad jazz had there been such strong divisions in pop music that ran along precise lines of dress, lifestyle and even social class. Ged McKenna recalls:

> I went regularly during the early seventies. There was a core group of us who were real die-hards and were there most nights some weeks, though how we afforded it, I have no idea. The place was run by a guy called Don, a military looking bloke with a dark moustache. At kicking out time he could always be heard 'come on now, talk as you walk'. It never varied. (McKenna to Brocken, 2008)

There were two bars at The Moonstone – one to the right at the foot of the stairs with the larger bar, down more stairs – this was where the bands played. This lower bar had a long bar which curved at the end where the glasses were washed. The stage was in the corner at this end, only a step up from the small, square dance floor.

Several local rock bands played at The Moonstone – some were better than others – but the major group for many of these 'troggs' were Restless, led by guitarist and brief singing partner of Elvis Costello, Alan Mays. Ged McKenna remembers:

> I guess the stand out band for me was Restless, who used to do a lot of West Coast stuff and had a gorgeous girl singer called Sheila; longish hair and floaty

frocks. I did a bit of roady-ing for them. A bloke called Alan [Mays] used to run it and I remember trying to persuade him not to split the band up. The biggest gig they got was supporting Stackridge at The Stadium. In the latter days, there was a band called Vicious who appeared around 1975 [...] The singer was a thin, spotty bloke with long, straggly hair and he had serious attitude: probably an early sign of the rise of Punk. Later in the '70s, Roger Eagle had ceased putting on gigs at The Stadium and we all stopped going there. By then for me it was past its best – or maybe I was just past caring. (*ibid*)

Invariably when Restless appeared at The Moonstone, the venue was packed. Following the end of an evening's sessions and depending upon which night one visited, 'troggs' would often move onto the Cavern, the Stadium, or perhaps on selected nights the Mardi Gras.

The Liverpool Stadium and Triad Promotions

In 1970 Roger Eagle was a budding rock entrepreneur and he formed Triad Promotions to bring concerts to Liverpool's somewhat neglected rock community. Eagle, although originally hailing from Oxford, was a former deejay at the Twisted Wheel club in Manchester, and was legendary for his knowledge of blues and soul music. As for Triad, Eagle claimed immediately that he was 'not in it for the bread' – very much a statement associated with that era in popular music history – and that he wished to offer an alternative to the usual concerts in Liverpool where, according to *Liverpool Echo* writer Sue Faulconbridge (7 October, 1970) 'the audience are rooted in their seats at the Phil or at the University, to listen with mute appreciation to their idols'. Eagle continued:

My own personal profit is about 5% per cent of the takings. The groups get 70%, as opposed to the 50% or 60% most promoters offer. We don't believe in pushing people around, so we won't have a deejay telling them what to do. If they want to they can dance in the aisles and move out of their seats. That's why we don't have reserved seats, so people feel they can move if they want. (Eagle to Faulconbridge, 1970:10)

The comment concerning deejays is an interesting one in that it suggests that some (many?) in Liverpool felt that deejay culture was very unquestioning. This was confirmed by one interviewee who many years later felt 'as if the deejay was always in charge in Liverpool' and that 'if you liked music that was not soul music then you were in trouble as to where to go'. Roger Eagle was renowned for his love of blues, R&B, and soul music but as a former deejay he appeared to understand that his promotions at the Stadium were distinguished by abandoning such a search for obedience. He also stated in the above interview that he did not like drink 'and if you have a bar there are bound to be one or two drunks who really spoil it for everyone else [...] I've seen a drunk audience and I've seen a stoned audience and I know which I'd rather have' (*ibid*, 1970:10). This contrasts greatly with the cabaret and country music scenes in Liverpool and expresses a level of self-consciousness about the kind of event that was being presented at the Stadium. Eagle was attempting to define the activity not simply via what it appeared to be, but also via what it was most certainly not. It was an announcement that if one did not really like what he was saying then one should not attend these music events at the Stadium. Musical absolutism was constantly challenged by Roger Eagle's presence in Liverpool, even though on a more personal level, he was known to be something of a musical absolutist.

It was during the late-summer of 1970 Eagle contracted himself to the boxing stadium, with the proposal to stage rock concerts at least once per month and his first promotion at the Liverpool Stadium under the name of Triad Promotions was on 19 September 1970 when he brought an Island Records package to Liverpool. Blues-rockers Free topped the bill, and were supported by Mott The Hoople, Bronco and (as a stand-in for the absent Fotheringay) CBS band Trees. It was a highly successful evening with over 2,000 fans in attendance. The gig had not been overly advertised and instead word-of-mouth had spread among the various rock communities on Merseyside and North Wales: the event was to become an important 'tribal gathering'. The alternative underground press, together with Liverpool's own Probe Records, set-up stalls in the foyer and London deejay Andy Dunkley played 'cool sounds' in between the acts. But word had not only spread about the gig *per se* but also about the live potential of support act Mott The Hoople and it was they who were eagerly anticipated. Ultimately, via this rumour-based expectancy, this band, rather than chart-toppers Free, left the audience baying for more. From that moment onwards the Liverpool rock community 'adopted' Mott The Hoople (and fellow Island artists Quintessence) as one of 'their bands' – some years before their recording of Bowie's 'All The Young Dudes' – and Roger Eagle as 'their' promoter. Much more was to follow in the years to come. As for that first Stadium gig, Eagle was to remark to the *Liverpool Echo*:

> The first concert [19 Sept] was good from the point of view of music, but not so good for light shows and food. The next one will have a really good light show, and more exciting food – curries and so on. [As for Triad] there's a sort of symbolic meaning in the name as well if you like. It stands for the promoter, the groups, and the audience; the three groups that have to work together for a really good gig. (*ibid*)

O'Connor's Tavern

Perhaps the first 'rock' pub in Liverpool was O'Connor's Tavern, where from 1969 rock groups took over where the Liverpool Scene poetry and music collective had left off. Bands like Easystreet, the Electric Rhythm Boys, Medium Theatre, Marseille, Nutz, and (later) Nasty Pop and Deaf School appeared at the renowned Thursday night residency slots, along with guests ranging from local bands to visiting Londoners such as Pete Brown, Lol Coxhill and Graham Bond. Even a young Freddie Mercury was to play one of his formative gigs at this venue in a student-led rock band. One of Liverpool's genuine alternative groups emerged from the underground scene at O'Connor's: Medium Theatre. This group was more of a collective, living together communally in Liverpool and playing long uninterrupted pieces full of changing moods and tempos. When they finally disbanded in the mid-1970s it was for some the end of an era.

The 'scene' based around O'Connor's Tavern tended to represent the taste cultures of the bohemian area of the city, Liverpool 8. By the late-1960s there were many cheap flats to be had in this area and, alongside a diverse Black population, the community had bound itself together in a spirit of opposition. In the mid-1970s O'Connor's was host to a small anarchist-inspired open-air festival, on open wagons, in Pilgrim Street. One group, the Accelerators, based in a Bentley Road, Liverpool 8 squat performed at this event and were probably the nearest Liverpool ever came to having a punk band; the group continued for several years from their L8 address. Such artists surrounding O'Connor's were very self-aware and, linked to the Liverpool School of Art, were showing early signs of post modernity. A reciprocal relationship was developing between the worlds of visual arts, rock music, graphic design, fashion, photography, etc. helping to fashion new musical objects out of the detritus of rock. For some, the distinctions between art and pop began to erode in mid-1970s Liverpool, and this cross-fertilization enabled new sets of creative spaces to develop: from galleries to artists' studios to recording studios and ultimately to the new venue of Eric's. Bill Drummond, Steve Hardstaff, Pete Fulwell, Roger Eagle and many others came under the spell of archetypal art school band Deaf School. This group celebrated a sense of theatre and spectacle, leaving behind other more pedestrian rock outfits and it was the collective surrounding this scene, together with the remnants of the Liverpool Stadium franchise, that set out launching the now world famous Eric's club in 1976. Music was once again central, but in a *bricolage* of vernacular ways.

The Cavern (and Mardi Gras)

Prior to the advent of the Triad promotions at the Stadium, what 'heavy' bands there were in Liverpool could usually be found at the Cavern. By 1970 the Cavern had become a split-level club – catering on the upper floor for a more soul-oriented fan and in the original basement venue, live rock music. Billy Butler was effectively running the club for local businessman Alf Geoghegan at this time and recognized the niche market for 'some of this underground music'. The fact that the Cavern was practically the only club serving this market in 1970 is one of the reasons why the local hippie grapevine soon came to recognize Butler's promotions, and the Cavern once again proved to be a magnet for an alternative popular music scene. Several important progressive and/or heavy rock bands played at the Cavern around the 1970-73 period including Wishbone Ash, Nazareth and Stray.

By 1970 it was difficult to actually get into the Cavern without a member's card. Licensing regulations were punitive and, being licensed for alcohol, the Cavern was officially designated 'a members-only club' and was required to provide evidence that non-members had been signed-in. So disorganized was the Cavern by this time, that it was tricky to actually become a member of the club and as for attempting to get access when under-age, this was an horrendous experience and many were stopped at the door by the bouncers, who also, it seems, took pleasure in allowing the more 'well-dressed' mods into the upper level, while denying 'troggs' access to the cellar. It was a very hit-and-miss affair, subject to the moods of those on the doors, yet young rock fans still queued to get in simply because there was very little else in the city at that time catering for the underground rock music they so loved – until the arrival of Roger Eagle, of course. Even rock concerts at the University of Liverpool's Mountford Hall could be difficult to access. Some concerts were deemed 'open access', others were for 'students only' and in the case of the latter, one had to be, yet again, signed-in, this time by a student carrying a union card. Les Parry recalls:

> To be honest, you had to be pretty dedicated to be a rock fan. It was probably the easiest thing in the world to find a venue that was playing Motown: youth clubs, school dances and all that – even the Ice Rink had soul nights – I remember Arthur Conley playing there. But it was really hard to find a venue dedicated to rock, and to actually get in there, if you were under-18 was very difficult. I remember almost prostrating myself in front of a student trying to get into the Union to see Taste. It was a students-only night but I'd gone along because I really liked the group and I asked to get signed-in. It took me ages and it didn't endear me to the student population very much. Then there was the Cavern, I'd hang around outside feeling stupid and try to slip past Paddy on the door. But it didn't always work. I remember one night trying to get in to see Little Free Rock, but ended-up hearing them from outside in Mathew Street – a very depressing experience. I can't tell you how happy I was when the Stadium gigs started. (Parry to Brocken, 2008)

When Billy Butler moved to the Mardi Gras club he and his business partner Chris Wharton made another attempt at 'progressive' nights. Word soon spread that Butler and Wharton were attempting to appeal once again to this alternative crowd – and the fans duly followed the pair to the Mardi Gras in their droves, leaving the Cavern somewhat surplus to requirements. Billy Butler remembers getting 'six projectors upstairs in the balcony, a camera and a screen over the stage, and we booked all the big name bands' (Butler to Brocken, 1996). By 1970 such 'big name bands' filled the pages of the *Melody Maker:* once again an authority of taste for young people in the early-1970s as it had been in the 1930s, and *Melody Maker* journalists such as Richard Williams, Karl Dallas, and Chris Welch were regarded as arbiters of 'serious' rock taste. Butler and Wharton regularly scoured *Melody Maker* for prospective groups. They took several financial risks, but were able to present some of the top 'underground' bands of the early-1970s such as Audience, Lindisfarne, Uriah Heep, Argent, Genesis, Van Der Graaf Generator, Thin Lizzy, and others. Eventually the Cavern was to close on 27 March 1973 to make way for a proposed Merseyrail ventilation shaft (which never actually appeared). It was a sad ending but the club had outlived its usefulness in practically every sense. Owner Roy Adams obtained the premises directly opposite in Mathew Street, opening it at first as the 'New Cavern' and then re-naming the venue 'the Revolution'. For a while, the New Cavern attracted remnants of the rock audience and local bands such as Strife were regulars at the venue. Strife had emerged from the Klubs and eventually signed recording deals with both Chrysalis and Gull. But as discotheques virtually took over all night club performance spaces, within a short space of time the venue was like any other in the city; it was, however, from this problematic site that the 'Eric's club night' was to evolve.

Summary

Popular music is often set as a kind of allegory of the consumer society, a place of absolute iconism and iconography, a place of passivity. Popular music adherents, we are told, are little more than inert automatons. But such impressions are simplifications of the transformations that can take place when popular music artefacts present to us notions of the sublime. Analysis of popular music reception, music and formats, informs us of why any reflection on art should not come to bear exclusively on the sender. It is surely acceptable to analyse the ways in which the receiver is affected, how feelings are received and experienced, how works are judged. Perhaps it is this approach – one of understanding how networks of vernacular art come to take shape – that can ultimately assist us in understanding how didactic art forms have been effectively supplanted by co-creative ones. Any examination of the audio cultures surrounding popular music dissemination and reception in Liverpool confirms myriad modes of listening. Research uncovers a host of shared practices and concerns. The retailing of recorded sound, the significance of radio, and word-of-mouth socialization patterns all provide creative spaces for cultural competence. Some listeners live in one or several subcultures with a specialized language, others use their listening to gratify other needs, other senses.

By looking at such pathways in Liverpool, the ways in which popular art is negotiated and understood, we no longer solely consider how a work comes about, but rather question the experiences of people in their coming together. These experiences are seminal and indeterminate, alternative and conventional. For decades in Liverpool, popular music activity has correlated with lived experienced and spoken in languages that that were understood. But one authentic language did not exist and it is impossible to discern one singular long-term trend in the musical history of the city. There was an inconsistent kaleidoscope of smaller and larger units which, at times linked, and at other times did not link. This fragmentary discourse represents the real historicity of Liverpool, for in an age of audio eclecticism the genuineness of an event surrounds the relative freedom to choose from a communal repertoire and to develop musical and social connections conditioned by the situations in which people meet the music, rather than by the so-called 'quality' of the music itself. Such choice is not only integral to understanding popular music, but also to our understanding of ourselves. To which mode of listening the listener adapts depends upon what listeners find of interest and choose to hear: modes of utilization, intercession, and arbitration, rather than production, are at the very heart of such choices. We are faced with the inevitable discursive point when coming to understand perhaps how the Beatles developed: things fall together, things fall apart. There is/was no centrality, only networks, connections, contingencies, convergences. Keith Jenkins states: 'I think there are no centres as such, but local patterns of dominance and marginality, which are all historiographically constructed and which must be historiographically read' (K. Jenkins, 2003:44). Jenkins is correct; equally, in this inter-connecting jigsaw, each and every individual has an important role to play.

Epilogue

By the age of nine years I was able to play all of the tracks from the Beatles' *Please Please Me* album on my tennis racket. Peter Randall and I spent the summer holidays of 1963 standing on the depressed part of the pavement in front of his dad's garage, imagining that we were on stage as the Beatles. Our two-part harmonies on 'P.S., I Love You', 'Do You Want to Know a Secret?', and 'Misery' were excellent – at least to our young ears. We knew all the words, could harmonize, and I was able to play all of George Harrison's solos note-for-note. It was the beginning of a new life for a painfully shy boy such as myself. Standing on Bowley Road, Stoneycroft, belting out the hits of the day created an aesthetic dimension from which I have never wanted to escape. In a short space of time I had the confidence to join the St James Church Choir in West Derby (only a short distance from the Casbah), mix with other people both young and old, and emerge at least partially from my debilitating introversion.

Around this time, I think it was late-autumn 1963, I was leafing through one of my father's order books one evening. It was one of those red-lined account books in which he would take orders for the following day's bread and cakes, but flicking through the back I noticed a couple of rhyming couplets in another's hand. My father informed me that it had been written by one of his many 'van lads', evidently smitten by Merseybeat. It occurred to me that I could use my Beatles and choir-boy experiences to write songs. My first effort was entitled 'Tired' and opened with the line 'You said you'd meet me there at five, you turned up at six' – I then rhymed 'six' with 'tricks' and was delighted. I thought that this was pretty hot stuff, but kept it to myself. My older sister Anne and I were members of the Co-Op Pathfinders Youth Club in Stoneycroft and one night she spilled the beans to the leader (who was, I think also the shop manager). I was mortified, but reluctantly agreed to sing it (I knew I could sing). It was probably the first time I had ever been congratulated for anything. Within a few weeks I was singing at Blair Hall on Walton Road in a competition organized by the Co-Op Society, where each Pathfinder club would entertain the massed ranks of parents. I sang two songs and Peter Randall backed me on piano. I was told afterwards that the Beatles had also played Blair Hall. I remember thinking I was glad that this information had not reached me before I went on stage.

I inform the reader of this little vignette not because I would like an A&R man to consider these songs from over 40 years ago (I can't remember how they go, in any case), but because I wish to stress that the Beatles meant just about everything to me. I never heard them sing a bad song, I never thought that they were anything other than utterly brilliant, and as I grew into adulthood and watched the group disintegrate I felt that John especially at least had one good friend, even if he didn't know it. The Beatles not only gave me some kind of narrative structure around which I could live my life, but also revealed to me a world of communication that I had hitherto not even realized existed – as a group they were truly a transcendental signifier. But I do not wish to universalize these sentiments – these were themes of great topical relevance for me, but they might not even be recalled at all by Peter Randall, never mind the massed ranks at Blair Hall.

Rock criticism needs to develop self-consciousness and reflexivity. In the place of consensus-based historical determinism there ought to be more discursive space. The use of such a framework to critically analyse discourses provides a means by which to explore and understand the multiple positions in which popular music meaning exists. By analysing significant creative spaces via discourse analysis researchers are able to explore new ways of examining popular music affect. Deena Weinstein even states that 'critics and their audience, in common with many other adults, have never fully grown-up; they persist in their youthful snobbery and need it confirmed continually' (2004:307).

So this work exists as neither a critique nor a confirmation of the Beatles, but as a questioning of the efficacy of existing popular music historicism. Historians are not here to provide answers via unequivocal linear generalizations. Histories of popular music should be concerned with the pursuit of contemporary significances, the questioning of empiricism by theory, and the documenting of various repertoires and interpretative strategies used by myriad participants. In doing so, the popular music historian can then at least attempt to explain how these repertoires and strategies come to be adopted and adapted in different social settings and periods.

Appendix

Cover versions known to have been performed by the Beatles a-z

Act Naturally	Russell, Morrison; Buck Owens '63	Live '65, Help, TV
Ain't She Sweet	Yellen, Ager; Gene Vincent '56	Tony Sheridan, session '69
All Shook Up	Blackwell; Presley '57	Quarry Men
Almost Grown	Berry	Live (as per Macdonald)
Alright, Okay, You Win	Peggy Lee '59	with Johnny Gentle '60
Anna (Go To Him)	Alexander '62	PPM, BBC, Live
Apache	Lordan; Shadows '60	Live '60
Baby it's You	Bacharach, David, Williams; Shirelles	'61 Live '61-3, PPM, BBC
Baby Let's Play House	Gunter; Presley '55	Quarry Men tape
Baby (Please Don't Go)	Olympics '58 (see W)	Live '60, rec '65
Bad Boy	Larry Williams '59	Live? BBC '63, rec '65
Beautiful Dreamer	Foster; Whitman circa '54	Live '62, BBC '63
Be-Bop-A-Lula	Vincent, Davis; Gene Vincent '56	Quarry Men, Hamburg, session '69
Begin the Beguine	Cole Porter	Live '60
Besame Mucho	Valazquez, Shaftel; Coasters	Live '62, Star Club, Decca, BBC
Blue Jean Bop	Vincent; Gene Vincent '56	Live Cavern '61-2
Blue Moon of Kentucky	Monroe; Presley '54	Quarry Men
Blue Suede Shoes	Perkins; Perkins, Presley '55	QM, Btles live '61-62
Bonie Moronie	Larry Williams '57	QM, Btles live '61
Boppin' The Blues	Perkins '55	Live Cavern '61-62
Boys	Dixon, Farrell; Shirelles '60	Live, PPM, Star, BBC
Bye Bye Love	Everly Bros '57	with Johnny Gentle '60 'Let It Be' sessions '69
Carol	Berry '58	Live '60, BBC '63

Cathy's Clown	Everly Bros '60	Live '60
Chains	Goffin, King; Cookies '62	Live, PPM, BBC
Clarabella	Pingatore; Jodimars '56	Live '60-62, BBC '63
C'Mon Everybody	Cochran '59	Quarry Men, Beatles
Come Go With Me	Dell-Vikings '57	Quarry Men
Corrine, Corrina	trad arr Turner '56, Peterson '60	Live '60-61
Crying, Waiting, Hoping	Holly '59	Live, Decca, BBC '63
Cumberland Gap	trad arr Donegan '57	Quarry Men '57-59
Dance In The Street	Gene Vincent '58	Live '60-62
Darktown Strutters' Ball	trad arr Joe Brown '60	Live '60-62
Devil In Her Heart	Drapkin; Donays '62	Live, WTB
Dizzy Miss Lizzy	Larry Williams '58	Live, BBC, Help
Don't Ever Change	Goffin, King; Crickets '62	Live, BBC '63
Don't Forbid Me	Pat Boone '56	Live '60-62
Don't Let the Sun Catch You Cryin'	Ray Charles '60	Live '60-61
Dream Baby	Walker; Orbison, Shannon, Channel '62	Live, BBC '62
Everybody's Trying To Be My Baby	Perkins '58	Live '61, BFS, Star, BBC
Everyday	Holly	Grundig rehearsal tape
Fabulous	Charlie Gracie '56	possibly '60: McC set list
Falling In Love Again	[*The Blue Angel*], Dietrich	Live, Star Club
Fools Like Me	Jerry Lee Lewis	Quarry Men
Freight Train	trad arr Cotton; McDevitt '57	Quarry Men
Glad All Over	Bennett, Tepper, Schroader; Perkins '57	Live, BBC
Gone, Gone, Gone	Perkins '59	Live '60
Hallelujah, I Love Her So	Ray Charles '56, Cochran '60	Live, Star Club
Harry Lime Theme, the	[*The Third Man*], Karas '49	Silver Beatles [stripper]
He'll Have to Go	Jim Reeves '60	with Johnny Gentle '60
Hey Baby	Bruce Channel	Cavern tape '62
Hey Good Lookin'	Hank Williams '51, Perkins	Live '60-61
High School Confidential	Jerry Lee Lewis '59	Quarry Men, poss. Silver B
Hippy Hippy Shake	Chan Romero '59	Live, Star Club, BBC

Hit the Road, Jack	Ray Charles '61	'Beatmakers' Oct '61
Honey Don't	Carl Perkins '56	Live '62-64, BFS
Honeymoon Song, the	[*Honeymoon*] Theodorakis '59	Live '61, BBC '63
Hound Dog	Leiber, Stoller; Presley '56	Quarry Men, Beatles
How Do You Do It?	Mitch Murray for Adam Faith	session 4/9/62
Hully Gully	Olympics '59	Live '60-62
I Forgot To Remember To Forget	Kesler, Feathers; Presley '56	Live '62, BBC
If You Gotta Make A Fool Of Somebody	James Ray '61	Live '61-2, Cavern tape
If You Love Me, Baby	see 'Take Out Some...'	Tony Sheridan '61
I Got a Woman	Ray Charles, Presley, Haley	Live '61, BBC
I Got To Find My Baby	Chuck Berry '60	Live '61, BBC
I Just Don't Understand	Ann-Margret '61	Live '61-62
I'll Never Let You Go (Little Darlin')	Elvis Presley '56	Live '60 – McC set list
I'm Gonna Sit Right Down and Cry Over You	Thomas, Biggs; Presley '56	Live '60
I'm Talking About You	Chuck Berry '62	Live '62, Star Club
I Need Your Love Tonight	Elvis Presley '59	with Johnny Gentle '60
I Remember	Eddie Cochran '59	Live '60-61
I Remember You	Frank Ifield '62	Live, Star Club
It's So Easy	Holly, Petty; Holly '58	Quarry Men, Moondogs
I Will Always Be in Love With You	query	Grundig rehearsal tape
I Wish I Could Shimmy Like My Sister Kate	Olympics '61	Live '61-62, Cavern
I Wonder if I Care as Much	Everly Bros 'b' side '57	Live '60 – McC set list
Jailhouse Rock	Leiber, Stoller; Presley '57	Quarry Men, Beatles '60
Jenny, Jenny	Little Richard '57	with Johnny Gentle '60
Johnny B Goode	Chuck Berry '58	Live '58? BBC '64
Just Because	Elvis Presley [version] '54	pre '61: Everett vol. 1
Kansas City/Hey Hey Hey	Leiber, Stoller; Penninman	Live '61, Star, BBC, BFS
Keep Your Hands Off My Baby	Goffin, King; Little Eva '62	Live '63, BBC

Lawdy Miss Clawdy	Lloyd Price '52; Presley '57	Quarry Men
Leave My Kitten Alone	Little Willie John, Turner, McDougal '59; Preston '61	Live '61, BFS [ex]
Lend Me Your Comb	Twomey, Wise, Weisman; Perkins '57	Live '61, Star, BBC '63
Let Your Baby Be Mine	query	Grundig rehearsal tape
Little Queenie	Chuck Berry '59	Live '60, Star
Lonesome Tears in my Eyes	Johnny Burnette Trio '56	Live '61-2
Long Tall Sally	Penniman, Johnson; Little Richard '56	QM, Beatles, E.P. BBC
Lost John	trad arr Donegan '56	Quarry Men
Lotta Lovin'	Gene Vincent 'b' side '57	possible '60: McC set list
Love Me Tender	Darby; Presley '56	Live [John Cochrane]
Lucille	Penniman, Collins; Little Richard '57	QM, Beatles, BBC
Maggie May	trad Vipers '57	Quarry Men, LIB '69
Mailman Blues	Lloyd Price '54	Quarry Men
Mailman, Bring Me No More Blues	Buddy Holly	Live [John Cochrane]
Matchbox	trad, Carl Perkins '57	Live '61, Star, BBC
Mean Woman Blues	Demetrius; Presley '57 (& others)	Quarry Men
Memphis, Tennessee	Chuck Berry '59	Live '61, BBC, Star, E.P
Midnight Special	trad. Arr. Donegan Quarry Men	Morecambe and Wise ATV '63
Money (That's What I Want)	Gordy, Bradford; Strong '60	Live, Decca, WTB
Moonglow	Stoloff '56	Live [stripper]
Moonlight Bay	Alice Faye '40, Doris Day '51	Morecambe & Wise ATV '63
Mr Moonlight	Jackson; Dr Feelgood and Interns '62	Live '62, Star, BFS
My Bonnie	Woods, Fuller 1881; Ray Charles '58	Tony Sheridan
New Orleans	Gary US Bonds '60	Live '61
Nobody's Child	Coben, Foree; Donegan, Snow	Quarry Men, Sheridan
No Other Baby	Bishop; Vipers '58	Tony Sheridan

Nothin' Shakin' but the Leaves on the Trees	Eddie Fontaine '58	Live '60, Star
Ooh! My Soul	Little Richard	Live '61, BBC
Over the Rainbow	Gene Vincent [version]	Live [John Cochrane]
Peggy Sue	Buddy Holly '57	Quarry Men
Peggy Sue Got Married	Buddy Holly	post-LIB session 1970
Poor Little Fool	Sheeley; Ricky Nelson '58	with Johnny Gentle '60
Puttin' On The Style	Guthrie; Donegan '57	Quarry Men
Railroad Bill	trad arr Donegan '57	Quarry Men
Ramrod	Duane Eddy '58	Quarry Men
Raunchy	Freeman, Bill Justis '57	Q.Men, Btles '60
Red Hot	Ronnie Hawkins '59	Live '61
Red Sails in the Sunset	Kennedy, Grosz; Turner '59, Ford '60	Live '60, Star
Reminiscing	King Curtis, Buddy Holly '62	Live '62, Star
Rock and Roll Music	Chuck Berry '57	Live '60-66, BFS
Rock Island Line	trad/Ledbetter, arr Donegan '56	Quarry Men
Roll Over Beethoven	Chuck Berry '56	Q.Men, Btles, WTB, BBC
Roses Are Red	Byron, Evans; Bobby Vinton '62	Pete Best solo '62
Saints, the	trad arr Haley '56	Tony Sheridan '61
Sawdust Dance Floor	Carl Perkins	Perkins-Beatles session '64?
Searchin'	Leiber, Stoller; Coasters '57	Live '58, Decca
September in the Rain	Dublin, Warren '37, Washington	Live '61, Decca
September Song	Weill, Anderson; Houston '38	stripper S. Beatles
Shakin' All Over	Heath; Johnny Kidd and Pirates '60	Live '60-61
Sharing You	Bobby Vee '62	Cavern rehearsal tape '62
Sheik of Araby	Smith, Wheeler, Snyder '21; Domino '61	Live, Decca [*Anth*]
Sheila	Tommy Roe '62	Live Hamburg, Star
Shimmy, Shimmy	Bobby Freeman '60	Live '60-63, Star
Short Fat Fanny	Larry Williams '57	Quarry Men

Shot of Rhythm and Blues, A	Arthur Alexander '62	Live '62, BBC
Shout	Isley Brothers '59	Live '60, ATV (RSG) '64
Side By Side	Woods, Kahn 1927; Kay Starr '53	BBC '63
Slow Down	Larry Williams '58	Live '60, E.P. BBC
So How Come No One Loves Me?	Bryant; Everly Bros '61	Live '61, BBC '63
Soldier of Love	Cason, Moon; Alexander '62	Live '62, BBC '63
Some Days We'll Remember	Grundig rehearsal	Live '60-61
Some Other Guy	Leiber, Stoller, Barrett '62	Live '62, BBC
Speedy Gonzales	Hess; Pat Boone '62	Hamburg [Clayson]
Stuck on You	Elvis Presley '60	McC set list, Johnny Gentle '60
Summertime	Gershwin; Cooke '57, Charles '58	Quarry Men
Sure to fall (in love with you)	Carl Perkins '56	Q.Men, Btles, Decca
Sweet Georgia Brown	Bernie, Pinkard, Casey '25; Coasters '57	Sheridan '61
Sweet Little Sixteen	Chuck Berry '58	Q.Men, Btles, Star, BBC
Take Good Care of my Baby	Goffin, King; Bobby Vee '61	Live '61
Take Out Some Insurance on Me Baby	Shingleton, Hall; Reed '59	Tony Sheridan [see 'If You Love Me Baby']
Taste of Honey, A	Marlow, Scott; Lennie Welch '60	Live '62, BBC, PPM
Teenage Heaven	Eddie Cochran '59	Live '60
Tennessee	Carl Perkins '56	Q.Men, Btles, '61
That'll Be The Day	Buddy Holly; Crickets '57	Quarry Men acetate, Gentle tour
That's Alright Mama	Crudup; Presley '54	Q.Men, Btles, Decca
(There's a) Devil in his Heart	Drapkin; Donays [see 'd']	Live '62, Decca, Star, WTB, BBC
Think It Over	Buddy Holly	Carroll Levis
Thirty Days	Chuck Berry '55	Live '61
Three Cool Cats	Leiber, Stoller; Coasters '59	Q.Men, Btles, Decca

Three Steps to Heaven	Eddie Cochran '60	Live '60-61
Till There Was You	Meredith Willson [The Music Man], Peggy Lee '61	Live '62 Decca, Star, WTB, BBC
To Know Her [Him] is to Love Her	Spector; Teddy Bears '58	Live '61, Star, Decca, BBC '63
Too Much Monkey Business	Chuck Berry '56	Live '61, BBC
Tutti Frutti	Penniman; Little Richard '57	Bill Harry
Twenty Flight Rock	Eddie Cochran '57 [The Girl Can't ...]	Q.Men, Btles
Twist and Shout	Berns, Russell, Medley; Isley Bros '62	Live '62, E.P. BBC, PPM, RVS
Well, [Baby Please Don't Go]	The Olympics '58	see 'b'
Well Darling		Grundig rehearsal
What'd I Say	Ray Charles	Gentle tour, [John Cochrane]
What's Your Name	Don & Juan '62	Cavern rehearsal tapes
Where Have You Been All My Life?	Mann, Weil; Alexander '62	Live, Star
Whole Lotta Shakin'	Lewis '57	'Beatmakers' '61
Who Slapped John?	Gene Vincent	session '69
Why (Can't You Love Me Again)	Sheridan, Crompton	Tony Sheridan
Wild Cat	Gene Vincent '60l	Grundig rehearsal, Gentle tour
Wild In The Country	Elvis Presley [*movie*]	Live '61: Pete Best
Will You Love Me Tomorrow	Goffin, King; Shirelles '61	Live
Wooden Heart	trad Presley '60 [*G.I. Blues*]	Live '61-62
Words of Love	Buddy Holly '57	Q.Men, Btles, BFS, BBC
World Is Waiting for the Sunrise	Seitz, Lockhart '19; Les Paul and Mary Ford '49	Grundig rehearsal
Worried Man Blues	Donegan '57	Quarry Men
You Don't Understand Me	Bobby Freeman '60	Live '60
You Can't Catch Me	Chuck Berry	Live as per Bill Harry
Young Blood	Leiber, Stoller, Pomus; Coasters '57	Live '59-63, Decca, BBC

You Really Got a Hold On Me	Robinson; Miracles '62	Live '62-63, WTB, BBC
You're My World	Cilla Black '64	session – part only
You'll Be Seeing Me		Grundig rehearsal
Your Feet's Too Big	Benson, Fisher; Waller '39, Checker '61	Live '61 Star
Your True Love	Carl Perkins '57	Q.Men, Beatles
You Win Again	Hank Williams; Lewis '58	Q.Men, Beatles

Abbreviations:

[*Anth*] – *The Beatles Anthology* Apple 07243 4 92969 9 2
ATV [RSG] – *Ready Steady Go* TV programme
BBC – performances at the BBC, radio and TV
Decca – Decca audition
Everett vol. 1 – Walter Everett 2001, p. 53 (see bibliography)
[John Cochrane] – diaries of, discussed in Leigh (1984), *Let's Go Down the Cavern, The Story of Liverpool's Merseybeat*, London: Vermillion
McC set list – Gottfridson 1997, p. 15 (see bibliography)
PPM, WTB, BFS, LIB – Beatles albums
RVS – Royal Variety Show
Star – Star Club tapes
Tony Sheridan, Sheridan '61 – Polydor sessions

'Grundig rehearsal'

In 1960, a rehearsal was tape-recorded at Paul McCartney's Forthlin Road address. The recording featured early versions of songs later recorded by the Beatles in the studio. It also included a number of cover versions and some were later included on the first disc of The Beatles' *Anthology*. The tape included titles such as 'Well Darling', 'Johnny Johnny', 'That's The End', 'I Don't Need No Cigarette Boy', 'Matchbox', 'One After 909', 'Cayenne', 'Hello Little Girl', 'That's When Your Heartaches Begin', 'Wildcat', 'I'll Always Be In Love With You', 'Some Days', 'Hallelujah I Love Her So', 'You'll Be Mine', 'The World Is Waiting For The Sunrise', 'I'll Follow the Sun', 'You Must Write Every Day', 'Movin' And Groovin'', 'Ramrod', and 'An Important Number'.

A few extra potted notes re covers

1. 'Baby, Let's Play House': This Elvis Presley cover version is one of two songs recorded during the Woolton fête of July 1957 (on the day John first met Paul) by the Quarry Men. The second song recorded was 'Puttin' On The Style'. After extensive audio restoration, excerpts from both songs were included in the BBC radio documentary *The Day John met Paul* broadcast on 26 June 2007; 'Come Go With Me', 'Cumberland Gap', 'Railroad Bill' and 'Maggie May' were also performed, but not recorded, that day.

2. Quarry Men tapes: Although tapes of the Quarrymen exist, they have yet to surface.

3. 'Young Blood' was recorded at the *Decca* audition, but has not been located.

4. *Live at the Cavern* tape recorded mid-1962: This was purchased by Paul McCartney on 29 August 1985 at auction. The tape contains 18 songs, mostly covers. Those covers are: 'Hey! Baby' (Bruce Channel), 'If You Gotta Make a Fool of Somebody' (James Ray), 'Sharing You' (Bobby Vee), and 'What's Your Name' (possibly Don and Juan's doo-wop hit of the same title).

5. 'Sheila': October 26, 1962, BBC: Occasionally at their BBC sessions, the Beatles taped songs that were not used in the broadcast. This cover of Tommy Roe's Buddy Holly sound-alike is one of them, and though a poor-fidelity live version that the group taped a couple of months later in Hamburg was issued as part of the *Star Club* tapes, this would presumably be better sounding. It is likely, however, that the tape was erased and/or has vanished.

6. 'Three Cool Cats': January 16, 1963, BBC: taped at a BBC session, but not broadcast. There is also a version of 'Three Cool Cats' from their 1 January 1962 Decca audition.

7. 'Three Cool Cats' 2 July 1963, BBC: another version of this Coasters song, taped at a BBC session in July 1963, but not broadcast.

8. *Beatles-Carl Perkins session* 1 June 1964: Carl Perkins claimed that he and the Beatles recorded in the studio together on 1 June 1964. The songs they did vary according to the account, but might have included 'Blue Suede Shoes', 'Honey Don't', 'Everybody's Trying to Be My Baby', 'Your True Love', 'Sawdust Dance Floor', and possibly others. No tape has ever surfaced and it seems probable that if the session took place, it was not taped. Perkins recalled staying in the studio until almost three in the morning, but no Beatles recording session officially ran past midnight until 13 October 1965.

9. 'You're My World' studio outtake, 3 June 1964: not a Beatles original, but a song that had just made no. 1 in the UK for Cilla Black. It has been variously reported that this cover lasts only 33 seconds – possibly an ironic version?

10. 'Sun King' session, 24 August 1969: As mentioned in the *Anthology 3* booklet, when the Beatles recorded 'Come And Get It' they warmed up with three rough covers: 'Ain't She Sweet' (released on *Anthology 3*) 'Who Slapped John' and 'Be-Bop-A-Lula' – these latter two recordings have yet to surface.

11. 'Peggy Sue Got Married', 3rd January 1970: McCartney, Harrison and Starr recorded the song 'I Me Mine': this was their last ever recording session as Beatles. After recording 'I Me Mine', the Beatles recorded this cover which apparently was taped, but has not thus far been heard. *The group had not only set in motion their recording careers as Quarry Men/Beatles via the recording of Buddy Holly material, but likewise brought it to an end: a striking musical, temporal and social continuity.*

Bibliography

Adams, Roy (2004), *Hard Nights, High Dives to Low Dives, the Cavern and the Nightlife*, Liverpool: cavernman.com

Ankrah, Joe (2004), interview

Atwood, Vince (2007), discussion

Barnard, Stephen (1989), *On the Radio: Music Radio in Britain*, Milton Keynes: Open University Press

Beadle, Jeremy (1993), *Will Pop Eat Itself?* London: Faber & Faber

Beare, Peggy (1998), interview

Belchem, John (2000), *Merseypride: Essays in Liverpool Exceptionalism*: Liverpool: University Press

Bethell, Billy (1999), interview

Biggs, Bryan [ed.] (1998), *Live From the Vinyl Junkyard: The Ultimate Mix*, Liverpool: Bluecoat and Liverpool Art School

Bimson, Joan (2008, 2009), discussion, email correspondence

Bird, Brian (1958), *Skiffle: The Story of Folk Song with a Jazz Beat*, London: Robert Hale

Bolger, Paul (2008), *Postcard Photographers of Liverpool and District 1900-1939*, Southport: Stations UK

Bourdieu, Pierre (1984) with Jean-Claude Passeron, *Reproduction in Education, Society and Culture*, London: Sage

Brocken, Michael (1996), *Some Other Guys! Some Theories About Signification*: *Beatles Cover Versions*, Liverpool: Mayfield

Brocken, Michael, (2000), 'Coming Out of the Rhetoric of Merseybeat' in Inglis, Ian [ed.], *The Beatles, Popular Music And Society*, London: Macmillan

Brocken, Michael (2003), *The British Folk Revival*, Aldershot: Ashgate

Brocken, Michael (2004), 'There's Gold in Them There Hills – the Geoff Speed Archive' in *English Dance & Song*, autumn edition

Brocken, Michael (2006), 'Was It Really Like That? 'Rock Island Line' and the instabilities of causational popular music histories', in *Popular Music History* 1/2 London: Equinox

Brocken, Michael (2008), *Liverpool City RLFC: Rugby League in a Football City*, London: LLP

Brooker, Peter [ed.] (1992), *Modernism/Postmodernism*, London: Longman

Brown, Mark (2008), 'Historian Says Beatles Were Just Capitalists and Not Youth Heroes', *Guardian*, 9 October 2008

Butler, Billy, interview 1996

Caradog Jones, D. (1934), *The Social Survey of Merseyside*, Liverpool: University Press

The producers (1993), *Celebration*, Liverpool: Granada TV

Charter, David (2007), 'Human Passion Shines Through Music', *Liverpool Daily Post*, 5 June 2007

Charters, Gordon (2008), 'The Orrell Mandoliers', *Liverpool History Society Journal* 7, Liverpool: LHS Publications Subcommittee

Cohen, Barry (2009), email correspondence

Cohen, Harvey G. (2008), 'Dawn of the Jazz Age: Sir Duke Ellington's Adventures in Britain', *Independent*, 13 November

Cohen, Sara (1991), 'Popular Music and Urban Regeneration: The Music Industries on Merseyside', in *Cultural Studies* 5/3

Cohen, Sara (1997), 'More Than the Beatles: Popular Music, Tourism and Urban Regeneration', conference paper, Liverpool: Institute of Popular Music

Cohen, Sara (2005), 'Country at the Heart of the City: Music, Heritage and Regeneration in Liverpool', in *Ethnomusicology* 49/1

Cohen, Sara (2007), *Decline, Renewal and the City in Popular Music Culture: Beyond the Beatles*, Aldershot: Ashgate

Cohn, Nik (1970), *AwopBopaLooBopAlopBamBoom*, London: Paladin

Connor, Frank (2004), mayfield-records.com

Conner, Frank (2009), interview

Cotterell, Dave [dir] (2007), *Cunard Yanks*, Liverpool: Souled Out Films

The editors (1977), *Country Music Spotlight* 1/1, Ellesmere Port: Wakefield

Cox, Christopher and Daniel Warner [eds] (2004), *Audio Culture: Readings in Modern Music*, London: Continuum

Cox, Peter (2008), *Set into Song: Ewan MacColl, Charles Parker, Peggy Seeger and the Radio Ballads*, Cambridge: Labatie

Critchley, Arthur, discussions 2006

Dallas, Karl (1982), 'Lonnie Donegan & Skiffle', *The History of Rock* 7, London: Orbis

Davies, Hunter (2002), *The Beatles: The Illustrated and Updated Edition of the Bestselling Authorized Biography*, London: Cassell Illustrated

Docherty, Thomas [ed.] (1993), *Postmodernism: A Reader*, Hemel Hempstead: Harvester Wheatsheaf

Duckworth, Ted (1997), interview

Dunn, Justin (2006), 'Farewell to Brookside Theme Writer Dave', in *Wirral Globe*, 18 October

Du Noyer, Paul (2003), *Wondrous Place*, London: Virgin

Ellis, Peter (2007), interview

Epstein, Brian (1964), *A Cellarful of Noise*, London: New English Library

Evans, Mike (1974), 'Stag Keeps it Local' in *Melody Maker*, 13 July

Everett, Walter (2001), *The Beatles as Musicians – The Quarry Men through Rubber Soul*, New York: Oxford University Press.

Farson, Daniel (1964), *Beat City* documentary TV programme shown 24 December 1963, London: ATV Rediffusion

Faulconbridge, Sue (1970), 'Pop Goes the Eagle', *Liverpool Echo* 7 October

Finnegan, Ruth (1989), *Hidden Musicians: Music-making in an English Town*, Cambridge: University Press

Fishel, David, Liverpool.com

Flannery, Joe, interviews and conversations with Mike Brocken 1996-99, 2007

Fowler, David (2008), *Youth Culture in Modern Britain*, London: Palgrave Macmillan

Fox, C. and P. Gammond, A. Morgan, A. Korner [eds] (1960), *Jazz On Record*, London: Grey Arrow

Frith, Simon (1996), *Performing Rites: on the value of popular music*, Cambridge [USA]: Harvard University Press

Garner, Clive (1988), *Music and Memories of the 1930s*, Liverpool: BBC Radio Merseyside broadcast

Garner, Clive, interview 1997

Gottfridsson, Hans Olof (1997), *The Beatles from Cavern to Star Club: The Illustrated Chronicle, Discography & Price Guide 1957-1962*, Stockholm: Premium.

Hardy, Bob (2003), merseybeat.org

Harker, Dave (1985), *Fakesong: The Manufacture of British 'folksong' 1700 To the Present Day*, Milton Keynes: Open University Press

Harry, Bill (1992), *The Ultimate Beatles Encyclopedia*, London: Virgin

Hassan, Ihab (1993), 'Towards a Concept of Postmodernism' in Docherty, Thomas [ed.] (1993), *Postmodernism: A Reader*, Hemel Hempstead: Harvester Wheatsheaf

Hatch, David and Stephen Millward (1989), *From Blues to Rock: An Analytic History of Pop Music*, Manchester: University Press

Hewison, Robert (1981), *In Anger: Culture in the Cold War 1945-60*, London: Methuen

Higginson, Steve (2005), 'The History of Black Music in Liverpool' in *Diverse Liverpool* 1, Liverpool: Fortis Media

Higginson, Steve and Tony Wailey (2006), *Edgy Cities*, Liverpool: Northern Lights

Hinds, Bill (2009), email correspondence

Hoare, Ian (1974), 'All Shine On' in *Let It Rock* 18, London: Hanover

Hoggart, Richard (1957), *The Uses of Literacy*, Harmondsworth: Penguin

Holt, Bill (2009), email correspondence

Horn, David (2009), email correspondence

Hudson, Brian (2006), 'University Jazz and the Mersey Sound: Student Days in Liverpool, a Memoir', *Popular Music History* 1/2 London: Equinox

Inglis, Ian [ed.] (2000), *The Beatles, Popular Music And Society: A Thousand Voices*, London: Macmillan

Jayston, Bert, discussions, 1997, 1999, 2002

Jenkins, Keith (2003), *Re-thinking History*, London: Routledge

Jenkins, Tricia (1994), *Let's Go Dancing: Dance Band Memories of 1930s Liverpool*, Liverpool: IPM

Johnson, Kenny (2009), interview

Johnson, Les (2009), interview

Jones, Mike (2009), email correspondence

Lane, Tony (1987), *Liverpool: Gateway of Empire*, London: Lawrence & Wishart

Laing, Dave, with Karl Dallas, Robin Denselow and Robert Shelton (1975), *Electric Muse: The Story of Folk into Rock*, London: Methuen

Leigh, Spencer with Pete Frame (1984), *Lets Go Down The Cavern: The Story of Liverpool's Merseybeat*, London: Vermillion

Leigh, Spencer (compiled 1991), *Speaking Words of Wisdom: Reflections on the Beatles Complied by Spencer Leigh*, Liverpool: Cavern City Tours

Leigh, Spencer and John Firminger (1996), *Halfway To Paradise: Britpop, 1955-1962*, Folkestone: Finbarr International

Leigh, Spencer (2002), *Sweeping The Blues Away: A Celebration of the Merseysippi Jazz Band*, Liverpool: IPM

Leigh, Spencer (2003), *Puttin' On The Style, The Lonnie Donegan Story*, Folkestone: Finbarr International

The editors, *Liverpool Echo*, 9 February 1924

The editors, *Liverpool Echo*, 1932

The editors, 'Launching Pad for a New Mersey Scene', *Liverpool Echo*, 1973 http://www.liverpool08.com/archive/index

Lyon, Roger (2009), discussion

McKenna, Ged (2009), interview

MacKinnon, Niall (1993), *The British Folk Scene: Musical Performance and Social Identity*, Buckingham: Open University Press

Marwick, Arthur (1998), *The Sixties*, Oxford: University Press

McManus, Kevin (1994), *Nashville of the North: Country Music in Liverpool*, Liverpool: IPM

Melly, George (2001), interview

Moy, Ron (2000), A*n Analysis of the Position and Status of Sound Ratio in Contemporary Society*, Lampeter: Edward Mellen

Malcolm Munro's autobiography

Nott, J (2003), *Music For The People: Popular Music and Dance in Inter-War Britain*, Oxford: University Press

Olaseinde, Oludele (2009), discussion

O'Toole, Mick: interviews and discussions 2007, 2008 and 2009

Palowski, Gareth (1989), *How They Became The Beatles 1960-64*, London: MacDonald

Parry, Les, discussion 2008

Parsonage, Catherine (2005), *The Evolution of Jazz in Britain, 1880-1935*, Aldershot: Ashgate

Pemberton, Sharon and Rosie Boateng (1996), *Who Put the Beat in Merseybeat?*, Liverpool: True Colour TV documentary

Percival, Robert, www.stthomasu.ca/~pmccorm/liverpooljazz2

Peters, Alan (2003), groovin'.com

Peters, Alan (2004), merseybeat.org

Peters, Alan (2009), email correspondence

Pettit, Emma (2008), *Old Rare New: The Independent Record Shop*, London: Black Dog

Power, Albie (2003), interviews, discussions

Preedy, Bob (2004), *Rockin' and Rollin' with Radio Caroline North*, Wetherby: Broadcasting History

Priestley, J.B. (1934), *An English Journey*, London: Mandarin (1994 edn.)

'Quickstep' (1933), *Liverpool Echo*, 8 December

Reynolds, Simon (1990), *Blissed Out*, London: Serpent's Tale

Reynolds, Simon (1998), *Energy Flash: A Journey Through Rave Music and Dance Culture*, London: Picador

Richards, Alan (2009), interview

Richards, A. and R. Franz [eds.] (1980), *Social Sounds: Merseyside's Guide to Social Club*, 5 and 6, Liverpool: Social Sounds

Sann, Paul (1957), *The Lawless Decade*, New York [USA]: Bonanza

Scott, Dave (1997), discussion

Sellors, Frank, www.bothy.co.uk, accessed 28 December 2008

Shank, Barry (1988), *Dissonant Identities: The Rock 'n' Roll Scene in Austin, Texas*, Hanover [USA]: University Press of New England

Smith, Sandra (1999), discussion

Speake, John (2008), interview

Speed, Geoff (1971), 'Interview with Lonnie Donegan', *The Folk Scene*, BBC Radio Merseyside

Speed, Geoff (2009), interview

Straw, Will (1991), 'Systems of Articulation, Logics of Change: Communities and Scenes in Popular Music' in *Cultural Studies* 3/3

Swallow, Norah E. (1974), 'Country Music at the Shakespeare Club, Liverpool' in *Oakie*, 31, Bradford: Oakie Enterprises

Sytner, Alan (2003), interview

Taylor, Timothy D. (2004), 'Bad World Music', in Washburne, Christopher J. and Maiken Derno [eds], *Bad Music: The Music We Love to Hate*, London: Routledge

Thompson, Phil (1994), T*he Best of Cellars: The Story of the World Famous Cavern Club*, Liverpool: Bluecoat Press

Tosh, John (1984), *The Pursuit of History; Aims, Methods and New Directions in the Study of Modern History*, London: Longman

Wakefield, Derek (1977), 'Editorial', *Country Music Spotlight*, Ellesmere Port: Wakefield

Washburne, Christopher J. and Maiken Derno [eds], *Bad Music: The Music We Love to Hate*, London: Routledge

Weinstein, Deena (2004), 'Rock Critics Need Bad Music' in Washburne, C. & Maiken Derno, *Bad Music: The Music We Love to Hate*. London: Routledge

Wenner, Jan (1971), *Lennon Remembers*, Harmondsworth: Penguin

Whitcomb, Ian (1972), *After the Ball*, Harmondsworth: Penguin

Willis-Pitts, P (2000), *Liverpool, The 5th Beatles: An African-American Odyssey*, Colorado [USA]: Amozen

Woods, Fred (1979), *Folk Revival: The Rediscovery of a National Music*, Poole: Blandford

Wooler, Bob (1961), 'Well Now – Dig This!' in Harry [ed.], *Mersey Beat*, Liverpool: Harry

Wooler, Bob (1997), interview following 'Liverpool Sound Seminar Series', Liverpool: IPM

Wright, Jade (2009), 'The Day the Record Stores Died', *Liverpool Daily Post*, 24 March

Young, Phil and Colin Hunt [compilers and editors] (1997), *It's Sound: A Celebration of Radio Merseyside*, Liverpool: Bluecoat Press

Index